New Vision Ministries Presents:

ME & GOD
Together At Last

By Eric Johnson

Most of the scripture verses from God's word within this book have been blended with the Holy Spirit's anointing and modern clarity to enable the reader to understand and apply the truth to their lives.

Copyright 2013 by Eric Johnson

ISBN: 1449970559
EAN-139781449970550

TABLE OF CONTENTS

TABLE OF CONTENTS -EXPANDED

IN THE HAND'S OF THE MASTER 324

READING GOD'S WORD 334

A CLOSE EXAMINATION OF ISAIAH 55:6-12 352

THE TABLE OF CONTENTS FOR BOOKMARKERS

DEDICATION

One day I was thanking God for my two daughters Erika and Courtney. They work so hard at everything they do. They bless me so much. Raising them has truly been one of the most rewarding privileges in my life. I love being around them and spending time with them. They are the source of a tremendous amount joy in my life. I always tell them how proud I am of them and how special they are to me. One day, I asked God to give them a very special blessing. I asked God to give them an out of this world type of blessing, something so grand that they cannot even contain it. A few moments later the spirit of the Lord came over me and said,

"I already have blessed them…
I GAVE THEM YOU."

I was so humbled at that moment. I am so thankful to God for giving me the opportunity to raise those kids and be next to them all the days of my life.

I've told my youngest daughter Courtney nearly everyday of her life, "She is the best girl in the whole town." I tell my oldest daughter Erika that she's my "GREEN PEPPER GIRL". When she was a baby, I once used a green pepper to get her to trust me and take her first steps toward me. There have been thousands of steps of faith, love and trust since that day over twenty years ago.

I thank the Lord for my wife Michelle. Her heart is as big as an ocean. She loves people like no one else on the planet. She amazes me in so many ways. I wish everyone on earth could meet her. Something leaps in my spirit every time she enters the room. I love you honey.

What am I accomplishing by all of this? I'm preparing three women in my life for a future of God's salvation, grace, blessings and love. I'm teaching them to trust God wholeheartedly. I'm teaching them that they are very special people to me and to God.

INTRODUCTION

In the process of writing this book I asked myself, "What qualification do I have to write a book and will people take me seriously?" Most authors have a substantial amount of education. Some have studied literature and writing for many years. Some have a Dr. or PhD in front of their name. Some have already written many books and are very well know. I don't have any of those qualifications or any impressive credentials. When I took my confusion to the Lord, he always came back to me with one word....LOVE!

God doesn't call the *qualified*...he *anoints* the called.
God's not interested in what *you have*...he wants *your heart*.

It's a privilege and honor that God chooses to use us for his many specific purposes. The truth is: God has *called* all of us to glorify him in different ways. **Every one of us has a purpose and destiny that can only be fulfilled by surrendering to the influence of God's Holy Spirit.**

Have you ever felt God calling you to something greater than you could have ever imagined? What he planted in your spirit was so radical and outrageous, you weren't sure if you could share it with anyone. Your first thought was, "ME GOD? Do you have the right person? Are you sure about this? Aren't you aware of all my hang-ups and deficiencies? Here let me remind you of them. Are you sure you know what you're doing?" There were many biblical men and women that have asked those same questions, "What qualifications do I have? I'm not holy enough or worthy to do the work of the Lord." But God used shepherds, fisherman, tax collectors, prostitutes, thieves and murderers to glorify him. God kept one word continually in front of those people...LOVE.

Being "CALLED" simply means God spoke to you and then you reacted to his promptings. We've all been *called* to glorify God in many different ways. We've all been *called* to love the Lord with all our heart, mind, soul and strength. We've all been *called* to love others with actions and words.

I decided to write down my spiritual attributes instead of my personal qualifications. Here is a list of what I came up with.

I am a child of God. I am holy, righteous, pure, blameless and
accepted in God's sight, based off Christ's actions for me.
I am more valuable to him than all the treasure in this world.
The spirit of Christ lives in me.
I have the fullness of God dwelling in me through his Holy Spirit.
God gives me inside information regarding everything I
need to know about his character, forgiveness and love.
He unravels the mysteries of life in front of
me by giving me spiritual vision and wisdom.
I am complete IN CHRIST.
I do not lack anything from my heavenly Father.
I'm capable of everything God wants me
to accomplish...because he literally lives in me.

Since God chose to lavish his love and forgiveness on me, then I am the perfect candidate to write about it. Since God chose to unleash his miracle working power through me, then how can I not write about what he has done? Since God sent his son Jesus Christ, to give his life as a payment for me, then how can I not write about his saving grace and how he has healed me in every way a person can be healed.

God has *called* everyone of us to glorify him in everything we do. We were supernaturally adopted into his family the moment we said, "Jesus...I believe and receive everything you've accomplished for me." We are children of God. He has called us by name to a purpose and destiny that will fulfill all our dreams.

GOD STILL SPEAKS TO US

*God's preparing YOU for the greatest manifestation
of HIMSELF...that the world has ever seen. You and I are the
ones he has chosen to channel his wondrous power through.*

My wife Michelle is a communicator. She can talk to anyone, anytime and anywhere...AND SHE USUALLY DOES! God has created all of us to be communicators. He has specifically designed us for that purpose. He did that because he is a master communicator as well. God has been speaking to people since the beginning of creation. Powerful things happen when God speaks and miraculous things happen when people speak as they are directed by the Spirit of God. Even today, God still speaks to us. The question is:

Are you listening to the voice of God?

God wants us to listen to him and understand who he is. He wants us to know what he's all about. He unravels the mysteries of his nature to us in many unique ways. He has valuable information about himself and us that he's trying to communicate to us. He is desperately trying to get our attention. You might be thinking,

> "Well if that's the case, why doesn't God just write it out in the stars one night so we can all plainly see that there is a God and here is his message to us? Then no one would be able to deny God's existence and his message could be clearly seen by everyone in the world."

That definitely sounds like a great idea to me too. You simply want God to speak to you in a very clear and profound way so you can understand him. That's not asking too much is it? Except now you're asking God to speak to you in a *particular way*. That leads me to this question: Have you researched any of the other avenues by which God has already communicated to us with?

God speaks to people in a number of different ways. One way God has spoken to us, very clearly, is through the prophets of the Holy Bible. Unfortunately, reading the word of God has become none existent, something our grandparents used to do. Christians, our bibles have collected dust long enough. People have owned bibles all their lives that still look brand new. The cover is not worn and the spine is not bent at all. The pages are still crisp and new, untouched and unread.

God cannot speak to us through unread bibles.
Words given to us by God that have never been believed in.
Promises spoken by God that have never been trusted in.
A victorious, abundantly thriving life that will never be discovered.

Beloved, it's time to change. As you slide that bible off the shelf, you'll probably hear in the supernatural realm the sound of a sword being slid out of its sheath. Won't you let it save you and your household? Won't you let it heal you? Won't you let God's word prosper you? It's time to ask God to give you a hunger for him again. Ask him to give you a desire and passion for his word.

Jesus told a story in the bible about a man named Lazarus and a rich man. Both men died and Lazarus went to Abraham to be comforted and the rich man went to Hell. The man in Hell asked if he could go warn his five brothers about this terrible place. He didn't want them to make the same mistake he did. Abraham responded:

They have the writings of Moses and the words of
the prophets to listen to and believe. Luke 16:29

This rich man knew he would soon see his brothers in this horrific place of torment, if they did not humble themselves, fall to their knees and cry out to God. Since the man in Hell knew he could not leave, he asked Abraham if he would send Lazarus to his house to warn his brothers of this horrific place. Abraham said, *"If they do not listen to Moses and the Prophets, they will not be convinced even if someone rises from the dead and talks to them." Luke 16:31*

- God spoke to the prophets and the prophets told the people what God wanted them to know. Hebrews 1:1
- God spoke to people as the Holy Spirit moved on them, to speak and write what he wanted us to learn. I Thessalonians 2:13; 4:8
- God spoke to the Jews and the Gentiles two thousand years ago through his son Jesus Christ (Hebrews 1:1). Jesus spoke in synagogues, temples, streets, hillsides and anywhere people would listen. Jesus said, *"I do not speak on my own behalf, I speak what my heavenly Father wants you to know." John 12:49*
- Even today God still speaks to us. He doesn't give up trying to connect with us, because he loves us so much.

God is an expert at communication and relationships. He speaks to people all the time. Many people are hearing from God all over the world, but unfortunately he's not being heard by everyone. He speaks to people today even more than he did in biblical times. Are you interested in what God has to say? Are you listening to his voice? Here are many scriptures that tell us if we will pursue after God we will find him.

*My sheep hear my voice. I know them and they follow me
and I give them eternal life. John 10:27 & 28*

*Everyone who hungers and thirsts after
righteousness will be filled. Matthew 5:6*

Draw near to God and he will draw near to you. James 4:8 ✱

*Those who come to God must believe he exist and he
rewards those who constantly seek after him. Hebrews 11:6*

*Ask and you shall have God's power, seek and you will find God's love,
knock and God himself will open the door for you
and invite you into his presence. Matthew 7:7*

These scriptures beg the questions:

Are we doing our part?
Are you passionate about knowing your creator?
Is he on your mind every moment of the day,
like someone your passionately in love with?
Do you have a burning desire to know God intimately?
How much effort have you put forth in discovering your creator?

The bible promises that people who *seek* after God, will *hear* from God. People, who are *desperate* for more of God in their life, *receive* more of his presence in their life. People who chase after, are hungry and thirsty for more of God, *will be filled.* Matthew 5:6; John 6:35

Look at all the things people chase after in this life; money, fame, power, pleasure, things, friends and the list goes on and on. Some people are successful at finding these things and others are moderately successful. Do you measure success by the number of possessions you have? True fulfillment is not found in things. Your value is not determined by your title, position, possessions or bank account. We spend our lives chasing after *things* when we should be chasing after our creator who understands us, loves us and completes us. I've wasted enough of the time God has given me chasing after things. My focus has changed to my savior the Lord Jesus Christ and I'm determined that my priorities are going to intertwine with God's agenda and his will for my life.

Many people don't seek after God because they don't believe it's possible to have a close relationship with a God that you can't see, touch or hear. So they simply don't put forth any effort in finding out who their creator is. This is true on the Christian side of the coin as well. Many Christians know God and they put their faith in his Son Jesus Christ. They're on their way to Heaven. But they don't grow close to him for many different reasons. They haven't experience the life of God that's within them. They feel as distant from God as the stars in the sky.

Here are some reasons people don't draw close to God:

- It could be because of dysfunctional relationship issues from the past which effects how they respond to love or authority.
- People who have been hurt in the past many times have a smaller circle of trust. This can cause a person's faith to be shallow and ineffective at many different levels.
- The things in this world, keep people distracted, frustrated and hurt.
- There doesn't ever seem to be enough time in their lives to discover how passionate God is about them.
- Perhaps they know God is real, but they want to be the predominate controlling authority in their life.

There are many reasons Christians and non-Christians
don't pursue after God the way they should.

The truth is...you're as close to God as you want to be.

If you'll put forth any effort at all in researching, seeking and
understanding God, then he will reveal himself to you. The simplicity of
it all is this:

YOU HAVE TO WANT TO KNOW HIM.

God is already doing his part. He desires to have a passionate
relationship with his creation. God's voice is echoing throughout the
universe...do you hear him?

Here I am. I stand at the door and knock.
If anyone hears my voice and opens the door,
then I will come in and be with them forever.
Revelations 3:20

CHAPTER 1

FAITH

Do any of these words describe your faith?

Is your faith average, comfortable, on the fence, hidden, lukewarm, doubtful, fearful, embarrassed, complacent, scarce, mediocre, angry, frustrated, fading or childish (meaning immature, selfish and ungrateful)? Has your faith pretty much been the same year after year with no real major changes to speak of?

Do any of these words describe your faith?

Has your faith been hungry, desperate, thirsty, bold, dynamic, passionate, confident, optimistic, positive, engaged, revealing, hopeful, radiant, mountain moving or childlike (meaning completely trusting God)?

Every single person in the bible who has ever taken a step of faith was pleasantly surprised when God showed up behind them in all his glory, majesty, provision and power.

That's why all those stories about people of faith are in the bible, to encourage us to set aside our fear, anxiety and embarrassment and take those crucial steps of faith towards God. They chose to trust God despite their circumstances and questions. Many of them lacked self-confidence and felt very small and insignificant, just like we do many times. These people made a decision not to trust in their own abilities and resources. They put their trust in God and his supernatural provision. As you understand more about God and the fullness of his nature, it's easier to trust him, pray to him with complete confidence, worship him with your whole heart and love him with all your mind, soul and strength.

STORY – Green Pepper Girl

When my daughter Erika was little, she was learning to stand, balance and take single steps. She loved green peppers so much that I decided to use one to get her to walk two or three steps in a row. I held the green pepper in front of her, but I kept it just beyond her reach. She was holding on to the bed with one hand and reaching for the green pepper with the other hand. Finally, she let go of the bed and took a step towards the pepper. She wanted that pepper so bad that she was willing to let go of the safety and security of the bed. I moved the pepper just a little beyond her reach again and with each step she took, she got farther away from the bed and she was walking for the first time in her life. She took four steps and then I gave her the pepper. WOW! SHE TOOK FOUR STEPS! She had never done that before. It has been over twenty years since then and I still remember that event like it happened yesterday. Even though she is now a young woman, I still call her "MY GREEN PEPPER GIRL."

Allow God to speak to you from your spirit as you read these words.

ENTER INTO GOD'S SABBATH REST
compiled by Eric Johnson

Here I am, come closer. I will not let you fall.
Take my hand and we'll go through this together.
I will reveal myself to you in such a new and profound
way that you will never again doubt my love for you.
If you'll just chase after me I will show you
wonders that you cannot even imagine.

Reach out to me my child and take those steps of faith.
I have many special gifts specifically designed for you.
I will pour them out to you because I can see in your heart
that I am your source for everything you encounter.
Out of everything I created, no one loves me back like you do.

I am the Lord. I am beyond your natural thinking.
You cannot comprehend me with your mind, but I am coming to you
now. Do you hear my foot steps? Do you feel the ground shake as I
walk? Do you hear it thunder in your spirit when I speak?
Do I promise and not act? Everything in all creation exists
because I spoke. I will remove the veil from your eyes so
you can see, understand and know my true nature.

Cry out to me all of you who labor relentlessly
and are burdened with life and I will give
you rest for your tired and wounded soul.
You have never experienced the kind
of rest that I am about to give you.
You run, toil, work and worry; but I'm going to
give you a supernatural rest that looks into
the storm and says, "PEACE BE STILL."
My rest will give you complete confidence as you trust in me.
My rest will give you an undeniable assurance
that I have you in the palm of my hand.

As surely as I am the Lord...I WILL GIVE YOU REST.

(I just love when the Holy Spirit takes the pen out of my hand
and begins to write what God wants to say to his children.)

This book is not only MY message to YOU about GOD. It's GOD'S message to YOU about YOU and HIM being united together forever.

Maybe you just don't feel God the way other people do. It always seems to be other people who are spiritual, blessed and filled with God. You attend church and want to be closer to God, but you're just not hungry for God like other people seem to be. If you're not hungry for the things of God, then ask him to put a hunger inside you and then seek him as he stirs the Holy Spirit within you.

God is already doing everything he can to draw you to him. He already desires a close, intimate relationship with his creation. That's why he put his spirit inside of every born-again Christian. We just need to realize who we already have in us and then let him come out of us. When we understand how passionately God loves us, then we will pursue him with more enthusiasm and confidence. God is already pursuing after us, we need to stop chasing after everything this world has to offer and turn towards him. Turn to God, trust him and be changed completely by his love and passion. Make a choice to stop running and turn to a love that will never reject you, hurt you or abandon you.

That first step toward him is something God requires. Taking that first step of faith in any situation shows God that we *want* him, we *need* him and we *trust* him. That first step of faith confirms to God that we are going to fully rely on him and believe in his promises for our situation. It shows God that we're hungry for more of him. We need to chase after God, diligently seek after him, hunger and thirst for more of him. Won't you put forth the effort today to seek him more, because God wants us to catch him?

I will be found by you says the Lord. Jeremiah 29:14
God is passionate about his relationship with you. Exodus 34:14
Call to me and I will answer you and show you
great and mighty things. Jeremiah 33:3
Those who hunger and thirst after righteousness
shall be filled. Matthew 5:6

LISTENING

It may not be time for God to hear our prayers...it may be time for us to listen to him...so we'll understand that there's a better way to pray.

Have you ever been talking with someone, then all of a sudden you realized they are completely monopolizing the conversation. You could hardly get a word in during the conversation. The word conversation means there is an exchange that takes place between two individuals; an exchange of thoughts, ideas, feelings and opinions. If only one person is doing all the talking during a conversation then there is no longer an exchange or interaction between the two parties. If you're the one doing all the talking then you're never going to learn anything.

Is listening a major part of your prayer time with God? We need to stop asking God for everything on our celestial Christmas list and listen to his voice. What if someone you really loved only came to you when they wanted something? How would that make you feel? NEWSFLASH! God is the most important speaker in the conversation between you and him. I want to hear his side of the conversation. God tells us in his word:

Be still and know that I am God. Psalm 46:10

BE STILL...but tonight all my favorite TV shows are on.
BE STILL...but all my friends will be on the internet tonight.
BE STILL...but we have to go to this party and tomorrow we have to do something else and the next day I have to do this other thing.
BE STILL...but I have this long list of things I need to tell God about.

During all this busyness God is patiently
waiting and whispering to us...BE STILL.

It sounds so simple doesn't it? Doesn't being *still* sound easier than being *busy*. So why do many people find it so difficult or maybe even impossible to do? We've all been talking to God for some time, now it's time for us to listen to him. Get on your knees and ask the Holy Spirit to speak to you. When we are silent before God, it shows God he's the most important person in the conversation. Remember your time is the most valuable thing you can give someone. So *be still* and hear the voice of God. God loves, he cares, he is patient and he is waiting.

STORY - The Cast Iron Bell

One evening I was teaching the young people at our church about hearing God's voice. I brought a cast iron bell to church with me to help in my object lesson. I had one person come up front with me and stand next to the bell. I told everybody in the room to lift up their right hand and to keep their hand raised as long as they could hear the ring of the bell, then to put their hand down when they could no longer hear the ringing.

I gave the bell a real good tug on the rope. I wanted them to remember that sound. That old cast iron bell shot out a loud long ring in the room. The reverberation rang out a long time and after about ten seconds some people in the back row put their hands down. After about fifteen seconds everyone's hands were down, except for mine and the other person next to me. We were standing right next to the bell. Our ears were only a few inches away from it. We could still hear the vibration very clearly. Twenty seconds had passed and our hands were still up. Twenty five seconds and we could still hear a faint ring. Finally after about thirty seconds had passed, we could no longer hear the ring. Everyone was surprised that we were able to hear the ring for such a long time. We could hear the sound of the bell when no one else in the room could hear it.

How close are you to God? Do you hear his voice when no one else does? Can you feel his presence even when the world is spinning out of control? Do you feel the Holy Spirit prompting you when no one else in the room knows he's there?

Jesus said, "My sheep hear my voice and they follow after me."
John 10:27

Many times we hear people speak but we're not really listening to them. Good listeners have their complete attention focused on the speaker. Have you ever talked to someone while they're watching TV? They might be able to appear like they are listening to you and watching TV. But as soon as you ask them a question and they don't respond, then you realize that you've lost them. They're not listening to you anymore. **One of the main reasons people don't hear from God is that they simply don't take the time to listen to him.** People design their lifestyles to be extremely busy. People fill every moment of their lives with stuff to do, places to go and tasks to accomplish. Sometimes the stuff is important, sometimes it's not really all that important and sometimes the stuff is just plain meaningless. People never stop filling their lives with things to do.

Short term and long term goals are something we should plan and pursue. But where does God fit into your plans? With such busy lives, is God lucky to get a few minutes left over at the end of a long day or maybe only a few minutes at the end of a long week? In a twenty four hour day, does God get the last two minutes at the end of the day just before you go to sleep?

We are the ones who lose out when we don't spend time with God. Sure there are a lot of people talking to him and asking for things they need or want. Many people give God advice, directions and their opinion on how things should happen. But how many people kneel before God and remain quiet? **How many times do we go before God and just wait on him and let him decide what the topic of conversation is going to be. Maybe he wants to lead you in a specific direction when you pray.** Have you ever waited for God's Spirit to lead you during prayer? You can waste a lot of time in prayer by taking the lead yourself.

Who is the most intelligent person in the
conversation between you and God?

That question always reminds me to wait on God and listen for his voice. The Holy Spirit knows how to help you pray the perfect prayer for any specific situation.

*Pray in the Spirit on all occasions with all
kinds of prayers and requests. Ephesians 6:18*

*Build yourselves up in your faith by praying with the Holy Spirit.
Jude 1:20*

Most of our prayers are for God to change our heath and heal us. Many times our prayers are for God to increase our finances or our position at work. We focus on how God needs to improve our situation or to prosper us in some way. I believe we should be more focused on God making a change *in us* and not just *our circumstances.* That's why we should let God direct our prayers. We should *be still* and listen to his voice. He knows what the most important topic is concerning your life.

A lot of people's problems would be fixed if they would just let God first deal with their heart. Allowing God to influence your thoughts and your emotional realm will help you experience more peace and less fear, more joy and less anxiety, more love and less strife. So surrender the topic of conversation to God and allow the Holy Spirit to teach you, lead you and change you.

Faith - 15

DO YOU HAVE FAITH IN YOUR RELATIONSHIP WITH GOD?

Good relationships require good communication, great listening skills and meaningful time together so that you can understand each other completely. There are over one-hundred and fifty thousand words in this book. Four of the most important words in this book are:

SPEND TIME WITH GOD.

God wants an intimate relationship with you and that requires time and attention. Don't let life's cares and worries steal your valuable time away. God wants us to research, understand and trust him completely with our time, energy and thoughts.

God wants the spirit of wisdom and revelation to come upon you so you will understand him completely. He wants you to be spiritually enlightened beyond your natural wisdom and know the hope of his calling and the riches of his glorious inheritance he has set aside for us to enjoy. The greatness of his universe making power is inside of those who have made Christ their Lord. Ephesians 1:17-19

Folks it's time to hear from God. **God's message to us is that he radically loves us. We are the focal point of his passion. We are the object of his affection.** Stop running from God and turn to a love that will change you completely.

The bible is God's love letter to mankind. The Old Testament talks a lot about war, famine, disease, devastation, destruction and death. But that's what happened when disobedient, rebellious people sinned and turn their backs on God. God doesn't punish people with a supernatural sledge hammer. Sometimes people walk or even run out from under his umbrella of grace and protection. If you'll read the bible closely you'll find out it's more about relationships than anything else. Specifically connecting you with God in such a new and radical way that you:

Know him completely.
You understand him intimately.
You trust him with everything.
You serve him with a heart driven by love.

Does your faith have no direction or point of reference? Is it kind of like dry desert sand, blown around by the wind of this world? Do you feel like God is a thousand miles away most of the time? Maybe you're in a continual state of fear and anxiety because of this uncertain world we live in. If you feel this way, you're really no different than anyone else out there. The important thing is not to stay in that place. Those anxious feelings of fear and unrest are quite real. Don't ignore them, respond to them, the way God directs us to.

> *Cast all your cares upon your heavenly Father*
> *because he cares for you. I Peter 5:7*

You might be thinking, "Come on, let's be real, it can't be that simple. I've got serious problems and I need some tangible answers to resolve these problems. It could take years of therapy to work through my issues. How can a scripture in the bible written thousands of years ago help me today? I need real tangible help like anti-depressants!" Well you could believe that and go in that direction and let me know how it works for you. More than likely you'll have the same problems years from now, because you didn't confront your issues from a supernatural perspective. God created us as supernatural beings. This body of flesh is wrapped around a soul and a spirit, all created by God. All the problems you encounter have a supernatural solution. **God's word works. Reading about, meditating on, believing in and speaking out God's promises are vital habits we need to pursue.** These habits will produce a lifetime of incredible benefits for you. God is always faithful to his word.

> *Here is my definition of what faith is.*
> *To put your complete confidence in God's love, grace*
> *and provision in such a profound and radical way; that*
> *it challenges the way you think, believe, act and speak.*

God wants to take our faith from where it is today and unleash it on tomorrow's task and challenges. The bible says we should mature in such a way that we get off the diet of milk (like a baby) and move on to a diet of solid food or meat (like a mature adult) Hebrews 5:12. I guarantee, whatever you're putting your trust in today, God wants that trust to be placed in him. **God wants your faith to be so bold and radical that it makes a historic impact on you and the world you live in. God wants your faith to take a chance with him. Challenge God with your faith, give him room to operate and show himself mighty and strong.** Faith is like a roller-coaster ride, you're going to be both fearful and excited at the same time of the great unknown ahead. Not knowing the outcome, but trusting God anyways is what faith is all about. Here are some important questions regarding your faith.

- When was the last time God's life transforming power...transformed your life?
- When was the last time you experienced God's miracle-working power on a consistent basis?
- Do you allow the faith walk that you're on to lead you and influence your decisions everyday?
- Does your faith make you more nervous than it does the enemy?
- Does your faith shake the foundation of this world or does this world shake the foundation of your faith?
- Does your faith make demons quiver, knowing that at any time a prayer could come out of your mouth and alter their plan or remove them from the created universe forever?

Most modern day Christians have put their faith in everything else but God! These include; their jobs, their health care cards, their optical and dental insurance, modern science and all the prescription pills they could possibly stand. They trust in their own abilities and resources because they are easily perceived by their five senses. Their eternal security is in their retirement plan. They've modified Philippians 4:9 to say, *"My 401K plan will supply all my needs according to its riches and power."*

Wherever your treasure is...there will your heart be also. Matthew 6:21

Faith believes there is a way through your situation when there doesn't seem to be a way out at all.
Faith believes when others are laughing at you.
Faith believes that the impossible through you, is possible through God.
Faith takes a chance even when there seems to be no chance.
Faith takes a step even when you might look silly.
Faith trusts God, not money, people and things.
Faith trust in God's resources and abilities, not your own.
Faith is dynamic; it needs to be put into motion.
If your actions are always following close on the heels of your faith, then your faith will always be leading you somewhere.
Your faith should be influencing your mind, attitude, emotions, mouth and actions until you see a manifestation of God's power released from within you.

Faith is the substance of things hoped for and the evidence of things that can't be seen yet. Hebrews 11:1

In Mark 12:44, Jesus tells us a story of a man who brought a very large sum of money into the sanctuary and gave it all to the church. Then an old woman came in and gave only a few coins. Jesus asked a question to his disciples, "Who gave the most?" Jesus answered for them, "It was the woman". The women gave money she desperately needed. The other guy still had plenty of money. This old woman gave money she needed to survive on. It may have even been needed for her very next meal.

This is not a story of tithes or offerings; it's a story of faith. This woman trusted God to provide for her. She was a woman of faith. This wasn't a contest about who gave the most, like they usually have between the boys and the girls at vacation bible school. Jesus could see the love, compassion and giving heart of this woman. She put her faith into action by giving her last two cents and trusting God for all her needs. This woman took a chance with her faith. This kind of faith caught Jesus' attention that day. Have you ever taken a chance with your faith? Anyone can say they have faith, but *"Faith by itself, if not accompanied by actions, is dead." James 2:17*

STORY – Pray For Everyone In The Front Row

One Sunday morning during praise and worship service, the Holy Spirit spoke to me and told me to pray for everyone in the front row where I was sitting. I asked God why? Then I questioned if that was really him speaking to me. I wasn't really worried about how I looked in front of people, praise God I've matured beyond that a long time ago. I just wanted to know if that was really God speaking to me to do exactly that. The more I resisted the more I felt my spirit shaking inside of me. Finally, I just did it! I started to pray for everyone in the front row during the regular morning worship service.

When I got to this one particular person, I prayed even more fervently. I felt God saying, "Right here, this is the person. Pray with all your heart and my spirit will be stirred within them." After praying for them I returned to my seat.

After the service that morning, I saw that same person on the stage with one of the ministers of music. They were hugging each other and crying together. I found out later that there was a huge family fight between those two people. But right then on stage they were reconciled, forgiving and loving. I believe it was my prayer that helped break down the walls of bitterness and offense.

God knows what he's doing when he asks us to do something. The question is: Do you know what you're going to do when God ask you to do something? The answer should be,

> "Yes Lord...here I am...your servant...I'll do it."

God longs to see our genuine faith-filled actions, so people will see our good works and glorify him (Matthew 5:16). The foundation of our faith begins with the knowledge of God's total and unconditional love for us (Galatians 5:6). The New Testament is constantly describing how awesome, complete and unconditional God's love is towards us.

Another awesome foundation for our faith is that we have complete forgiveness through our savior, so there is now peace between God and us (Romans 5:1). **We don't have partial forgiveness or momentary redemption until the next time we mess up. Jesus perfected our eternal redemption forever (Hebrews 9:12,10:14). Knowing we are completely and constantly clean, pure, blameless, justified, righteous and holy before God is mind blowing!** This type of forgiveness is what should propel our genuine, passionate, faith-filled actions. If your actions are a by-product of fear, condemnation, guilt, a set of biblical laws or church rules, then your faith will never be motivated by grace, mercy, forgiveness and love (Titus 2:11 & 12). This is why your motive for why you do what you do is so vitally important.

CHRISTIANITY and RELIGION can look very similar alongside each other, but the difference is what's motivating you to do the things you do. Is your faith motivated by your five senses or are you lead by God's Holy Spirit that lives in you? Are you more in touch with your emotional realm than you are with the new spirit God has deposited in you? Is what you see in this physical world more real to you than God's truth and the supernatural realm?

> *God has filled you with new life so your faith,*
> *hope and love will flourish abundantly, through*
> *the indwelling of his Holy Spirit. Romans 15:13*

Christian soldier, let your faith inter-mix with your confidence, hope and actions and then stand back and see the glory of God erupt out of your spirit. **Your actions will always follow your beliefs and God's presence, power and glory will always follow your faith-filled actions.**

CHAPTER 2

REBELLION - DISOBEDIENCE - SIN – REPENTANCE

The bible says that God's goodness and love draws people to repentance (Romans 2:4). The bible is God's love letter to us. It's a letter of grace and mercy that we don't deserve. The bible also contains stories of God's wrath and anger. There are some awful events that have happened to people in the bible. All these things happened to people because of their own actions; specifically when they rebelled, were disobedience and sinned against God. God forgave people in the bible all the time. People would seek God out and receive his forgiveness and then they would fall into sin again. They would seek his face and then later they would rebel. They would fall on their knees and repent, then later grumble and complain against him. God must really be patient with his creation to put up with that type of constant wayward thinking. God loved the people he created and he gave them plenty of chances to come back to him. Eventually, because of people's rebellious hearts and sinful life, God didn't give them what they deserved, he gave them exactly what they desired, complete separation from him.

How long will people wipe their feet on God's grace and mercy?
How long will people dance to their sinful heart's desire
on the floor of God's forgiveness?
How many times will people slap God's loving hand and reject him?
How long will he wait for people to come to their senses,
love him back and follow him completely?

SIN

Nobody has to teach someone to sin. It is clearly inbred in people to want their own way, complain, gossip, lie, have a raging temper and criticize others. People naturally tend to be SELF-centered rather than OTHERS-centered. Sin is not taught it just comes out of people. No one has to teach you to lust it just comes into your mind through distorted desires. Through the fall of Adam and Eve sin and death entered into the entire human race. Even though God provided everything people needed, they still wanted more. Satan made sure people wanted more than what God had to offer and he was successful at perverting that concept. Satan also tried to offer Jesus more:

I'll give you all the kingdoms of the world
and they will bow down to you. Matthew 4:9

Satan wants you to desire for more than what God has provided. That shows God you're completely dissatisfied with his provision. That way you'll wander from the truth and seek whatever the world has to offer you. That leads to all manner of haughtiness, ingratitude, being unthankful and sin.

Most people keep themselves so busy that they never have any time to think about God and focus on his true nature. They don't seek after a true personal relationship with him. The sin never satisfies the emptiness in their lives. That emptiness they feel should have been filled with God, their creator that they never had time for. **Busyness is a major tool in the enemy's arsenal.**

God could have destroyed the earth right after the fall of Adam and Eve, but he didn't. God continued to love Adam and Eve regardless of their choice to disobey him and sin. Instead of destroying the earth or destroying Adam and Eve, God sacrificed two animals as a blood covering for their sins. Through the Old Testament law the blood of animals was continually shed for the sins of the people. Goats, sheep, lambs, bulls and many others were brought to the altars to be sacrificed for the sins of the nations. But the sinning never stopped...and surprisingly, it never even slowed down.

At one time mankind was wiped off the face of the planet because of the rampant sin that was taking place. I'm sure this crushed God to have to do this. Since that's all that was coming out of mankind's soul was sinful thoughts and actions, God destroyed sin by destroying mankind. God knew that it wasn't the best way to destroy sin and it's power. God hated the sin that separated his creation from him, so he devised a way to deal with sin once and for all. God knew it was going to require his very own blood to redeem the world. So God's ultimate plan was put into place. Remember when Abraham told Isaac, *"God himself will provide the sacrifice" (Genesis 22:8)*. Abraham was prophetically saying:

GOD HIMSELF WILL <u>BE</u> THE SACRIFICE.

I AM THE WAY

Salvation comes no other way. Under no other name can people be saved, only by believing in the Lord Jesus Christ. Acts 4:12

STORY – The Bird

One time there was a little bird in my garage flying around and frantically trying to escape. He kept flying into the window over and over. I could see that eventually this little bird was going to hurt himself. I went over and opened the large garage door and waited for the bird to fly through the opening and be free. But he didn't do that, he just kept flying into the window over and over and scratching frantically at the glass. I went over and opened the second garage door next to the other one. I thought surely he would fly through either one of the big openings now, but he didn't. He was so sure the window was the way to freedom, but it wasn't. He was confused, frustrated and panicking now. I had to go over there myself to direct him to the other openings. Finally he flew through the garage door and was free.

The disciples said, "Master show us the way," and Jesus said to them, "I am THE WAY to find God, God has filled me with his TRUTH and I have his LIFE giving spirit in me. ***No one can ever be reconciled to God except through me."*** *John 14:16*

No one can be *redeemed* except though Jesus blood. Ephesians 1:7
No one can be *adopted* into God's family except though Jesus lineage. Ephesians 1:5
No one can be *righteous* before God except though Christ's righteousness. Romans 3:22
No one can be *accepted* by God except though Jesus payment. Eph. 1:6
No one can be *holy* in God's sight except though Jesus sinless life. Ephesians 1:4
No one can be *blameless* except though Jesus sacrifice. Ephesians 1:4
No one can be *justified* except though Jesus actions. Romans 5:9

Sinners become saints based on what Jesus accomplished at the Cross of Calvary. When a person's faith meets God's grace then they receive God's gift of salvation and become children of God. **People don't get saved by a change in their actions. They get saved by believing in the name of the Lord Jesus Christ and by accepting everything he accomplished for them through the atonement of his blood. Born-again Christians are saved by believing in Christ's**

actions. The lost (people who are not born-again in their spirit) don't need to *ask* Jesus into their heart or *ask* God to save them. God wants them saved more than anything! People shouldn't *ask* God (in the form of a question) to save them or *ask* God if he will save them. Of course God wants you to be apart of his family! He's been whispering into your ear ever since you had ears and this is what he's been saying,

"I love you. Stop running, turn to me and discover who I am and all the many facets of my character. An extremely high price has already been paid for you. I don't care how bad you've been, I want you back. I want you with me...reconciled, whole and healed. I want you and me to be together forever."

Don't ask God if he will save you. That's ridiculous, of coursed he wants you saved! God has already made his decision about us. He loves us unconditionally. God is proposing a question to everyone who is lost, "Will you accept my free gift of salvation?" It was always God's plan and Jesus purpose to redeem you.

That little bird may have died in my garage if he would have never responded to my promptings. He just couldn't believe the way to freedom was another direction. He kept hitting the window over and over. He thought this had to be the way, but it wasn't. I didn't want him to die, I wanted him to live. That's why I took the time to provide a way to freedom by opening the door and even prompted him to go in the right direction. **God has opened his arms wide to receive all of humanity into his heart.** He's whispering to people in their thoughts to stop, listen and turn to him. He wants us to understand that there's a new life to experience IN CHRIST.

People come up with *their own way* of reconciling themselves to God, but it's not *the way*, through the Lord Jesus Christ. *Their way* is through religious practices or performing traditional rituals. People try to determine *their own path* to God based on their improved performance, their own works or their own goodness (Romans 10:3 & 4). This false sense of security people blanket themselves with is based; on incorrect teaching, traditions, feelings and their own personal opinions.

There is a way that seems right and logical in a person's mind, but in the end, it leads your soul to destruction and death. Prov. 14:12

Even the disciples, who had spent so much time with Jesus, had to be told point blank from Jesus own mouth, "I AM THE WAY! You're looking at him! I'm it! The search is over! I am the long awaited Messiah!"

God sent his Holy Spirit to overshadow the humble and highly favored Virgin Mary and she conceived the Lord Jesus Christ. Jesus birth, life, death and resurrection have been prophesied in hundreds of messianic scriptures in the bible. The fully God and fully human person of Jesus Christ was finally here on earth so that he could reconcile mankind to God.

Have you ever wondered why the bible is full of all those genealogies of Christ? The Old Testament lists all of Adam and Eve's children up to Noah. The book of Genesis continues with the genealogies of Noah's family up to Abraham, Isaac and Jacob. The Old Testament continues with countless genealogies, with who begot whom and who begot them. Who married whom and who their children were. Why would they put all that boring stuff in the bible? Who wants to read all that? The gospels in the New Testament review the genealogies leading up to *one man*, Jesus Christ. God was giving us an entire family tree in the bible that pointed, in the end, to our one and only messiah, redeemer and savior. **You see God did not what anyone to miss the most important person in all of history ever born...HIM.**

Jesus is the once and for all, absolute and only blood sacrifice for all the sins (past, present and future) of every person in the human race.

When Jesus said from the cross, *"Father forgive them, for they know not what they do" (Luke 23:34).* He was not only talking about the Romans who were crucifying him and the Jewish leaders who insisted on his death. He was talking about ALL OF HUMANITY. Remember Jesus said:

No one takes my life. I lay it down on my own as a ransom for the entire world. John 10:18

When Jesus was suffering, bleeding and dieing on the cross, no one was TAKING anything from him, he was GIVING to us. He was giving us forgiveness, salvation, eternal life, freedom, healing, wholeness, rest, righteousness, acceptance and a home in Heaven.

Jesus was essentially saying:
Here is my body and my blood, Lord I give my life as a ransom for THE ENTIRE HUMAN RACE. Place your anger, wrath and judgment towards sin on me and forgive them of all their sins.

God certainly didn't want anyone to miss the message about what Jesus did for the human race. He wants it known to all people throughout the entire world.

> *Go and make disciples in every nation and baptize them by the*
> *authority of the Father and of the Son and of the Holy Spirit,*
> *and teach them to obey everything I have commanded and remember*
> *I will always be with you in your spirit. Matthew 28:19 & 20*

SIN - SAINT - SIN - SAINT - SIN - SAINT

People are defiant by nature. They rebel against their creator and his authority. Like a defiant two year old child, they simply want their own way. If they want something they take it regardless of the repercussions. This rebellious nature (inside of people) fights against God's nature, his promptings and his voice. The power of sin directs people to concentrate on themselves, worry about themselves and satisfy themselves. The power of sin is completely and thoroughly, one hundred percent selfish, stubborn and rebellious. People do not want to be held accountable for their actions or submit themselves to someone's authority.

> *You stubborn stiff-necked people, why are you are always*
> *resisting the Holy Spirit's promptings. Acts 7:51*

Only a humble, broken and surrendered person will get on their knees before God and admit to him that they've sinned against him. It's the most humbling thing a person can ever do.

Godly sorrow brings repentance that leads to salvation. II Corinth. 7:10

That tugging or drawing that this scripture is talking about is a supernatural prompting from God. Don't resist God, get rid of that haughty arrogance or your heart will begin to harden over time. You will hear and feel God's tugging less and less, until finally you don't feel him at all. That's a terrible condition to be in.

> *Because of your stubbornness and your unrepentant heart,*
> *you are storing up wrath against yourself for the day of God's judgment.*
> *This is when his righteous judgment will be revealed. Romans 2:5*

Stubborn hearts won't bow before the Lord. Bowing down acknowledges the position, honor and authority of the person you're bowing to. That's not very popular in this fast paced, me first, look out for number one society we live in. But that's exactly what it's going to take to touch the heart of God.

Sin only satisfies for a moment, but the repercussions can be for a lifetime and eternity. Sin always takes people further than they ever wanted to go. People give up their spouses, children, homes, jobs, and most regrettably *their souls* for the pleasures of sin. Sin that remains hidden is sin that remains in control. Whatever you're hiding from people is not hidden from God. Get free from it now, don't wait! The enemy wants to divide and conquer, he wants to isolate and infiltrate. Repentance brings sin into the light of God's love, grace and forgiveness. Repentance taps into the power of Christ's blood, exposes sin and sets people free from their sin. **God doesn't redeem people half way. The redeeming power of Jesus blood makes such a radical change in people's lives that Jesus calls it being "BORN-AGAIN" in your spirit.**

I'm about to reveal something to you that's incredible says the LORD. Your sins, that were as red as scarlet, shall be as white as snow cover field. Red as crimson, they shall be white like a lambs wool. Isaiah 1:18

If we will confess our sins, he is faithful and just and will forgive our sins and purify us from all unrighteousness. I John 1:9

God loves you just the way you are, but refuses to leave you there. God wants his creation to respond to his love by examining the emptiness in their lives and allowing his spirit to prompt their heart. Don't cleave to sin but release it through the power of Christ's blood. God wants people to move on to a life of freedom and fulfillment. God loves people but not their sin. God loves what he created. His grace and mercy extend out over us like an umbrella, further than we deserve.

What if you fail God and turn back toward your old sinful life? Many Christians can get caught in a roller-coaster ride of, sin one day and saint the next, then sin again another day and repent the next. Saints of God, you are dead to sin (in your spirit). **Sin may have influence over you through your emotional realm and flesh, but it no longer has complete control over you like a master has over their servant.** You have been freed from that *old nature*. You have a *new nature* now and a brand new identity IN CHRIST.

We need to understand how horrible sin is in the eyes of God. We need to hate sin because God hates anything that's going to harm you. God hated sin so much that he sent his son to free us from it, by way of THE CROSS. Jesus paid a huge price for your freedom. When you walk in that freedom everyday, then you're glorifying God. When you turn from sin and say to yourself, "I'm free from sin", you're saying to God, "THANK YOU for the blood of Jesus Christ and for salvation." When a Christian person falls into sin, they need to get back up and confess to God that they forgot who they were for a moment. You're a royal child of the king of the universe. You wear a robe of righteousness on your shoulders. God's given you a ring of comfort and joy. He's crowned you with grace and mercy. He's completely filled you with his spirit, presence and power. Don't ever forget that!

Is it OK to continue in sin since we are under God's grace?
By no means! Our old sin nature died in our spirit, so how can
we willfully participate and enjoy it any longer? Romans 6:1 & 2

Your old sin nature died the moment your spirit was touched by God.
Don't let the external power of temptation and sin hypnotize your mind
and control your words and actions. Your spirit, mind and body are no
longer instruments of wickedness, so offer yourselves as a joyful
servant to your heavenly Father, because he has rescued you out of
darkness and placed you in his kingdom of light. You are now a child of
righteousness. Sin is no longer your master because you live under
God's umbrella of grace. Romans 6:11 & 14

Get off that hilly roller-coaster ride of sin, saint, sin, saint, sin, saint. When we sin God's grace is there to pick us up, dust us off and help us to continue going forward. God's grace teaches us to turn from sin (Titus 2:11 & 12). Christians love God and love other people and they would never even think to or want to hurt another person. But we need to figure out how much God loves us and then love ourselves. Don't be in love with yourself, in an arrogant, haughty way. But love what God created. He created you. He loves you. You need to love yourself. Don't hurt what God loves. Run away from sin and walk into complete freedom through God's grace.

Flirting with sin periodically and dabbling in it occasionally goes against your new nature of being IN CHRIST. Envision yourself the way God sees you. You're his child, the apple of his eye, treasured more than anything else he has created. God loves you and you need to love what he loves and that includes you. We respond to God's love by forsaking our old way of thinking and walking in our new, fresh, abundant thought-life. **Born-again Christians have the life of God in their spirit.** Don't go down the path of sin and hurt what God loves…which is YOU!

Get rid of everything that hinders your thought life and the sin
that so easily entangles and captures your flesh. Hebrews 12:1

THE SINFUL CONDITION OF PEOPLE AND REPENTANCE
What! My sin is not that bad!

God doesn't care about the condition you're in when you come to him...the important thing is...that you come to him. *Be reconciled to God (II Corinthians 5:20).* Take some paper currency out of your pocket. Then crumble it up. Next, throw it on the floor and jump up and a down on it. Now pick it up and look at it. It might be dirty and wrinkled. It may be torn and faded. But guess what? During all that time IT NEVER LOST IT'S VALUE! No matter what people have said or done to you and no matter how deep in sin you've fallen, you never lost your value in God's eyes. God loves you. You are his creation and his treasure.

God tells us how treasured and valuable we are to him in his word. He also explains to people that they are sinners in need of a savior. People get into trouble when they don't understand both of these significant messages. Many unbelievers don't understand they are sinners in need of a savior. They think they're very moral people and they might be according to the world's standard, but they're not going to be judged by the world's standard, they're going to be judged by God.

No one knows a person's heart better than God, so people would be wise to listen to him. God repeats himself throughout the bible that he wants sinners to be saved. Many people don't have a clear understanding of how severely evil sin is. Most people compare themselves to other people to justify their supreme morality. The problem with that is you're comparing yourself to the flawed nature of sinful people. People look at others and say, "They're worst then me. They've killed someone, where I'm only guilty of being jealous." ALL SIN....IS SIN. It doesn't matter if a ten foot high wall is hindering you or a two hundred foot high wall is blocking your way. The only way through it is by Christ's blood.

Jesus made peace between God and mankind by tearing down the dividing wall between them. Ephesians 2:14

People get into trouble when they start comparing their sins to other people's sins. For instance, many people would say that jealousy is not as bad as murder, but jealousy is the first step in the direction of murder. Do you know how many people have been murdered in the world because of jealousy? The very first murder on the face of the earth happened because Cain was jealous of his brother Able. See how ugly jealousy is. JEALOUSLY BEAT A MAN TO DEATH! That same jealousy that people say is not that big of deal and is just a small issue, was the cause of envy, hate, revenge and finally murder. Jealously is a horrific sin.

People shouldn't waste their time categorizing their sins to make themselves seem better than others. Justifying their morals in their own mind by comparing them to a world that chases after sin is ludicrous. It may satisfy their moral conscience temporarily but it does nothing to ensure their salvation, eternal life and a home in Heaven.

I'm A Good Apple

It's like going to an orchard and collecting apples. Let's say there are some apples with spots on them and others have slight deformities. Some have a few bug holes in them and some have fallen to the ground and are bruised. So you gather what you think are the best apples and you put them in your basket. Compared to all the other apples in the orchard those are definitely the best. When you are leaving the orchard you see this big beautiful apple tree in the farmer's front yard. The apples are huge, spotless and perfect. All the apples that you thought were good in your basket, now actually look awful in comparison to the tree you just discovered. Once you saw the perfect apples in the farmer's front yard all the "GOOD APPLES" in your basket are now not so perfect and maybe even horrific in comparison.

My point in this story is this: The apples in the orchard are like the people of this world. Some seem good and others seem bad. The apples in the basket are the people who think they are going to Heaven because they are not as bad as other people. The apple tree in the farmer's front yard represents God's perfect standard of holiness. This story is a simplified example of what I hear people do all the time. They compare themselves to others to determine whether they will gain access to Heaven. The apples that were gathered into the basket in the story were no where near perfect when compared to those from the perfect tree out front. People are using the wrong comparison for God's standard of holiness. Even if you had God's standard of holiness written out so you could try to obey it, you could never maintain that level of performance. Only one person has ever fulfilled "THE LAW" and that was the Lord Jesus Christ (Matthew 5:17).

People are always comparing their sins to other people's sins, but their using the wrong measuring device to justify their goodness. People's *small sins* will always look a little more polished when they compare them to other people's *big sins*. All they're really left with in the end is one big basket of sin that has already been atoned for by God through his son Jesus. Here's a great question to consider: Since God has already dealt with mankind's sin through the blood of Jesus, why not accept his free gift of salvation?

Unsaved people make themselves feel better about their sinful condition through interpersonal comparison. In essence they are saying, "In comparison to other people's sinful life styles, MY SINFUL LIFE IS PRETTY GOOD." When you boil it all down it's a BIG POT FULL OF PRIDE. It comes right down to this foolish reasoning. They justify in their own minds that:

MY SIN...IS REALLY NO SIN AT ALL.

When people reach this stage of thinking they're going on a Sunday stroll through a MINE FIELD! People arrive at this mindset through deception, confusion and then finally pitiful arrogance.

If anyone says he is without sin, he makes God out to be a liar.
I John 1:10

(BECAUSE)

Everyone has sinned and fallen short of the glory of God. Romans 3:23

In all their pride the wicked do not seek you Lord.
In all their thoughts there is no room for God. Psalm 10:4

Am I trying to say that unsaved people need to act better to be accepted by God and get to Heaven? ABSOLUTELY NOT! Any good deeds performed to gain access into Heaven...is sin. Any righteousness people try to obtain outside of the righteousness of Christ is evil. Pride, haughtiness and self-righteousness is the root of that type of thinking.

The bible says it like this:

Our own self-proclaimed righteousness is like filthy rags to God.
Isaiah 64:6
God gives us righteous standing before him
that cannot be earned by works. Romans 4:6
If righteousness could be gained by our performance
then Christ died for nothing. Galatians 2:21

Let's say a person resented a co-worker who had made some insulting comments about them in front of everyone. Now every time they see that person they get this feeling in their spirit about them. They feel anger, resentment and ill will towards them. Anger when left unchecked can lead to hate, and hate can lead to revenge, which could lead to wanting to hurt that person severely or even murder? Do you know how many disgruntled employees have walked into their place of work with a gun and began shooting people? They became offended and hurt and then with hatred they finally killed because of the sin in their heart. Sin wants to control the heart and take people places they've never been before. Hate, revenge, unforgivness, jealously, strife and anger are all sin at any level.

That hate that came into this person's heart at the beginning...IS SIN.
That rage that began to grow a little more everyday...IS SIN.
Their heart, that had no room for forgiveness, IS SINFUL.

Finally, that person's actions came into alignment with their hate and they committed murder. When people read about the murderer in the paper the next day, there will be many people who will say, "I would never have murdered someone like they did." That's when they start comparing other people's evil with their *so called goodness*. IT'S NOT FAIR TO COMPARE! Those same readers, at sometime in their life, may have hated to the same degree in their heart, but they just never followed through with it in their actions.

Have you ever been angry at someone's peculiar driving techniques when you were out on the road? Did you shake your fist at them? Did a curse word come out of your mouth? Were you ready to get out of your vehicle and fight with them? Maybe you even had the thought for a moment to try to run them off the road. Where did all that anger and wrath come from? You were fine a minute ago...OR WERE YOU?

When people get squeezed whatever is on the inside of them is going to come out. Unbelievers can try to hide their sin nature that's down it their heart. They might think it's very small and insignificant but God sees it. He's trying to get them to realize that a tremendous price has been paid for their sin. **God has made peace with mankind through his son's blood (Ephesians 2:12). Sinners have been reconciled to God (Romans 5:10).** Acceptance of that free gift is the most important decision people will ever make in their lives.

When unbelievers stand before the Lord they will be completely guilty of sin no matter how much they try to sweep it under the rug. Every person who is not a born-again Christian will be guilty when they stand before a holy God. Technically the SAVED person is just as guilty as an UNSAVED person, but the SAVED person knows their sin, guilt, judgment and condemnation were transfer to Christ on the cross. God's wrath and judgment has *passed over* the person who has accepted Christ as their Lord. The UNSAVED person is just as saved as the SAVED person; it's just that the unsaved person never accepted Christ as Lord. **The saving work was accomplished for everyone all at the same time.** *Jesus Christ died for the sins of the whole world. I John 2:2*

No one is good enough to get into Heaven by their own merits. People shouldn't try to gain access by their own goodness and righteousness. That's why God gave Moses The Ten Commandments. God in essence was saying, "Here are some laws to remind you of mankind's depravity and sinful nature." The Ten Commandments were given to people to drive sinners to repentance and receive God's forgiveness. They weren't given as requirements for us to fulfill to find God; they were given as a way to find THE CROSS.

The LAW OF GOD chases sinners to the CROSS OF CHRIST.
Galatians 3:24, Romans 3:28

At the cross of Christ is where lost souls find, accept and receive the salvation of the Lord. Trying to keep *The Law* through your own efforts to gain access, favor or salvation is a stench in God's nostrils (Philippians 3:9, Galatians 5:4). This is what religious people spend their time doing. Any good works people do on their own, to be accepted by God, is a filthy dirty stench to him (Isaiah 64:6). Any thing you do to maintain (by your own efforts) some kind of right standing before God, devalues Christ's sacrifice for you. **God is at peace with us because of the blood of Jesus.** God has covered Christians in a robe of righteousness earned for us by Jesus Christ.

Many Christians believe God is responding to them based on their own goodness or commendable actions and that's wrong. **All Christ's goodness, righteousness, holiness and purity was deposited in you when you became a born-again Christian.** That's what God is responding to. He's responding to the new born-again spirit that's in you. God will respond to your good actions (driven by faith) when it's based on Christ's good actions (the atonement). When you try to promote *your* goodness or *your* performance, as a way to God or as a reason for God to respond to you, then you just stepped into *performance-based religious works.* **Works are awesome. Your actions are extremely important, but your relationship with God is not determined by your perfect performance, awesome works or good deeds. Your relationship with God is a sealed deal because of your belief in what Christ did for you. John 10:28**

There are no good qualities you possess that made God decide to offer you salvation. God loved you when you were a dirty, rotten, no good sinner. You were sinning in your actions because it was your nature to sin. Isn't that amazing that God loved you when you were a child of wrath and darkness. You were in the worst possible condition you could ever be in when God's love encompassed you and whispered in your ear, "I love you, come to me. Stop running and known me as your heavenly Father."

The righteous of Christ:
...is not based on anything I've accomplished. Romans 3:21
...comes to us by having faith in the completed work of Jesus. Rom. 3:22
...seals us for all eternity. Romans 4:11
...is a gift from God. Romans 5:17
...has made my spirit alive. Romans 8:10
...places spiritual weapons in my hands. II Corinthians 6:7
...is like a supernatural impenetrable breastplate that covers my heart.
   Ephesians 6:14
...is like a tree in me that produces good fruit. Philippians 1:11

All born-again Christians are covered in the RIGHTEOUSNESS OF CHRIST. Don't cover yourself with your own robe of righteousness; it will have holes and tears in it. The material will smell like it has been soaked in raw sewage. You may even sprinkle a little bit of Jesus on top of those works you're doing to make yourself seem very religious. But it's that haughty puffed up attitude that's hurting you. Some religious looking Jews were arguing with Jesus and claimed they knew God and their father was Abraham. But Jesus said:

Your father is the Devil! John 8:44

God knows why you do what you do. You can't fool him. Ask God to search your heart and see if there are any self-righteous, ritualistic, religious motives in you. It's your ability to confess your short-comings, weaknesses and faults that God rejoices in. **Once God has deflated you of all your glorious virtues (through self-focus) then you'll be able to understand the fullness of God's grace toward you. God has already completely dealt with your sin issues by way of the cross.** Let go of what you're holding on to. It's hard to receive anything when you're holding on to a lot of worldly baggage. Let it go! The burden you've been caring is heavy and cumbersome. You weren't designed to carry it.

Unbelievers are living in the *neutral zone* right now. God's judgment, condemnation and wrath towards their sin was placed on Christ's body at the cross. But if people decide to go and stand before God without accepting Christ's payment for their sins, then they will accept the full punishment for their sin nature. We Christians have an awesome message for the world:

Christ accepted the punishment for your sins, by surrendering his life for yours. Now accept his payment for your sins, by surrendering your life to him.

Unsaved child of God, your sin, if left unconfessed and unrepented, will lead to complete separation from God for all eternity. On the other-hand, your confessed sin, that you turn from and repent of, will lead to eternal life and a home in Heaven. So, where are you going to let your sins lead you? Your sins can lead you to Heaven if you understand that you've been released from them. When you're standing before the throne of God the most important question at that moment will be: Did you accept the blood covering of Jesus Christ for your sins or did you reject the most holy, righteous, precious blood that was ever shed for you?

All sins, past, present and future, for all mankind, were placed on and paid in full by the Lord Jesus Christ. People's acceptance of that payment is the crucial element of their salvation.

All the medicine in a hospital will not kill an infectious disease unless people receive it into their body. Jesus' death on the cross was the sufficient, complete and necessary atonement required by God. **God didn't need Christ's sacrifice...we needed it.** God required that a holy, righteous, sinless sacrifice be made. It's also required by God that each person *understands* and *receives* that payment individually.

NEW NATURE - NEW SPIRIT - NEW YOU

The whole world is under the control of the evil one. I John 4:19
The wicked say, "God will never hold me
accountable for my sins." Psalm 10:13
People flatter themselves too much to detect or hate their sin. Ps. 36:2

People who are not born-again refuse to believe in the God of the Bible
because they do not want to be held accountable for their actions.
The problem with that theology is that regardless of what they think,
believe or want, in the end they are still accountable to God.

Ignoring the whole topic of God, the bible, Jesus, sin and salvation is in essence rejecting God, his word and the Messiah. Unsaved people don't want to consider the possibility of being judged by God. However, humanity has already been judged and it's been found guilty.

Whoever believes in Jesus does not need to walk in condemnation ever,
but unfortunately whoever does not believe, stands condemned already.
John 3:18
Sin entered the world through one man (Adam) and death through sin
came to all people, because ALL HAVE SINNED. Romans 5:12
Through the disobedience of one man (Adam)
all people were made sinners. Romans 5:19

Most of the world is just waiting for the pending punishment of sin. Does the world care? They might, if we will take the good news of the gospel message to them. What a wonderful thing that Jesus Christ has done for us when he stepped forward two thousand years ago and said:

I'll pay for their debt of sin…
BECAUSE I LOVE THEM.
I'll suffer and allow myself to be put to shame and tortured…
BECAUSE I LOVE THEM.
I'll shed my blood for their sins, past, present and future…
BECAUSE I LOVE THEM.
I'll take the punishment for the sins of the whole world
upon me at the cross… BECAUSE I LOVE THEM.

Jesus could have called down twelve legions of angels to save him
and take revenge for him. HE COULD HAVE SAVED HIMSELF...
BUT INSTEAD, HE CHOSE TO SAVE US (Mark 15:31).
He chose to love us even when facing a torturous death on a cross.

Jesus said, "No person can take my life from me...
I lay it down on my own." John 10:18

Because of that day over two thousand years ago when Jesus suffered and died on the cross, ALL SIN has been imputed to Christ (II Corinthians 5:19). The good news is EVERYONE ON EARTH IS SAVED! But not everyone has *received* the salvation of the Lord Jesus Christ. People are SAVED by the actions of the Lord Jesus Christ, not their own actions. **Every person who has ever became a born again Christian was saved by a change in their beliefs, not a change in their lifestyle.** We are saved by grace through faith. It doesn't have anything to do with your outstanding performance or glorious virtues (Ephesians 2:8). Now go tell unbelievers that they're ALL SAVED and all they have to do now is *just believe.*

Most unbelievers feel God would never accept them based on their current life style or previous failures. But the Good news is, God already loves them and accepts them. The unbelievers are the ones who aren't accepting him. Wouldn't that be horrific for a person to be lost for all eternity, separated from God forever, when the payment for their ticket to Heaven has already been paid in full? God's wrath and anger for our sins were placed on Christ. God's wrath and anger were completely appeased through the sacrifice of Christ (Isaiah 53:10). Sinners just need to accept God's love, believe his words and receive his free gift of salvation.

God was actually in Christ, reconciling the world to himself,
no longer counting people's sins against them. II Corinthians 5:19
Through the obedience of Jesus many people
will be made righteous. Romans 5:19
If you confess that Jesus is Lord and truly believe this
in your heart... YOU SHALL BE SAVED! Romans 10:9

Now that's a big deal! Don't take these scriptures lightly. Confessing Jesus with your mouth and believing with your heart is a very big deal. These scriptures don't mean that you are simply aware of the historical Jesus and the many things people said he did. These scriptures are talking about coming into agreement with everything Jesus said, stands for and accomplished.

Radical supernatural transformation happens when we come into agreement with everything Jesus said, stands for and accomplished.

This is not patty-cake Christianity; this is an obvious impartation of the Lord Jesus Christ into your life. People are going to sense that something is different about you, because SOMETHING IS COMPLETELY DIFFERENT ABOUT YOU! A change has taken place in *your spirit* at the core of who you are. Your spouse, family, friends and co-workers will begin to notice these changes coming out of you through your words and actions. You can't hide true Christianity under a bowl. You can't live it out in a box or hide it throughout the week at work. It shines from within you like a brilliant light. **It should be radically obvious to people around you that you are different from the rest of the world. Not just in your actions and words but in your *nature* deep down in your spirit.** That's where those outward changes are manifesting themselves from. Galatians 5:22 & 23

You are a light in this dark world. A city on a hill cannot be hidden. People don't light a lamp and put it under a bowl. No...they put it on a stand and it gives light to everyone around them. Matthew 5:14 & 15

True Christianity bears fruit just like a fruit tree does. The fruit is the evidence that the tree is a fruit tree. The fruit on the tree doesn't make the fruit tree a fruit tree. The tree was a fruit tree long before it bore fruit. It's the fruit trees nature to produce something good. It can't help but produce good fruit, because that's the type of tree it is.

People will see your good works (fruit) *and glorify God. Matthew 5:16*
You will recognize the children of God by the fruit (good works)
they produce. Matthew 17:16

The Holy Spirit is constantly teaching us God's thoughts on every subject. The Holy Spirit teaches us how to respond to; people, a situation, sickness, sin, problems, persecution, attitudes and much more. Do we fail and fall sometimes? YES...of course. We're all in the process of letting Christ live through us at different levels. When we fail, we just need to get back up on our feet and walk in the fullness of Christ once again. God knows at one time we were just dust on the ground, but now we are a spirit-filled being he dearly loves.

We are complete IN CHRIST. We do not lack anything in our spirit.
The life of God is in us and we need to grow in our awareness
of HIS NEW NATURE that compels us from within.

The law of Moses could not free you from your sins. But through
Jesus, everyone who believes is free from all sin. Acts 13:39
God treats us much better than we deserve. Because of Jesus Christ,
God freely accepts us and sets us free from our sin. Romans 3:24
Because of God you are in Christ Jesus, who has become for us wisdom
from God. Because of Christ we are in right standing with God.
Because of Christ we have been made holy before God.
Because of Christ we have been set free from sin. I Corinthians 1:30
I urge you, as aliens and strangers in this world, to abstain from sinful
desires which wage war against your mind and body. I Peter 2:11
Do not conform to the evil desires you had
when you were a child of darkness. I Peter 1:14

Some verses in the bible tell us we are free from sin and some tell us that we wrestle or war against sin. So which is it? Are we free from sin or are we slaves to sin?

When a person becomes a born-again Christian their
old sin nature died and their new spirit is supernaturally
alive because it's been touched by God. Romans 6:11

We Christians have a new nature in our spirit. We had an old sinful nature, but that nature is gone now. This new nature produces new fruit. This good fruit that we produce is a bi-product of being IN CHRIST. It comes out of our spirit in Christ-like thoughts and actions. The reason we still sin is not because we have an old nature in us. That old sinful nature is now gone (II Corinthians 5:17). However, we still have a body we must live in. Nothing happened to our body when we were saved (I Corinthians 15:51-54). But our spirit was totally transformed when we accepted Christ as Lord. **Our spirit that was completely dead became completely alive the moment God touched it.**

You have the life of God in your new born-again spirit.
Your body is a vessel for this new life to flow from. John 6:63

Christians sin because they make bad choices. Those bad choices go completely against their new nature. The good news is the body does whatever the mind tells it to do. Here is some more good news:

We have the mind of Christ. I Corinthians 2:16

Do not conform any longer to the pattern of this world. Your mind can be transformed and renewed by reading God's word. Then you will be able to walk in God's good, pleasing and perfect will. Romans 12:2

The grace of God, that brings salvation to everyone, teaches us to turn from ungodliness and sinful pleasures and that we should live soberly, righteously and godly. Titus 2:11 & 12

<u>When we come to the realization that:</u>

We are new creations IN CHRIST.
God has placed a new heart in us that is sensitive to him.
The Holy Spirit lives in us and speaks to us in our mind.

Then we can live this life full of victory by understanding that our old sin nature is gone and we now have the life of God in us. We are free from sin and the condemnation of sin and not lacking any good thing in our spirit.

Your faith will begin to blossom through a revelation in your mind about all these good things; love, peace, joy, authority, power and the anointing that God has planted in your spirit. Philemon 1:6

The Holy Spirit is our teacher, counselor and helper. If we're not sensitive to the Holy Spirit's desire to be involved in our lives, then we cannot be taught, counseled and helped. This will severely hinder your growth and maturity. We stop growing when we refuse to change. A Christian can get themselves into all types of trouble when they no longer listen to or are lead by the spirit of God. The Apostle Paul tells us that we should walk with the spirit of the living God and not in the flesh of our own human desires and emotions (Galatians 5:16). The Spirit of God is in every born-again Christian. God is <u>FOR</u> us. Jesus is <u>WITH</u> us and the Holy Spirit is <u>IN</u> us. What an awesome combination we have in us, around us and working through us. We have so much of God around us that we can never escape him. We have the fullness of the Godhead in us. Colossians 2:9 &10

SATAN'S LIES ARE NEUTRALIZED BY GOD'S TRUTH

Don't listen to the tempter (the Devil) when he comes knocking at the door of your mind. Those old sinful thoughts that may try to influence you came from a completely different *you* with an old dead nature. Remember, the *old you* is gone and the *new you* (through the Spirit of Christ) has come to live in you and stay forever (II Corinthians 5:17). Unfortunately, Christians do allow themselves to listen to the twisted whisper of the enemy. We are supposed to combat his lies, deceptions and temptations with the truth of God's word. We need to actively fight against those temptations by renewing our minds daily with God's truth. James 4:7

Satan tells us the lie. *(But God's truth tells us how to combat it.)*

- They shouldn't talk to you that way. *(If your enemy curses at you and ridicules you then pray for them. Matthew 5:44)*
- You deserve to be treated better than that. *(Pray for those who despitefully use you and persecute you. Matthew 5:44)*
- Don't take that from them. *(Bless people who curse you. Luke 6:28)*
- Let them know exactly how you feel. *(Keep a bridal on your tongue. James 1:26)*
- Give them a piece of your mind. *(The mind led by the spirit is full of life and peace. Romans 8:6)*
- Don't talk to that person ever again. *(Where envying and strife is, there is confusion and every evil work. James 3:16)*
- They don't care about you. *(Do good to those who hate you. Lk 6:27)*
- They don't love you. *(Love hopes for the best in others. I Cor. 13:7)*
- They don't deserve your love. *(If a person says they love God but hates others, how can the love of God be in them? I John 4:20)*
- You deserve that, take it, do it. *(God's grace teaches us to deny ungodliness and worldly lust. Titus 2:11 & 12)*
- God won't hold you accountable for that. *(Whatever master you obey...his servant you become. Romans 6:16)*
- You're only human. *(You are a new creation and you have the life of God in your spirit. II Corinthians 5:17)*
- After all, you have to vent and let it out. *(Your tongue is like a roaring fire that can burn down an entire forest with one angry sentence. James 3:6)*

Remember a garden is a great place to grow vegetables, fruits and also WEEDS! Any seeds good or bad will grow great in freshly tilled and fertile soil of a garden. Any plants that you allow to remain in the garden will flourish. We can't stop the enemy from scattering seeds in the garden of our thought life, but we don't have to allow the seeds to take root and grow.

My wife and I were out in our flower garden one day and she said, "Is this a weed or a flower?" "That's a good question", I told her. It was hard to tell if it was something we should leave alone and let it grow or pull it up by the roots. We need to ask the Holy Spirit, "Is this thought a weed or a flower?" We need to ask the Holy Spirit, "Do I need to nourish that thought by meditating on that?" We need to get our spiritual shovel out and dig up some of the plants we've allowed to grow.

When I was growing up we always had a large vegetable garden that my dad would have us weed throughout the summer. A great tool for doing this was the hoe. With the hoe you could reach the weeds very easily and uproot them even if they were close to the good plants. Usually we simply uprooted the weeds and let the sun shine scorch and kill them in the heat of the day. But my dad told us to go back and gather the weeds lying on top of the ground and throw them away. This had to be done, because even though the weeds were pulled up and laying flat on top of the ground, over a few days the roots would shoot out little roots back into the ground and the weeds would start to grow again. I've seen weeds re-root themselves and thrive many times. In a similar way, evil thoughts die hard if we do not address them immediately with the truth of God's word. Don't just stop thinking about that evil thought, but kick the Devil in the butt by telling him who you are IN CHRIST. Then throw him out your front door and let him know your body is a temple for the Holy Spirit to live in. Then push him down the stairs with a shout of victory from your mouth and finally chase him out of your yard using the authority Jesus gave you. **Let the enemy know you mean business (James 4:7)!** Your mind is too valuable to rent out space to him and his weeds don't need to be anywhere near your garden.

We need to hoe our spiritual garden with the word of God. We pull up weeds and their roots when we listen to the Holy Spirit. **The bible talks about a *root of bitterness* (Hebrews 12:15) and it can take over your garden if you allow anger, strife and unforgiveness to remain deep within you.** A garden full of weeds looks awful. Don't let those weeds choke out all the good fruit that's trying to grow in your life. Don't let anger grow in your heart. Don't let jealousy and pride flourish. Don't let offense and strife be like wild vines that take over everything. Unforgivness may seem like a small plant but the roots grow deep and wide just under the surface.

There are many people who spend a lot of time judging and criticizing others, but never willing to take a close inward look at themselves. The world is full of easily offended people whose rage is ready to consume the next person who bumps up against them. They will shut you out of their life in a micro-second and never talk to you again. I've seen it in the church also, so don't hide from it or ignore it. Confront evil with the light of truth and expose that behavior. God wants Christians to have a beautiful thriving garden for everyone to see and enjoy.

How do Christians let themselves get into this sinful lifestyle? One slow sinful drop at a time. Similar to how a small drop of water can eventually destroy a whole house. A water leak can rot wood, it can destroy drywall and rust pipes. All this can happen before you are even aware it has taken place. By the time you discover the problem, it's too late. The water has already done a lot of damage. My point is, Christians sometimes fall into sin. They make terrible choices when it comes to their attitude, thoughts and actions. **Christ lives in us, but sometimes we make the choice to not express (in our behavior) that Christ lives in us at any given moment throughout our day.**

If you want to glorify God with your life, then allow the Holy Spirit that's inside of you to lead you in works of righteousness. That's when we are at peace. That's our destiny. That's when our new Jesus DNA will burst forth from within us. As born-again, spirit-filled Christians, that's our natural state. When we sin we are in complete disarray. It goes against everything that's in us. But remember…WE DIED TO SIN. It is no longer our nature to sin. **Our old sin nature is no longer our master to the extent that we *have to obey it*. You were meant for something greater. You were meant to display the life of Christ. The Holy Spirit's job is to remind us that we really are pure in God's sight and are made for good deeds…not sin.**

If anyone has Christ living on the inside of them, then they are a NEW CREATION. The OLD NATURE has been done away with and the NEW LIFE of Christ has come to permanently reside in us. So allow Christ to express himself through you. II Corinthians 5:17

GO AND SIN NO MORE

One time I walked down stairs into my living room, and to my complete surprise, there was a huge bump in our living room ceiling. There was literally a six foot round, one foot deep sagging bump in my ceiling. I pushed up on the soft drywall and knew, THIS WAS BAD! I knew I not only had an extensive drywall problem to repair, but I also had to find the leak that caused this and repair the roof as well. When it rained, water leaked through the roof and onto the roof rafters, then it would drip down onto the flat drywall area in the attic space. The water began to soften and deteriorate the drywall from the back side (the attic side). I couldn't tell anything was happening from the living room side. The water was slowly weakening the drywall every time it rained. I never could tell any damage was being done until there was a total failure in the drywall with this huge sagging dip. By the time I saw the problem a tremendous amount of damage had already been done. It was a slow deterioration process, but in the end, it was clearly noticeable for everyone to see.

In a similar way, this is what happens to us spiritually when we allow things to go unchecked by the Holy Spirit. Our faith is hindered when we allow things to remain in us that have no right to be there. Little things like hurts or offenses, if left unchecked, can take root in our lives. **We allow them to grow freely when we meditate on them often.** This is when a Christian can get themselves into all kinds of trouble. It can actually cause a lifetime of destruction if not confronted with wisdom from God and the truth of his word. The bible calls it, *giving the enemy a foothold.* Have you ever tried to push a car in the winter time when the ground was slippery? If you could just get a foothold some place you could push the car. If you could just get your foot to grip on a little edge of pavement or in a pot hole, you would have some power and influence over the car. See how important a foothold is for making progress. The same is true with a mountain climber. They are constantly looking up to see what the best path to take is. They don't want to climb themselves into a DEAD ZONE where there are no footholds. A mountain climber is in constant need of footholds to make progress. Many times a foothold is just a small little bump that a climber can capitalize on. The bible tells us, *"Do not give the enemy a foothold"* *(Ephesians 4:27).* Any sin you're holding onto is a foothold for the enemy and it allows him to make progress in your life.

Get rid of all bitterness, rage, anger, brawling and evil communication.
Ephesians 4:31

Get ride of all selfishness, jealousy, malice, sexual impurity,
lust and any other evil thoughts. Colossians 3:5-9

People fall into sin all the time. Non-Christians sin until their hearts are full. They can't get enough. Christians have been freed from the curse of sin and the law of sin. But many choose to go back and be a slave to it once again. The best way I can describe it is like this; non-Christians leap into sin, Christian's trip and fall into sin. Christians sometimes choose to get angry, be jealous, hateful, unforgiving and lustful. When they do this they allow their first line of defense to be overtaken. The first line of defense is our thought life. Evil thoughts just seem to pop into our minds sometimes, you can't help it. Meditating on those evil thoughts is where the danger lies. Eject that thought from your mind instantly. Don't allow the enemy to secure a foothold. Take that thought captive to the obedience of Christ as it says to do in II Corinthians 10:5. Don't allow a *root of bitterness* to overcome you. It can steal years of joy, peace, growth, maturity and victory from your life. It can wreak havoc in your thought life, personal life and spiritual life. That's not the life you were designed to live. Stubbornness, selfishness and strife are not *fruits of the Holy Spirit*. Christians need to allow Christ to come out of them, because that fulfills our purpose and that's how God is glorified.

We are NEW CREATIONS at the core of our spirit,
regardless of how we choose to act at any given moment.
Expressing Christ in our thoughts, words and actions
is the way we find complete fulfillment in our lives.

Christians no longer desire to sin because of the new spirit that was placed in them. Righteousness has been deposited in the core of our nature. Does your mind and body fail some days? Of course it does. But your new spirit that God planted in you will never fail. It is continually giving you Christ-like desires in your heart. You know your not happy deep down in your soul when you're angry with someone. You know there is uneasiness in your spirit when you are bitter and harbor unforgiveness. Christians who do sin simply need to come into agreement with what Christ has already accomplished for them. I usually pray something like this:

> Here's my sin Lord. I'm leaving it at the cross where it has already been dealt with. Your forgiveness has covered all my past, present and future sins. I want to walk in the freedom that was secured for me at the cross. In Jesus name, Amen!

I've heard some people simply say, "Thank you Jesus...for your blood."

THE CALLOUSED HARD HEART

Jesus Christ has already completed all that was necessary for us to have healing, peace, forgiveness, restoration, wholeness and unity with God. If God wants so many positive things for people, then why do they spend a lifetime running from him? I believe the answer is a calloused heart. Don't harden your heart to the Holy Spirit. If you do, his voice will get softer and softer until you don't hear him at all. That's the worst possible condition a person can be in.

The people's hearts have become calloused, they hardly hear with their ears and they have shut their eyes to the truth. Otherwise they might see God clearly, hear his voice, understand with their hearts and then they would be healed. Matthew 13:15

From your calloused heart comes a flood of iniquity. Psalm 73:7 They close up their calloused hearts and their mouths speak with arrogance. Psalm 17:10

When people push away from the Holy Spirit's love, promptings and voice, they harden their hearts to him. Ignoring the Holy Spirit grieves him deeply. Let's say a form of pride sweeps over you, this soon leads to a haughty, judgmental spirit. The bible says:

God opposes the proud...but gives grace to the humble. James 4:6

This scripture is not saying God dislikes pride or even hates it. It's saying because of your spirit of pride you are now in DIRECT OPPOSITION TO GOD! I hope you understand how dangerous a prideful, haughty, hardened heart can be. Religion can lead to sin real quick and that can cause you to be judgmental of everyone around you. **Having a judgmental spirit is a way of diverting the attention from your broken heart and instead focusing on the faults of others.** It's always easier to point your finger at someone else rather than turn and examine your own heart. God does not want his children walking around depressed, discouraged and frustrated by numbing themselves to the Holy Spirit that's inside them.

Why are you so focused on the speck of sawdust in your friend's eye, and you pay no attention to the large beam in your own eye. Matt. 7:3

You strain the gnat out of your friend's soup but eat the camel that's in yours. Matthew 23:24

*In their own eyes they flatter themselves too
much to detect or hate their sin. Psalm 36:2*

People blanket themselves with a false sense of righteousness by esteeming their own virtues and focusing on what's wrong with others. This manufactured self-righteousness is like an umbrella people put over their head and this will keep the rain of God's grace from falling on them. You can't soak in God's grace if you're full of yourself. This is the core of religious thinking and it is a stench to God. God says it's like a pile of filthy rags (Isaiah 64:6). The reason God despises your own righteousness so much, is because it doesn't lead to the godly sorrow type of change and maturity he wants to see in you. **You can spend the rest of your life pointing out people's faults because there are plenty of imperfect people around. We need to allow the Holy Spirit to search our heart so we can grow, mature and express God's *new nature* living on the inside of us.** That's how we glorify God. Releasing God's nature on people also pleases us. You'll be a much happier Christian when you are led by your *new nature*. You'll be frustrated, miserable and discouraged when you let your flesh, emotions and your five senses make all your choices for you.

The Holy Spirit was given to us to teach us, minister to us, help us and counsel us. A person who refuses to listen to the Holy Spirit will have less and less sensitivity to God. When Christians allow their hearts to become calloused, they decrease their spiritual sensitivity to God's voice. Jesus said, *"I will send the Holy Spirit and he will fill you with power from Heaven" (Luke 24:49).* **The power of God's spirit is in us!** Trying to live this Christian life without tapping into the power of the Holy Spirit would be like a fireman charging into a burning house with a squirt gun. The fireman needs the full force and volume of the city water system to overcome the fire. You can't live a incredible, victorious, powerful Christian life without plugging into the power of God's Holy Spirit. **When you close yourself off to the Holy Spirit's teaching and leading, the bible just becomes information without wisdom and words without supernatural revelation.** You also won't be passionate about reading and understanding God's word. Operating by your own strength and power is called religion and it will leave you tired, run down, dry and disillusioned.

The person without the Spirit (or the person who ignores the Spirit of
God) *does not accept the things that come from God, for they
seem foolish to them and they cannot understand them
because they are spiritually discerned. I Corinthians 2:14*

We need to listen to the Holy Spirit.
He's our life line to not only surviving but thriving.

Do not put out the Spirit's fire, when he's trying to <u>teach</u> you.
Do not put out the Spirit's fire, when he's trying to <u>speak</u> to you.
Do not put out the Spirit's fire, when he's trying to <u>pray</u> through you.
Do not put out the Spirit's fire,
when he's trying to <u>love</u> someone through you.
Do not put out the Spirit's fire, when he's trying to <u>worship</u> through you.
I Thessalonians 5:19

Another way people allow their hearts to become calloused and
hard; is by not allowing God to heal their heart. God designed hearts to
be soft and sensitive, they are the most fragile and vulnerable part of us.
Hurting people can't heal themselves. They only know how to put up
walls to protect themselves. Walls don't heal people, they divide people.
When that pain and hurt is allowed to go unchecked it can lead to all
kinds of dysfunctional thinking and eventually dysfunctional living.
Proverbs 23:7

*God heals the brokenhearted and binds up their wounds. Psalm 147:3
The Lord is close to the brokenhearted and saves
those who are crushed in spirit. Psalm 34:18*

I believe most of us could benefit from some form of professional
counseling by talking to a therapist or a psychiatrist. It's a good idea to
get advice and direction from people. But God does more than help us,
he heals us from the inside out. Only God can heal our heart because he
created us. I ask God all the time, "Heal the things in me that I don't
even know need healing."

*Come to me, all you who are weary and burdened with life and I will
give you rest. Take my yoke upon you and learn from me, for I am gentle
and humble and you will find rest for your hurting soul. Matt. 11:28 & 29*

*I will give you a new heart and put a new spirit in you.
I will remove your heart of stone and give you a
supernaturally sensitive heart of flesh. Ezekiel 36:26*

God will heal YOU, restore YOU, fix YOU,
encourage YOU and counsel YOU. So that you can
glorify HIM, praise HIM, thank HIM and love HIM.

GOD'S ANGER AND WRATH WAS APPEASED
AT THE CROSS OF CHRIST

God doesn't want anyone to perish. He wants everyone to
find and enjoy salvation through the Lord Jesus Christ. John 3:16

God knows Christians are not perfect, but we are forgiven and that's EVERYTHING! **We can't keep track of every sin we've committed and God doesn't expect us to. That would be impossible!** Even the good deeds we should be doing and aren't doing are called sin in James 4:17. You don't have to come to God with all the many things you've done wrong everyday. He just wants you to understand that Christ has already accomplished everything that was required for the complete payment of your sins.

Christ went <u>once for all</u> into the most holy place and <u>freed us</u>
<u>from sin forever.</u> He did this by offering his own holy, precious,
sinless blood instead of the blood of goats and bulls. Hebrews 9:12

In accordance with the will of God, we have been made holy
(consecrated and sanctified) *through the sacrifice of the*
body of Christ, <u>once for all.</u> Hebrews 10:10

God was actually in Christ, reconciling people to himself,
<u>not imputing their trespasses to them anymore</u> and has committed
to us the ministry of reconciliation. II Corinthians 5:19

Jesus is not going to offer his body or blood over and over the way the Old Testament priest did. They entered the temple year after year to try to cover the sins of the people with an animal sacrifice. Christ died once for all, <u>to do away with sin through the perfect sacrifice of his holy blood.</u> Christ was sacrificed once <u>to take away the sins of many people</u> and he will appear a second time, not to bear sin, but to celebrate the salvation of those who are waiting for him. Hebrews 9:25-28

Christ died for sins <u>once for all, the righteous for the unrighteous, to</u> <u>bring you to God and to make your spirit righteous before him.</u> Jesus was put to death in the body but made alive by the Spirit. I Peter 3:18

If we walk in the light, as he is in the light, we have fellowship with each other and the blood of Jesus <u>removes our sins completely from us.</u> I John 1:7

I will be merciful towards their unrighteousness and their sins and iniquities I will never remember again. Hebrews 8:12

Here are what all these scriptures are screaming out to us.

Christ died once for ALL PEOPLE!
Christ died once for ALL SIN!
Christ died once for ALL TIME!

One drop of Christ's blood was enough to take care of every sin that was ever going to be committed by mankind for all time.

Are you always troubled in your soul and fearful? Do you have an argumentative personality? Are you an easily offended person whose rage and wrath is ready to fight with people when they come against you? It might not be a physical put up your fist and fight kind of rage. It might be a violent rage you keep hidden deep down in your soul. You might not let it out for everyone to see, but it's there doing its destructive work in you.

If you're a Christian and you find yourself in this dreadful condition, then meet Christ at the cross and lay your baggage there. We need to release sin at the cross and walk away from it guilt free. Don't allow the enemy to bark at you with his condemning words because of your faults and failures. Your sins are covered with the blood of Christ. **Your spirit is saved, purged, sealed, sanctified and righteous. The enemy can't touch your spirit. Your spirit can no longer sin (I John 3:9). The enemy can only tempt you in your thought life and try to get you to react to some of your old desires. Many Christians walk around with guilt and condemnation over sin in their emotional realm because they don't understand and receive God's complete forgiveness that took place in their spirit. That's why understanding in your mind what has taken place in your spirit is so vitally important. Many churches have failed dreadfully in teaching these truths.**

The forgiving work has already been accomplished by God through Jesus. We are already forgiven for *all our sins.* All of the sins that you committed in the *past* and all your sins that you commit *today* and all the sins that you will commit in the *future*, <u>WERE ALL IN THE FUTURE</u> when Jesus died for you two-thousand years ago. We have been forgiven. We are a forgiven people. But like anything else we get from God, we have to do the *accepting* and *receiving* part. We need to walk in the fullness of God's grace and have complete confidence in what Christ accomplished in the atonement. Whatever word you want to use is fine, but they all really mean the same thing. Confess, repent, come into agreement with, acknowledge; all these words really mean that we are to lay all our condemnation from sin at the CROSS OF CHRIST where the saving work has already been accomplished and walk away from it completely free forever.

---

*God sees you as righteous, holy, pure and clean. These attributes
(which are found in your spirit) are NOT based on YOUR actions;
they're based on CHRIST'S actions for you. Your actions didn't
get you saved, your belief in Christ's actions is what saved you.
You are who you are based on your NATURE not your ACTIONS.
Your actions will always follow close on the heels of your _flesh_
or your _spirit_. Which-ever one dominates you the most
will control your thoughts, actions and inevitable your life.*

Your spirit that was completely dead was resurrected when you became a born-again believer. **Your spirit is now pure, holy, righteous, forgiven forever, purged, sinless and sealed. That's something to get excited about!**

God gets excited when we take that challenging, difficult inward look at ourselves. When you come to the cross of Christ, that's a time when God is happy to stand next to your sin, because that's where it was attached to his son. **God's wrath and anger against sin was poured out on Christ so there's now peace between you and God.** Remember God loves you and his Holy Spirit will lead you away from the power of sin as it tries to attach itself to your mind, mouth, attitude and actions.

*It is by God's grace that we have been saved through our belief in
Christ's actions. It is a completely free gift from God and it would no
longer be a gift if you felt you deserved it, earned it or maintained it
through your perfect performance. Your salvation is not maintained
by your actions, secured by your attributes or based on
your own personal righteousness. Ephesians 2:8 & 9*

*God's grace teaches us to deny ungodliness and worldly lust
and to be righteous before the world in our actions because
we are righteous before God in our spirit. Titus 2:12*

God is the one who came up with the forgiving plan of salvation and the only way is through his son Jesus Christ. Don't let the enemy use embarrassment or shame to keep you from coming before God. If the enemy has whispered in your ear, "You're not good enough to come before God." Then tell him, "You must be talking to the *old me*. **The *new me* is forgiven, holy, righteous, pure, accepted, blameless and clean before God.** Forgiveness is a gift we receive from God. You can't earn it through behavior modification or works (Ephesians 2:9). Like any gift, you need to open it, accept it, receive it, enjoy it and then be thankful for it.

The bridge of salvation was designed and built by God to bring you to him. Each board that was put in place to build this bridge was paid for by Christ's blood. When you first accepted Christ as Lord and walked over this bridge, you may have noticed that every board had the word GRACE engraved on it. You can't cross a bridge that's not completely finished because it won't be structurally sound and it could collapse. **Christ is not giving people bits and pieces of forgiveness throughout their lives.** He paid the complete price for you long before you accepted him as Lord. At the end of Jesus life he cried out those three wonderful words from the cross, *"It* (the bridge) *is finished!"*

The world has tried to come up with countless ways of dealing with sin. Even many Christians today are still trying to figure out how to deal with people's sin issues. Pastors scream at the top of their lungs for people to stop sinning, but that doesn't ever seem to work. God came up with the only way to redeem us and that's through the blood sacrifice of his son Jesus Christ. **One drop of Christ's blood was more than enough to pay for ALL the sin of ALL mankind for ALL time. Don't ever underestimate the thoroughness of that cleansing process in your spirit. Your new born-again spirit is wall-to-wall, floor-to-ceiling filled with God.**

STORY - Take Care Of Your Plumbing Problems

When I was a teenager, my dad and I had to dig up our house sewer line. We soon discovered that some tree roots had grown over to the sewer line and those roots latched on to that cool moist sewer pipe. The roots were literally drawing the moisture through the clay porous pipe. They grew right down along the length of the pipe, following the moisture. We found a very small crack in the sewer pipe and one very small white root made its way into the crack. When we broke open that section of pipe we saw that one little root had just exploded in growth when it entered the pipe. There was a large cylinder shaped mass of roots clogging up the entire pipe. They all formed from that one little root. Nothing could flow freely in the pipe anymore. We had found the problem and fixed the clog in the pipe.

When Christians sin it is extremely uncomfortable for them because they have Christ's spirit in them. They feel like this free flowing pipe-line between them and God has been clogged up. Just like the little white root caused a huge household problem; the enemy always takes advantage of every opportunity to make you feel guilty, condemned and worthless. He makes you feel like God is not talking to you anymore, like God has turned his back on you. The enemy wants you to feel distant from God. Don't continue to listen to the enemy's ranting. Direct him to the CROSS OF CHRIST. If he wants to continue with the subject of your sin, then the conversation will have to take place at the base of the cross. He probably won't want to go there with you because he doesn't want to be anywhere near the blood of Jesus.

The Holy Spirit will lead you in your quest of living a complete and full life IN CHRIST. We need to let the Holy Spirit teach us, counsel us and guide us by responding to his promptings and voice. Sit down with the Holy Spirit and have a Holy Ghost chat. If you've sinned, the Spirit of God will remind you that **you are a redeemed, reconciled, forgiven, sanctified, sealed and accepted...because Jesus made peace between you and God.**

The God of the universe that created all things wants to hear from YOU! That just blows me away that God listens to little old insignificant me. God wants to hear about your problems, cares and worries. But he also wants us to be sensitive to his promptings and listen to his solutions to get out of those problems. **People want God to listen to them when they pray because they have a need and they want God to move in their situation. But God wants us to listen to him every moment of everyday, counseling us in our thoughts, teaching us new words to speak and directing our hands to glorify him. God loves us so much; he has literally placed his fullness inside of us. Colossians 2:9 &10**

The Holy Spirit will show you how much God loves you...
now enjoy his affection and attention.
The Holy Spirit will show you God's complete forgiveness...
now rest in the security of that thorough cleansing.
God has deposited his love, power, spirit and anointing in us...
now walk in that truth.

I am filled with such great joy knowing that
my children are walking in the truth. III John 1:4

Faith is our positive response to what God
has already accomplished for us by grace.

When the evil one comes to condemn you, here is a full proof plan to refute the condemning power of Satan. This will work for all born-again, blood-bought children of God.

Ok Devil, if you want to bring up my sins…then fine…let's look at them. Let's go and look at my sinful life. Let's go on a spiritual walk down that road of Calvary. Come here Satan and follow me, don't lag behind. Do you see the cross on that hill over there? Let's go a little bit closer. Why do you seem so afraid? You see the cross is where my sins were nailed. Christ's body became the ultimate, once and for all sacrifice for my sins. Do you see his blood on the cross? Why are you shaking? Come closer if you want to see my sins because they're all right there. You're the one who wanted to condemn me for them! So I thought I'd show you where they were dealt with once and for all. You want me to take up a life of sin again! Then here let me take them from the cross. They won't seem to come off the cross but now my hands are covered in Christ's blood. Do you want to see what is left of my sins…all that remains is his holy, sinless blood.

You can now chase after the enemy with the blood of Christ. He doesn't want to be anywhere near it. It was the blood of Jesus Christ that Satan sought after so fervently and eventually it destroyed his hold on all mankind.

THE CROSS
by Eric Johnson

As I walked down the path into the woods, I noticed a man up ahead.
When I reached him we walked together for a while.
We talked about who I was, my life and a lot about my past.
He began criticizing me about a lot of things I had done.
He began accusing me and condemning me for every sinful act.
I felt awful as I began revisiting in my mind the things
I had done. I wondered how he knew so much about my past,
it was like he was there at every evil moment. After a few more
accusations from him, an unusual smile came over my face.

I turned away from him and walked out of the woods and into the field.
He stayed close behind me with his relentless condemning mouth.
I just smiled and walked to the top of the hill.

All of a sudden he was completely silent.
He stood there frozen, looking straight at the wooden cross.
I said, "Come a little closer if you want to get a good look at all my sins.
They were nailed to that cross some time ago. Why do you stand back?
Why are you so afraid? You are the one who brought up my past,
so come closer if you want to get a good look.
All those sins you mentioned are here nailed to the cross.
I've visited here before and Jesus told me,
"OLD THINGS HAVE PASSED AWAY
AND BEHOLD I MAKE ALL THINGS NEW!"

"Do you want me to take them down from the cross?"
I pulled but the cross would not let go of them.
When I held out my hands and took a step toward him he jumped back.
Then I saw the blood on my hands, blood from the cross.
"If you want to touch my sins, you're going to have to go
through the blood of Jesus first, and I know you can't do that.
SO BE GONE WITH YOU!" When I took another step towards him
he fled back into the woods. The accuser comes back every now
and then and when he does, I just ask him if he wants to
go on another walk with me...to a hill...called Calvary.

Supporting scriptures

*There is no condemnation for those who are in Christ Jesus
because God sent his Son, in the likeness of sinful man,
to be a sin offering for us. Romans 8:1-3*

*Don't let your mind be controlled by the philosophies of this world,
but allow the Holy Spirit to transform and renew your mind.
Then you will be able to understand God's perfect will
for your life and please him in every way. Romans 12:1 & 2*

*Your body is a temple for the Spirit of God to reside in.
You are not your own, you were bought with a price.
Therefore honor God with your body. I Corinthians 6:19 & 20*

*Because Christ lives in you, you are a new creation, your OLD
NATURE is completely gone and your NEW NATURE is here to stay.
God in his great love and mercy has reconciled the world to himself
through Christ Jesus. He's no longer counting our sins against us. God
made him who had no sin, to be sin for us, so that through Jesus Christ,
everyone could be righteous before God. II Corinthians 5:17-19*

*My OLD NATURE has been crucified with Christ. It is completely dead.
Now that Christ lives in me, I'm a new creation with a NEW NATURE.
Galatians 2:20*

*Jesus bore our sins in his body on the cross, so that we might die to sin
and live for righteousness. We were like sheep that had lost their way,
but now we have been saved by our shepherd. I Peter 2:24 & 25*

**The sacrifice of the Lord Jesus Christ on the cross was the
necessary payment to appease God's wrath and anger towards sin.
There is now peace between God and mankind. That is the greatest
message you could ever share with anyone. The WAR IS OVER
between God and us!**

*God is at peace with mankind because of
Christ's atonement at the cross. Romans 5:1*

THE NEW YOU

Whatever it is that's keeping you from getting closer to God; sin, fear, embarrassment, anxiety, worry, pride, control, stubbornness, arrogance, the love of money, worldly education, family members or being overly self-conscience. LET IT GO, GET RID OF IT. It's not worth missing out on a glorious faith-filled life with God. We sometimes feel distant from him because of wrong thinking and confusion, but the truth is, **we Christians have the fullness of God's Spirit living in us.**

WE ARE NEVER DISTANT FROM GOD.

Maybe you feel dry and empty in your soul. Maybe you let some sin issues creep in. Maybe you got a little bit religious, puffed up and judgmental toward everyone else, but not mature enough to take an inward look at yourself. Ask the Holy Spirit to take a good look at you. Do you know what he will say? He will say:

> I love you. God loves you. Christ laid down his life for you. Operate in this complete love that I have planted in your spirit. Don't hold me at a distance any longer. I adore you. I'm jealous for you and I'm not apologizing for it. My love has completely overtaken your spirit. I want you to understand this in your mind, walk in my love and shine like children of light.

Remember God has completely forgiven you of your sins. God chooses to forgive us because he loves us and we choose to accept his complete forgiveness because we believe the truth about his nature. God says he actually forgets about our sins in Hebrews 8:12. When he looks at you, he chooses to not see your sins any longer. Shouldn't we do the same thing, don't meditate on your failures (Hebrews 9:14,10:2). **Look to a future overflowing with complete forgiveness, being made righteousness, radical freedom, extreme confidence and eternal security that can not be stripped away. God says in his word:**

> *I will blot out your transgressions for my own sake*
> *and remember your sins no more. Isaiah 43:25*

Sin is no longer an issue between God and you because the Lord Jesus Christ was punished for your sin. If you don't feel like Christ was punished enough for your sin, then you don't understand how precious, holy and sinless his blood was. **Christians are covered in the righteousness of Christ! Now that's something to celebrate! When**

God looks at us, he sees his child that he loves, forgiven, accepted, healed, pure, holy, anointed and complete. God is completely at peace with us. His presence doesn't withdraw from us when we sin. If God could get you to fully understand these life transforming concepts about yourself, then it would radically and drastically change your relationship with him.

Forgiveness is God's gift to us, you can't earn forgiveness. You can only receive it and walk in it. Jesus paid a huge price for your salvation, so don't diminish its worth by trying to pay for it or even maintain it by some works of your own. **Accept Jesus Christ's blood covering for your sins as the complete and final end to Satan's hold on you…FOREVER!** The only communication between you and Satan from now on is going to be something like this.

Satan you are defeated by the blood of Jesus! I am forgiven and have been set free from sin forever! When Jesus said, "IT IS FINISHED", he also meant, YOU ARE FINISHED! Your work here in my spirit is done. My spirit is completely redeemed and sealed and you can't touch it! I've been around your mountain far too many times. Our friendship is over! Our relationship has been supernaturally severed. If you come back to hang around me, then you're going to have to just sit there and watch me praise God and bless his name. By the way, I'm going to tell others about the supernatural change that has taken place in me so they will know there's more to this life than what you have to offer. So here is a word from my mouth to your ear:

I REBUKE YOU SATAN!

Our life together, our friendship and this conversation is over!

Jesus' last words from the cross were "IT IS FINISHED". Be secure in the finished work of Christ and rest in his redeeming work that was accomplished for you. IT WAS FINISHED…FOR YOU…HIS BELOVED.

If we confess our sins, he is faithful and just and will forgive us our sins, and purify us in our spirit…from ALL unrighteousness. I John 1:9

*The arm of the Lord is never to short to save
or his ear to dull to hear our cry. Isaiah 59:1*

*There is no condemnation for those who are in Christ Jesus
who walk not after the flesh but after the Spirit. Romans 8:1*

Satan condemns Christians who sin and conversely the Holy Spirit prompts Christians who sin. There is a tremendous difference. The enemy will provide plenty of guilt and condemnation in regards to sin to drive you away from God. **The enemy wants you to believe you're not worth God's time and you've disappointed God so many times that he will never accept you again. Satan wants you to believe that you're always on the verge of losing your salvation.** Don't get me wrong, you should feel bad when you've sinned, because it goes against your *new nature* of being IN CHRIST. You should hate sin in the same way God hates it. God HATES all sin, but he doesn't hate you. He can't hate you, HE'S APART OF YOU! That's why he designed a once and for all type of sacrifice (Jesus' blood) that would appease his wrath towards sin. **God designed a bullet-proof plan of salvation for us, not a wavering, fragile salvation that's based on our performance, virtues or sinlessness.**

God is not responding to you based on your actions,
he's responding to you based on Christ's actions
through the atonement. You know what…
you really don't want it any other way.

The cross of Christ is a great place to visit. That's where God's wrath, anger and judgment toward your sins were imputed to Christ. But let's not forget what happened at the tomb where they laid Jesus' body. The tomb of Christ is a phenomenal place to focus on. The power of God's own hand raised Christ up from the dead. God's very own hand has raised you from the dead also! You were dead in you transgressions and sins but now you have been raised up with Christ and are seated with him in Heavenly realms (Ephesians 2:6). **This means the exact same power that raised Christ from the dead is inside of every born-again Christian.**

This is the exceeding greatness of his power that has been given to us who believe, according to the working of his mighty strength which he wrought in Christ when he raised him from the dead and set him at his own right hand in Heaven. Ephesians 1:19 & 20

We were buried with him through baptism into his death. But just as Christ was raised from the dead to glorify the Father, we to may live a new life in Christ that glorifies God. Romans 6:4

*If the Spirit of him who raised Jesus from the dead is living in you,
then he who raised Christ from the dead will also give life to your
mortal bodies through his Spirit who lives in you. Romans 8:11*

INCREDIBLE! INCREDIBLE! INCREDIBLE!

It's all about new life! Your old spirit is gone; therefore your old life is gone. Or at least it can be or will slip away eventually as you renew your mind in God's word. As you begin to understand what has happened in your new born-again spirit…then you will start acting differently. **The enemy wants to remind you of the old you. He wants you to stay focused on who you were. But the Holy Spirit is constantly revealing to us who we are now that we are IN CHRIST.**

---

*God has so much for you to discover in your NEW LIFE in Christ.
You don't have time to constantly be going back and reflecting on
your OLD life, OLD nature, OLD thinking and OLD habits.
You have a completely forgiven spirit now. The Holy Spirit uses
the truth of God's word to draw us away from our OLD WAY
OF THINKING and he leads us into a NEW WAY OF LIVING
based on the LIFE OF GOD that's in us.*

THE CHOICE IS HEAVEN OR HELL
*God will love you even as you turn and leave his presence
forever and walk into a Hell that you chose over him.*

A person only has two choices for all eternity, HEAVEN or HELL. Sounds like a very easy choice doesn't it? If it's such an easy choice to make, then why did Jesus say,

*Despite all my warnings many will travel down the road the leads to
death and destruction…ut the few who will listen shall have
eternal life and a home in Heaven. Matthew 7:13 &14*

If going to Heaven is a completely free gift that God extends to everyone, then why do so few people accept that gift? How did Jesus know that a majority of the people would choose Hell instead of him?

---

*Everyone says they want to go to Heaven for all eternity, but they
won't spend one minute of their life researching how to get there.*

Many people just hope they will make it there by being a good person, but that's a foolish way to believe when it comes to your eternal security. Heaven and Hell are supernatural places so you have to go to a supernatural resource to understand them. Hell was not even created for people. It was prepared for the Devil and his demons. People aren't supposed to go there; it was never designed for our punishment. Unfortunately people choose to go there everyday. Could God stop people from entering Hell? YES! After all he's God! But it's not his choice to make; it's each individual person's choice to make. God is screaming at the top of his lungs to people, CHOOSE ME! CHOOSE HEAVEN! CHOOSE ETERNAL LIFE! Unfortunately many people aren't listening. They've tuned God out and desensitized themselves to his promptings. People choose to go to Hell everyday by rejecting the Lord Jesus Christ as their savior. You don't have to be a card carrying Satanist to go to Hell.

Simply reject God over and over for the rest of your life.
Ignore him every time he prompts you to seek after him.
Reject the Lord Jesus Christ and his payment for your sin.

IT'S YOUR INDIVIDUAL CHOICE TO MAKE.
He can't make the choice for you. If it was up to God EVERYONE WOULD GO TO HEAVEN, he said so himself.

The Lord is not willing that anyone would perish,
but that EVERYONE would enjoy his salvation. II Peter 3:9
God wants everyone saved by knowing that the Lord Jesus Christ is
their redeemer and he gave his life as a ransom for all. I Timothy 2:4-6

One of the most popular responses from people when you ask them if they're going to Heaven is, "Oh yes, I'm a good person compared to others." That's their first mistake. People think being a good person is the requirement for getting into Heaven. The second mistake people make is this: They judge and compare their sinfulness to other people's sinfulness. They try to elevate their performance by comparing themselves to other people's failures. Once again, it's not even your *own goodness* that gets you into Heaven. The third mistake people make when it comes to their eternal security is this: It's not their judgment that matters. It's God's judgment that matters. **People need to find out what standard God is going to use when judging them. Not so they can meet that standard, but so they will realize they could never meet his standard.** If you're relying on your efforts to gain favor with God and access into Heaven, then you've just insulted God and rebuked the sacrifice of the Lord Jesus Christ.

The standard God is going to use to judge whether you're good enough to get into Heaven is this: ABSOLUTE PERFECTION, IRREFUTABLE HOLINESS and SINLESSNESS IN EVERY AREA OF YOUR LIFE. Sinless with every thought you've had, holiness in every word you've spoken and righteousness in all your actions. How are you doing so far? Not so good maybe. You can't meet God's perfect standard of holiness, that's why we needed the Lord Jesus Christ.

I always thought Matthew 7:13 & 14 was talking about the number of people who will make it into Heaven and Hell. There will be this huge number of people who would go to Hell and very few that would go to Heaven. But it says wide is the *gate* to Hell and narrow is *the way* to Heaven. It doesn't matter how narrow a mountain ledge is, everyone on the face of the earth could cross it if we all scooted over one person at a time. A gate is a way to get some place. So this scripture is talking about *the requirements to get through the gate*. Many people are using the wrong standard to get into Heaven. This wrong standard is developed through performance based religion. Religious people believe their goodness will get them into Heaven or their awesome works will secure their place there. That's the wrong standard; they're trying to enter through the wrong gate. Many people will be deceived in this way, that's why Matthew 7:13 & 14 calls it a wide gate.

The flip side to Matthew 7:13 & 14 is this; there is also a narrow gate that seems too good to be true. This small gate is *not performance based* and many people have a hard time with this, but really they shouldn't. It's actually the best way and the only way to get into Heaven. **This small gate doesn't require you to be perfect, holy, righteous, blameless and sinless. It requires Jesus to be perfect, holy, righteous, blameless and sinless...and he was and is.** Jesus said he was THE WAY to get to God his Father (John 14:6). He is the narrow gate that only requires that you trust in him (John 10:9).

WOW! That's totally awesome! That just took all the pressure off us! All we have to do is believe. Believe the words that Jesus spoke. Believe in the things he did and believe in the atonement he secured for us. People tend to think they need to add something to their salvation. But if you try to add something of your own to this salvation then it's no longer a completely free gift from God, earned for you by Christ's actions alone. You're devaluing Christ's sacrifice and mocking God's grace.

God imputes righteousness without human effort. Romans 4:6

Romans 11:6 clearly explain this concept; if salvation, righteousness and justification are somehow a by-product of our own efforts, then there is no room for God's grace in your life. The Apostle Paul repeatedly made this point in the book of Romans, that salvation and justification are acquired by faith in God's grace. We are saved by believing Christ is our savior and that's it (Romans 10:9 & 10). We are not saved by our actions, works, or by maintaining any of the Old Testament laws. We are also not saved by conforming to any New Testament performance based scriptures. The action based verses we find in the New Testament reveal to us the character of God. Since Christ now lives in us, we will soon be walking in the spirit and displaying those same character attributes. That's the salvation God wants us to understand, experience and enjoy. This is the only type of salvation we can truly rest in.

Paul continually bombarded the Jews with the fact that salvation has been extended to us by God's grace. The only part we have in salvation is the faith part (the believing part). Many religious people cannot accept the fact that all we have to do is *believe* to receive this salvation (Romans 5:2). By *believing* you received God's peace when it came into your heart. By *believing* you received Christ's righteousness and holiness. Even though believing sounds simple and it's all we have to do, it's still a major role at the point of salvation and in our daily walk of faith. Mark 11:24 tells us to *pray* and *believe* at the same time, so does Matthew 21:22. This means it's possible to pray and *not* believe at the same time. Believe God's word, trust him with all your heart, have complete confidence in the atonement of Christ and let the Holy Spirit lead you into this new life IN CHRIST.

Sometimes there is a fine line between Christianity and religion. Throughout your Christian walk, don't ever step over that line into performance-based faith and action based salvation. Don't lean on your own righteousness, you'll end up bickering with everyone, frustrated with people, tired, dry and disillusioned in your faith. You'll always be condemned in your conscious because you can't ever seem to live up to God's perfect standard of holiness. **If you could live your life perfectly holy, righteous and sinless; you wouldn't have needed a savior.** Religious people don't ever feel like they do enough to please God. The truth is…you don't have to do anything to please God. He's already at peace with you because of Christ's blood. Ephesians 2:13 & 14

God's standard of holiness is so high, he knows we could never meet the requirements. That's why Jesus came to earth to become our savior. He became a man with flesh, bones, thoughts and emotions. Jesus looked at all the people and saw they were like lost sheep with no direction, no purpose, no real life to speak of and no savior. **Then Jesus said to God, "Impute their sin to me! Place their sin and your wrath towards sin on me. I'll take the punishment for them." That's God's phenomenal message to everyone! Christ has made peace between God and the world! Colossians 1:20; Luke 2:14**

Many unbelievers I've talked to have said, "A loving God would never throw me in Hell. "God doesn't throw people into Hell. He saves people from Hell.

See how much twisted thinking there is out there about Heaven, Hell and God. Heaven and Hell are supernatural places, so we need to go to a supernatural source to find out more about them. The horrific reality is that people choose to go to Hell everyday. God gave people a free will to decide who they want to be with for eternity. God's heart is crushed when people choose Hell over being with him in Heaven forever.

As surely as I live, declares the Sovereign Lord, I take no pleasure in the death of the wicked, but rather that they turn from destruction and live. Ezekiel 33:11

My Father's will is that everyone who looks to the Son and believes in him shall have eternal life, and I will raise him up at the last day. John 6:40

God is heartbroken when people choose Hell over him. Many people will say to God, "But I didn't know Hell was real, otherwise I would have not rejected you!"

When you reject God's word…you reject him.
When you reject what the prophets that God spoke through said…then you reject him.
When you reject Jesus Christ and his teachings…then you reject God.
When you reject the Holy Spirit's promptings…then you reject God.
When you laugh at that Christian co-worker's message of salvation…then you rejected God.
When you turn the TV station away from a minister of the gospel…then you reject God.

Jesus said, "Anyone who listens to you…listens to me. Anyone who rejects you…rejects me, and anyone who rejects me, rejects my Father who sent me to save them." Luke 10:16

God sent Jesus to teach us, heal us, die for us and save us. So we could FIND God, KNOW GOD, LOVE God and COMMUNE with God.

Jesus said, "Don't you believe that I am in the Father and the Father is in me? The words I say to you don't come from me, but from my Father who lives in me." John 14:10

No one goes to Hell by accident. People go to Hell because:

They desensitized themselves to the Spirit of God.
They harden their hearts to God's promptings.
They are openly defiant against God.
They've broken his commandments. By the way, everyone of us has!
They refuse to acknowledge their sin nature
and that they are in desperate need of a savior.
They will not humble themselves, bow down and repent of their sins.
They do not accept Christ's payment for their sins.
They continually reject Jesus as their Lord.

The people's hearts have become calloused. They refuse to listen to the truth and they have closed their eyes to the light. Otherwise they might see with their eyes, hear with their ears, understand with their hearts, repent and God would heal them. Acts 28:27

It won't be a mistake or accident when people go to Hell. People are responsible for the decisions they make regarding their life and their eternal security. There won't be anyone else around to blame for the choices they've made.

Let's take a look at how people dilute their sexual sin for a moment. Many people might be able to proclaim that they never cheated on their spouse, but while they're walking around tooting their self-righteous horn, ask them this question: "Have you ever committed adultery in your heart?" Jesus says whoever looks at someone and lust for them, has already committed adultery in their heart (Matthew 5:28). Have you been completely clean in your thought life regarding this issue? Some people might have the restraint to not outwardly sin in their actions, but their thought life may run wild in its pursuit of lust and pleasure.

God will bring to light what is hidden in darkness and will expose the motives deep within a person's heart. I Corinthians 4:5

God's trying to tell the lost, "THEY ARE SINNERS IN NEED OF A SAVIOR!" People need to clearly understand this. There are people who have been so angry with others that they actually had the thought in their head, "I want to kill them!" They had the thought in their mind but they didn't follow through with it in their actions because it's against the law. Spending the rest of their life in prison is not the career path they envisioned for themselves. So they conclude that they're a "GOOD PERSON" because they didn't follow through with murder. WRONG! People murder other people in their heart all the time and this is how they do it. They determine in their mind:

I'm not going to talk to that person ever again!
They'll never hurt me again!
I am writing them out of my life forever!
They don't deserve my love and friendship!
I will never forgive that person for that!
I hate them!

Even Christians have a hard time with their emotions and their flesh. There is a war raging in their minds that no one can see. These thoughts of hate, anger and offense did not come from their new born-again spirit. They came from their wounded soul and it took over their emotional realm. When people think like this they sin against God. Anger and offence are like an out of control fire raging in their heart. They chose not to forgive and they sinned in their thought life. **God obviously sees everyone's actions but he also knows our intentions, thoughts and motives.** Jesus did this all the time when people came to him. He discerned what was in their heart.

Knowing their thoughts, Jesus said,
"Why do you entertain evil thoughts in your heart?" Matthew 9:4

Jesus knew what they were thinking and asked,
"Why are you thinking these things in your heart?" Luke 5:22

God's truth judges the thoughts and the attitudes of our heart.
Hebrews 4:12

Unsaved person, are you ready to go and stand in judgment before God with your heart, nature, spirit and thought life completely exposed before him? The enemy blinds people so they can't even understand what is in their own heart. But deep down inside is a sin nature that has been there since they were born. It comes out of people in the ugliest ways.

The people's hearts are darkened so that they call the evil things that they do good and they call God's goodness evil. Isaiah 5:20

This is why people shouldn't look at other people and judge whether or not they are good enough to get into Heaven.

- First of all, it's not mankind's judgment that counts.
- Secondly, people's perspective on who is good is twisted by the world we live in.
- Third, you can't ever be good enough to get into Heaven by your own merits or deeds.

God is going to look at *your nature* to decide if you will enter into Heaven, *not your actions.* Do you have his Spirit abiding in you or do you have the *old sinful nature* there inside of you. **If *your actions* could get you into Heaven, God wouldn't have needed to send his son to die for you.**

You see...the arrogance that presumes the innocence of our sin...is sinful as well.

Heaven was designed and built by God, so we need to research his requirements for access and membership. The President of the United States lives in the White House. Go try to gain access to his residence without going through the proper procedures and see what happens. Now how much greater is God than the president? This seems to be everyone's problem. People fabricate their own ideas about what God's requirements for access to Heaven are. Many people believe they are going to get into Heaven based on their own virtues, attributes and deeds. But God doesn't impute righteousness by works. Romans 4:6

Maybe your simple rule is: ALL GOOD PEOPLE WILL GO TO HEAVEN. According to the bible, acceptance into Heaven is not based on your judgment or your goodness. Our judgment of who is good is severely blinded by the darkness of this world. We can try to determine that this person deserves to go to Heaven and that person deserves to go to Hell, but the truth is; only God can see into a person's spirit. God knows whose spirit has been born-again and supernaturally transformed.

The truth is no one will fool God. Besides, God is not interested in how good you are. **Goodness is not his requirement for access into Heaven. Goodness is an attribute of being IN CHRIST. Goodness is a by-product of what God has placed in your spirit (Ephesians 5:22).** You can't ever be good enough or do enough good deeds to gain access into Heaven. Any righteous deeds we try to proclaim as good, outside of God's glory, are like filthy rags to a holy God. The bible doesn't say our sins are like filthy rags, it says our *own self-proclaimed righteousness* is like a bunch of filthy rags (Isaiah 64:6). This concept is so important for people to understand. You need to grasp this to effectively evangelize to lost souls. They're going to have plenty of questions and we need to be able to answer their questions correctly. It will be very easy for God to decide who makes it into Heaven and who doesn't. He will ask you a few questions similar to these.

What did you do with Jesus' blood? Colossians 1:20
What did you do with the bread of life that I gave to you? John 6:51
What did you do with the drink of living water Jesus gave you? Jn. 4:10
Did you embrace the Lamb of God who takes away the sins of the world? John 1:29
Did you accept Jesus teachings or did you reject the truth? Luke 10:16
Did you follow him when he said, "I am THE WAY to make it to Heaven?" John 14:6

God's requirement for access into Heaven is the blood covering of his son Jesus Christ. You have to believe, accept and confess that Jesus' death on the cross has completely appeased God's wrath towards your sin.

You see the whole world has already been charged and convicted as guilty, evil and sinful. There is no doubt in God's mind about it. What is awaiting the unsaved is their eternal punishment for their sinful nature. **The awesome news is Christ has already received the punishment for them and God has accepted that payment in full. People who do not accept Christ's payment will have to pay for their sins themselves.**

The wrath of God will grind the unrighteous to powder on the day of judgment. Matthew 21:44

The one who believes in Jesus is not judged, but anyone who does not believe is judged already, they have been convicted and will receive their sentence because they did not believe in and trust in the name of God's son Jesus Christ. John 3:18

The truth is, many people we walk by every day are like convicted criminals. They might as well be wearing an orange jump suit with a number across their back. The earth is their prison while they await their eternal punishment. The world does not recognize that they have been found guilty of their sinful condition. That's why God gave mankind the

Ten Commandments, so people would realize they've broken them and that's O.K. because there was no way they could have ever kept all those laws in the first place. **THE LAW was put in place to let people know they could never be perfect through their own efforts and they are sinners in need of a savior. God did not give people the Ten Commandments (or any of the Old Testament biblical laws) as a pathway to Heaven. Obeying these laws will not get you into Heaven or even closer to the front door.** The Ten Commandments are a pathway to the cross of Christ. God wants sinners to acknowledge the state of their sinful condition, repent and accept his son as the complete sacrifice for ALL SIN…for ALL PEOPLE…for ALL TIME.

I do not challenge the grace of God, because if righteousness is fulfilled by the works of my own hand, then Christ died in vain. Galatians 2:21

The law was not made for a righteous person, but for the lawless and disobedient. It was given to wake up sinners, murders, unholy and ungodly people. I Timothy 1:9

Religiousness happens is when your beliefs are driven by your own merits, emotions, works and strength. Folks we need to stop being religious. **Religion does not impress God; religion only impresses the person who's religious.** God hates religion. Christianity is not a religion. True Christianity is about experiencing continuous intimate fellowship with God.

Religious people try to reach God or Heaven through their OWN HAND. Christianity is about God reaching out to his people through his OWN SON.

There is a big difference. You can't reach God through you own efforts. He's beyond your reach. You can only touch God supernaturally through THE WAY that he provided. Jesus said,

"I AM THE WAY" for mankind to reach God.
"I AM THE WAY" to be redeemed from a life of darkness.
"I AM THE WAY" for you to be transferred into the kingdom of light.
"I AM THE WAY" to make it to Heaven.
"I AM THE WAY" to possess eternal life.
"I AM THE WAY" to have peace with God.
"I AM THE WAY" to be completely free from sin.
"I AM THE WAY" for you to know God as your loving Father.
(John 14:6)

Jesus said he is the spiritual bread that has came down from Heaven, so people would see it (understand him), eat it (receive him into their spirit), have eternal life (here on earth) and a home in Heaven forever (John 6:48-51). God is continually reaching out to us and trying to draw us to him. Don't make the monumental mistake of turning from his promptings.

> *Because of the increase in wickedness...*
> *the love of many will grow cold. Matthew 24:12*

The evidence that people have sinned against God in their thoughts and actions is overwhelming. People can't hide their sinful nature from God. Can anyone honestly say they've never sinned in thought, word or deed? Many people sweep their sin under the rug and use the excuse, "I'm only human." Actually you're a created being wrapped around a spirit. People were never designed to fornicate, lust, hate, lie, cheat, steel, curse, commit adultery and kill. But unfortunately mankind chose to turn from God, be disobedient and rebel against his truth and his nature. **All sin is basically not trusting God.**

The word pervert means to think, speak or proceed with action in a wrong or opposite manner in which something was originally designed to be used. When we choose to sin, we are perverting the mind, body and soul to be used in a way that it was not originally designed for.

At one time God destroyed the entire earth by a flood because of the sinful condition of mankind. Only one man and his family loved God and were saved from the flood. **God does not exist for us, we exist for him. Everything was created to glorify God. God holds back his wrath towards mankind because it was appeased through Christ. God responds to us now through a New Covenant of love, grace and mercy.**

> *Just as a mother hen holds out her wings to gather her chicks under*
> *them, God desires that his children come back to his loving arms.*
> *Matthew 23:37*

Can you image how painful it must be for God to watch so many people hurting themselves by their sinful behavior? Everyone running around in disarray, not seeking God, self-centered, stubborn, self-righteous people. Everyone wants to be the predominate controlling force that directs their lives. The average person spends approximately thirty seven million minutes on this plant and they spend very few of those minutes loving God back. Jeremiah 2:32 is one of the saddest scripture in the bible. This is the heart of God breaking before the prophet Jeremiah:

My people have forsaken me…for so many days. Jeremiah 2:32

Since God can see directly into people's hearts, he knows sinners are in need of a savior. No one is fooling God… that's a fact!

If you claim to be sinless, you're only fooling yourself. We need to listen to God, because he possess the truth that will set us free. I John 1:8

Everyone at some time has sinned against God in their thoughts, words and actions. Fortunately God has secured a way for people to be reconciled to him, but he has left the choice up to us.

That has to be the cruelest thing to experience, to see your very own creation turn their back on you and walk into an eternity full of darkness, completely separated from God forever. People who make that choice have been monumentally deceived.

I've heard a lot of people say, "God is a forgiving God and that's what I'm counting on when I stand before him." Well you have to believe in the Lord Jesus Christ, he's the one who secured that forgiveness for you. Many people think they'll have the opportunity to beg God for forgiveness when they are standing before him. They're willing to gamble their entire eternal security thinking that they'll have the opportunity to do that? All they're really doing is coming up with reasons why they won't repent *right now*, turn from sin *right now* and believe *right now*. They're not fooling anyone but themselves and they're certainly not going to fool God. Everyone has a different version of the same excuse but it all boils down to this:

I will not humble myself before God.
I will not repent and turn from my life of sin.
I will not obey God.
I just want him to leave me alone so I can live my life the way I want to.
I will determine my own morals and live by my own truth.
I've already invented my own fantasy of Heaven
and what the requirements for access are.
I will not accept the Lord Jesus Christ as my savior.

When we are driving down a road and see a warning sign, we obey the instructions that are given because our safety can depend on our obedience to those signs. We don't question the signs. We don't doubt the signs. The signs are there for our protection. God has given us many signs and warnings in his word that are critical to our eternal survival.

THE BRIDGE IS OUT AHEAD... what are you going to do about it?
STOP...being so busy and do some research about your creator.
YIELD...yourself to God, his voice and his promptings.
There is only ONE WAY...to Heaven and that's through Jesus Christ.
DETOUR AHEAD...God doesn't want you to continue down the road you're on.

Slow down, stop and read the signs God has placed in front of you. Understand and believe the truth on those signs he's given you. Don't continue to ignore his promptings and warnings. Your eternal security depends on it.

Many will drive down the wide road that leads to destruction. But I say to you, take the narrow road that I am leading you to. Only a few will follow THE WAY, but it will lead you to eternal life. Matt. 7:12-14

When people are speeding down the freeway, everybody thinks they are just fine because everyone else is going the *typical ten over the speed limit* with them. But when the police are behind you, YOU ARE THE ONE THAT'S CAUGHT! Try telling the police officer that, "Everyone else on the highway was speeding also." See if that gets you off the hook. You're the one who is guilty and will pay the fine. Trust me, you don't want to pay the fine for your sins, you want Jesus to pay it and he already has paid for them *in full*. People just need to CONFESS, BELIEVE IN, and RECEIVE Christ's sacrifice as the complete payment for their sins.

We were at a gas station one time, and we saw the young man there who was dating my niece. I think he was only getting a few dollars worth of gas. I told my wife to go and have him fill up his tank and put it on our debit card. He could have been arrogant and prideful and said, "No thanks, I'll pay for my own gas." But that would have been ludicrous. Instead he received it with joy and excitement and he came over and gave us each a huge hug. He was so happy he lifted me up off the ground. He loved that we did that for him. Why do people reject the free gift of salvation that God has so graciously offered them? They need to run to him, cleave to him and accept him as their Lord.

HEAVEN
How can I be so homesick...for a place I've never been?

Heaven is real. It's not a fairytale land. It's not a fictitious place or some fantasy in a person's mind. Heaven is beautiful, it's beyond our imagination. It's a supernatural place. God has done many incredible things in my life that are beyond my comprehension and Heaven is going to be the most awesome exhilarating place we've ever experienced. It's being prepared specifically for us. There's no separation in Heaven. **Heaven will be filled with God's children all united in God's love.** I think as people enter this supernatural place, they will immediately fall to their knees and receive a love that they were never able to completely comprehend on this earth. It was always available for us to fully experience, but our earthly thinking and paradigms just wouldn't allow our hearts to completely receive God's love. Leaving the natural realm and entering Heaven will be incredible. I believe it will be like taking off a thick, heavy soaking wet robe that we've been wearing for a long time. We will be released from every burden and weight we've been carrying. The world is an environment that is constantly pulling at us, but when we step into Heaven, I believe we will experience a freedom that will make us feel like flying. That's the type of freedom and love we're going to experience in Heaven together. I look at how beautiful God created the earth and I can only imagine what God is preparing for us in Heaven.

How can the natural mind conceive what God has prepared for those who love him? But God has revealed these mysteries to us through his Holy Spirit. I Corinthians 2:9 & 10

SPIRITUAL VISION - Heaven

Not long ago, God gave me a vision of Heaven that I will never forget. Jesus and I were standing in Heaven and I was gazing down on the awesome beauty of it all. We were on a balcony overlooking the supreme majesty of this spectacular place. There were buildings everywhere, like miniature castles with bright, white polished stone. The buildings were dazzling as I gazed down on this unbelievable place. Then Jesus touched my shoulder and said, "There is more...look higher." I turned to look at what he was pointing to and it took my breath away. This magnificent place we were gazing at continued up this huge slope. I was only looking at the base of Heaven. The buildings became even more magnificent as they marched upward. Every edge and every corner sparkled like the sunshine on a lake. It looked like the buildings were translucent and lit from within. I will never forget that vision and I am going to see it again one day, standing right next to my savior.

Many years ago, when we first walked into the church we attend now, we were greeted by loving caring people. They hugged us and loved on us the entire time we were there. Their beautiful smiles and warm hearts were swiftly received. It was something we hadn't ever experienced before. When we left that day we knew we found a new home church. We wanted to go back and experience that love again. We didn't even want to leave that day, we just wanted to stay there and be around those beautiful loving people. This is just a small sample of the love we are going to experience in Heaven in an exponentially mind blowing way. The love of God is going to be incredible in Heaven with everyone loving each other unconditionally, radically without limits. I'm ready to go right now! I look forward to that day with all my heart.

STORY – Take My Breathe Away

One time we went on vacation to Lake Michigan when my daughter Erika was only about four years old. These beautiful one-hundred foot high sand dunes separated the camping areas from the lake. My daughter had a hard time walking in the sand so I picked her up in my arms. As we approached the top of the sand dune and saw the sun hitting the big, beautiful, sparkling waters of Lake Michigan, I heard my daughter open her mouth and take in a loud breath of air. The view literally took her breath away! Since I was carrying her I was able to hear that breath perfectly. It made such an impression on me that I still remember it today.

Children of God, when we step into Heaven what God has prepared for us is going to take our breath away! It's going to surpass every beautiful place on earth we've ever seen! It's going to radiate with the light of God's glory and the undeniable presence of his love! It's going to be spectacular! It's gong to be for us to enjoy forever!

THERE'S ETERNAL LIFE IN THE KINGDOM OF GOD
God has given us eternal life through Christ. If you have the Son you have this new life in you, but anyone who does not have the Son of God does not have any life inside their spirit. I John 5:11 & 12

God wants his creation to come to a pivotal turning point in their lives...surrender...and live the life of a supernatural transformed born-again being. That's a phenomenal supernatural event. All the angels rejoice when one sinner comes to God. There is a full blown party in Heaven when one sinner finds the Lord. Salvation is something we get to celebrate everyday for the rest of our lives. Christians have their eternal destiny secured forever!

But as great as that is...there is more. Your heavenly Father continuously gives to his children. When Jesus spoke about eternal life he was talking about something we receive at the point of salvation. **Eternal life is more than a ticket to Heaven; it's a license to bring Heaven down here to earth! We Christians have eternal life *right now* here on earth to experience! It's actually in us!**

Anyone who believes in the Son HAS eternal life... John 3:36

Many Christians believe the main goal of salvation is getting your sins forgiven and escaping the flames of Hell. Now that's a huge benefit for Christians and if that was the only benefit it would be worth it all. But that's only the beginning of this amazing journey of faith. Eternal life is actually the goal of salvation. Born-again Christians possess eternal life right now here on earth. It's in their spirit. It's not something we're waiting to obtain.

Jesus Christ suffered for our sins, the just for the unjust, the righteous for the unrighteous, the sinless for the sinner, so that we might be brought back into fellowship and intimacy with God. I Peter 3:18

The barrier of sin had to be broken first so we could have eternal life starting right now here on earth (Eph. 2:14). Jesus had a perfect relationship with God and through his sacrifice perfected our relationship with his Father. Our relationship with God is absolutely perfect. The hindrances of sin, the barrier of sin, the guilt of sin, the condemnation of sin and the shame of sin have been completely removed from our spirit. Hebrews 1:3

This is eternal life, that they may <u>KNOW GOD</u> in his complete fullness. John 17:3

Eternal life is being <u>reconciled</u> to GOD. II Corinthians 5:18
Eternal life is being <u>accepted</u> by GOD. Ephesians 1:6
Eternal life is being outrageously <u>loved</u> by GOD. John 3:16
Eternal life is being completely <u>forgiven</u> by GOD. Jn. 1:29; Heb. 2:17
Eternal life is being in constant <u>relationship</u> with GOD. Ephesians 3:19
Eternal life is <u>passion, intimacy and commitment</u> for God and from God.

God wants us to completely understand the glorious inheritance <u>WE HAVE IN US</u>. Ephesians 1:19
We are children of God and joint-heirs with Christ. Romans 8:17
The kingdom of God has come to live IN US. Luke 11:20
The secrets of the Kingdom of God have been deposited IN US. Mark 4:11

We are to always be kingdom focused, kingdom driven and kingdom minded. I believe God gives us supernatural understanding, wisdom and visions that are beyond the world's comprehension and surpass our wildest dreams. How do we maintain this kingdom mentality? You'll hear these three words all throughout this book.

<u>Surrender</u> yourself to God completely.
<u>Submit</u> yourself to God's plan and ideas for your life.
Completely <u>humble</u> yourself to the most loving, kind, forgiving, uplifting person you've ever met.

You will find me when you seek after me with all your heart. Jeremiah 29:13

When we read, understand and grow in the knowledge of God, then our actions will come into supernatural alignment with our spirit.

That's the moment the kingdom of Heaven will come flooding out of your belly like a river of living water. John 7:38

God chooses to use people as vessels to operate through. Why? Because he wants to, that's what pleases him. A supernatural, all powerful, all knowing God wants to connect with you. You're his creation! You're his child! You're his passion!

Isn't that the most amazing relationship you could ever step into? When I finally understood what eternal life was, it just blew me away. When our humility, surrender and submission makes a supernatural connection with God, then he can transform us completely with his Holy Spirit. **The Holy Spirit establishes God's kingdom in us and then through us.**

The Holy Spirit will teach us everything we need to know about life, each other and ourselves. Remember our faith should be moving forward even when we have unanswered questions. Don't fear what you don't know. The Holy Spirit will reveal to you any information you're unaware of, if it's required you need it. He will fill in the large gaps of information you don't understand. That's his job. He's our teacher, counselor and our comforter.

You won't ever have all the answers. That's what faith is. Faith is not knowing but trusting in God anyways, moving forward and establishing the kingdom of Heaven.

Are you <u>kingdom focused</u> or are you <u>barely get by focused</u>? Are you just <u>surviving</u> or are you <u>thriving?</u> Are you a <u>spectator</u> or are you a <u>participator</u>? Allow God's kingdom to manifest itself through your positive faith-filled thoughts, words and actions. Have you ever touched a wool blanket that was full of static electricity? You can get a petty good zap from static electricity. **Holy Ghost filled Christians are full of supernatural electricity and when we touch something in this physical world it gets zapped by the kingdom of God.** Christian soldier, you really do have the kingdom of God within you, now release it into your world. Give people a radiant revelation of God's kingdom and then enjoy the journey.

TRANSFORMATION AT SALVATION

In Luke 19:2, a man named Zacchaeus was a tax collector and a thief. He was a selfish self-centered man. His soul was filled with pride, arrogance and evil. When Jesus came walking down the road, he told Zacchaeus, "I want to go to your house today." Jesus went into Zacchaeus' home and into his heart that day and changed him completely. You see Zacchaeus' treasure became something different that day. It changed from gold coins to his savior's forgiveness. It changed from selfishness to selflessness. He was transformed from a thief to a generous man. The day Zacchaeus gave away all the money he had was the day he became the richest man alive. The hand of God touched his spirit and he was completely transformed at the core of his nature.

In God's kingdom:

The biggest liar…will broadcast the truth in love.
The adulterer…will be faithful and true.
The coldest heart…will be the most passionate servant.
The biggest failure…will be the greatest minister.

God thoroughly and completely changes people. He removes the cold hard heart of carnality and gives people a new soft heart that's sensitive to him (Ezekiel 11:19). God changes angry, hateful, selfish, jealous, stubborn, arrogant, wicked, lustful people into new spiritually born-again children of God. Christians are certainly not transformed into God's little perfect robots. Our minds and bodies have not been made perfect, only our spirit has been purged, sealed and perfected forever (Hebrews 1:3, 10:14, Ephesians 1:13). When unbelievers make the choice to confess their sin to God and believe in the name of the Lord Jesus Christ, a supernatural lightening bolt hits their spirit. God won't make the choice for them, but once they do, you can't stop the flood gates from being opened. God will come pouring into every area of their spirit. Whether or not he flows out of their spirit and into their daily life is a choice people make every day.

God is passionate about you; he created a universe for you to gaze upon at night. He gave us the earth as our home and he gave us each other to enjoy. **The only time God was ever selfish is when he created you, because he created you for him. You are the object of his love. He adores you. He has placed his fullness inside your spirit so he could always be with you.**

God directed me to write <u>THE GIFT</u> one Christmas season, because almost all the attention that time of year is focused on; Santa Claus, shopping, getting presents, long lines, Christmas trees, lights on the house, all the big parties and much more. A lot of these activities lead people into a season of frustration, anxiety and stress. None of these things or activities are wrong, but we need to focus on the actual reason for the CHRISTmas season. Is your CHRISTmas...CHRISTless? Why is the person whose birthday we're celebrating rarely ever mentioned? Unless you happen to be in church, then it's OK to bring up the name of Jesus Christ, the savior of the entire world. God gave the world the greatest gift they could ever receive, so why are so many people not interested. When we take CHRIST out of Christmas...THEN WHAT'S THE POINT! People would be so different if they would try to include Jesus Christ in their Christmas. Find out who this man really is. Read the words he said and what other people said about him.

The birth, life, death and resurrection of Jesus Christ is something every born-again Christian should celebrate everyday. Jesus had a miraculous supernatural birth and so did we. We have been born-again through God's spirit, from his imperishable seed (I Peter 1:23). We are a completely new creation. The old person was kicked out of our spirit and a new person now resides in us (II Corinthians 5:17). We used to be children of the devil, he was our father. We were children of disobedience, children of darkness and wrath (Ephesians 2:2 & 3). But now we have been transferred into the kingdom of light. The glory of God shines from within us. We celebrate the life of Christ everyday we rise out of bed. Christ was conceived as the Holy Spirit overshadowed the Virgin Mary. We have that same spirit in us, giving us new life, an abundant life and eternal life.

THE GIFT
by Eric Johnson

I hurried down the stairs on Christmas morning and saw
the beautifully decorated tree glowing with many lights.
My excitement turned to concern when I
saw only one small gift under the tree.
Where were all the many things I had asked for?
Even though I was disappointed, I still
remained curious about the one little gift.
I opened the package and found it was empty.
I sat there hurt, confused and I was just as empty inside.
Didn't I deserve any of the things I had asked for?
After a few moments the Spirit of the Lord swept over me.
He said, "My child, I do love you more than you
can even comprehend right now. Look deeper into the box."
Then I saw it! It was a beautiful picture of the baby Jesus in a manger.
"That is my gift to you, but it is not a gift unless you
open your heart and receive Christ into your life."
I knelt there beside the tree for a while.
It was hard for me to understand everything about God.
But faith began to grow in me and I received
God's gift of Jesus Christ that morning.
I accepted Christ's sacrifice for my sins and I felt
an incredible flow of God's love come over me.
A heavy burden was lifted from my shoulders that day
and I knew Heaven would be my home for eternity.
A moment later I opened my eyes and saw with a new vision.
The star on the top of the tree was the guiding
star leading everyone to the Savior.
The tree trunk and branches seemed to form the cross where Jesus was
suspended between Heaven and earth for the sins of the world.
The lights on the tree represented saved souls
who were shining like stars in the sky.

THEN I NOTICED ALL THE GIFTS UNDER THE TREE!
The gifts were all sizes wrapped to perfection with decorations
and bows. I opened the biggest one first, it was the love of the Lord
and I felt it all over me. The second gift was joy;
I could feel it even before I had it completely opened.
The next one was peace, it surrounded me immediately.
There were many packages that were filled with forgiveness.

I looked around the room and there were packages everywhere.
Patience was in one and kindness was in another one.
The Lord had given me so much already, more than I deserved.
Goodness and gentleness, faithfulness and self-control.
The Lord just kept on giving. I had never realized
how much I was loved by God.
He always wanted to give me so much of him
and all I had to do was let him in.
The gift of Jesus Christ is the greatest gift
I have ever received in my life.
I knew I would never celebrate another
Christmas season or another day without him.

What do we receive after God's forgiving grace comes flooding into our spirit? EVERYTHING! We get it all! A peaceful mind, a calm spirit, assurance of his continual presence, an eternal hope of Heaven, we get to enjoy an abundant eternal life here on earth. God sanctifies us and anoints us to establish his kingdom. God's miracle working power can flow through us freely. After our salvation experience we receive a spiritual sensitivity to God that comes through humility, surrender and submission. We acquire spiritual vision so we can perceive things from a heavenly perspective. We receive spiritual hearing so we will be able to know God's voice. All of your spiritual senses come alive when Christ comes into your heart. (Please read I Corinthians 2:11-16)

God will take out your heart of stone formed by the world
and he will give you a heart full of the life of God. Ezekiel 36:26

Christians can operate in all of God's divine gifts when we understand the full measure of God's grace and believe in the monumental cleansing of the atonement of Christ. The pipe has been unplugged. **The dam has been released and a teeming river of living water is coming at us with the full force of Heaven behind it. God will blow people away with everything he has planned for them. Normal no longer exists in the life of a Christian because we live in a different dimension. God is a supernatural being and we also are supernatural beings wrapped in a body of flesh. Your connection with God is the most important relationship you'll ever encounter.** For the first time you will feel completely alive and conscious of God's presence, his glory, his voice and his promptings. Now go and saturate the world with the goodness of God, the grace of God and the love of God.

CHAPTER 3

GOD'S HEALING TOUCH

Many people are baffled by the subject of healing and how God operates in this supernatural platform. They ask questions like:

Why doesn't God still heal people today?
If God's such a great miracle worker,
then why doesn't he heal everyone who's sick?
Why aren't Christians closing down hospitals all over the world?
Why do you hear about some people being healed and others not?

My response to these questions is: GOD HAS ALREADY HEALED THEM! Jesus took the stripes on his back for our healing over two thousand years ago. Jesus accomplished everything that was required by God on the cross for all the sins of mankind, past present and future. Look at it like this, the entire world is saved from sin. However, many in the world choose not to receive Christ as their savior. The necessary work has not only been accomplished for our SALVATION, but our HEALING, REST and RIGHTEOUSNESS have all been atoned for through Christ. **God would no more want you sick and in bed than he would lost for all eternity without him.** We just need to make a choice to accept that complete truth and walk in it.

When people first accepted Christ as their Lord and savior, they made a choice to accept God's forgiveness, love and grace into their lives. In the same way, we have to choose to be healed. That sounds pretty simplistic doesn't it? Everyone who's sick wants to be healed. *Wanting* **to be healed and** *choosing* **to be healed are two completely different mindsets. We can only understand, believe and receive when we have a complete revelation of God's nature, power and intentions.** Let's examine four awesome truths in the bible that God wants us to fully grasp.

- God LOVES us, it's up to us to receive his love, walk in his love and extend it to others. Without a complete revelation of God's true nature we cannot walk in the fullness of his love.
- We are FORGIVEN, it's up to us to receive it, walk in that forgiveness and extend it to others. Without a complete understanding of the thoroughness of God's forgiveness, we will never feel like we are completely clean and accepted by him.
- God has given us all the FAITH that is necessary to accomplish everything he has destined for us to do. It's up to us to trust in him and rely on the FAITH he's given us.
- We ARE HEALED by his stripes (Isaiah 53:5, I Peter 2:24). Everything has been completely accomplished for our healing. It's up to us to choose to be healed. It's up to us to receive it, believe it and walk in supernatural healing. Whether or not these truths penetrate into this physical world we live in depends on if we cooperate with the laws of faith God has established. The necessary work has been completed. **The atonement of Christ completed the healing work for everyone at the same time.** It's up to us to trust in the atonement of Christ and *choose* to be healed. People who believe God wants them sick, don't truly understand his nature.

God has already healed everyone. Just believe it, receive it and walk in it. Let's examine our part in receiving healing. Some people are healed and some people are not healed. We know God is not lacking in power, strength or ability. That's a fact! In fact, Jesus healed almost everyone he came in contact with. There were only a few places where Jesus could not heal the sick and that was in his hometown. Some people there cast doubt and unbelief into other people's minds. This caused people's confidence to wavier and Jesus could not do many miracles there because of others.

OBJECT LESSON – Pop Can

Try this interesting object lesson. Set an empty pop can flat on your palm. Then place your other palm on the other end of the can. Now put the can up close to your chest so you will be able to push with a lot of inward force to crush the can. Were you successful at crushing it? It's very hard to crush a can by pushing on it from end to end.

Now grab a second identical empty can and hold it as if you're going to drink from it. Now squeeze your fingers and thumb together to crush the can. Wasn't it much easier to crush the can that way?

Although the cans were the identical size, shape and construction, one seemed weaker and the other seemed much stronger.

God has given us all an equal measure of faith (Romans 12:3). Some people seem to have bold strong faith, while others seem to have weaker, timid faith, similar to the two cans in the object lesson. One can appeared to be stronger than the other one, but we know the cans were identical.

Some of us trust God completely with the faith he's given us and some of us don't. Some of us fully rely on God with the faith that he has given us and some us don't. We all have the same size faith, but how much do you trust in and rely on that faith? How much do you lean on it no matter what your circumstances are? **People trust God at many different levels and there are as many different levels of trust as there are people.** There is only one kind of faith and that's the FAITH OF GOD that comes from him. We have the same faith as Jesus right now in our spirit (I John 4:17; Galatians 2:16 & 20). How are you ever going to do the same miracles Jesus did unless you truly believe this (John 14:12-14)? Having a complete revelation about this truth will catapult you into a completely new supernatural dimension.

Remember, you only need faith the size of a mustard seed to move a mountain (Matthew 17:20). So we know it's not the size of our faith that matters. What matters to God is the type of faith we have. God already knows the type of faith he has planted in us. We are the one's who gradually understand a little more everyday, the type of faith he has placed in us. Let's briefly examine love, forgiveness and faith and then we will come back to the subject of healing.

Love

God's deep, unwavering, nature is to love us with all of his heart, with all of his soul and with his entire mind. God loves us one hundred percent right now as we are. Now that's a hard pill to swallow because we know ourselves better than anyone. We know all our faults and everywhere we've failed and we remind ourselves of those failures constantly. **But the truth is, God will not love us any better when we become better. He will not love us more when we do more for him. God loves us unconditionally.** If you're trying to earn God's love, then you don't understand his nature. God is the very essence of the attribute of love (I John 4:9 & 10). Jesus came to earth to show us how much God loves us.

We all received the fullness of God's love when we became filled with his spirit (Romans 5:5). We are completely filled to the rim with God's love in our spirit. We express that love with words, thoughts and actions to varying degrees everyday. Some people release God's love on others like a raging waterfall. They love without restraint or conditions. Some people severely restrict God's love. They let God's love flow out of their soul like a dripping faucet with limits and conditions attached to it. We have a choice to make. We can EMBRACE what Jesus said, BELIEVE IT, ACCEPT IT, RECEIVE IT and WALK in God's love. Or we can reject the TRUTH, turn from it, ignore it, twist it, limit it and turn away from it. **We all make a choice about God's love everyday. Many people walk away from God's promptings and reject the most valuable love they could ever experience. God leaves that one critical, life transforming choice up to us.**

Forgiveness

If we confess our sins then he is faithful and just to forgive us and cleanse us from all unrighteousness. I John 1:9

God wants us to believe in the completed work of Christ on the cross. Everyone is already one hundred percent SAVED FROM THE CURSE OF SIN because Jesus submitted himself to his father's plan and the saving work at the cross. People can hear the gospel message, receive it into their hearts and accept this salvation. Or they can walk away from that good news and reject the sacrifice that Christ has made for them. BUT HE'S ALREADY ACCOMPLISHED THE SAVING WORK FOR EVERYONE! God wants people to accept the completely free gift of his LOVE and SALVATION. The entire world has been SAVED from the curse of sin. But the entire world does not RECEIVE that salvation or WALK in it.

If you accept God's forgiveness, yet walk around with the shame and guilt of sin, then you don't truly understand the depth of what was completed for you at the cross of Christ. You may believe the crazy lie that you're a terrible sinner and God would never accept you. Maybe you're on a roller-coaster ride of sinning one day then repenting another day, then sinning the next day and repenting the day after. You can choose to believe that God is in Heaven with a club in his hand and when you mess up he's there to let you have it. There's a lot of twisted thinking out there. **Many Christians are not walking in the complete forgiveness that was accomplished for them through Christ.**

If you *believe* in the Lord Jesus Christ and *accept* his blood covering for your sin, then you shall be saved from:

The POWER of sin. Romans 6:7, 11, 22
The CURSE of sin. Galatians 3:13
The PENALTY of sin. Romans 3:24
The GUILT and CONDEMNATION of sin. Romans 8:1
The CONSCIOUSNESS of sin. Hebrews 9:14,10:2 & 22

If my house is completely clean, then it's much easier to keep it clean because I would notice if anything was out of place and I would want it to remain clean because it looks so good. I don't want it to go back to the way it was, dirty and messy. If my house was dirty then it's much easier to leave yesterdays clothes on the floor and dishes on the end tables because the rest of the room is already a complete mess.

If you're a born-again Christian then your spirit was saved, filled with the Holy Spirit, sealed from sin, cleansed and perfected forever. Did you know that one-third of you (your spirit) is completely clean and cannot sin? Your spirit is wall to wall Holy Ghost. Your spirit sings to God all the time. Your body might not be doing this but your spirit is. When we focus on our body and emotions we sometimes feel like failures, but when we focus on what's true about us in our spirit, we can release the life of God that's in us and we will feel empowered to overcome the flesh.

Faith

If you really believe that your faith can move mountains, then God combined with your faith will do it. We need to embrace our faith, trust in our faith and fully rely on the faith God's given us. That's how we tap into God's miraculous power.

Without faith fully relied on, leaned on and trusted in...
it is impossible to please God. Hebrews 11:6

Healing

Now here we are again at the most popular topic
in the Christian community...HEALING.

The topic of healing is pursued more than any other facet of Christianity. Can you imagine what would happen if we pursued after the face of God as much as we cry out for his healing hand?

Let me state this as plainly as I can. Jesus accomplished all that was necessary for OUR TOTAL AND COMPLETE HEALING, when he shed his blood for us.

JESUS BLOOD

The BLOOD OF JESUS sealed the New Covenant between God and mankind. This covenant secured for us the following:

OUR HEALING – We are healed from physical diseases, mental and emotional disorders. Matthew 8:17, I Peter 2:24

OUR FORGIVENESS – We are one hundred percent forgiven of all our past, present and future sins. Eph. 1:7, Heb. 1:3, 8:12, 9:26, 10:11 &17

WHOLENESS – We are not lacking anything. We are complete in Christ. I John 4:17

RIGHTEOUSNESS – We are covered in the righteousness of Christ (Romans 5:19). We were literally made righteous (in our spirit) before God. II Corinthians 5:21

CLOSENESS – We are close to God because he actually lives in us. Ephesians 2:13

RECONCILIATION – God is not mad at anyone. He's not displeased with you. II Corinthians 5:18, Ephesians 2:16, Colossians 1:21

PEACE - We have peace with God because God truly is at peace with us. Ephesians 2:14, Colossians 1:20

A NEW HEART that's sensitive to God's nature. Jeremiah 31:33 & 34

We are ACCEPTED by God because of Christ's blood. Ephesians 1:6

He is MERCIFUL towards our unrighteousness. Hebrews 8:12

JUSTIFICATION - God treats us just as if we've never sinned because Jesus never sinned. We are 100% cleansed in our spirit (before God) for all eternity. Romans 5:9, Hebrews 1:3

We are ETERNALLY REDEEMED praise the Lord! Not temporarily redeemed until we mess up again. Hebrews 9:12, I Peter 1:18 & 19

We have INTIMACY with God that has been extended to us. Heb. 8:11

We have ACCESS to the Father. Ephesians 2:18, Hebrews 4:16

In the Old Testament book of Numbers, God told Moses to fashion a bronze snake on a staff. He told him to lift the staff up high before the people so when they got bit by snakes, that were everywhere in the wilderness, they would be healed. Just as Moses lifted up the bronze snake in the wilderness, in the same manner, Jesus was lifted up on the cross for our healing. John 3:14, Numbers 21:4

In the same way that Moses lifted up the snake in the desert (on a pole), *so the Son of Man* (Jesus) *must be lifted up* (on a cross). *John 3:14*

These signs will accompany those who believe: In my name they will drive out demons; they will speak in new tongues; they will pick up snakes with their hands; and when they drink deadly poison it will not hurt them. They will place their hands on the sick and they will be healed. Mark 16:17-19

I have given you authority to trample on snakes and scorpions and to overcome all the power of the enemy. Nothing will be able to harm you. Luke 10:19

Don't you find it interesting that when Jesus spoke on healing, he uses the snake to describe to us the power we have available within us? It is those same snakes that bit the Israelites in the wilderness back in the time of Moses, that come to us today in the form of sickness and diseases (poisons in our bodies).

Jesus asked two blind men, "Do you believe I am able to heal you?" "Yes Lord," they replied. Then he touched their eyes and said, "According to your faith, it is done". Matthew 9:28 & 29

It's not whether God is <u>ABLE</u> to heal you. Genesis 18:14
The challenge is not if he <u>CAN</u> heal you. Psalm 103:3
The question is not if God <u>WILL</u> heal you. Mark 16:18
The mystery is not whether God <u>WANTS</u> to heal you. III John 1:2

The answer to your prayer, salvation and total healing is in the finished work of Christ at the cross.

God <u>HAS HEALED YOU</u> through the blood of Jesus that was shed for you. Believe it and walk in it, just as you would walk in the LOVE he has given you. Just as you walk in the FORGIVENESS he so graciously has extended to you. Just as you would walk by FAITH and not by sight. BELIEVE IT and RECEIVE IT just as you would any other gift from God, which include the following; SALVATION, the covering of Christ's RIGHTEOUSNESS, RESTING in Christ, the PEACE that surpasses all understanding, the ASSURANCE of a home in Heaven and all the other many promises God has given us. We know that through the work of our Lord Jesus Christ, all these things were accomplished for us. The choice is up to you, will you walk in that complete truth about yourself or will you wonder in the wilderness.

Story:

One time my whole family was over at my brother's house opening up Christmas presents. My brother's wife Stephanie was really sick. Practically everyone in the room was telling her to take different types of medicine and to try this new over-the-counter drug on the market. Finally, just before we were about to leave my wife said, "Why don't we pray for Stephanie?" That was a great question she proposed to a room full of born-again, blood-bought, fire-baptized, Jesus loving prayer warriors.

Why do we try to solve our problems in this world through natural remedies? We're all guilty of it. We share with each other:

How the doctor helped us.
How taking a certain pill helped.
How drinking fruit juice for a week helped us.
How gargling with honey and lemon juice helped.
How a specific diet helped us.

Last time I checked, we Christians have a phenomenal promise in the bible that says:

By HIS strips we ARE healed. Isaiah 53:5, I Peter 2:24
(It's already a completely atoned for supernatural fact in our spirit.)

We Christians are supernatural beings and we should seek out God for his supernatural solutions to our problems. **Christians should feel much more comfortable operating in the supernatural realm rather than in the natural realm, but that's typically not the case.** God wants us to pray and believe to such a degree that his power erupts out of our spirit and into our circumstances. When we do this, the supernatural realm pierces into our physical world and we get to experience a mighty manifestation of God's power as it strips away our diseases and depression. We need to believe and not doubt, agree with each other in prayer, anoint one another with oil, fast and take communion. These are all points of contact that allow us to literally reach into the supernatural world and draw our blessing out into the physical realm where we can benefit from it.

We have to do more than believe God *can* heal us or *wants* to heal us. We have to believe that God *has already healed us* in the supernatural realm. We draw that truth out of that realm by operating in the laws of faith that God has given us. **Do you know how many people have died from diseases and tumors with the healing power of God right there inside of them? God has already made his** decision about our healing, salvation and rest. His answer is **BE HEALED, BE WHOLE and BE FREE!**

There are hundreds of scriptures about healing in the bible. God obviously wants us to *receive* the healing that Christ secured for us. There must be something we're doing wrong because so many people are not receiving the healing they're so fervently praying for. We know Jesus Christ has accomplished everything that we need to be healed, but there are many things that can hinder us from releasing God's power from within us.

Healing seems to be at the top of everybody's list when it comes to prayer requests. But God has many other priorities he wants to accomplish in our lives as well. We may feel that our healing or someone else's healing is of the highest priority, but we need to listen to the Holy Spirit, he knows what God's priorities are for us. **If we focus on the Holy Spirit and his leading during prayer, then we will be tremendously more effective in releasing God's power.**

- God wants us healed, but he also wants us to believe in his word.
- Yes God wants us healed, but he also wants us to not doubt him. James 1:6
- Yes God wants people healed, but more importantly he wants them to confess Jesus Christ as Lord and be saved. Matt. 9:2; Mark 2:4-6
- Yes God wants people healed, but he first wants them to confess their faults to one another. *Confess your faults to one another and pray for each other so that you may be healed. James 5:16*
- Yes God wants us healed, but he also wants us to be united together in love.
- God wants to heal us, but he also wants to hear from us on a daily basis, not just when we need something from him. We need to seek God's face to know him intimately, not just his healing hand. Your faith will begin to work by knowing God's nature. Galatians 5:6
- Yes God wants us healed, but he also wants us to have the right motives when we ask. *When you ask you do not receive because you ask with wrong motives. James 4:3*
- Yes God wants us healed, but he also wants us to connect with him with a passionate heart and with an intense hunger in our soul. *Love the Lord with all your heart, with your entire mind, with all your soul and with all your strength. Mark 12:30*
- Yes God wants us healed, but he also wants us to be doing things that are pleasing to him. *Do not merely listen to the word and so deceive yourselves but do what it says. James 1:22*

It's easy to focus on what you need or want when you pray. Our prayers can become self-centered so fast without even realizing it. We've been so inwardly focused our whole lives and this habit can be difficult to break. When the Holy Spirit prays through us, he prays the perfect prayer one hundred percent of the time.

The Holy Spirit helps us when we are confused and don't know what to pray for. He will pray with us and through us with words from Heaven. The Holy Spirit makes intercession for the saints according to the will of God. Romans 8:26 & 27

So how are you going to pray? Are you going to pray to God for your own priorities and objectives for the day or are you going to allow the Holy Spirit to direct, prioritize and pray the perfect prayer through you? For instance: What if you're praying for your friend at work who was just diagnosed with cancer, but the Holy Spirit is trying to lead you towards an issue between you and your spouse. If you want God's will and agenda accomplished in your life, then listen to the Holy Spirit, he knows how to prioritize your prayer life. The Holy Spirit wants to be involved in every aspect of your life, not just the areas you give him access to. You'll be much more effective in prayer when you are sensitive to the Holy Spirit's leading and direction. He will lead you in the exact words that need to be spoken.

Spouses the way you treat each other could hinder your prayers. I Ptr. 3:7
The Holy Spirit wants to direct your prayers. Jude 1:20

We need to be praying the right prayers for the right reasons. The only way that's going to happen is by allowing the Holy Spirit to lead us into spirit-filled prayer and give him the opportunity to pray through us. He knows the will of God and he knows the perfect prayer in every situation. Based on everything God has taught me about himself, grace, salvation, healing and the atonement; here is one of the most effective ways I have found to pray.

A HEALING PRAYER

Father you've already anticipated this problem before the doctors even found it. Nothing is catching you by surprise. I believe that by Jesus' stripes I have already been healed. **I don't have to get you to heal me.** Prayer is not about me making you heal me. Prayer is not about me convincing you or even begging you to do something that you already want to do and *already have done* for me through the atonement of the Lord Jesus Christ. You've already provided for my healing in the spirit realm. You placed the same power that raised Christ from the dead on the inside of me. **Father, help me to respond in faith instead of fear.** I command all doubt and unbelief to leave my mind. My faith is connecting right now with what you've already provided by grace. What's true about me in my spirit is now manifesting itself in the physical realm and into my body. So I open my mouth and release the life giving power of your healing words. I speak out against this sickness and command it to leave my body. The power of God is rising up from my spirit right now and my body is going to glorify you. No sickness can attach itself to me, because I'm a child of God. No germ can touch my body and live. Everything I need has already been accomplished through your grace and now I just need to rest in that truth and give thanks to you all day long.

STORY – In The Middle Of The Aisle At The Hardware Store

One time my wife and I were at the local hardware store and she was developing this incredible headache. The pain got so intense that she asked me to pray for her right there in the middle of the store. So I prayed for her right there in the aisle with customer's shopping all around us. We didn't let the people around us intimidate us; we were more interested in seeing a manifestation of God's power than anything else at that moment. We didn't care if people saw us, how we looked or what they thought. We were desperate for a manifestation of God's healing power. Do you know what happened next? SHE RECEIVED HER HEALING RIGHT AT THAT MOMENT, IT WAS AWESOME! God can operate in that type of faith and complete trust in him. God wants to be glorified on the earth and he was glorified in the middle of the aisle at the hardware store.

You'll never release God's power from within you by being embarrassed about him in front of people. God wants you to tell people about him (Matthew 28:19 & 20). He wants you to glorify his name before everyone. What is there to be embarrassed about? A person who loves God should not fear what people think.

Is embarrassment hindering your prayer life? If you're quiet, shy and timid in your faith, then the Holy Spirit wants to change that about you. Remember when Moses said, *"Lord I can't speak good in front of people."* Then the Lord said, "WHO MADE MAN'S MOUTH…DID NOT I!" (Exodus 4:11) If you're bashful then the Holy Spirit wants you to open your mouth. Isn't it just like God to use our weakest attributes to magnify his awesome power. He'll use the most backward, soft spoken person to speak his glory out of their mouth. If you're not a dancer then the Holy Spirit will get your feet moving. The Holy Spirit laughs at people who say, "I can't sing good." He knows there's a praise in your spirit that cannot be silenced. The Holy Spirit takes those quiet, shy, backwards people and he prompts them with the awesome message of salvation when they're around others. The Holy Spirit is constantly nudging us in our emotional realm to glorify God with our spirit.

Be obedient to what the Holy Spirit is leading you to do, even if it's way out of your comfort zone or embarrassing. There is always a reason for why God does what he does and you will always benefit from it. I'm not a writer but some how these words are leaving my spirit and being put into written form. I'm simply writing about how great God is, what he's done for me and what he's spoken to me. I am writing about his awesome nature and the mighty works of his hand. I'm doing what the Holy Spirit is directing me to do.

Why has God done so many miraculous things in my life? Is it because he likes to show off? Is it because he likes me more than you? Is it because I've been holy enough to attain his favor? Of course not! God's loves us all exponentially greater than we can even imagine. **His love for us is a constant, unwavering and unchanging attribute of his nature.** He's not mad at us when we fail. It's God's nature to be patient and compassionate. His favor surrounds us like the air we breathe. He's pleased with us because we are his children…period!

By nature I am a quiet person, but in my spirit I'm a loud mouth. My spirit is constantly nudging me to open my mouth and glorify God. There's an urgency in my spirit to tell others of his goodness. Is embarrassment keeping you from being healed? Are you so connected to this physical world that you can't leave it for one moment and operate in your supernatural God given faith that's down in your spirit?

*Don't be embarrassed about serving God and don't be quiet
about your faith. God's plan of salvation is the most important
message you could ever share with anyone. Someone shared it
with you, so openly and boldly proclaim the Lord's love,
grace, forgiveness and salvation to the world.*

THE PRAYER OF FAITH SHALL HEAL THE SICK
(James 5:15)

Another thing I learned from the hardware store miracle is that God is glorified through our confident, spontaneous, uninhibited prayer. I believe God wants us to be in our prayer closets (Matthew 6:6), but he also wants us to pray outside of our closet and in the public square. When someone comes to you with a prayer request, try to pray for that person right at that moment, no matter where you're at. WHY WAIT? **God's power is available *in you* when we display our bold, unashamed, child-like faith *in him*.** He's searching throughout the world for that type of faith. The power of God has already been deposited in every born-again Christian. **Our spirit is completely filled with God's power; faith draws it out of our spirit where we can benefit from it.** Maybe you feel like you have strong faith but God doesn't seem to ever answer your prayers. Please examine the following questions carefully:

- Do you believe your faith is below average? (around a C- grade)
- Are you embarrassed about your faith in front of others?
- Do you mix doubt in with your faith?
- Do you speak confident faith-filled words and do you think positive faith-filled thoughts?
- Is your faith out of shape, rarely used and exercised?
- Do you believe prayer is about persuading God to do something for you?
- Do you believe God's YES answer to your prayer is based on how holy you've been?

You may be a person of faith, but you may have mixed it with your own emotional (carnal) attributes, thereby making it shallow, weak and timid. Do you use your faith as a platform to condemn and judge others? That's what religious people spend their time doing. Do you try to get God to respond to you based on everything you've done for him? Once again, that's what religious people do. **Christians are constantly** reacting to life based on what they see, hear and touch with their physical senses. However, we are spirit-filled beings as well, and we need to counter act what happens to us in this world by acknowledging what is true about us in our new born-again spirit. Then we can proceed with confident faith-filled words and actions according to that truth. Prayer is our confident response to what God has already done by grace.

If the "PRAYER OF FAITH" can heal the sick like it says in the book of James, then we need to find out what the "PRAYER OF FAITH" really is. Maybe we shouldn't be so focused on the word *prayer* but we should be concerned about the *faith* that's motivating that prayer. I've heard pastors scream at their congregations about how they need to spend more time in prayer and on the surface that may be true. But telling people they need to spend a certain amount of time in prayer every week borders on churchified-religiosity. People can slip into mundane religious duties so easily without even realizing it?

Knowing God intimately is far more important than fulfilling a certain time slot in prayer everyday. Knowing God as your Father should be more important than succumbing to a daily ritual. Close, intimate fellowship with God should be something we enjoy ALL DAY LONG! We are never severed from his presence. People think prayer is the time when you speak to God or when he speaks to you. But the truth is, God speaks to us all day through his Holy Spirit. He reveals his divine character and goodness to us constantly. We can meditate on his goodness even as we perform other daily tasks. God wants us to be in constant communion with him because he loves us so much. Religion limits you to fifteen minutes a day with God, but an intimate, fervent, passionate, Father-child relationship is unlimited in its application. God wants to spend his entire life with you starting right now; you don't have to wait until you get to Heaven for that communication and intimacy to begin.

There's a lot of confused, misguided people praying to a God that they really don't even know. **We don't need more prayer; we need people to understand God and that he wants to connect with us. We need to have a full revelation of what happened to our spirit when God touched it.** The type of love that God filled your spirit with will compel you to seek his face, thank him continually and love him with all your heart. If we would teach people this, then we wouldn't have to beg them to come to church or to come to the mid-week service. We wouldn't have to plead with them to come to a special prayer meeting or a revival service. Experiencing the depth of God's love is going to compel you to do things you would have never done before.

Remember the story of *The Woman With The Issue Of Blood*, Jesus said, *"Your faith has healed you (Mathew 9:20)."* Why did Jesus say that? Was it actually her faith that healed her or was it God's power? It was her positive response (faith) tapping into the power of God in her. Here are three key elements in her story:

- First she made a positive statement of faith, *"If only I could just touch the edge of his cloak, then I would be healed."* Jesus wasn't even on the scene at this time when faith first began to rise up in her.

- Second, she had to push through the crowd. This required desperation, hunger, determination and persistence. Do you mix these four character traits with your faith or do you mix doubt, unbelief, embarrassment, discouragement and guilt with your faith? Don't let these negative thoughts dilute the perfect God given faith that's in you.

- Then Jesus asked the question, *"Who touched me?"* The third thing she did was say, "It was I." She proclaimed her miracle to the people in the crowd around her. Are you ready to proclaim your miracle to your Christian and non-Christian friends? Maybe you'll look silly if it doesn't happen. Maybe you'll look silly if it does happen. Who cares! Don't be so concerned about how you'll look in front of people when the Holy Spirit prompts you to receive.

Are you willing to take a chance on God? Are you ready to take a step of faith in a situation where if you fail, everyone will be laughing at you. If you fail everyone may say, "You must not be as spiritual as you think." If you're ready to take a step of faith despite all those fears and questions, then you've just positioned yourself in an atmosphere that releases power out of your spirit. God loves when our faith tramples on our emotional hindrances. God delights in faith-filled people who fully rely on him with complete confidence. So get ready for a phenomenal supernatural adventure that the faith of God produces.

For a Christian, it should be easier to have a miracle than a problem. The miracle to your problem may erupt by simply changing the way you think about your problem. Do you talk to God about your problems or do you talk to your problems about your God? Sounds like a clever cliché , but actually it's a faith altering truth we need to apply to our lives.

Story - Are You Speaking In The Wrong Direction?

One time I had an aching knuckle in my index finger that had been hurting me for months. I told God all about it everyday. I told him how much it hurt me and I was tired of this pain. I prayed for him to heal it constantly. I always wondered why God wouldn't do anything about it. Then I read about how Jesus spoke to a fig tree (Matthew 21:18-22) and he also told us to speak to our mountain (problem or sickness) in Mark 11:23. Jesus even commanded the wind and the waves to be still (Matthew 8:26). Jesus was kind of a wild, radical and confusing guy sometimes, but when it came to miracles he did produce results thousands of times. People just couldn't understand why he did some of the things he did. Jesus was always dominated by the spirit of God, while others were dominated by their circumstances and emotions.

I was ready to be healed from this constant pain in my finger and I was willing to try to understand this new concept about releasing faith. I held my index finger up to my mouth. Then I began to speak faith-filled words into my knuckle. I told my physical flesh that it was going to have to bow its knee to the creator of the universe (That's kind of crazy!). I commanded my body to react to the power of God in my spirit (That's radical!). My knuckle was going to have to listen to my faith-filled words until it realized that it had no choice but to obey (Now that's powerful!). Instead of talking to God about my knuckle I spoke to my knuckle about my Lord. I told my pain that my healing has been secured through the blood of the Lord Jesus Christ.

A supernatural contract has been written and sealed in blood that has secured my immediate inheritance. It's the most powerful contract that has ever been written between God and mankind! As I removed my finger from my lips the pain was no longer there. I just started crying out to God. WOW! Praise you Lord! How could such a simple concept about healing have escaped me for so long?

God was tired of listening to me complain. He wanted me healed, but I needed to operate in the supernatural laws that he's established. The correct information allowed me to finally enjoy the healing Christ secured for me.

One time I bumped into a pastor friend of mine and his wife at a big chain merchandise store. He had been telling me about his endless list of aches and pains. After about fifteen minutes of "PAINFUL TALK", I said, "Let's pray together right now." So I prayed for him right there at the front of the store. I may even have shocked the pastor; they did seem kind of surprised and reluctant. **Would you be willing to pray for someone right in the middle of a store, at a school, in a crowded cafeteria, at work, on a street corner, or in a line at an amusement park? Are you so in touch with your emotional realm (carnal) that you can't lay aside your concerns, worries and embarrassment and operate in faith?** Allow the Spirit of God to erupt down inside of you and then let it out of your mouth with a PRAYER OF FAITH like it says to do in James 5:15. **God wants to say something through your mouth and show the world he is Lord.** God says to us in his word:

Open your mouth wide and I will fill it. Psalm 81:10

God is looking for people who will proclaim his goodness,
stand firm and make a declaration out of their mouth:

SICKNESS: you traveled down this road with me many times…
BUT OUR JOURNEY TOGETHER IS OVER!
PAIN: I've learned to accept your touch everyday…BUT NO MORE!
DEPRESSION: I've placed you on top of my head everyday like a hat,
but from this point on I'm going to wear peace like a crown.

Speak it out with such passion and tenacity
that you begin to believe it in a greater way.

---

*When the Holy Spirit comes out of your mouth, it will be
wonderful, miraculous and supernaturally life changing.
It will always be a restoring healing encouraging word.*

God wants our minds sharp and alert and he wants our faith to be bold and unwavering. The way I see it, I've wasted too much time with lukewarm, reluctant, fearful, passive, emotionally driven faith. When I get to Heaven I want to have accomplished everything that God trusted me with. There's an opportunity to glorify God everyday because God literally lives in you.

Don't' look back at your life and say:

I wish I would have invited that person to church.
I wish I would have prayed for that person right at that moment.
I wish I would have told them about Jesus.
I wish…I wish…I wish…I wish…

Turn those wishes into a reality by being obedient to the Holy Spirit's promptings. Turn those WISHES into a HOPE. Then you'll be able to say:

I hope that person I invited to church will be there this Sunday.
I hope God manifests himself in that person's life through my prayer.
I hope that person understood my testimony and the gospel message I shared with them.

I hope you're beginning to understand the kind of faith that God delights in. It's already *in us,* we just need to let it *come out of us.* The faith God gave us is perfect, pure and clean. When we mix faith with our doubts, questions, embarrassment, worries and our other emotional hang-ups, it becomes diluted and useless. Faith wants to lead you on a powerful, anointed, victorious and abundantly overflowing journey. Don't let any lingering negative attributes keep you from enjoying the journey. A mountain moving manifestation of God is a by-product of our positive faith-filled thoughts, words and actions.

Let a passionate prayer of faith burst out of your spirit and then watch in amazement as God's glory engulfs your words.

STORY – My Wife's Soar Throat

One time I came home from work and my wife had an extremely severe sore throat. She could not swallow at all and she had not eaten anything all day. She was crying when I got home from work and she asked me to pray for her. When I touched her throat, I didn't pray aloud so my wife could hear me, I just began to pray in my spirit to God.

I said, "Lord your grace is sufficient. There is no one like you Lord. We are your created beings. You said to pray, ask, believe and to not doubt and that's what we're doing Lord. Our healing comes from the completed work of Christ on the cross, through the shedding of his blood. So we look to the cross and receive complete healing right now and we will continually give your name praise and glory. We pray this according to the authority and truth of Jesus words and actions…Amen."

My wife left the room and returned a few minutes later still crying. I asked her if her throat still hurt and she said, "NO…IT DOESN'T HURT AT ALL! " She was crying with tears of joy. She started swallowing over and over to show me. Then she immediately went to the refrigerator and started pulling all kinds of stuff out of it to eat. Her throat was healed! God's power manifested itself in a phenomenal way. PRAISE THE LORD! GOD IS GOOD TO US!

This is what I call getting an experience with the word of God. **Put God's word in you then believe it and speak it until you see a manifestation.** God is faithful to his promises. His answer to his promises is always YES! (II Peter 1:3, II Corinthians 1:20) Here are some phenomenal scriptures God has given us to meditate on, believe in and pray. These are from the bookmarker I've compiled _GOD'S HEALING WORD._

GOD'S HEALING WORD
complied by Eric Johnson

If anyone is sick, have the church pray over
them and anoint them with oil and the prayer of faith will heal
the sick. Confess your faults to each other and pray for each
other so you may be healed. The prayer of the righteous
is powerful and effective. James 5:14-16
Oh Lord my God, I cried out to you for help and you healed me. Ps. 30:2
I will not die but live and proclaim what the Lord has done. Ps. 117:17
Trouble and distress have come upon me
but the truth in your words are my delight. Psalm 119:143
The Lord will perfect that which concerns me. Psalm 138:8
Those who know your name will trust in you, for you Lord
have never forsaken those who seek you. Psalm 8:10
Lord you hear the cry of the afflicted. You listen
to their prayer and encourage them. Psalm 10:17
He sent forth His word and healed them.
The Lord himself has rescued them from the grave. Psalm 107:20
Your light will break forth like the dawn and your healing
will quickly appear. Then righteousness will go before you
and the glory of the Lord will be your rear guard. Isaiah 58:8
They went from village to village preaching the
gospel and healing all that were sick. Luke 9:6
I am the LORD who heals you. Exodus 15:26

Jesus took our sickness and carried our pains, he was
pierced for our transgressions, he was crushed for our iniquities;
the punishment that brought us peace was upon him
and by his stripes we are healed. Isaiah 53:4 & 5
The Lord says, I have heard your prayer and
seen your tears and I will heal you. II Kings 20:5
Oh Lord my God, I called to you for help and you healed me. Ps. 30:2
It is the Lord who forgives all your sins and heals all your diseases.
Who redeems your life from the pit and crowns you
with love and compassion. Psalm 103:2-4
Don't be so anxious about the cares of this world. Instead pray
with thanksgiving, then the peace of God which passes all
understanding, will keep your hearts and minds
at rest as you trust in Christ Jesus. Philippians 4:6-7
Humble yourselves under the mighty hand of God and he will lift you
up. Cast all your cares to him because he cares for you. I Pet. 5:6-7
When you keep your thoughts fixed on God and trust him
completely, he will keep you in perfect peace. Isaiah 26:3
Peace I leave with you, my peace I give to you. The Lord your God
has given you a supernatural peace in your spirit. So don't let
your hearts be troubled and don't be afraid. John 14:27
Do not fear for I am with you. Don't be discouraged for
I am your God. I will strengthen you and uphold
you with my mighty hand. Isaiah 41:10

Trusting in the promises of God is the beginning of an extraordinary journey in life. When you get your mouth, life and thinking in alignment with the word of God, it will catapult your mediocre, stagnate, religious faith into the kingdom of light.

Be fully persuaded that God has the power to do what he promised.
Romans 4:21

Receive God's word into your spirit. Commit the scriptures to memory,
believe them whole heartedly and speak them out of your mouth
continually. God is searching for faith on the earth
so we can see his promises fulfilled in our lives.

CHAPTER 4

SPIRITUAL MATURITY
AND SUPERNATURAL GROWTH
God's power will be released through the faith he has given to us...
when we engage the faith he has given to us.

The problem is always us...it's not God. From Genesis to Revelations, God wants his children to connect with him. God has very specific directions on how he wants us to interact with people, what he wants us to think about and how to use our mind, mouth and body for his glory. **Not so we have to live under a bunch of rules and regulations to please him, but so we can experience God's fullness, rest and freedom. There are many places in the bible where God gives us specific directions about what to think, say and do so that the supernatural power of God can be released from our born-again spirit.**

A scientist named, Sir Isaac Newton, discovered that for every action there is an equal and opposite reaction. Have you ever watched a game of pool being played and the very first hit of the game is the cue ball breaking up the other fifteen balls on the table? The initial action is the cue ball headed quickly towards the collection of assembled balls at the other end of the table. When the cue ball arrives it releases all of its energy into the fifteen other balls. When we release our faith into a particular situation, then God's power can be released from within us.

All throughout scripture God promises that his power will manifest itself in our positive thoughts, faith-filled prayers, encouraging words and loving actions. The bible is filled with this ACTION/REACTION biblical truth. You can turn anywhere in the bible and see this happening. Let's look at Psalm 37:3-6

<u>If we will:</u> *Trust in the LORD and do good.*
<u>Then God says we will:</u> *Dwell in the land and enjoy safe pasture.*
<u>If we will:</u> *Delight ourselves in the LORD.*
<u>Then God says:</u> *He will give you the desires of your heart.*
<u>If we will:</u> *Commit our way to the LORD and trust in him.*
<u>Then God says:</u> *I will do this. I will make your righteousness shine like the dawn, the justice of your cause like the noonday sun.*

This ACTION/REACTION concept is found everywhere in the bible. The Apostle Paul said, "Faith without works is dead." It's the same ACTION/REACTION concept. God wants us to act on or put into motion the faith he has given us.

<u>God wants us to:</u>
TRUST in the faith that he has given us.
RELY on the faith that he has given us.
LEAN on the faith that he has given us.
USE the faith that he has given us.

Our faith should never be; cold, stagnate, quiet, idle, afraid, asleep, timid or passive. **God wants us to do something with the faith he has given us, so that his power, which he deposited in our spirit, can be released into this physical world.** Your miracle and your faith are actually intertwined like a DNA strand in your spirit. Your faith and miracle need to blast off like a rocket internally from your spirit, then they need to enter the gravitational orbit of your mind (where your belief system can direct your faith-filled miracle), then it can pierce into this physical world through your thoughts, words and actions. **If you don't ever step out in faith, then God will never have the opportunity to be glorified by the power, authority and anointing he's placed in you.** Actually God has already responded through his grace to every need we'll ever have. His anointing is like rocket fuel in your spirit and your faith is the spark that puts your miracle in motion. His power will manifest itself when faith comes bursting out of our spirit. The power originated from heaven and now it's in you waiting for some type of spark to ignite it.

In the book of Jeremiah 29:12 God says through his prophet:

If you will call to me, then I will answer you.
When you seek me, I will be found by you.

For every faith-filled action you have, God has already responded by grace to that need. We're not waiting for God to do something; he's waiting for us to do something through faith. Are you waiting for God to do something miraculous, even though he's already done something miraculous in you? The fuel is already in your spirit and God is anxiously anticipating your spark of faith to ignite it.

When we open our mouths, God opens his mouth. When we shake our fist at the enemy, God's fist hits the center of our enemy's camp. When we're in the dungeon, chained and shackled and we start worshiping God, then the prison foundation walls will start to shake and we will be set free. When we charge forward towards our giant in the name of the Lord Almighty, God will strike down that giant for us. Because of these biblical truths and the laws of faith it seems like God is responding to us right at the moment that we need him the most. It seems like God is showing up just in time to save the day. But God has already anticipated all our needs before we even had a need. Forgiveness and salvation were provided for people to reach out and grasp at anytime in their lives. That awesome gift was always there waiting for them. Here are some additional gifts God has given us.

God has already anticipated that people would need:

SALVATION - That's why he sent his son to die for us. God required pure, holy, righteous, sinless blood (his blood) to be shed for us.
HEALING - It's already a completely atoned for supernatural fact. Are you operating in the laws of faith to command it to come forth?
LOVE - The love of God is the single most important thing you'll ever open your heart to. The human heart will harden without his love.
PEACE - We can be free from all mental diseases, depression and anxiety. We can triumph over fear, abuse and discouragement. Did you know what's true about you in your new born-again spirit is more powerful than anything that has ever happened to you in this world?
THE HOLY SPIRIT - God deposited the fullness of his divine nature into us. Because we have his Holy Spirit we have the life of God inside of us. He's our comforter, encourager and counselor.

God has already anticipated every need we will ever have. Will we take advantage of the divine gifts he has deposited in us...is a question we answer everyday through what we practice.

How long has it been since you've had the power of God manifest through your faith? God has given us thousands of promises in the bible that release his power into our situation, but he asks us to put our faith into motion first. God wants to unleash his kingdom on this earth through us, but he requires our cooperation to release this power and glory from within our spirit.

Put aside what the world thinks about you. Don't be embarrassed about being a Christian. Trust in the Holy Spirit when he prompts you to do something. Don't let your hands remain idle, God designed those hands of yours to serve others and glorify him (Matthew 10:42). God has filled our hearts with his love. God has given us ears that lean towards his instructions. God has given us a mouth to speak bold, confident, positive, faith-filled words. **Be bold in your faith and the power of God will be released from that spark. You certainly don't want to miss out on anything the creator of the universe has planned for you.**

For I know the plans I have for you, declares the LORD.
My plan is to prosper you and to protect you.
Your entire future is in the palm of my hand. Jeremiah 29:11

UNDERSTANDING CHANGE AND TRANSFORMATION
Jesus said, "You must be born again." John 3:7

Change is typically not comfortable, that's why people resist it so much. We resist it especially when it comes to making changes in our thinking, actions and habits. When change comes knocking at our door, we usually don't answer it. It's that wall of resistance that God is trying to break down in us. Yes that's awesome that you're spending time reading the Bible and in prayer, now BE TRANSFORMED BY IT!

What exactly is God interested in changing about you? JUST ABOUT EVERYTHING! Most people hate change, but in God's kingdom it's an awesome thing. I hope you understand that when you became a born-again Christian, your spirit was completely transformed at the point of salvation. When we read our bibles we discover the truth about those changes that have already taken place in us. When we read our bibles something in our new spirit leaps and says, "This is my new identity IN CHRIST...NOW WALK IN THAT TRUTH." **Understanding in your mind what has taken place in your born-again spirit is the key to loving God, yourself and others.**

We go out to our vegetable or flower garden every few days because we're anxious to see the changes that have taken place. We love to see changes take place in our babies, children and in our families. In the exact same way, God loves to see changes in us. He loves to see changes coming out of us that are a direct result of his spiritual influence. God wants us to understand a little bit more everyday about this new nature in us. He wants us to trust him with the changes he has planned for us.

Are you becoming more Christ-like in the way you treat others? We become more Christ-like when we understand the truth about who is living in us. These truths are revealed to us when we read God's word. God's truth is like a supernatural seed that is planted in us. That seed is designed to produce fruit on your branches. Seeds always produce something, it's a natural and supernatural law. Isaiah 55:11

God fills every person who accepts Jesus Christ as Lord with his very own Holy Spirit. The Holy Spirit is interested in teaching, counseling and changing you. Your love for God should produce a humble heart that is willing to learn, grow and mature at any cost. **Everyone who allows the Holy Spirit to influence them...will experience the power of Heaven in their lives.**

Jesus said, "I will fill you with power from the high Heavens."
Luke 24:49

Wouldn't you agree that's a great change? Being filled with God's spirit, with his power, with knowledge and wisdom is a phenomenal change. Reading God's word injects the truth into our brain and changes how we process information. It changes our motive for why we do what we do. Blood-bought, born-again, Holy Spirit filled Christians are already changed and transformed on the inside. The Holy Spirit is trying to reveal to you that an awesome transformation has taken place in your spirit.

Let's say a person receives all kinds of great instruction from a friend, parent, co-worker, pastor or counselor. But they never apply that great advice to their life by following through with it. They want to do things their way. It's that stubborn nature in people that sometimes says, "I'll figure it out on my own. I'll do it my way." The bible says:

A person who accepts counsel is wise. Proverbs 12:15

Out of the mouth of God flows wisdom, knowledge and understanding. Proverbs 2:6

Anyone who trusts in the Lord and listens to his instructions will be blessed and prosper. Proverbs 16:20

If you would have listened to me, I would have poured out my heart to you and made my thoughts known to you. Proverbs 1:23

When a person becomes born-again in their spirit, God literally waves a supernatural wand over their head and transformed their dead spirit into a living, breathing, supernatural spirit full of the life of God. A total transformation happens deep within their nature (II Corinthians 5:17). Now the Holy Spirit's job is to whisper into their mind everyday about all the new radical changes that are evolving in them. These new changes will flow against our old thought patterns, old habits, old emotions, the flesh, even our five senses. **Your flesh through the influence of the world will tell you to satisfy yourself, but your new spirit through the influence of God's Holy Spirit will prompt you to live a God glorifying life.**

We need to do our part and lower the wall of resistance to learn about all these new changes that have taken place in us. Surrender to the Holy Spirit's promptings. The Holy Spirit does not twist our will and break it. He teaches us about our new identity. For a Christian, these changes should actually feel very comfortable because we are fulfilling our perfectly designed purpose. We become more like Christ (in our thoughts and actions) when we surrender our heart to the Holy Spirit's voice. **Our born-again spirit is identical to Jesus' spirit right now while were here on this earth and for the rest of eternity. I John 4:17, I Corinthians 6:17**

Being born of the Spirit means we possess an amazing life within us. Being a born-again Christian means we are different on the inside. Now we need to let Christ come to the surface and live differently on the outside. His new life in us produces peace and rest in every thought and action.

The less we resist the Holy Spirit, the faster we'll understand the depth of what it means to be IN CHRIST. The more we understand the nature of God, the more we trust him with this new life he wants to live through us.

Don't conform to the pattern of this world, but let yourself be transformed by renewing your mind in God's word, then you'll understand, God, his nature and what he wants you to do in every situation. Romans 12:2

This type of transformation is going to change most of the thoughts you have and many of your conversations with people. People are going to notice something is different about you. **They're going to wonder what's up with you and that will be your opportunity to explain to them the tremendous changes that have taken place in you.**

Maybe the old crowd you hung around with is confused about your new life and desires. Maybe you did a lot of stuff with the old crowd that you shouldn't have. That's OK, when you confessed your sins to God; he was faithful and forgive your sins (I John 1:9). Nobody wants to be known as a "Goody-Two-Shoes" in front of everyone. That's perfectly fine, because you're not good. *"No one is good but God (Mark 10:18)."* You're forgiven, reconciled and redeemed! You are a completely new creation in your spirit. Explain to those people that you're no *better* than they are…your just *better off*…now that you've accepted God's forgiveness and you have the life of God inside you. Explain to them they have the same opportunity to receive Christ also. Do you love your friends enough to do that?

If you're saved, you have God's spirit in you and your unsaved friends and coworkers don't. That scares them. When they see you, they see God in his fullness living through you. That change is confusing to them. When unbelievers resist you their resisting God's spirit that's inside of you. They want things to continue the way they were. People are comfortable with their repetitious controlled life styles. Even though it may not be the perfect life they wanted, they've figured out they can survive like this. If God ever gets their attention and they listen to that whisper in their ear, he will come flooding into their lives and radically change them forever. That's what unsaved people fear; they don't want to be different from their friends, family and co-workers. They want things to remain the same, comfortable and familiar. Even born-again Christians can become comfortable being led by their flesh, emotions and five senses.

The gospel message to the unsaved (and the believer) is that God has made peace between them and him through the blood of Jesus (Isaiah 53:4 & 5). God is the most important person you can ever have peace with. That peace between you and him is extremely valuable. Allow God's peace to radiant from the core of your nature, then watch as it influences your thoughts, words, actions and then finally your world.

Don't just be hearers of the word...but be doers of the word. James 1:2
The Lord has awakened my ear to hear and do what is wise. Isaiah 50:4

Being a DOER OF THE WORD does require a lot of changes in your thoughts, words and actions. But look at the benefits; power, anointing, favor, blessings, rest, contentment and completeness IN CHRIST. God has filled each believer with peace, joy and love. We have something the rest of the world is desperately seeking after and that's hope for the future and all of eternity. WOW, GOD IS GOOD! The changes God has planned for us are awesome! **Open your arms out wide, look up to Heaven and say, "Here I am Lord...immerse me in your life changing presence."**

The awesome thing is God's already given us all these divine blessings. They were deposited in our new spirit the moment we confessed Jesus as Lord. We just need to come into agreement with what God has already accomplished in our new born-again spirit. Philemon 1:6

Change sometimes means acting the opposite of how the world teaches us to act. The world has a "ME FIRST" mentality and there is no doubt the world loves to be served. We love to be served at restaurants, we love to have people clean our houses and deliver our paper to our door step. We are a pleasure driven society and we love all the comforts of this world. Jesus said, "*I did not come to be served, but to serve others and to give my life as a love ransom for everyone" (Mark 10:45).* The world will tell you to get even and give people a piece of your mind. But Jesus said, "*Love your enemies, do good to those who hate you, bless those who curse you and pray for those who mistreat you (Luke 6:27 & 28)."* People chase after many things to satisfy their needs and find their identity. But God says: *You would be wise to take care of your soul.* How would it benefit you if you possessed all the wealth of the world but your soul was lost for all eternity? Mark 8:36

I love those words Peter said to Jesus:

Where else shall we go Lord? You alone have the words of eternal life.
John 6:68

Being a DOER OF THE WORD means you're ready, willing and open for these phenomenal changes God has made in your spirit. Don't be controlled by your feelings, emotions or by peer pressure. Listen to the voice of God inside of you. It's a familiar voice that will calm those raging storms in your heart. It's an encouraging voice that instills peace from within. God wants you to enjoy the new life that's within you.

My ways are not like your ways and my thoughts are not like your thoughts. As high as the Heavens are above the earth, so are my ways higher than your ways and my thoughts wiser than your thoughts says the Lord. Isaiah 55:8 & 9

How do we understand God's ways? How do we understand what his will is for our lives? By reading and interpreting the word of God correctly. The bible was written by the Spirit of the living God as he moved upon the hearts of his willing authors. II Peter 1:20 & 21

We thank God continually because when you received the word of God, which you heard from us, you accepted it not as the words of men, but as it actually is, THE WORD OF GOD which is at work in the people who believe. I Thessalonians 1:13

Anyone who rejects this instruction does not reject man but God, who speaks to us through his Holy Spirit. I Thessalonians 4:8

When Jesus prayed to God on the Mount Of Olives he said, *"Not my will, but yours be done" (Luke 22:42).* Jesus was not questioning what God's will was, nor was he questioning if this was really what God wanted him to do. Jesus submitted to his Father's will, authority and his nature and we need to do the same.

Humility, surrender and submission sound like weak words to the world. But in the kingdom of God, they are a beautiful fragrance to offer to him. Those qualities command his attention.

I'M A NEW CREATION

Put off your old self (your old thought patterns) *that corrupt your heart through selfish desires and be made new in the attitude of your mind. Put on a new self* (new thought patterns that understand the new spirit that's in you) *created to be like God in true righteousness and holiness. Ephesians 4:22 & 24*

Are you receiving this? **Your spirit is righteous and truly holy, just like God's. Everything you will ever DO, SAY and BE in this Christian life should be flowing out of your new born-again spirit.**

Many Christians have those days where they feel like complete failures. They try to act like Christians are supposed to act and they try to talk like Christian talks. You can run out of steam real quick by operating in your own strength and flesh. But that can eventually work out to be favorable, because now that you've exhausted your flesh, emotions and your carnal self, you can now operate through the Holy Spirit. **Allow him to lead and empower you and this Christian life will require a lot less effort on your part.** God loves when we come to the end of ourselves, because that's when he can pick us up, dust us off and say, "Now let's walk in the spirit together."

Being a born-again Christian should be very easy. Someone else is in charge of your life now. If you're a good listener, a lot of the changes God is making in you should come about with very little effort on your part. **Your new Christ-like attitude and philosophies are a bi-product of surrendering to the changes that have taken place in your spirit. Christians have a totally transformed supernatural spirit in them full of God's life, power, love and peace!**

Everything Christians do should be driven by their new God powered, Holy Ghost energized, Jesus filled spirit. It's difficult to live this Christian life by using your natural strength, energy, talents and abilities. You're sharing your body with three divine characters now; the Father, the Son and the Holy Spirit. That's where your power, strength, thoughts, peace, love and rest come from.

God wants you to walk hand in hand with the Holy Spirit and in your new God given nature called THE FULLNESS OF CHRIST. You didn't resist God when you accepted Christ as your personal savior, so don't resist his Holy Spirit that's living in you right now. He will prompt you when you approach those teachable moments throughout your day. It's how much we resist the Holy Spirit that determines how long it will take to mature. Are you so busy throughout the day, that you never take the time to listen to him? If this is the case, maturing could be a very slow process for you. In Deuteronomy 1:6 God asked the Israelites:

How long will you be on this mountain?

How good a listener are you? God is constantly revealing his character, love and wisdom to us. More than likely, you've had hundreds of these teachable moments within the past month. **God is constantly trying to minister to you and through you and reveal himself in a**

greater way. Did you miss those moments or did you latch on to those teachable moments with him?

God has already completely and thoroughly changed your spirit at the point of your salvation. Now God wants you to understand what took place in you and submit to the changes he wants to make in your thoughts, words and actions. YOUR MIND (your thought processes) is the <u>BRIDGE</u> between YOUR SPIRIT (the 100% perfected, saved, holy, sanctified, righteous part of you) and YOUR BODY (your words and actions).

KNOWING who you are IN CHRIST, precedes BEING who you are IN CHRIST. Understanding about these changes that have taken place in our spirit is how we become the best possible representative for God to glorify himself through.

Think of it like this: Jesus is holding on to a rope and guiding us through this life. By holding on to this rope we will all get to our destination point, which is Heaven. Let's say this rope is very long, some Christians are at the end of the rope (and some Christians literally are at the end of their rope) far from Jesus and some are at the front of the rope, close to Jesus. The ones who are close to Jesus feel the power of his love stronger than ever and they reflect that love toward others. They clearly understand the forgiveness that was so graciously given to them and they in turn extend forgiveness to others. Their worship is different because they completely understand who it is they are worshiping. They extend the same love and grace to others that they have been given. They know they have died to sin in their spirit and they no longer want to live with sin in their flesh. They seek first the kingdom of God and his righteousness. The life of God that's in them influences and completes them. Their senses are sharp, they hear God's voice and they're sure of his calling. If you're holding on to the rope that's great, you're going to Heaven, but eternal life is something we possess right now here on this earth. Jesus said:

I have come that you might experience a supernatural life filled with an abundance of God's presence and power. John 10:10

Have you ever met a miserable Christian who was frustrated, short tempered, fearful or always negative? They worry all the time and have little or no peace. The reason is because they refuse to listen, change and mature as the Holy Spirit leads them. That's the condition they were in when God called them OUT OF DARKNESS! He certainly doesn't want them to remain there. Some people are maturing so slowly in their walk of faith that there is very little evidence that they're a born-again Christian. Those people should have matured their way out of that state of mind and those character attributes a long time ago. Don't get mad at them. Don't throw your bible at them, but teach them who they are IN CHRIST. Don't attack their actions or *the process* that we're all in. **A continual practice of wrong behavior is an indicator of how little time a Christian has spent renewing their mind with God's word. Not just reading God's word, but renewing their mind with the truth about their new born-again spirit.**

When your mind changes the way it processes information, then it's beginning to be renewed. When your mind is able to fight off negative thoughts, then it's being renewed. When you read about and understand God's nature a little more everyday, then you're renewing your mind. **A Holy Spirit filled Christian is the most powerful resource on the planet. Whether or not that power is ever released is a process of renewing your mind. READING, RENEWING and RELEASING is how God's word manifest itself in our lives.**

God's word was literally manifested in the flesh of the Virgin Mary's womb and became the Lord Jesus Christ (John 1:14). A divine seed of truth became God in the flesh. All because one person said, *"Let your truth be in me...according to your word" (Luke 1:38).* Are you planting seeds of truth that are producing divine manifestation everywhere that you go?

When you made a decision to accept Christ as your Lord and savior, Christ made a decision to live in you. Christ is IN YOU, God SURROUNDS YOU and the Holy Spirit is operating THROUGH YOU. This supernatural trio will challenge and change you from head to toe. We need to RECEIVE CHRIST, WALK IN CHRIST, LIVE AS CHRIST and EXPRESS CHRIST. We need to tell God:

Not my will...but yours be done. My OLD WAY of thinking must decrease so your NEW WAY of living can increase in me.
(Adapted from John 3:30)

This is how we renew our mind and become
a person who chases after the heart of God.

Please God in every way by bearing good fruit in all your deeds and growing in the knowledge of him. Colossians 1:10

IT'S TIME TO BE TRANSFORMED AND GROW

Saints of glory, God wants to be good to you. He has so much to pour out to his people, but he will not force himself on anyone. He will not make your choices for you. You have to decide how much of God you want in your life. ALL of him…is in ALL of you…but you're the one that regulates the flow of God in your life.

Are you going to put your faith on everyday like a watch on your wrist or are you going put it on like a suit of armor completely covering yourself like a mighty warrior?

Examine the following questions:

Do you only partially rely on God?
Do you put your complete confidence in him?
Do you limit him in certain areas of your life?
Is God only allowed in certain rooms in your house?
What type of Christian are you; a spectator or a participator?
Do you just want to attend church
or is your hearts desire to *be the church?*
Do you glance through your bible during Sunday service
to appease your religious conscience?
Is your emotional realm influenced so much by this world that
you rarely step out of that realm and enter the realm of faith?

WHAT we do is important…but WHY we do
what we do…is even more important.

The bible says that FAITH without WORKS is dead. But WORKS without FAITH are dead also. The two must walk hand in hand together so that genuine faith will produce genuine works.

We are flooded with a staggering amount of information everyday. Are minds are constantly being bombarded by radio, TV and all kinds of other visual and listening devices. We are inundated with newspapers, magazines, e-books and text messages constantly. We absorb all the information the internet has to offer us. People are continually being saturated with the local news, metropolitan news, national and world news. There are thousands of news stations and weekly talk shows on TV everyday. Our computers, TVs and cell phones have become digital billboards constantly flashing in our faces with all the information the world has to offer. Our car stereos are constantly blasting in our ears. I'm not against communication and information, we need to research things, learn and be informed. But what about the information God wants to give you? Have you taken any time out of your day to tune into his frequency?

When you feel God tugging at your soul, don't run away from that. He's trying to speak to you. He's trying to reveal himself to you. Don't let your heart grow cold and hard. The bible says God will, *"...remove that cold stony heart and give you a new heart of flesh"* *(Ezekiel 11:19)*. If you'll surrender your heart to God, he'll change it. He'll give you a heart that's sensitive to his Spirit, willing to listen, a humble heart, a heart that wants to learn, grow and love. Jesus said you'll be such a completely different person that you are literally birthed in the spirit realm as a *new creation* in Christ Jesus (I Corinthians 6:17). Unsaved person, let God into your heart. Christian person, let God have complete access and influence in your heart and life.

When you jump into a pool of water you get completely wet, nothing about you is dry anymore. Most people want to just dip their big toe in the river of Christianity to see if the temperature is comfortable for them. They don't want to make any big waves with their faith. God wants us to jump off the dock, trust him, take the plunge and fearlessly go all the way in.

We need to love the Lord with all our heart, with our entire mind and with all our soul. Then do you know what God will do? He will transform all your heart, your entire mind and all your soul. **God wants ALL OF YOU and he wants to give you ALL OF HIM.** He will change your heart, mind, soul, thoughts, words, attitude, motives, even your hearing and your vision will become acute to the supernatural. You'll perceive things differently about God, yourself and others. He'll change how smart you are. God will change you in every area that you surrender to him. He will change your kids and grand kids, even into your fourth and fifth generations. His life transforming power will pierce into your family's lineage and change the destiny of your history forever. Acts 11:14

When God wants to use you for service and his purposes he will prompt you to start preparing. You might not think you're ready, qualified or worthy, but God knows you better than you know yourself. God knows what his spirit, that's in you, is capable of. You see authority overcomes communication issues, love cast out fear, passion overcomes lack of training and the truth erases our doubts. God will exalt us to a place and position where we can glorify him and lead others into his presence.

God knows your short comings. He knows you have issues. Don't remind God of those little things that he can most definitely take care of. When the Holy Spirit prompts you to prepare for service, just concede and obey. God works through the little things that you and I do. Just do the little things that you can do and allow room for God to operate in that. Look at all the great things God did in the bible with the small things people had.

- David's sling and a stone brought down a roaring giant. I Samuel 17
- Moses' staff separated the Red Sea. Exodus 14:22
- A small bowl of oil and flour was all an old woman had during a famine and she never ran out of either. I Kings 17:12
- A widow's oil was increased so that she was able to pay her creditors. II Kings 4:4
- You might only have five loaves and two fish, but in God's economy that feeds five thousand people. Matthew 14:19

The sling, staff, bowl, oil, loaves and fish didn't have any power in them. It was people's faith that tapped into God's supernatural multiplier. **If you will dedicate whatever is in your hand towards God's purposes, then he can supernaturally multiply it.** Don't look at your hand or at yourself and say, "I don't have enough for God to use. I don't have enough skill, education, ability, or any other good qualities." That's not faith…that's the flesh talking…that's carnal thinking. **You can't use your five senses to perceive the things of God. You have to use your spirit. Faith is not relying on your abilities and resources; faith is relying on what God has deposited in your new born-again spirit.**

God has given everyone abilities to glorify him. Just take a step of faith with what you have and see God use it for his glory. I had a small pencil in my hand, but with God's spirit pushing it along; it became this phenomenal book of power, love and encouragement for everyone to read. Just dedicate whatever is in your hands to God and he will glorify himself in everything you touch.

THE SUMMIT
by Eric Johnson

The mountain before me was enormous.
I began my climb steady and sure.
Soon I ran into obstacles. Some places I slid back down the
mountain, almost to my death. The mountain seemed to be winning.
I could feel the force of the mountain trying to keep me from my goal,
but I fought my way through. Finally the summit was in view.

It was then that the climb became the most difficult.
The steep loose rocks made the final journey seem hopeless.
I slid down the rocks again.
I was hurt, I was tired and I was beginning to lose hope.

Suddenly, I felt a hand on my shoulder.
I turned quickly and there I saw him. It was Jesus!
I grabbed his hands and knelt at his feet.
He said to me, "Oh my child, I've been reaching out to
you the entire journey but you pushed me away and
went your own direction." I cried at my Savior's feet,
then he lifted me up and we drifted off the mountain.

Instead of rising to the top of the summit,
we glided down to the base of the mountain.
Jesus said to me, "If you say to this mountain be cast into
the sea and do not doubt in your heart...it shall be done."
I stood there looking up at the mountain.
It was an enormous towering obstacle. I asked myself,
"Did I have enough faith?" Then I looked at Jesus. Two eyes
looked back at me who had been where I was before.
He had felt fear and loneliness. He had been hurt and unloved
by others. With my eyes still focused on Jesus, I said in a
loud voice, "MOUNTAIN BE CAST INTO THE SEA!"

The earth began to shake furiously.
Rocks and boulders tumbled all around us.
Something of incredible size and power was
happening behind me, but I kept my focus on my Savior.
I heard water and waves splashing up. Then there was a great calm.
I stood there looking into the eyes of Jesus.
Love, Joy and Peace came over me that I could not explain.
I did not have to look back anymore.
I knew God had removed the mountain.

Do you have a tremendous obstacle in your life that seems to be the size of a mountain? When we stand there and look up at these mountain sized obstacles, the questions that immediately come to mind are:

Why did this happen to me?
How do I even begin this climb?
Which way do I go?
How long will it take?
Will I have enough strength?
Emotionally, how do I even begin to handle this?

Immediately all those questions that form in your mind can lead to a lot of fear, doubt, anxiety and frustration. When we have unanswered questions, that's when faith should begin to rise up inside of us.

From our perspective a mountain is tall, steep, difficult and scary. From Heaven's perspective a mountain looks very flat. A change in how you believe will change your perspective on things.

Set your mind on things above (the truth and promises of God) not on earth below. Colossians 3:2

The things we see and hear can get us down, depressed, discourage and fearful. All these feelings stifle our forward motion IN CHRIST. God wants us to perceive things from a heavenly perspective. God has a supernatural solution that can penetrate right into your situation. Our problems can become opportunities when they're attached to a promise from God.

I can do all things through Christ who strengthens me. Philippians 4:13

This is a verse that we all have read many times, but we need to stop and study that verse and let it really sink into our soul and mind. You either really believe that scripture or you don't believe it. There should be no middle ground or gray area when it comes to God's word.

The POWER is in what you believe about God's word.
The POWER is in what you believe to be true in your spirit.
The POWER is in what you believe Christ accomplished for you.
The POWER is in what you believe to be true
about your heavenly Father's nature.

Many people don't know if they can do all things through Christ. A lot of times people lack self-confidence and self-esteem. But that's exactly what Philippians 4:13 is talking about. Our confidence shouldn't be in US it should be IN CHRIST...IN US.

Let's examine what we know:

We know that God's word is the final truth on every subject.
We know that nothing is too difficult for God. That's a universal fact!
We also know that we are IN CHRIST.

If Christ is in us, through the Spirit of the living God and there isn't anything he can't do, then we are capable of anything God wants us to accomplish. Now walk in that truth, celebrate that and he will give you strength to do it.

One time my daughter wanted to try to do something that she never tried before. I told her, "YOU CAN'T DO THAT! " WOW! That was a big mistake on my part! She was mad that I didn't believe in her and that she could do it. I immediately told her, "You will *never* hear me say that again." You can do all things through Christ who strengthens you. You really can.

Jesus said, "I tell you the truth, if you have faith as small as a mustard seed, you can say to this mountain, 'Move from here to there' and it will move. NOTHING WILL BE IMPOSSIBLE FOR YOU." Matt. 17:20

How much faith does it take to move a mountain or to heal the sick or even raise the dead? How much faith does a person need to unleash God's miracle working power from within them? According to this scripture the answer is, NOT VERY MUCH FAITH AT ALL. I had a hard time understanding this for a while. Don't we need our faith to be super-sized? Didn't Jesus always rebuke people because of there lack of faith? Doesn't Jesus want us to have great faith? The Holy Spirit finally revealed it to me in this way.

The kind of faith that impresses God is the faith that he gave you. Human faith can have plenty of fear and self-consciousness mixed in with it. The faith God gave you is bold and trusts in him completely. If you're worried about being embarrassed in front of others, then your faith will probably never accomplish much because you're using human faith that operates by sight. Human faith relies on your five senses and emotions. The faith God has given you is release by his spirit that's in you. The Apostle Paul said:

God has given every person the full measure of his divine faith.
Romans 12:3

When it comes to releasing that faith, the Holy Spirit will teach you <u>WHAT</u> to say, <u>WHEN</u> to say it and <u>HOW</u> to say it. That doesn't mean ramming Jesus down everybody's throat that you come in contact with. It means *speaking the truth in love.* Jesus was always looking at the *type* of faith people had. It was as if he could see right into their heart.

When Jesus entered the city, a centurion came to him and said,
"Lord, my servant is critically ill and tormented."
Jesus said," I will go to your house and heal him." The centurion
answered, "Lord, I am not worthy that you should come to my house,
but speak the word only and my servant will be healed. You see I am a
man of authority and I have many soldiers that I give orders to. I say to
this man go and he goes and to another come and he comes and to my
servant do this and he does it." When Jesus heard this he marveled and
said to the people around him, "I have never found such great faith in
all of Israel." Then Jesus said to the centurion, "Go and this miracle
will be done for you, just as you have believed." A day later the
centurion found out his servant was healed in the same hour
that Jesus spoke those words. Matthew 8:5-13

Jesus compared the mountain, which depicts your specific need or problem, to your faith, which only needs to be the size of a mustard seed. The type of faith that God has given you is strong enough to destroy a mountain and then move it out of your way. Jesus used the size comparison between the mountain and the mustard seed to show how important it is to use the faith that's in your spirit, not your human faith that operates outside of your spirit. From a supernatural perspective the faith that God has given you is more like the size of a mountain and your problems are the size of a seed. Envisioning the solution to your problem from this perspective will help release the pure, perfect, bold and powerful…faith that's in you.

DOUBT AND UNBELIEF

You can fool some of the people some of the time, but you can never fool God. He will not be mocked (Galatians 6:7). God is not interested in how religious you act and look. Religion is not attached to a universal power source like God. God is looking for genuine faith-filled people to operate through. He's looking for people who desire to live out the life of Christ from their spirit. God doesn't care if you fail some days. Trying and failing is better than not trying at all. The Holy Spirit will teach you and encourage you along the way…that's why he lives in you.

You can tell a lot about someone's faith when pressure and persecution comes. Just see what they run to. Do they run to the doctor for their healing? Do they run to a prescription drug for peace and to escape reality? Do they run to food or sex to mask their pain and problems? Many people just simply run away from everyone; including their family, friends and church. Why is it the last place people run is into the arms of their heavenly Father? Why don't people run to the word of God to seek his supernatural solution for their situation?

Maybe one reason people don't go to God first is that deep down inside, THEY DOUBT that God can do anything about their situation or THEY DOUBT that God would do anything for them because they failed him so many times in the past. THEY DOUBT God will answer their prayer because they haven't been holy enough. They've asked God for things before and their prayers went unanswered, so THEY DOUBT he will help them now. Maybe the reason people don't run to their bibles is because THEY DOUBT it will have any real effect on their life in any tangible way.

Jesus said, "If you have faith and do not doubt, you shall not only do
what I did to the fig tree, but you can also say to this mountain,
'Be removed and cast into the sea', and it shall be done for you."
Matthew 21:21

If a person doubts then they shall not receive anything from God.
James 1:6 & 7

Jesus said, "When you don't doubt my words
they are full of life, truth, power and peace." John 6:63

Doubt and unbelief hinder our faith and cripple our prayers. Mixing doubt and unbelief with your faith is like pouring a large bucket of water on a small candle flame. It's like having two separate teams of horses hitched together and pulling in opposite directions. All that awesome power pulling against each other is reduced to zero. DOUBT WILL SUBDUE YOUR FAITH, it's a spiritual law and there is no way around it. Look at what happened when Jesus visited his home town.

One day Jesus was teaching in his home town and many who heard him were amazed. They said, "Where did this man discover all these truths?" They asked, "Where did this man get all this wisdom and power to perform miracles?"

(Here comes the doubt about Jesus their Messiah.)

"Isn't this the carpenter we all know? Isn't this Mary's son and the brother of James, Joseph, Judas and Simon? Aren't his sisters here with us?" And they took offense at him. Jesus said to them, "Only in his hometown, among his relatives and in his own house is a prophet without honor." He could not do many miracles there, except lay his hands on a few sick people and heal them. He was disappointed because of their lack of faith. Mark 6:1-6

They had all heard about the great teachings and awesome miracles Jesus had done everywhere. But doubt cast a dark shadow on everyone's faith. They started questioning who he was and his deity. *Isn't this the son of Joseph and Mary? Aren't his brothers and sisters here with us?* They had a difficult time understanding how Jesus could be the Son of God. They thought, "How could he come from God? He was born and raised here. Is he truly the Messiah who has done all these tremendous miracles in many other towns?" Their unanswered questions birthed *doubt* and *unbelief*. Jesus used the word *believe* over one hundred times in the gospels, especially in the book of John. Jesus longed for people to *believe* that his Father was God and that God sent him here.

Jesus answered and said to them, "This is the work of God, that you believe in me who God has sent." John 6:29

Jesus said, "Anyone who believes in me has everlasting life." John 6:47

Jesus spoke to the crowds and many believed in him. John 8:30

*Jesus said, "I am the resurrection and the life, anyone who
believes in me, even if they were to die, will live with me forever."
John 11:25*

*Don't let your heart be troubled,
you believe in God, believe also in me. John 14:1*

*God the Father loves you, because you have loved me,
and believe that I came from him. John 16:27*

*We believe and are sure that you are the Christ
our Messiah, the Son of the living God. John 6:69*

Doubt and unbelief crushes our faith and severs the flow of God's power in our lives. Jesus could not do many miracles in his own hometown because of unbelief. Jesus possessed unlimited healing power from God. That power was right in front of them, ready to explode when their faith touched him. But that didn't happen that day. Instead their doubt and unbelief mocked him. When we start doubting God, we start questioning the power and authority of everything he governs. We'll even start believing we came from a fish that crawled out of the ocean millions of years ago. God will not operate under a QUESTION MARK. God operates in the EXCLAMATION POINT after the words, "I BELIEVE!"

I might not be able to see a way through this terrible situation…but I BELIEVE!
I don't know how God is going to accomplish that promise he made…my job is to just BELIEVE!
I may not understand everything about God…but I BELIEVE!
I've prayed and now I'm going to be patient…and just BELIEVE!

God's power flows through people who are confident in God's nature towards them. People who doubt God ask him these questions all the time:

God, are you really able to do that?   God, do you really exist?
Are you really close to me?   Do you love me?
God, do you care about me?   Do you still hear me?
Are you watching over me?
Are you able to do what you promised in your word?

God sent Jesus here to earth to crush all doubt, wipe away our tears and to reconcile us to God. God doesn't ever want us to doubt his love. Doubting God's love for you will hinder every other relationship you have in this world. Christian soldier, LETS NOT DOUBT! Let's charge forward into new territory together. Doubt retreats from the enemy and runs off the battlefield. Faith charges forward with comrades shoulder to shoulder running together, breaking through the enemy's battle lines and jumping over the barriers they've built. **God has positioned his children with supernatural authority to demonstrate his glorious power here on earth.** God wants to show himself mighty, strong and victorious through his faith-filled children. It will be the fight of your life…but it will be worth it.

Your faith is dynamic; it should always be moving forward and accomplishing something. Faith doesn't sit still; take a day off or take an extended vacation. Let your faith absorb into your mind and eventually it will come out of your mouth and penetrate into your mess.

I believe God has given everyone a complete measure of faith like it says in Romans 12:3. The critical issue is, how much do you rely on that faith? Do you rely on it completely, partially or barely?

God can look into people's hearts and see their faith, but he can also see their actions and hear what they say. **The faith of God that's in you will move your mouth in such a way that it makes Heaven overflow and the earth soak it in.**

A man came to Jesus and knelt before him. He said, "Lord, have mercy on my son for he's a lunatic. Many times the demon in him has thrown him into a fire or a river. When we brought him to your disciples they could not cure him." Then Jesus answered and said, "What a faithless generation you are, I'm not going to be here much longer to teach you about spiritual things. Bring the boy to me." Jesus rebuked the devil and he departed out of him and the child was completely set free. Then the disciples said to Jesus, "Why couldn't we cast the demon out of the boy?" Jesus said, "Because of your unbelief. If you have faith the size of a mustard seed, you can say to a mountain, 'Go throw yourself into the sea and it shall be done.' Nothing shall be impossible for you. This kind of unbelief only comes out by prayer and fasting." Matthew 17:14-21

When the disciples saw the lunatic and how crazy he was, they must have said, "Can we really cast this demon out?" When they were not able to cast the demon out of the boy, they went to Jesus and asked why. He said, *"Because of your unbelief."* Jesus was telling his disciples, this kind of unbelief only comes out through prayer and fasting. The disciples had already cast demons out of many people before this. The problem was they got their eyes focused on this man's violent, thrashing, demonic behavior. They mixed doubt with their faith and it rendered the power of God useless to them.

Many times a Christian's first response is fear, doubt, worry, hurt and anger instead of faith, confidence and hope. We are emotional beings and we've been operating in the flesh using our five senses all our lives. This is how we've always perceived everything in life. But a Christian has the supernatural life of God in them. We need to respond to life using our new spirit. If you let your emotions and physical senses dominate your mind, then your spirit won't be able to manifest the power of God from within you. Romans 8:6

FAITH VERSES FEAR
Jesus said to them, "Why are you so fearful?
How is it that you have no faith?" Mark 4:40

If you're worried, scared, fearful or anxious, then join the crowd. We've all experienced those feelings in our faith. Those emotions are a part of being human. But we are also supernatural beings and we have the life of God in us. What we focus on and do right after those emotions come sweeping over us is vitally important. You can choose to stay in that pool of despair or you can:

Cast all your cares upon God because he cares for you. I Peter 5:7

Stepping out in faith can be a fearful thing. You could look crazy, funny and get laughed at by people. You might get ridiculed by co-workers because Jesus is your Lord and savior. Sadly enough you may even become the outcast of your family because they're not willing to go where God's taking you.

Fear will usually be right along side your faith,
but we cannot let fear control what the Holy Spirit
wants to do THROUGH US, IN US and AROUND US.

Here are three different ideas on operating in faith and fear. I've heard it taught these three different ways. First, I've heard it said this way:

1. You can't have faith, if you have fear. They can't co-exist together.

I understand what the speaker was trying to convey to people. He was trying to tell us to be bold in our faith. I believe the scripture in II Timothy 1:7 when it says that God did not give us a spirit of fear but of power, love and a sound mind. Fear cannot penetrate our spirit. Our spirit has been perfected and sealed by God (Ephesians 4:30; Hebrews 10:14). Fear does however penetrate our emotional being; it shows up in our thoughts and words all the time. **Fear keeps a majority of Christians from doing what God wants them to do.** We have to live in this world and in this body of flesh with our emotions always right there with us. Our emotions will always be there with us wherever we go. We're not supposed to hide our emotions or stop having them. But we're not supposed to let our emotions dominate our thoughts and rule over us. I believe the other two statements (2 & 3) capture the reality of this confrontation between faith and fear. The second way I heard it taught is like this:

2. You'll have faith and fear at the same time, but let your faith outshine your fear.

That's very true as well and I agree with that concept. I believe this way of teaching is much closer to what we experience during those crucial FAITH verses FEAR moments. **What's happening in our spirit should override the fear that's in our head.** Our five senses are best friends with the fear monster that tries to control us, but we are supposed to walk by faith and not by sight (II Corinthians 5:7). We're supposed to confront our circumstances base on what's true about us in our new born-again spirit. The third way I've heard it taught is like this:

3. There is no such thing as stepping out in faith, we will always be stepping out in fear.

I laughed when I heard the speaker teach it this way because I could totally relate to this. Many times when God leads me to do something in front of people, I get extremely fearful, but I do it anyways. Fear will always be with you because it's an emotion that quickly latches on to your five senses. **As long as you have a brain you will have fear, but fear can never attach itself to your spirit (II Timothy 1:7).**

Hopefully as you read God's word and allow the truth to dominate your thoughts, fear will have less and less power over you.

Faith and fear are usually present simultaneously because they operate in similar environments. Faith and fear both operate when you don't have all the answers. Faith and fear are both present when your future is uncertain and when you don't know what the outcome is going to be. Faith and fear are both fueled by what we believe to be true.

Trust in the Lord with all your heart, mind and soul. You shouldn't rely on your physical senses when trying to perceive God. Love, trust and perceive him with all your heart as he guides you through this life. Proverbs 3:5 & 6

Faith steps out even when we are uncertain. Faith goes forward even when we don't have all the answers or any answers. Faith is surrendering every bit of control to God. Jesus gave us five words of faith that we can recall in those moments when fear starts to overwhelm us.

Don't be afraid...just believe. Mark 5:36

God is always searching for someone with bold, unwavering, steadfast, strong, child-like faith. The reason he's looking for people with that type of faith is because that's the type of faith he placed in us. **The faith you have in God came from him.** We use *his faith* (which is perfect) to put faith in what Jesus did for us. Faith trusts the Holy Spirit to teach us, guide us and speak through us. We literally have *the faith of Christ in us* (Galatians 2:16 & 20). **We actually have the exact same faith Jesus has.** I probably just blew your mind away with that statement, but it's true. We don't just have faith "IN" God and his Son. We have the faith "OF" Christ, which is from God (Romans 12:3). If you'll get your mind around that concept, your faith will never again be weak, timid or frail. It will never be embarrassed or quiet ever again. This is a truth you must grasp so you can stand strong, charge forward, be resilient and never back down.

Life will test your faith everyday. All you have to do is wake up in the morning, get out of bed and the process begins. Life continually throws many challenging circumstances our way. Shower those difficulties with the truth of God's word. Stand firm on the promises that God has made.

When the truth in God's word becomes more real to you than the world you live in...then that's when you'll experience a mighty manifestation of God.

We walk by faith in the spirit realm, not
by sight in the physical realm. II Corinthians 5:7
God did not give us a spirit of fear. He gave us a spirit filled with
power and love. He gave us a sound mind which helps us
to discipline ourselves to trust him. II Timothy 1:7

I loved helping my dad when I was growing up. It didn't matter whether he was working on a car, doing some plumbing work or fixing an appliance. I was always right there next to him, handing him the tools and watching how he fixed things. That's how it is with God and me. I want to be right there next to him, spending time with him, understanding the depth of his character and loving him. I want to know why he does the things he does. I've experienced him fixing me and repairing my soul countless times. He's given me all these divine tools called patience, self-control and love; and he teaches me how to release them out of my spirit. God is the pinnacle example of a loving father (Romans 8:15). **Communing one on one with God is the whole purpose of your life, your prayers and salvation.**

<u>Do you hear God speaking to you right now in your heart?</u>

"I need you to shine over there in that dark place, there is no light there. Can you do that for me? I know I can count on you. It will be scary going there, but I am going to fill you with my power and it will be like a shield to protect you. The world will try to tear you apart like a pack of wolves, but my Holy Spirit will guide you with words, thoughts and actions. When you feel weak, I will uphold you with my strength. When you feel powerless in your own abilities, I have given you my Holy Spirit; he will impart my power to you. My power holds the universe together. When fear comes upon you, my peace will overcome it. Don't ever forget, nothing will be able to snatch you out of my hands and nothing will be too difficult for you and I together."

<u>YOUR FAITH, YOUR MOUTH AND YOUR MOUNTAIN</u>

It's difficult to get around a mountain and it's extremely difficult to go over a mountain. That's why God compared the mountain to our faith in Matthew 21:21 and in Mark 11:23. Many problems we encounter in life are going to seem like mountain sized obstacles. But Jesus said, *"Tell the mountain to go and be cast into the sea."* I laugh every time I read that, but then I remember who my heavenly Father is, how much he loves me and what his spirit in me is capable of accomplishing.

MOUNTAIN GO THROW YOURSELF INTO THE SEA!

Those are some very bold words to say when you're looking up at a towering, intimidating mountain, but Jesus was talking about what your faith can accomplish in the supernatural realm and he's the master in that arena. I don't know what mountain is before you, but God governs the supernatural and the natural realm. **When Christians get a universe-size revelation of how big God is, then their mountains will fall before them.** You speak those faith-filled words from within you and the power of God will remove that mountain in front of you. God wants us to open our mouths and speak a word of truth into our situation. Open your mouth and speak out what the Holy Spirit has placed in you. When your faith and your mouth, get in alignment with God's word, then NOTHING WILL BE IMPOSSIBLE FOR YOU!

All things are possible for those who believe with their mouth,
thoughts and actions; because all things are possible
for those who act on their beliefs. Mark 9:23

OBJECT LESSON - The Power Of The Mouth

I have a great object lesson that I've built to show people how powerful our words are. I have a person come up in front of everyone and stand on a board. Then I blow air into a piece of hose which inflates a thick vinyl balloon under the board. After blowing about five deep breaths into the balloon, the person is lifted up a few inches off the ground. I can lift a two hundred pound person off the ground with just a few breaths of air. I like to use this unique object lesson when I teach on the power of what comes out of our mouth.

God loves to hear words come out of your mouth that
are a direct result of his Holy Spirit that's inside of you.
Imagine God saying this to you: MY words in YOUR mouth…
are just as powerful as MY words in MY mouth.

Think about that for just a moment and as you begin to understand what God is trying to convey to you, it will completely blow your mind away. **God's word spoken through your mouth will channel and release his power into your situation. Many Christians are living way below the level of anointing, authority and power God has deposited in them.** Do you know how many people have swallowed many of their miracles? Their miracle began in their spirit; it grew as they meditated on God's promises in their mind. Then they mustered up enough courage to get the words up and into their mouth and regretfully they never spoke it from their lips. They never spoke God's word (that was planted in them) out of their mouth. **Remember good saints of God, faith is not only knowing the word of God is true, real, active, living and powerful, but faith is released when we act on those beliefs. The word of God is the most powerful resource you'll ever hold in your hands or speak out of your mouth.**

- People who believe that their prayers are powerful, spend time on their knees before God.
- People who anticipate and expect to see a manifestation of God's power among the body of believers, are people who love to go to the house of God.
- People who believe that the word of God is powerful and life transforming, read it continually and speak it out of their mouths.

Do you see how your actions will always follow your beliefs and God's word will transform your belief system.

You can't speak what you don't know.

God wants us to HEAR his promises spoken. John 5:24 & John 12:47
God wants us to READ his word. Luke 4:16
God wants us to MEDITATE on his truth. I Timothy 4:15 & 16
God wants us to BELIEVE his word. John 2:22
God wants us to SPEAK his word. Acts 4:29
God wants us to QUOTE his word. Philippians 1:14
God wants us to MEMORIZE his word. I Corinthians 15:2
God wants us to CONFIRM his word. Mark 16:20
God wants us to STUDY his word. II Timothy 2:15
God wants us to RECEIVE his word. I Thessalonians 2:13 & Luke 18:13
God wants us to CONTINUE in his word. John 8:31

The word of God must be very important if he wants believers to do all of this with it. Jesus said:

The words that I speak to you come directly from my Father. John 14:10
The words that I say are filled with God's power and life. John 6:63

Jesus was in close communication with his Father all the time.
We begin to understand how close God is to us when
we read scriptures like these:

God said, "I will never leave you or forsake you." Hebrews 13:5
Nothing will ever be able to separate you from the love of God.
Romans 8:39

I will stick closer than a brother. Proverbs 18:24

We put our faith into action in a number of ways: worship, prayer, believing, thanksgiving, fasting, communion, praise, witnessing, assembling together, reading God's word, testifying, trusting, giving, loving and finally SPEAKING. If speaking God's word is such a powerful thing, then why don't more Christians do it? The answer to that question is everything I have previously mentioned in this book. Unbelief, doubt, fear, embarrassment, negativity, anxiety, being busy and distracted will all quench the Holy Spirit that's trying to speak through you.

Stepping out in faith can be a very scary thing. If God doesn't show up you could look really silly or even look like a spiritual failure. Anytime God wants to do something through your FAITH…FEAR and ANXIETY are always close by and ready to overtake your faith. You can do many things in faith even when these other attributes are present. The Holy Spirit will teach you how to overcome these negative, faith killers. You keep learning from him and soon those hindrances will diminish to nothing.

Don't be frightened by those who oppose you. Philippians 1:18

(BECAUSE)

I appointed you to go and bear fruit that will last forever. John 15:16

You will never succeed at anything if you don't take a chance on failing. But here is some good news…no one is a failure in God's kingdom.

Look at all the ordinary fearful people in the bible who by faith, stepped out of their comfort zone and did many miraculous things for God's glory. Here are some questions to consider:

When was the last time you put your faith into action?
Is your faith moving your mouth?
When was the last time you experienced an awesome manifestation of God's power because of what the Holy Spirit spoke out of your mouth?

We have complete confidence in God because when we ask anything according to his will, we know God hears our prayers and we know he will take car of our situation because we trust in him. I John 5:14-15

Jesus said to the devil, "IT IS WRITTEN! Man shall not live by eating bread alone, but by meditating on the truth that God has spoken." Matthew 4:4

Remember: God's word in our mouth
is just as powerful as God's word in his mouth.

Jesus said, "Whoever will <u>say</u> to this mountain, be removed and cast into the sea and does <u>not doubt</u> in their heart, but <u>believes</u> that the things they <u>say</u> will come to pass, then they shall have what they <u>say</u>."
Mark 11:23

In Mark 11:23 Jesus said to <u>believe</u> and <u>not doubt</u> once and it has the word <u>say</u> in it three times. **Don't ever underestimate the power of God's word when it comes out of your mouth.**

God wants to hear his truth come out of your mouth in such a bold and confident way that it glorifies him and blesses you instantly. It pleases God to hear words of faith, trust and confidence come out of your spirit. Your response to the faith God has placed in you will be a moment you will remember for the rest of your life.

That's why reading God's word is vital for a believer. You can't speak what you don't know. **A daily intake of God's WORD, THOUGHTS and CHARACTER are essential if you desire to speak LIFE, VICTORY and POWER into your situation.**

When you open your bible…God opens his mouth.
When you open your mouth…God opens the windows of Heaven.
You could literally be one word away from your miracle.

The Lord stretched forth his hand and touched my mouth and he said, "Behold, I have put my words in your mouth." Jeremiah 1:9

The Apostle Paul told us to:
Speak the word of God courageously and fearlessly. Philippians 1:14

God's love, power and presence will cause you to speak positive, faith-filled words. Anyone can talk negative about what's wrong with people and life. **Christians have Christ in them; therefore we have the life of God in our spirit. Christ literally lives in us (Galatians 2:20). We are now full of love and self-control.** Our words, thoughts and actions are in the process of changing because we have a *new nature in us* (Romans 12:2). Christians need to speak positive faith-filled words of encouragement over people's lives. Speak words that God puts in your heart. Speak the word of God boldly out of your mouth. **The power of God in you will change what's coming out of you.**

Let God's spirit saturate your mind and then fill
your mouth with his glory. Romans 15:6

THE POWER OF YOUR SHOUT

There will always be someone around to tell you:

You can't do that!
You can't minister to people that way!
God can't use a person like you, look at what you've done in the past!
You wouldn't like teaching little kids!
No one has ever done it that way before!
You shouldn't worship God like that!
You can't pray for people right in the middle of the worship service!

There will always be people around that SHOUT YOU DOWN. There was a blind man named Bartimaeus who lived in the city of Jericho. He was at the roadside begging when he heard that Jesus was walking by. He began to shout to Jesus, so loud that it was embarrassing others around him. They rebuked him and told him to be quiet, but he shouted even louder (Mark 10:46-48). **But even a blind man could see that he needed Jesus.** Don't let others steal your shout. Make sure your shout is louder than theirs. Just before David and Goliath fought they shouted at each other, back and forth they shouted and exchanged words with each other.

Goliath shouted:
"Why do you treat me like a dog by coming at me with a little stone?"
Goliath cursed David and his god. "Come here," he said, "and I'll give
your flesh to the birds of the air and the beasts of the fields!"

David shouted to Goliath:
"You come against me with a sword and spear; but I come against you
in the name of the Lord. Today the Lord will hand you over to me and I
will strike you down and cut off your head. Today the Lord will give the
carcasses of the Philistine army to the birds of the air and the beasts of
the earth and the whole world will know that there is a God over Israel.
Everyone will see and know that it is not by sword or spear that the
Lord saves; FOR THE BATTLE IS THE LORDS and he will give all of
you into our hands." I Samuel 17:45-57

Even King Saul tried to shout David down just before the fight.
Saul told David:
"You are not able to fight this Philistine, you are only a boy and he has been a fighting man since he was young." I Samuel 17:33

David's brother Eliab tried to shout David down even before he spoke to King Saul.
When Eliab, David's oldest brother, heard David speaking with the men, he burned with anger towards him and asked, "Why have you come here? Your job is to take care of the sheep!" I Samuel 17:28

There are probably all kinds of people who shouted and laughed at David that day. Some were Philistines and others were his own people the Israelites. But he didn't let that deter him from what God put in his heart, *his destiny*. It would be a battle that people would talk about for thousands of years. When the Holy Spirit gives you something to shout about, don't let other people have the last word and don't let them shout you down. **Whatever the spirit of God has put in you, let it break forth out of your mouth like the sound of a trumpet.**

Start confessing the Word of God:

BOLDLY…out of your mouth!
CONTINUALLY…out of your mouth!
EVERYDAY…out of your mouth!

Repeat this everyday until it saturates your mind.

I AM who God says I am.
I HAVE what God says I have.
I CAN DO what God says I can do.

The world operates under the thought pattern, *I'll believe it, when I see it.* In God's kingdom that doesn't work. You have to BELIEVE IT and SPEAK IT to SEE IT. Examine the following verse closely.

"Therefore I say to you, what things you desire, when you pray (This is the SPEAKING part), *believe* (This is the BELIEVING part) *that you receive them, and you shall have them.* (This is the RECEIVING part)
Mark 11:24

Once again we are to SPEAK, BELIEVE AND RECEIVE God's blessings & promises. God's ear is turned toward those who pray to him in full faith and confidence. **Until you make a decision to believe with**

all your heart and then act on it will all your mouth, nothing supernatural will ever happen.

Faith without the truth applied to it through our actions is dead.
James 2:26

The word of God is a spoken thing. It was written down on paper so we could READ IT, BELIEVE IT and then SPEAK IT.

Jesus said, "Anyone who believes n me, everything that I have done they can do also, and they shall do <u>even greater works</u> than me, because I'm going to my Father and whatever you ask in my name, you shall have it, that the Father may be glorified. John 14:12-14
Jesus said, "If you abide in me and my words abide in you, then you can ask for whatever you desire and it will be done." John 15:7

Your mind is the bridge between your faith and God's power.
Your mouth is the bridge between God's power and the world.

You are like a musical instrument that a musician can create a beautiful song with. God wants his glory to resonate from within you. He wants to hear confident, faith-filled, prayers come charging out of your mouth. He wants to hear a song of worship sung from your heart. God wants to hear positive faith-filled words flow out of you. **The main purpose of your mouth is to speak out the wonders of God. We are created vessels, spoken into existence by God's own breath. We are designed to speak the glories of God continually out of our mouth.** Fill your mind with the word of God and then open your mouth and let the Holy Spirit fill it. Let the word of God proceed out of your mouth and everyone around you will be amazed at God's glorious wonders.

CHAPTER 5

GOD LOVES YOU

I finally discovered how valued I was...when I met God's love.

Most parents have those baby books where they record when their baby first smiled at them or when they first rolled over from their back to their belly. Many times people just write down how much they love that new child of theirs. I was reading in my daughter Courtney's baby book a while back. She was only about seven months old when I wrote this:

Courtney you're so pretty. You have these big beautiful blue eyes and I just love looking into them. You smile all the time and make everyone around you smile also. You are a very quiet baby, you almost never cry. You have a beautiful voice and love to clap your hands. You are always content just looking around and exploring, you discover new things everyday. I love to watch you when you're sleeping. I love to see you enjoy all the many new experiences in life. I think you've finally discovered that your voice is beautiful. It's like you enjoy listening to yourself talk and laugh. You completely mesmerize me. Your face captures my complete attention. I can't keep myself from coming in the room and wrapping my arms around you and saying you're mine and I love you. You fill my life with such joy.

Your Dad

I was just bawling my eyes out when I read this. It brought back so many wonderful memories for me. It helped me to remember just how much I was completely in love with her. I loved both my daughters the moment I laid eyes on them. My love for them didn't have to grow or mature, it was instantaneous. I'm so glad I took the time to write about them. Now all these many years later they can read in their baby books and understand just how much their mom and I treasured our time with them.

It's the same way with God's word (the Bible); he has written a lot about how much he loves us. Here is what he's written about us.

MY LITTLE CHILD

You are my creation and you stand blameless before me. Rom. 5:1,6:1-6
I have chosen you and adopted you, because I love you. I'm so glad
you're a part of my family. You are very precious to me. Allow me to
influence you just as a potter shapes their clay. Jeremiah 18:6
I want you to know me as completely as I know you. Eph. 1:8 & 17
Because you are mine, my spirit lives in you. You shall have my mighty
power and favor with you all the days of your life. Eph.1:18, 2:5 & 6
I am anxious to hear your voice everyday. Ephesians 2:18, 3:12
I have forgiven you yesterday, today and tomorrow completely.
The debt and curse against any child of mine has been lifted. Col. 1:13 14
My grace and mercy will always be with you. Hebrews 4:16
My spirit in you will be like a counselor that leads you
throughout your day. I will teach you to have patience,
kindness, gentleness and self control. Galatians 5:22
I see so much potential in you. Philippians 2:13
You are the apple of my eye. Zechariah 2:8
I have placed my seal on you and I will not remove it.
Nothing will snatch you out of my hand. Ephesians 1:4 & 13, 2:19
Your face reflects the light of my love. Colossians 1:13
Your countenance will break forth like the dawn;
it will shine like the midday sun. Psalm 37:6
I have created you, formed you and redeemed you.
You are mine forever. Isaiah 43:1
I trust you with the secret knowledge of my kingdom. I Chronicles 4:1
I've placed my royal family seal on you, so that everyone
will know that you are a child of the king. II Corinthians 1:22
I have anointed and equipped you for every good purpose
that I have ordained for you. II Timothy 1:7, 3:17
When I look at you, I see a person completely free from sin. Just as if
you've never sinned. I have covered you with my righteousness. Rom. 5:1
Your new life contains the power of my spirit.
I will put my words in your mouth and I will cover you
with the shadow of my hand. Isaiah 51:16
Your thoughts will be like my own thoughts. Romans 8:4, 12:2
You are going to prosper and have a divine future. Jeremiah 29:11
Don't ever forget my child, that I choose you, you are royalty, you are
apart of my heavenly family. You belong to no one else but me. I Ptr. 2:9
Nothing will ever separate you from my love. Romans 8:39
Since your spirit has been purged from sin, your body, mind
and soul are now instruments of righteousness. Romans 6:13

My shield of favor will protect you all the days of your life. I Peter 1:3 & 4
I will lavish you with wisdom and understanding beyond your years.
You will know the mystery of my will and what pleases me. Eph. 1:8 & 9
You are my wonderful handiwork.
I am so proud to call you my own. Ephesians 2:10
When you call out to me, I will always answer you. Psalm 91:15
You wear a ring of comfort and joy on your finger. Jeremiah 31:13
You will rule over the many works of my hands
and I will lay everything at your feet. Psalm 8:6
I want you to resemble me by reflecting my love,
forgiveness and grace to others. II Corinthians 3:18
I will shield you with my hand of protection
as I lay it on your head. Psalm 3:3
I have crowned you with love and compassion; I will satisfy
your desires with my favor and blessings. Psalm 103:4 & 5
I will protect you all the days of your life
so that no harm will come to you. Psalm 91:10 &14
I will never leave you or forsake you. Hebrews 13:5

From your Father who loves you. John 3:16

There are so many wonderful things that God has said about us in the bible. I hope you're beginning to grasp how much God loves you. God promises in his word that if we will start taking the steps to understand his character, he will reveal himself to us in a way we can understand.

I read my daughters' baby books to them every once in a while so they will understand how much I love them. They love hearing about themselves and all the little things we noticed about them when they were babies. From the very first day I saw them, I loved them, because they are mine. They are mine to love, hold, nurture, teach and enjoy. They are a part of me. I get to help mold them and shape them into who they will become.

God loves us the way he does because we're his. You are his to hold, love, nurture, teach and enjoy. All the information you just read about yourself is from God's word (The Bible). God wouldn't have put it there if he didn't mean it. When we spend time seeking his face, reading about his character in the bible or worshiping him, then that's when he reveals his love to us in a greater way. Make sure you go back and read the words of _MY LITTLE CHILD_ as often as you can, so that your constantly reminded of how much God loves you.

This really happened to me. One morning many years ago when I was waking up out of my sleep, I had this incredible experience with God. I was standing in this thick cloud of fog wondering where I was. Then someone spoke to me out of the cloud, he asked me a question. His voice was loud and commanding. He said, "Who are you?" I knew then it was God speaking to me. I never had anything happen to me like this before. How was I going to answer God? I'd better tell him the truth for sure; I mean it was God speaking directly to me. What was the answer to the question he was looking for? I just spoke what was in my heart. I said, "NOT MUCH." Then the Lord said something to me that I'll obviously never forget for the rest of my life. He said,

"Did I send my Son…for NOT MUCH?"

At that moment it was like information was flowing into my head at a thousand miles an hour. God wrote a love letter to me as thick as a phone book. It was like he placed it on the top of my head and said, "Receive this now from me in your understanding." It was one of the most incredible moments of my life. Some type of channel had been opened and heavenly wisdom began transforming my mind. The information was about me. It was important knowledge about who I was in Christ. It was the most intense manifestation of God I had ever felt. At that moment I finally realized how much God loves and cares for me. God revealed to me the truth about his nature. I was just as awake, after he said that to me, as I am right now writing this book. The intensity of the meeting was so powerful...I'll remember it forever.

GOD JUST SPOKE TO ME!

It was the closest I had ever come to actually hearing the audible voice of God. I mean I really did hear the voice of God; it's just that I happened to be sleeping just before this event. He touched me with an undeniable love from Heaven that I'll never be able to describe in words.

The bible does describe this kind of love. I've compiled four bookmarkers that will help you understand how much God loves you. They are GOD KNOWS MY NAME, I AM, BY GOD'S GRACE and MY LITTLE CHILD. After that event, I never again doubted what God says about me in his word. I hope you understand that God loves you with the exact same relentless passion.

Faith works by love. Galatians 5:6
(You can only operate in faith if you're operating in love.)

Won't you try this today? Get down on your knees right now and allow the love of God to absorb into every area of your spirit. Let God fill every cell in your brain with the fact that he's completely in love with you. Tell God you want to completely understand how much he loves you and to fill you with his unconditional, unlimited and unwavering love. When he does this, AND HE WILL, the love of the Lord will take over every part of your character. **Your circumstances might be the same tomorrow but your heart will be different. All your hurts, heavy burdens, emotional strife and confusion will slowly dissolve as the love of God flows into your heart.** It's kind of like putting a garden hose, flowing with water, into a jar filled with dirt. The rush of clear clean water will eventually remove all the dirt from the vessel. There will soon be an overflow out of your vessel and it will have an undeniable effect on the people around you. It will be like a tremendous waterfall pouring into you and then flowing out of you (John 7:38). God's greatest desire is for you to UNDERSTAND his love, RECEIVE his love and then GIVE his love to others. **The love of God is the single most important discovery you'll ever make in life.** The world would be lost without the love of God. Let's read a little bit about God's love from I Corinthians 13.

THE LOVE CHAPTER

Love endures long and is patient and kind.
Love is never envious, it never boils over with jealousy.
It isn't boastful. It does not display itself in a prideful haughty way.
It's not conceited, arrogant or inflated with pride. It's not rude.
God's love in us does not insist on its own way.
It's not self-seeking, touchy, grouchy or resentful.
It takes no account of the evil done to it. Love pays no attention
to a suffered wrong. It grieves at injustice and unrighteousness
and rejoices when righteousness and truth prevail.
Love bears up under anything and everything that comes our way.
It's always ready to believe for the best in every person. It's hopes are
fadeless under all circumstances and it endures everything without
weakening. Love never fails. It never fades away or gives up.
I Corinthians 13:4-8

God has poured out his love into our hearts by the Holy Spirit. Rom. 5:5

May God strengthen you with his power in your spirit, because God has rooted and established you in love. You can know without a doubt, how wide, how long, how high and how deep are the dimensions of God's love for you. His love surpasses anything you've ever came in contact with before. Know this child of God; God has completely filled you with his love in your inner being. You have the fullness of God's divine nature residing in you. Ephesians 3:16-19

God's love is already in every born-again Christian. We just need to trust him with it, then it can burst forth out of you like a volcano. It may already be coming out of you in new ways and desires that were never there before. Reading God's word will help unleash God's love from within you. You have to know that all of God's love is in you before it can come out of you. The words *"God loves you"* echoed from every one of Jesus' actions. That's why he taught us, healed us and eventually died for us.

Even though the mountains could be shaken flat and the hills crumble to the ground, never will my unfailing love for you be shaken says the LORD. Isaiah 54:10

I used to demonstrate to my daughter Erika how much I loved her by saying, "I love you this much." Then I would hold out my hands in front of her and slowly spread them out as wide as I could. I used to do this all the time so she could see visually how much I loved her. God describes his love for us in a similar way. The following verse is God speaking:

As high as the Heavens are above the earth... so great is my love for you. Psalm 103:11

God's love is so vast, it really is OUT OF THIS WORLD! In this scripture God describes for us the physical dimensions of his love, just like I did with my daughter Erika. The speed of light travels at around three hundred million meters per second (300,000,000 meters/second). That equates to five trillion, nine hundred billion miles per year (5,900,000,000,000 miles/year). Now we need to multiply that figure by three hundred million (300,000,000) light years. That's the distance across the universe, at least that we are currently aware of. When we multiply those two figures together, we finally get the physical dimension of how much God loves us. Which is one quintillion, seventy seven quadrillion miles. Here is the actual numerical figure

(1,770,000,000,000,000,000 miles). When God holds out his hands and says, "I love you this much!" His hands would spread apart until they reached this distance of one quintillion, seventy seven quadrillion miles. **Do you know how far that distance is? If you did, it would revolutionize your perspective of God's love and it would change you instantly, drastically and constantly. God wants us to have a mind blowing, supernatural, radiant revelation of his love towards us.**

Sometimes God reveals himself to us in layers as we draw closer to him and sometimes God's love is like trying to take a drink from the Niagara Falls by standing under it with your mouth open. Either way is fine because both revelations are going to transform your life. As you begin to have a deeper understanding of how much God loves you, it will exponentially magnify how you love God, yourself and finally others. God says his children are to shine like the noonday sun and we are to be a light of love in this dark world.

God doesn't want you to doubt his love for one moment. When you understand his love, it will change everything about you, your world and the people around you. God's love will change how you think, talk and act. It will change how hard you laugh. It will change your perspective on life and your relationships with people. It will give you the patience you so desperately need while serving and caring for people.

I dare you to try to love God back as much as he loves you. Of course it's not possible but he'd love for you to try. All of your life is about trying to do just that. **God tells us that loving him is the greatest thing you will ever do with your life.** Jesus said this is the first and greatest commandment:

> *You should love the Lord with <u>ALL</u> your heart, with*
> *<u>ALL</u> your soul and with <u>ALL</u> your mind. Matthew 22:37*

God is patiently waiting for us to fall head over heels in love with him. Partial commitment means you haven't had a complete revelation of his love. God desires complete surrender with all our heart, mind and soul. **He has so much information to give us about himself, it's going to take one hundred percent of our heart, mind and soul to absorb it all.** God wants us to radiate with all his many character attributes as we walk out into the world and shine the light of his glory. I know for a fact how much God loves me. He's revealed it to me in so many unique and profound ways. The great news is, God loves you just as much as he loves me. The best kept secret in the whole world is this:

God loves people.

Most of the world doesn't understand the depth of that statement. People don't know it, they refuse to comprehend it and they never receive it. People think they have to earn God's love through behavior modification, but you can't. It's something given freely for everyone to receive. Even most of the Christian community believes you have to do certain things or act a certain way for God to love you. **God is not going to love you any better when you become better. He is not going to love you more when you do more good things for him.** You just can't stop God from loving you, but you can refuse to receive it or limit it. You can run from God and turn your back on his love. Remember you don't have to act a certain way for God to love you. Otherwise he wouldn't love any of us. The bible says:

God proved he loved us, because EVEN WHILE WE WERE SINNERS, Christ died for us. Romans 5:8

Why did God love us if we are all a bunch of rebellious, wayward, God rejecting, self-centered sinners? **Because God's love is not dictated by our actions.** God's love is something that's difficult to describe to people. It has to be experienced, like standing at the edge of the Grand Canyon. God's love is not controlled by evil. When we are disobedient, we will have repercussions for those actions because it gives Satan an inroad to our lives (Romans 6:16). But God's love for us is a constant force that surrounds us. **His love in our spirit is a catalyst for experiencing life and peace. Romans 8:6**

A greater understanding of how much God loves you will drastically accelerate your maturity level. This supernatural love from God is the catalyst of our Christian character. A catalyst is defined as a substance introduced into a process that modifies and exponentially increases the rate of change of the reaction. What a great word to describe God's love for us, IT'S A CATALYST!

God's love is the substance, that is introduced into the process of our lives, that exponentially increases the rate of how much we love, forgive and prefer one another. God's love is a catalyst and it causes a chain-reaction in us.

<u>To experience God's love in its greatest capacity:</u>

We need to READ about God's love.
We need to LEARN about God's love.
We need to UNDERSTAND how much God loves us.
We need to RECEIVE God's love with all our heart.
Don't reject it, turn from it or limit it.
We need to MEDITATE on the love of God throughout the day.
We need to RECIPROCATE God's love.
Love him back with the love he gave you.
We need to GIVE God's love to others. (Freely, unrestricted, unmerited and unconditional)

Jesus said the greatest thing you could ever do is:

Love the Lord with all your heart, with all your soul, with all your mind and with all your strength. Mark 12:30

The second greatest thing you could ever do, once you understand and are doing the first thing is this:

Love your neighbor like their one of your own family members. Matthew 22:39

If you ever wondered what God's will is for your life, it is all right there. **God's love is the catalyst for being in his will.**

Build yourselves up in your most holy faith by praying in the Holy Spirit and keep yourselves immersed in God's love. Jude 1:20 & 21

Today child of God, draw a line in the sand, go and write it on a wooden stake then drive it into the ground on your property. Write it on the walls of your house, write it on your clothes or on the bottom of your shoes with a permanent marker and pronounce to him:

TODAY GOD...I RECEIVE THE FULLNESS OF YOUR LOVE.

Your interpretation of God's loving nature towards you.... is the most important thought you'll ever have.

Now God can operate in that type of faith, passion and surrender. That's what he's been waiting for. God wants people to receive him into their spirit and then release him out of their spirit for others to experience. I've observed that many people, to various degrees, have built up walls around themselves to keep others at a safe distance. This seems to be an instinctive defensive mechanism built within people so that they don't get hurt. **God's love will rip apart every wall you've built, the moment you crack open the door to him.** He will fill that box you've created around yourself with so much of his love that soon it will burst wide open. LEARN about God's love, RECEIVE his love, ACCEPT it, MEDITATE on it daily, be CONFIDENT of it, be SECURE in it and TRUST in his love.

STORY – Love Letter

One time I was driving to work early in the morning. It was dark and raining which made it extremely difficult to see. There in my car, I was talking to God and letting him know that I felt like he was a thousand miles away from me. I wasn't feeling him close to me like other days. So I asked God a stupid question, I said, "God do you love me?" There was a ten second pause from Heaven. Then a semi-truck came speeding by very fast. As the back end of the truck went by, I notice in the lower right corner of the truck, there were three words written there. Someone used their fingertip to write these words on that dirty truck:

GOD LOVES YOU.

I thought to myself, WHAT! WHAT just happened here! God…is that you! Did you just write me a note on the back of that semi-truck? Did you have someone write it earlier and then time the truck to go by right when I needed to see that? Was it just a coincidence that I happened to be asking that question to you and then this truck went by at the exact time I needed to hear from you?

Instead of questioning God's response and asking him why he would ever take the time to ever love someone like me. I just decided to receive those three words that God had written to me and allow the truth to penetrate into my heart. GOD LOVES ME! It might as well have said:

GOD LOVES YOU ERIC DEAN JOHNSON

...because that's how I received it. My heart started filling up at that moment with the love of God. I couldn't understand what was happening to me. I was just completely overwhelmed with the power, presence and love of God. I started crying with tears of joy, receiving and understanding God's love in a marvelous and profound way.

Maybe you've been down that same road I was on that morning. I think we all have. We have those days when we just don't feel like God is close. I want you to start a new habit. I want you to say this when you first open your eyes in the morning.

GOD LOVES ME and I LOVE HIM and
I'M GOING TO GO and LOVE OTHERS.

God has his arms around the people of this world and he's saying to them, "I LOVE YOU...I CREATED YOU...YOU ARE MINE." We struggle, push away and run from the very thing that we so desperately need....THE LOVE OF GOD IN OUR HEARTS.

God is trying to capture the world's attention, look into their eyes and say...I LOVE YOU. Those who surrender to him and receive it... WILL BE CHANGED FOREVER.

LOVE PEOPLE

Love each other deeply from your heart. I Peter 1:22

Don't get tired of blessing and helping people. For in time you shall receive a great reward for your faith-filled words and actions. So take advantage of every opportunity in reflecting Christ's love towards others. Galatians 6:9 & 10

Be completely humble, gentle and patient when loving one another, because you are united in God's love through his Holy Spirit. Ephesians 4:2 & 3

God wants us to love one another because GOD IS LOVE and that's how we perfectly resemble him. Have you ever noticed the statements parents make when they see their new born baby for the first time? They say things like, "He has your eyes, she has your nose or he has your chin." We're anxious to see the resemblances of our children in us. In the exact same way God is waiting to see how we resemble him. Not with our nose, chin and eyes but with *our spirit*. **In our born-again spirit we're identical to God. He intertwined his spirit around our new spirit and now we're united with him (I Corinthians 6:16).** Our thoughts and actions are not identical to God's because were all in *the process* of learning about this love that's in our spirit. As we learn and mature we begin to love like he does. **God wants us to love and forgive like no one else on the earth. He wants us to express his character traits for the entire world to see.**

The world will chase after that type of love, if we would just extend it to them. We'll be able to look them straight in the eye and tell them, "GOD LOVES YOU", and they will finally begin to believe it. Then we'll be able to share with them the hope that we have in the Lord. We'll be able to share with them the gospel message of the Lord Jesus Christ in a way they will understand, believe and receive. That's the whole point of Christianity. God is reaching out TO YOU (his child) and then he reaches out THROUGH YOU (to others).

Religion is all about people trying to reach God through strict performance based works, rituals and doctrines.
New Testament Christianity is about God reaching out to his children through love, mercy and grace.

God is very specific on how we are to treat people. He continually tells us in his word to love others because that's how we resemble Christ. When your relationship with God grows deeper then your relationships with others will change as well. Your overwhelming love and compassion for others will be the evidence to them that you are a child of God.

When we completely understand and totally receive God's love, then we will be able to love others with that same unconditional love, regardless of how they treat us. That's what the word *unconditional* means; there's no strings attached, no requirements to fulfill and no list of conditions to meet. The love I have for other people comes from an overflowing source in me, put there by God. God is passionate about people and that same passion was deposited in our spirit when we were born-again. God's love should flow through us regardless of how we're treated or how others respond to us or even whether they choose to love us back.

Is your love for others based on their performance or is it based on the new nature that's in you. God's love in us causes us to hope for the best in people. We shouldn't look for the worst in them; the rest of the world is doing that. If you can't seem to find anything good in a particular person, then hope to see the best in them one day. God's love in us always hopes to make a tremendous impact on others.

God is love and love overflows with hope.
God hopes that people will turn from their wicked ways.
God hopes that people will love him back.
God hopes that his creation will humble themselves
before him. God hopes that we will seek his face,
understand his nature and know him completely.
God hopes for and envies our prayers.

STORY – Love Hopes For The Best

One time I made this collage of three pictures in a frame for my wife. The first picture was of her and I hugging together under a waterfall in Jamaica on our honeymoon. The scripture verse I put under that picture was from Proverbs 12:4 it says, *"A wife of noble character is her husband's crown."* The second one was a picture of our two daughters. The verse under that picture said, *"Her children will rise up and call her blessed."* The third picture was a beautiful photo of her and under that picture I put a scripture from Proverbs 31, *"She is clothed with strength and dignity. She speaks with wisdom and faithful instructions are on her lips. A woman who loves the Lord is a valuable treasure to find."*

When I first made this frame for her, those scriptures were a hope that I had for my wife one day. I held on to those scriptures and prayed them over her. I believed that my wife was going to be a Proverbs 31 woman one day. Today, all these many years later, the things I had hoped for have come to pass. My wife loves the Lord more than anyone else I know. She is a woman of noble character. She is clothed with strength and integrity.

Hope is a powerful thing. Many times hope is all we have to hold onto in life. **Hope is an attribute that we should mix with our faith, prayers and praise.** Hope is something we need to cling to and embrace everyday. Don't ever give up on anyone. Hope and pray for them. Hope for the best in people by loving them God's way.

LOVING PEOPLE GOD'S WAY

I try to be the most difficult person to offend. I try not to be easily provoked or angered. Sometimes I'm successful at it and sometimes I'm not. It depends on how much time I've spent renewing my mind in God's word and understanding that his character attributes have been placed in my spirit. **God's love enables us to repel the offenses that come our way.** One time someone told me that another person said something against me. I could have thought to myself:

> I knew that person didn't like me.
> I'll get back at them some way.
> I'll never talk to them again.

Instead, I told that person I was talking to, "No, they would have never said that about me. They must have meant something different. You must have misunderstood them or they probably didn't mean it the way you interpreted it." You see love hopes for the best in people, not the worst. God's love in us doesn't latch on to the negative but always hopes for a positive outcome.

If we would just love others the way God loves us...
the world would drastically change overnight.

God has supernaturally channeled his love into our hearts through his Holy Spirit (Romans 5:5). As we discover more about this love that God has placed in our spirit, then we'll be able to shower others with it at tremendous levels. The world desperately needs a mighty revelation of God's love.

STORY: A Kind Word

One afternoon as my wife's hospital shift was beginning, many of her co-workers told her about this extremely irritable and angry patient. No one went into his room unless it was absolutely necessary. Everyone knowing my wife's personality, knew she was completely up for the challenge. As soon as she went into this man's room he began barking at her constantly about everything. He insulted her and complained about everything and everyone.

But it was all to no avail, it was like rain dripping off a ducks back. My wife didn't allow his words to penetrate her, but her words did penetrate him. She was soft spoken and cordial. She got him some ice water and repositioned him so he was more comfortable. She showed him genuine care, concern and loved him with words and actions.

The other nurses were surprised that she was in his room for so long. They thought, "What was going on in there? Was he strangling her to death?" They didn't hear any yelling from the room any more. Finally, as she was coming out of the room, she turned and joked with the guy about something and the both laughed. The other nurses stood in amazement.

What had just happened in there?

My wife was displaying some biblical principles that never fail. A few scriptures that come to mind for this situation are.

A soft word diffuses a person's anger. Proverbs 15:1
Prefer one another above yourself. Romans 12:10
Love your neighbor like they're the most important
person in the world to you. Matthew 22:39
Be kind and compassionate to everyone. Ephesians 4:32
Don't be overcome by evil but overcome
evil with the love that's in your spirit. Romans 12:21
No weapon formed against you will ever succeed. Isaiah 54:17
Do not let any unwholesome words come out of your mouth but only
speak words that are encouraging for others to hear. Ephesians 4:29

The patient was hateful, abusive and offensive. He spent most of the day cursing at everyone. But God's love was flowing out of my wife's spirit; she was loving, patient, kind and compassionate. **The love of God drastically transforms people; don't subdue it, UNLEASH IT ON OTHERS!** It will change all of your relationships around you. God's love drastically changes how you think and respond to people. When you love people with the love of the Lord, you always hope for the best in others. Love disarms angry, frustrated, hurting people. It melts away those icy walls people build up around themselves. Love confuses and disarms our enemies (Proverbs 16:7). God's love will cast out that fear in you. His love in you will cause you to be patient, persevere and prevail. I Corinthians 13:7

You can only get as close to God...as the person you love the least.

I just love the wisdom behind that statement. You might want to read that sentence over and over until you completely understand it. God wants us to love people; he wants his love multiplied exponentially over the earth through us! There is a whole world of people out there to love and God wants us to go and *love them all!* It's going to take some of your time, energy and maybe even a little bit of money. You may also have to give up some sleep, but it will be worth it. **A life filled with loving people is a fulfilled, satisfying, successful and blessed life.**

We're not allowed to choose who we're going to love and who we're not going to love. We're not allowed to choose who we're going to forgive and who we're not going to forgive. Born-again Christians love people, they don't know any other way. It's ingrained in their *new nature* of being IN CHRIST. Blood bought, Holy Spirit filled Christians forgive people no matter what the offense. Forgiveness is not a choice we make, it's actually a part of our new nature. **Christians, who unconditionally forgive, clearly understand the debt of the sin that they have been forgiven of. Forgiveness is attached to our identity.** Forgiveness has become a part of who we are. It's not only something we do but it's a character attribute of who we are IN CHRIST.

Christians are forgiving people...because we are forgiven people.

It seems like the bible is always teaching us to respond to others contrary to how the world responds. For example:

If your enemy is hungry, feed him. Romans 12:20
If you love those who only love you, what good is that? Matthew 5:46
If someone strikes you on the cheek, turn to him the other cheek. Matthew 5:39
If someone takes your cloak give him your tunic also. Matthew 5:40

Jesus said, "Love your enemies and bless those who curse you, do good to people who hate you and pray for people who despitefully use you and persecute you." Matthew 5:44

Do you see what I mean? The wisdom of God is completely different from the wisdom of this world. **When you overwhelm people with love, you are revealing to them the heart of God.** Does God's love flow out of your heart like a river or does it drip from your tight lips like a leaky faucet? Let love flow out of your heart like a mighty flood, pushing forward, rising higher and moving into new areas. God's love is like a waterfall from Heaven which lands on us and spills out over into the community.

The bible has a lot to say about loving people God's way. The word love is mentioned over eight hundred times in the bible. Extending people the love of God is a privilege and something they will not soon forget. **The love of Christ coming out of you will challenge every emotion in you.** God's love is always *others*-centered and never *self*-centered.

Maybe you just can't love people that way. You just don't feel like you have it in you. How are you going to love people with this type of love? You're going to need some help. You won't know how to love many of the difficult people in your life but the Holy Spirit will show you how.

God has poured out his love into our hearts by
the Holy Spirit whom he has given us. Romans 5:5

I will send you the Holy Spirit and he will endue you
with power from the high Heavens. Luke 24:49

The Holy Spirit will show you how to love these hurting, dysfunctional, frustrated, difficult people in the world. **Remember, hurting people hurt other people.** You can't go by your feelings when loving people, you have to go by what God says from his word through your spirit. We have to respond with spiritual wisdom to the world's condition. **When people hurt you don't take it personal. They just don't know how to love others the way you do. The enemy wants you to be offended but God wants you to be a peace maker.** God can heal that broken, hurting person that is so difficult for you to love.

What good is it if you only love those who love you back?
Even a hateful person can do that! Matthew 5:46

*God wants you to be different when it comes
to loving difficult people, because you are different.
God wants you to love people like no one else on the planet,
because you are like no one else on the planet.*

STORY – The Hand Shake Song

Every Sunday in our church we have what is called "The Hand Shake Song". It's a time when you get out of your seat and go around and shake hands with everyone, hug them or give someone an encouraging word. We also get to meet new visitors at this time and fellowship with each other for a few minutes while a song is being played. One time God spoke to me just before "The Hand Shake Song" and I'll never forget what he said to me:

"Go and love my people for me. They don't understand how much I love them and I want to channel MY LOVE THROUGH YOU TO THEM. I can see that you have my spirit working in you and that you'll allow me to love them through you. Go and love every one of them for me."

WOW! What an awesome word from God! Now every Sunday just before "The Hand Shake Song" I hear those words ring out from my spirit, "GO AND LOVE THEM ALL." That crystal clear message that God spoke to me that day, is actually for all of God's children.

We're all striving to be vessels that God can flow through and loving others is an important part of that process. **God wants us to allow Christ (who lives in us) to express himself outwardly towards others, through our personalities, emotions, thoughts, words and actions.** If you always allow him to do that, then you will always be in the will of God. You will be fulfilled, complete and happy. You'll be content and at peace as Christ comes out of you. **Trust the person of Christ who lives in you and enjoy his accomplishments as he comes out of you through your words and actions.**

I've heard a lot of people say:
You don't know my neighbor. It would be scary to go over there and try to make amends with them. I don't know how they would respond to me. You don't know what my spouse did to me. That pain would be too much for me to confront again. You don't know what my angry child said to me when they ran out that door.

I'm afraid to make the first move.
I'm afraid of being rejected.
I'm afraid they might hurt me again.
I'm afraid they won't love me back.

<u>Here is what the Lord would say to that fear inside of you:</u>
MY perfect LOVE casts out fear.
MY LOVE damages fear.
MY LOVE crushes fear.
MY LOVE breaks the yoke of fear.
MY LOVE triumphs over fear.
MY LOVE melts away fear.
(I John 4:16-18)

So take a step of faith and trust God. He's all about restoring broken relationships. When we trust God and take those steps of love, then he will come sweeping into our situation with his ministering spirit. He will soften and change those hard hearts around you. God's love melts away the cold, icy heart.

God has committed to us the message of reconciliation
between himself and mankind. II Corinthians 5:19

<u>*STORY - Never Fight With A Red-Headed Woman*</u>

I remember one time my wife and I were fighting about something stupid. She was mad, frustrated and yelling at me. Usually I'm very patient, but this time I was fighting back just as hard. Then I got a revelation from God.

"Go to her, put your arms around her and just look
into her eyes until she sees how much you love her.
Nothing else matters more to her than that, and
don't let go of her, no matter what she says".

Now that's a dangerous thing to do to a mad, red-headed woman. So I did exactly that. I did exactly as the Holy Spirit instructed me. She fought back and struggled to get away from me, but after a few minutes, we were laughing, loving and forgiving. GOD'S LOVE MELTS HEARTS, it really does.

God's love comforts the offended heart.
God's love fills the empty heart.
God's love heals the broken heart.

My wife and I could have stayed angry at each other. We could have gone to bed mad. We could have allowed that anger to grow deeper and fester into hatred, rage and bitterness. We could have allowed our household to be a place of division and strife. We could have gotten a divorce and in the end we would have learned absolutely nothing about God's supernatural, unconditional, never ending love.

Be completely humble and gentle. Be patient when loving one another. Make every effort to keep the unity of the Spirit through the bond of peace. Ephesians 4:2 & 3

When the world sees your good works emulating from God's love, they will glorify your Father in Heaven. I Peter 2:12

God wants the world to look at his children, full, complete and operating in his love and say, "WOW…that's completely different from anything I've seen in a long time! I WANT THAT! I want to know them and what they're all about." **People are drawn to God's love, not rules, doctrines and church protocol.** There's not a person that has ever lived, that wanted to be unloved and unaccepted. People want to be loved, accepted and valued. Let the Holy Spirit soften their hard heart, that's what he specializes in (John 16:8). Our responsibility is to extend to people the love of God because we are ministers of reconciliation. You might be thinking:

Lord…it will be difficult to love everyone with the same unrestricted and unconditional love. How do I love people like this? This is a love I don't fully understand. It's a love that I never really expressed before. But Lord, I WANT IT! I want to know how to love others the way you love me.

It's that kind of hunger and desire that releases God's love from our spirit. God says his love for us is higher than the Heavens are above the earth. That means we can search out all the many facets of God's love for the rest of our lives and continually discover all the many unique ways that he loves us. God's love is so vast; it's hard to fully comprehend, but WE ALL SO DESPERATELY NEED IT. All of his creation longs for it because God designed us that way.

God has already placed his love in our spirit, but we are the ones who regulate the unraveling process of his love. We determine everyday the speed at which we want to learn about his love and express his love. God's love knows no limits...so don't limit it.

When God supernaturally fills you up and you begin to understand the extreme depth of his love, then you can't help but let it flow out to others. You'll love that difficult boss, or your distant spouse, that frustrated neighbor or that impossible teenager. It won't be through your own strength, it will be God operating through you.

GOD WILL SURPRISE YOU WITH THE NEW

When we became born-again Christians, we were given the Spirit of God to live on the *inside of us* so that Christ could come alive on the *outside of us* through our thoughts, attitude, words and actions. The spirit of Christ literally lives in us (Romans 8:9). Our old sin nature was completely pulverized and obliterated the moment Christ moved in. Our old spirit is now dead and our new spirit is dancing with new life. That's an incredible source of power we have in us. Our fleshly desires (that were driven by our old nature) are in the process of dieing, but we are dead to sin in our spirit (Romans 6:2,6,7,11). **The fleshly desires we have now are the residual effects of old thought patterns and habits. They will try to influence you when you meditate on them. How much time you spend thinking about the OLD self versus the NEW you, will determine how much victory you have over the flesh.** That's why it's important to keep learning about the NEW spirit that's in you. Don't ever forget that you're a child of the King. In the spirit realm you wear a royal robe, a beautiful crown, a gold ring and you carry a dazzling scepter.

Our old sinful nature was crucified with Christ. It was destroyed so that we no longer have to serve it as our master. Romans 6:6

Born-again Christians are taught and lead by a completely new nature. The Holy Spirit wants to break out of your soul like a run away freight train and release that new fruit that's in you. It's going to completely surprise your old way of thinking. The bi-product (fruit) of being filled with the Holy Spirit is love, peace, joy, gentleness, patience, kindness, goodness, faithfulness and self-control. God has already given us all the patience, peace, joy and love that we will ever need for this life. It's there deep down inside of us. How did it get there? It was transferred there through the Holy Spirit when you accepted Christ as Lord of your life. **You are now IN CHRIST and since Christ is not lacking in any of these attributes, then we also have all that we need for an abundant life and victorious living.** We just need to let that love, peace, patience and joy flow out of our spirit and into our mind, soul, mouth and actions. Your spirit has been touched by God. Your spirit is now alive, alert and in hot pursuit of God's desires. You literally have the life of God within you. You are a completely new creation IN-CHRIST. So get ready for a life filled with many new and exciting surprises.

All the different fruits of the Spirit that Galatians 5:22 & 23 speak of are the character attributes of God. They may not be something you understand completely. They are character attributes that come out of your new born-again spirit. The Holy Spirit will challenge you to respond to people or a situation with this new spirit that lives in you.

We Christians must rely on the Holy Spirit to lead us, counsel us and teach us. If we harden our hearts to his voice, then we cannot be empowered by him. In essence we would be saying to God, "Thanks for saving me, but I'll take over from here and guide myself through this Christian life". That would be crazy! You don't have a clue about what a divine and holy God could want from you.

Those who are in the flesh can not please God. Romans 8:8
Don't be fooled by the enemy, the work that God started in you
through his spirit, cannot be completed by trying to perceive
spiritual things through you carnal flesh. Galatians 3:3

We don't help the Holy Spirit the Holy Spirit helps us. You could read the bible and put your own spin on it. You could try to discern it for yourself, but that would lead to all kinds of trouble. Who knows the mind of Christ except the Spirit of God (I Corinthians 2:16). **The Holy Spirit helps us read and interpret the truth in God's word. We need the Holy Spirit to translate, decipher and filter everything we see, think, feel, experience and say in life.**

One of the bookmarkers I've complied is called *WHAT ARE WE TO DO WITH ONE ANOTHER*. It tells us how we are to treat one another. It explains what God's love in us will accomplish in our relationships around us.

WHAT ARE WE TO DO
WITH ONE ANOTHER?

Be DEVOTED to one another in LOVE.
We are to ENCOURAGE one another.
We are to FORGIVE each other.
We are to CARRY one another.
We are to REJOICE with one another.
We are to PRAY for one another.
We are to EXHORT one another.
We are to SHINE THE LIGHT to one another.
We are to be PATIENT with one another.
We are to be KIND to one another.
We are to be GENTLE towards one another.
We are to STAND FIRM with one another.
We are to be LIKE MINDED with each other.
We are to extend FAVOR to one another.
We are to GRIEVE with each other.
We are to CELEBRATE one another.
We are to be GOOD to one another.
We are to CARE for one another.
We are to HOPE with one another.
We are to BELIEVE with one another.
We are to be GENEROUS with one another.
We are to LOOK FOR THE BEST in each other.
We are to BEAR one another's burdens.
Be COMPASSIONATE to one another.
We are to HONOR one another.
Be THANKFUL for one another.
Live in HARMONY with one another.
ACCEPT and GREET one another.
We are to AGREE with one another.
We are to be UNITED with one another.
We are to SERVE one another in love.
Be HUMBLE towards one another.
We are to SUBMIT to one another.
Offer HOSPITALITY to one another.
We are to FELLOWSHIP with one another.

complied by Eric Johnson

SELF-CENTERED TO CHRIST-CENTERED
TO OTHERS-CENTERED

God is passionate about restoring the relationship between you and him. He is also passionate about restoring relationships between you and your family, friends and anyone else in your circle of fellowship. Why, because you are his ambassador (II Corinthians 5:20). You are his representative here on this earth. **God wants to manifest his divine character attributes through you. How you act will determine what people think about the God that you love, serve and promote.**

You should all live in harmony with one another. Be sympathetic, compassionate and humble. Live together like a closely knit family does. Do not repay evil with evil or insult with insult, but shower each other with compliments, encouraging words and blessings. You have been called to live a triumphant, exhilarating and blessed life. I Peter 3:8 & 9

Children of God, there are so many things we can glean from that one scripture. God knows what he's talking about. The bible is not God's self-help book so that we can improve our life and have better relationships. First God wants us redeemed and reconciled to him, then he wants us to reflect the light of his truth and character to others. This is challenging stuff he wants to accomplish in our lives. **There is spiritual warfare taking place every time you think a thought and every time you open your mouth.** Will it be blessings or cursing, will it be life or death? Will it be a positive thought or a negative word?

I have set before you life and death, blessing and cursing. I hope that you will choose life so that you and your family may prosper. Deuteronomy 30:19

You can change your family's future not only by the words you speak but also by the thoughts you think. You can sever those muti-generational curses by the choices and changes you make in your life today.

I Peter 3:8 & 9 is a clear promise from God. If you *do* what it says, you will *receive* what it promises. God cannot and will not back down on a promise. So if we love, live in harmony and be peace makers, then you'll walk in God's blessings all day long. Maybe you have some difficult people to love around you. WELCOME TO EARTH! Here is some good news. **God has put the fullness of his nature in you, to teach you everything you need to know about him.**

Loving difficult people is...DIFFICULT!
But God commands us to love them, so you know
his Holy Spirit will show us how.

This is how we know what love is: Jesus Christ laid down his life
for us and we ought to lay down our lives for each other. If anyone
has material possessions and sees someone in need but has no pity
on them, how can the love of God be in them? Dear children,
let us not love with words only but with actions propelled by
God's Spirit in us. I John 3:16-18

As God's love touches your spirit it will burst from your heart
and flow out to others. Everyone who loves unconditionally
without restraint has had a deep, inner heart transforming
experience with the love of God. I John 4:7 & 8

Anyone who understands that the fullness of God's love lives in their
spirit, will be able to love others beyond their own inner strength.
I John 4:21

STORY – Loving Others With Actions

The Northeast Blackout of 2003 was a massive widespread power outage that occurred throughout parts of the Northeastern and Midwestern United States and Ontario, Canada on Thursday, August 14, 2003. The blackout affected an estimated 10 million people in Ontario and 45 million people in eight U.S. states. At the time, it was the second most widespread electrical blackout in history.

My neighbors were all outside talking about it when I got home from work. It was also devastating to hear that none of the gas stations could pump any gas. My daughter called me and said her best friend's mom was completely out of gas and needed help. I had a full five gallons in the garage so I drove over to her house and gave her some. For just a moment when I was pouring gas into her car, some thoughts came to my mind.

You might need some of this gas later for
your own car or maybe for your generator.
This is a major multi-state power outage.
You don't know how long you're going to be without power.
You better keep your gas to yourself.

Then the word of the Lord came to me:

If anyone has material possessions and sees his neighbor in need, but has no pity on them, how can the love of God be in them? I John 3:17

So I aligned my thinking with the word of God. I said, "God is going to take care of me. I am not going to be without anything he wants me to have." Yes, this was a fearful time with many questions in my mind. But my faith and love are going to move forward and trust God. I serve a God who has an unlimited supply of resources. The more I pour out to people in need (love and gas), the more God can refill my supply. My faith was tested soon after that when my wife called me and said her friend at work had absolutely no gas and she had a forty minute drive home, could I come and help. I said, "Of course," and immediately went and gave her some gas.

Here is a word of wisdom about maturity. What God freely gives us; we should freely extend to others. That's why God gave it to us. God loves us and wants us to love others with our time, money, words, thoughts and actions. God has forgiven us and wants us to extend forgiveness to others (Ephesians 4:32). God has blessed us and wants us to be a blessing to others. God has many divine attributes that he has lavished on us and he wants us to operate in those gifts.

Freely you have received…so freely give. Matthew 10:8

STORY – God Will Supply All My Needs

Our Church owns a campground out in the middle of the country. It's about forty miles from my house. I was going to drive to the youth camp meetings all that week and I knew it would probably take an entire tank of gas to drive out there all week long. I only had about a quarter tank of gas and I was concerned about it. I began to just talk to God out loud and I said,

"Lord…I want to minister to these youths who have come out here to this revival. I'm here to pray for them, speak faith-filled words over them and encourage them. I'm here to serve you in any way I can. I'm not going to let my gas gauge distract me from my purpose. I'm doing the little things that I know how to do and I need you to come in and do the big things that you can most certainly do. My trust is in you completely. In-fact, I believe right now, as I actually touch my finger to the instrument panel and put it over the gas gauge, you can fill my tank up with gas."

WOW…that's pretty crazy! Maybe I shouldn't be doing this? Isn't this challenging God? I mean should I really expect God to fill my gas tank? Isn't my gas tank my own responsibility? But the Holy Spirit rose up in me and said,

"Move your finger to the full line on the gas gauge."

Was God going to fill my gas tank right before my eyes?
Maybe it was just my own voice in my mind, challenging God
for a miracle. Was I letting my emotions get ahead of my faith?
Isn't this border-line fanatical?

Then I heard that same voice again rise up in my spirit.

"Move your finger to the full line on the gas gauge."

I began to slide my finger from the quarter tank of gas mark to the full line. I did it over and over as if God was actually going to supernaturally fill my gas tank. **I didn't just obey what the Holy Spirit said, but I believed what the Holy Spirit said.** Did God fill my tank? NO! What happened? Didn't I have enough faith? Then God's word leaped out of my spirit:

God will liberally supply every one of my needs according to his glorious riches obtained for us through Christ Jesus. Philip. 4:19

I started laughing at my gas gauge. I thought to myself, this gas issue is a very little thing in God's eyes. If I can't trust God for a simple tank of gas, how am I going to trust him to miraculously transform these young people who I'm going to pray for tonight? How am I going to trust God to supernaturally intervene in the lives of these young people if I couldn't even trust him to get me there?

The gas wasn't the priority prayer for the moment. The youth were who I should be concerned about. Salvation and souls were what I should be focused on. I needed to focus my prayer on the bigger things that God was planning on doing that night in the lives of people. I was not going to do without anything God needed me to have, THAT'S A SUPERNATURAL FACT! **God is going to supply all of my needs because he promised he would and his promises are more real to me than anything in this life.**

We had a phenomenal service that night. God moved in ways that I'll never forget. Lives were touched and broken hearts were healed. God filled the entire sanctuary with his love and presence that night.

Did God move my gas needle from EMPTY to FULL? NO! Did I have the faith that he could do it? YES! Did I get down and disappointed when God didn't supply all my needs? NO! I walked by faith and not by sight (II Corinthians 5:7). God said it…so I believe it! I believed that my car could run on empty for as long as I needed it to. Even as I saw that gas needle move farther and father towards empty…I STAYED IN FAITH.

The very next day, someone at church handed me
cash to specifically go and fill up MY GAS TANK!

I never even said anything to that person about gas, being low on gas or not having any money for gas. How did this happen? Because of a promise God made to me.

My child, you can trust me to supply all your needs, based on
my compassion, love and my promises. Philippians 4:19

God saw!
God cares!
God loves!
God supplies!
God is in control of it all!
God is worthy to be praised!

I guarantee if there would have been other people in my car and I would have put my finger on my gas gauge and said, "God fill it up!" They would have laughed me right out of the car, maybe even if they were Christians. **I don't know how God is going to accomplish everything he promised us. It's not my job to figure it all out. My responsibility is to step out in faith, not doubt and believe that God will be faithful to his promises.**

In Matthew 9:23 a little girl had DIED and Jesus still went to visit her. We are talking no heart beat, no blood flow and no breathing. SHE WAS DEAD! Someone ran to tell Jesus not to bother coming to the house, the GIRL WAS DEAD! The people at her house were wailing and mourning over her because SHE WAS DEAD! When Jesus reached her house, he told them, *"She isn't dead, she's only sleeping."* The crowd must have thought he was crazy because they knew SHE WAS DEAD! There was a lot of DEAD TALK going around that day. Every word that came out of these people's mouths regarding this girl was about DEATH. But ETERNAL LIFE walked right through the crowd of DEATH. The giver of LIFE stepped into the house of DEATH. The people knew all about DEATH, they recognized it and they lived around it. That's why they didn't recognize THE AUTHOR OF LIFE.

Jesus said, "I am the resurrection and the life, anyone who believes in me, even if they were to die, will live with me forever."
John 11:25

Do you know how many dead people Jesus has raised to LIFE? Do you know how many dead spirits Jesus has touched and they leaped to life? The answer is...ALL OF THEM! That's his specialty. When he touches people their spirit leaps. Every dead person (dead in their spirit) that looks to Jesus Christ and says:

I believe you are the Son of God.
I believe you died for my sins.
I believe you rose from the grave.
I receive your salvation into my spirit...

...are RAISED FROM THE DEAD in their spirit through Christ.

Before we got saved, we were as dead as dead can be (in our spirit). But now we have been raised up from the dead, in a similar and supernatural way that Christ was resurrected.

A lot of people believe that God doesn't speak to people today like he used to. They believe God has already said everything he's going to say. A lot of people believe that God doesn't perform miracles today, like he's been doing ever since the beginning of time. I just laugh when I hear people who believe that way. They just haven't discovered God in his deepest dimension. God reveals himself to people who trust him, believe in him, obey him and release him out of their spirit through faith. **Faith is how God's nature and purpose are promoted and glorified on the earth.**

Don't hinder the flow of God's miracle working power in your life. We get into trouble when we stop the flow of God's love, mercy, grace and forgiveness. When we choose not to extend the forgiveness that was so freely extended to us, then we get ourselves into complete disarray and turmoil in the spiritual realm. It's in those key moments that we will either do one of two things. We will either give the enemy a foothold in our lives or we will release God's glory from our spirit. There's NO POWER when there's NO FORGIVENESS. There's NO POWER when there's NO LOVE. There's NO POWER when there's NO HOPE. Christians need to keep the free flowing river of God's attributes moving and operating in their lives. **God's character attributes were deposited in us so they could flow out of us.**

Forgive...just as God has forgiven you. Ephesians 4:32

The love of the Lord is unlimited...so don't limit it. Don't get yourself in the position where you hinder the free flowing attributes of God's character in your life. By limiting the outflow of Godly character to others you limit your ability to mature in Christ and grow towards your destiny. Understanding your identity IN CHRIST is directly connected with your maturity and purpose. God has filled you with his love so you can go and release it on others.

If you want unlimited growth, wisdom, power, anointing and peace in your life; then don't interrupt the flow of God's love, forgiveness, compassion, mercy and grace towards others.

Surrender to the Holy Spirit as he prompts you to love, forgive, help, encourage, listen to and understand people. How you treat others is an indicator of how much you've renewed your mind. **God will inject health and healing into your relationships when you love people beyond your own capabilities and extend to them God's grace, mercy and love from within your spirit.** I've seen and experienced disappointing behavior from Christians in my life. That must be extremely painful for God also. When we don't understand God's love in its fullness, then we will fail and fall more often. **God has a spectacular life planned for us to experience and it begins immediately as we understand what his divine nature in us is capable of.**

We have the supernatural presence of our divine God IN US. God himself, through the person of Christ, resides within us. Just BE YOU...BE IN CHRIST. Christians make being a Christian so much more difficult than it really is. We are IN CHRIST. That means we now want what he wants and that's how Christians find true fulfillment. It comes by expressing and letting the life of Christ come out of us.

God is passionate about you! Are you just as passionate about him? He longs to hear from us. He wants to hear your voice and look into your eyes. He watches you when you sleep at night. His thoughts about us are too numerous to count. When we finally *get it* and understand God's love, then we'll be able to *give it* to others unconditionally. For some of you it will take a lifetime to understand

God's divine character, the fullness of his love and the complete forgiveness he's made available for you. Others may mature very rapidly. It all depends on your level of surrender to the Holy Spirit and how much you understand that CHRIST COMPLETELY LIVES IN YOU. I've seen the Holy Spirit miraculously accelerate people's maturity when they are hungry, desperate and thirsty to learn about their new identity. This is because God feeds the hungry (John 6:35), he given water to the thirsty (Matthew 5:6) and he rewards those who diligently seek after him. Hebrews 11:6

Growth occurs when we absorb the truth about who we really are in our spirit and what we already possess in Christ.

LOVING OTHERS FROM THE BOOK OF FIRST JOHN

The book of I John has a lot to say about the love of God and reflecting his love to others.

God is light and in him there is no darkness.
If we claim to have fellowship with him but walk in darkness,
then we lie and do not live by the truth. But if we walk in the light
of his truth, we have fellowship with one another knowing
that the blood of Jesus purifies us from all sin. I John 1:5-7

Because we love God, we love to obey his commands. The person who says, "I know him," but does not do what God commands is confused and the truth has not completely renewed their minds. But if anyone obeys God's word, God's love is truly made complete in them. This is how Christ lives through us. Whoever claims to be a Christian should strive to emulate the characteristics of Christ. I John 2:3-6

Anyone who claims to be in the light, but lives in strife with others, is still in darkness. Whoever loves others lives in the light and no darkness will ever make them stumble. I John 2:9-10

If anyone has material possessions and sees someone in need, but has no pity on them, how can the love of God be in them? I John 3:17

This is a commandment of God: to believe in the name of his Son, Jesus Christ, and to love one another as he has commanded us. This is how we know God spirit lives in us. I John 3:23 & 24

Dear friends, let us always, fervently and unconditionally love one another, this is the type of love that comes from God's spirit inside of us. Everyone who has been born of God has been filled with his love. Whoever has a difficult time loving others hasn't had a radiant revelation of God's nature. This is how God has expressed his love towards us: God loves us so much that he sent his Son as an atoning sacrifice for our sins. Release God's love out of your spirit and it will have a tremendous effect on you and others around you.
I John 4:7-11

We love because he first loved us. If anyone proclaims that they love God but still has strife in their heart, then they have not had a clear revelation of the depth of God's true nature. I John 4:19 & 20

GO AND LOVE MY PEOPLE

Beloved, we're not going to be able to love others without using the love of God that's in our spirit. It has to come <u>FROM</u> God, <u>TO US</u> and then <u>THROUGH US</u> and finally <u>OUT TO OTHERS</u>. If you're running on empty, then stop and ask God for a refilling. You can only drive a car for so long without stopping and putting gas in it. Ask God for a refilling of his never ending supply of love, then go and love people the way God loves you.

Don't get tired of blessing and helping people. In time you will receive a great reward for your faith-filled words and actions. So take advantage of every opportunity in reflecting Christ's love towards others. Galatians 6:9 &10

When you squeeze an orange, orange juice comes out. When you squeeze and apple, apple juice comes out. When trials and disappointments squeeze a person filled with God's Holy Spirit, then God's love comes out. Patience comes out during frustrating times and peace comes out as the storm rages around you. **You are God's representative, ambassador and a minister of reconciliation.** God wants the world to see and experience his godly character attributes through you. The world won't be able to understand us, but they will be drawn to us and to God. **Loving other people glorifies God. We are the extension of God's heart here on earth.** Don't just love the ones that you *choose* to love or that *deserve* your love. GO AND LOVE THEM ALL like God commands us to do. The Spirit of God will teach you how.

Make my joy complete by being like minded, having the same love for each other that I have for you, be united in spirit and purpose. Do nothing out of selfish ambitions or motives, be more concerned about others than yourself. Don't be so consumed about your own life, but get involved in the lives of others. Your attitude should be the same as Christ's attitude. Philippians 2:2-5

Remember you are a light in this dark world. You are like a city that can be seen in the distance on a hill. Does a person put a bowl over a candle they've just lit (Matthew 5:14)? You have a constant flowing fountain of his love to draw from. Go and shine the light of Christ to everyone. Loving people is going to take some time out of your schedule. It's going to challenge you. But if you will listen to the Holy Spirit he will give you many creative ways to love others.

If you truly desire to be successful at loving people God's way... then you will be. So as often as you can, go and tell people that you love them and that God loves them. Then do everything in your power to show them that he really does.

WHERE HAS ALL THE LOVE GONE?

Where has all the love gone? I don't see it anywhere around. The world is filled with relationships with no love, no commitment, no communication and no forgiveness. Each person has gone their own way, with their own goals and desires. Each person has a, "What can I get out of this relationship," mentality. Relationships cannot survive like this and most of them don't.

Where has all the love gone? Communication between people has become shallow and superficial. There is no time to connect or bond with each other anymore. Our neighbors we live by are complete strangers to us. They are people we just give a quick hello to going from our car to our house.

Where has all the love gone? People hide behind many masks. There's no time to just get real with each other. The truth is we don't have it all together. People have unresolved issues that keep their relationships distant, shallow and weak.

Where has all the love gone? The world has twisted our love and deflated our passion. The world's love is self-centered and conditional. When did people forget how to love? If you reach out and get your hand slapped repeatedly, then eventually I guess you just stop reaching out. The world's love is cold and calloused. There are so many hard hearts out there. The light is fading fast. Will anyone be the first to open up their heart, reach out to someone and dare to love?

Where has all the love gone? The conclusion is, you can only trust yourself. People are unloving and unforgiving. They are completely focused on themselves and their own life. At their core they really don't even like themselves. They love money, houses, cars and possessions. They put their faith and hope in these things. They invest their time and energy into these things rather than love, compassion, sharing and concern.

Where has all the love gone? Many have turned their backs on the light, the truth and their source of hope. People don't seek after God. They don't trust him because they don't know him. They ask themselves, "Will God let me down just like the others have?" People have turned away from God's outstretched arms for far too long.

Where has all the love gone? It's in Heaven where it's always been. The source of love is in the heart of God. His love erases doubt, crushes fear, heals our pain and removes our sin. God's love came down from Heaven and showed us THE LIGHT, THE TRUTH and THE WAY. Reach out today and grasp hold of a love that will never let you go and soon you'll say, I know where all the love has gone…IT'S RIGHT HERE ABIDING IN ME.

WORLDLY LOVE

This world's love is shallow and cold. There is no fire in the world's love. You can't feel the warmth of it against you. It's a hypocritical love because it originates in worldly concepts and philosophies. This type of love has just enough patience to exist with people and no more than that. This type of love only gives when it's been given to. Just under the surface of the world's love is a raging fighting spirit filled with judgment, condemnation and wrath.

People camouflage themselves so well with this superficial worldly love. It has all kinds of conditions attached to it. This love can mask over a lot of hidden self-righteousness. It's a religious type of love that makes people feel good about themselves. It loves the least amount possible when tolerating people. It's out there in the world and it's in our churches as well. This type of love does not wrap itself in forgiveness. You have to earn its forgiveness. It's an ugly, lonely, pitiful way to love.

I've worked in the secular field for over thirty-five years and I've seen people who have allowed the world to vacuum out all their love, passion and hope. They have been hurt by the world and they've built walls around themselves so that no one will ever hurt them again. They won't share even the smallest things with others. The truth is, they can't give to others what they don't have in them. Their spirit is dead. They've never opened their mouth so the God could breathe his breath of life into them. They never opened their heart to him so he could make their spirit leap back to life. Their hearts are cold, empty and dark.

GOD'S LOVE

God reaches out to us everyday so that we can know and experience the fullness of his love. God's love strips away hate and disarms our enemies. Hate is crushed under God's love. The love of God causes us to forget any offenses and forgive completely. **Let God love you completely and radically with no limits. Receive his love into your heart and then you'll be able to love him back and finally truly love others.** This scripture has helped me tremendously when it comes to resting in God's love.

Come to me all you who are weary and heavily burdened and I will give you rest. Take my yoke upon you and learn from me, for I have a gentle and compassionate heart and you will find rest for your souls. My yoke is easy and my burden is light. Matthew 11:28-30

People who have been hurt by others don't trust like they first did when they were a child. They don't let anyone in behind the walls they've built. People have so many hang-ups when it comes to letting God love them. Remember when Jesus told the disciples:

Do not forbid the children to come to me,
for such is the kingdom of Heaven. Luke 18:16

These children just wanted to get close to Jesus. They wanted to be next to him, sit in his lap and touch the face of God. At first the disciples rebuked the children and the children didn't understand what the disciples were talking about. They didn't know there were rules and regulations about seeking God. THAT'S RELIGION! **Don't hinder God's free flowing love, power and presence because of pain, traditions, confusion and stubbornness.** Jesus told his disciples, "NO! NO! NO! Don't do that! Just let them come to me." God wants us to trust and love him without limits. He wants us to come seeking, searching and to be curious about his nature.

STORY - Do Not Forbid The Children

During the Sunday morning worship time at my church, I briefly opened my eyes during a song and I saw two little girls at the altar dancing and praising God. WOW! This was awesome! They had these big beautiful smiles on their faces and they were holding hands and dancing. It's sad to say, but I've rarely seen people this happy and free when worshiping God. I've been on stage a number of times looking out at the congregation, so I know what you see can be very discouraging. I thought to myself, "Oh God, if only we could all be that free when worshiping you." Those two little girls taught me a lot about communing with God at a deeper level. The church has become so self conscious, busy and distracted during worship, I thought it was definitely a lesson we all needed to learn.

To my great surprise, the pastor did not agree with me. He did not perceive in the spirit what I saw. He had the most disgusted look on his face. He whispered over to the deacon and then the deacon came down and stopped the girls from praising and worshiping God and ushered them back to their seats.

Oh church, some days we just blow it. We totally miss what God has planned for us. My wife says when we all get to Heaven, we're all going to be little five year old black children (referring to the pigmentation of the skin). Why...maybe because she's white (referring to her light beige skin tone). Maybe it really will be like that, just to teach us that skin color demonstrates the diversity of God's creativity. It's not a reason to hate and destroy one another. Why does my wife think we're all going to be children? Because children trust and love without limits. Children who are free in their spirit dance and enjoy life with each other. They believe with all their heart and that's exactly how God wants us to live out our faith. I believe Jesus was trying to teach his disciples something in this situation in Luke 18:16. Will we open our hearts and learn...is a question we answer everyday through our actions.

<u>God says to us in his word:</u>

Come to me my child, I will catch you. Believe in me and every word that comes out of my mouth. Every word I speak is the truth. In fact, it is impossible for me to lie. Only truth will come out of my mouth and every promise that I speak will come to pass. When I say, "I LOVE YOU", I really do. You can trust in my love. I will not reject you like the world has. I created you. I love your simple, unwavering trust that you have. Chase after me and I will catch you and show you my true nature.

If people would just let that word, written by the spirit of God, absorb into their heart, then a deep healing process would begin in them. Let Jesus' words wrap themselves around you like a blanket. Take them into your thirsty soul. Then he'll give you perfect peace and complete rest. He will give you rest on every side and in all circumstances. Hurting, controlling, dysfunctional people need to let down their guard, turn off the control force field they have around them and let God inside. Won't you let God heal everything about you today?

Moses said to God.... "<u>WHO AM I?</u>" Exodus 3:11

One of the very first things a Christian needs to discover is WHO THEY ARE IN CHRIST. The Bookmarkers *I AM / HE SHALL BE CALLED, BY GOD'S GRACE, GOD KNOWS MY NAME* and *MY LITTLE CHILD* will remind you of who you are everyday. Your identity is your foundation for your Christian life.

I AM

ABOUNDING IN GRACE II Corinthians 9:8 ● *ABLE* Philippians 4:1
AN AMBASSADOR FOR CHRIST II Corinthians 5:20
ANOINTED II Corinthians 1:21 ● *MADE RIGHTEOUS* Romans 5:19
THE APPLE OF GOD'S EYE Zechariah 2:8 ● *ALIVE* Ephesians 2:4
CLAY IN THE POTTERS HANDS Jeremiah18:6
ANXIOUS FOR NOTHING Philippians 4:6 ● *BORN AGAIN* I Ptr. 1:23
NOT ASHAMED II Timothy 1:12 ● *ADOPTED* Ephesians 1:5
BLAMELESS I Corinthians 1:8 ● *CHERISHED* Ephesians 5:29
BAPTIZED INTO CHRIST I Corinthians 2:15 ● *FREE* John 8:36
BLOOD BOUGHT I Corinthians 6:19-20 ● *BLESSED* Ephesians 1:3
A CHILD OF GOD John1:12 ● *CLEANSED* I John 1:7,9
A CITIZEN OF HEAVEN Philippians 3:20 ● *HIS* Isaiah 43:1
COMPLETE IN CHRIST Colossians 2:10 ● *CHOSEN* I Peter 2:9
A CONQUEROR Romans 8:37 ● *CALLED* I Peter 5:10
CRUCIFIED WITH HIM Galatians 2:20 ● *FAVORED* Job 10:2
DELIVERED Psalm 107:6 ● *DEAD TO SIN* Romans 6:11
FORGIVEN Ephesians 1:7 ● *A LIGHT IN A DARK PLACE* Acts 13:47
A FELLOW CITIZEN OF HEAVEN Ephesians 2:19
INSEPARABLE FROM HIS LOVE Romans 8:35
GIVEN THE HOLY SPIRIT II Corinthians 1:2 ● *HUMBLE* Philip. 2:24
GLORIFIED WITH HIM II Thessalonians 2:14
FULL OF THE FRUIT OF THE SPIRIT Galatians 5:22,23
GRANTED GRACE IN CHRIST JESUS Romans 5:17
GIVEN AN ABUNDANT LIFE I John 4:9 ● *SAVED* Ephesians 2:8
HEALED I Peter 2:24 ● *HEAVEN BOUND* I Peter 1:4
HIS HANDIWORK Ephesians 2:10 ● *ACCEPTED* Ephesians 1:6
HONORED II Timothy 2:21 ● *LIBERATED* Romans 6:23
HOLY Ephesians 1:4 ● *COMFORTED* Jeremiah 31:13
IN CHRIST I Corinthians 1:30 ● *JUSTIFIED* Acts 13:39
LOST, BUT NOW I'M FOUND Luke 19:10
A NEW CREATION II Corinthians 5:17 ● *CONFIDENT* I John 4:17
GUILTLESS AND NOT CONDEMNED Romans 8:1
PLEASING TO GOD Psalm 149:4 ● *THE HEAD* Deuteronomy 28:13
A MOUNTAIN MOVER Mark 11:22 ● *LOVED* John 3:16
MADE BY HIM Psalm 100:3 ● *NEAR TO GOD* Ephesians 2:13
NEVER FORSAKEN Hebrews 13:5 ● *JOYFUL* Philippians 4:4
NOT A SLAVE TO SIN Romans 8:1 ● *A LIGHT* John 8:12
AN OVERCOMER I John 5:4,5 ● *PEACEFUL* Philippians 4:7
PROTECTED Psalm 91:14 ● *PROVIDED FOR* Matthew 6:33
QUALIFIED Colossians 1:12 ● *YIELDED TO GOD* Romans 6:13
RAISED UP WITH CHRIST Eph 2:6 ● *WALKING IN HIS LIGHT* I Jn. 1:7
RECONCILED TO GOD Rom. 5:10 ● *A ROYAL PRIESTHOOD* I Ptr. 2:9
RENEWED II Corinthians 4:16 ● *A SAINT OF GOD* Psalm 34:9

SANCTIFIED I Corinthians 6:11 ● *A TEMPLE* I Corinthians 3:16
TRANSFORMED II Corinthians 3:18 ● *REDEEMED* Galatians 3:13
TREASURED Psalm 83:3 ● *TRIUMPHANT* II Corinthians 2:14

(FRONT OF BOOKMARKER)

HE SHALL BE CALLED

A GIFT FROM GOD John 3:16 ● *A SACRIFICE* Ephesians 5:2
THE BRIGHT AND MORNING STAR Revelation 22:16
IMAGE OF THE INVISIBLE GOD Col. 1:15 ● *MASTER* Mark 12:14
THE BEGINNING AND THE END Revelation 21:6
ARM OF THE LORD Isaiah 51:9 ● *AN OFFERING* Luke 4:34
A SURE FOUNDATION Isa. 28:16 ● *GREAT HIGH PRIEST* Heb. 4:14
MOST HOLY Daniel 9:24 ● *ONLY BEGOTTEN SON* John 3:16
LIGHT OF THE WORLD John 9:5 ● *KING OF KINGS* I Timothy 6:15
ADVOCATE I John 2:1 ● *ALMIGHTY* Revelation 19:15
AUTHOR AND FINISHER OF OUR FAITH Hebrews 12:2
BREAD OF LIFE John 6:35 ● *DELIVERER* Romans 11:26
THE ROCK OF MY SALVATION II Samuel 22:47
CHIEF CORNERSTONE I Peter 2:6 ● *I AM* John 8:58
EMMANUEL - GOD WITH US Matthew 1:23
LORD OF THE SABBATH Lk. 6:5 ● *RIGHTEOUS JUDGE* II Tim. 4:8
THE SON OF THE HIGHEST Luke 1:32
SON OF GOD Luke 1:35 ● *SERVANT* Philippians 2:7
FAITHFUL & TRUE Revelation 19:11 ● *MESSIAH* Daniel 9:25
GOOD SHEPHERD John 10:11 ● *OUR MEDIATOR* Hebrews 12:24
HOPE OF GLORY Colossians 1:27 ● *OUR SHIELD* John 6:51
TEACHER John 3:2 ● *OUR PEACE* Ephesians 2:14
LIVING WATER John 4:10 ● *LAMB OF GOD* John 1:36
LORD OF ALL Acts 10:36 ● *REDEEMER* Isaiah 59:20
OUR INTERCESSOR Hebrews 7:25 ● *PHYSICIAN* Luke 4:23
OUR REFUGE FROM THE STORM Isaiah 5:4
SAVIOR OF THE WORLD I John 4:14
RESURRECTION AND THE LIFE John 1:25
OUR ROCK AND OUR FORTRESS Psalm 31:3
WONDERFUL COUNSELOR, MIGHTY GOD,
EVERLASTING FATHER, PRINCE OF PEACE Isaiah 9:6
GOD MANIFEST IN THE FLESH I Timothy 3:16
THE WORD Revelation 19:13 ● *MAN FROM HEAVEN* I Corinthians 15:48
A QUICKENING SPIRIT I Corinthians 15:45
THE WAY, THE TRUTH AND THE LIFE John 14:6

JESUS CHRIST THE LORD

(Back Of Bookmarker)

I AM / HE SHALL BE CALLED was compiled by Eric Johnson

174   -   Me & God - Together At Last

These words are a phenomenal reminder of who we are IN CHRIST and who Jesus is to the world. There are many bookmarkers in my collection that I feel need to be read everyday and this is certainly one of them. The more we read and believe the more we will be transformed into the likeness of Christ. This bookmarker is an awesome collection of scriptural truths about us and our savior. Remember, your actions will always follow your beliefs. When you begin to believe what God says about you to be true, then you'll begin to act on those beliefs.

How a person thinks about themselves...is what they'll soon become.
Proverbs 23:7

I want you to start a new habit. First thing in the morning, I want you to stand in front of the mirror and read the *I AM* bookmarker I've compiled. I want you to look in the mirror and read that information about yourself. Let it absorb deep into your spirit. **If God can convince you, through his word, of everything you already divinely possess, then you'll start acting on those new beliefs about your true identity and the power and gifts of God will be ushered in through your actions.**

That's one of the reasons God has you reading this book right now, so that you will believe what God says about you to be true. God only speaks the truth, he cannot lie. If God says you're TREASURED, CHERISHED and LOVED by him, THEN YOU REALLY ARE! That's why I wrote this book, so that you would trust God completely with your life, believe in the truth of his word and know that he will be there for you everyday through his Holy Spirit. This book boldly proclaims what the Lord Jesus Christ has done for the entire world. If you'll go a little further in your faith, God will meet you there in *your* hunger, *your* desire, *your* desperation, in *your* expectation, in *your* hope and in *your* faith-filled positive words.

You'll start SPEAKING things you never spoke before.
You'll start DOING things you never did before.
You'll start THINKING things you never imagined before.
You'll start LOVING people who you never thought you could love.
Instead of holding on to offenses, you'll start FORGIVING people instantly and completely.

The truth about you and God being together forever, will set you free to live a God glorifying, victorious, powerful, thriving life. John 8:32

God loves us unconditionally, therefore there is nothing that you can do that would make him love you more and there is nothing that you can do that would make him love you less. God is love. It's his nature to love without caution or restraint or conditions. We will always be his to love.

His love is unchanging. He won't love us any better when we become better. He loves us one hundred percent right now as we are. God's love for us is higher than the Heavens are above the earth. His love does not change even if we have no plans to change. What needs to change is our ability to receive his love. **So the choice is yours, will you open your heart to him right now and receive more of his love than you've ever experienced before?** Give him your whole heart today child of God. Give him your obstacles and pain that stand in the way. He'll remove them and give you rest. God loves us one hundred percent as we are right at this moment. So let yourself be loved by him.

Allow God's love to engulf your heart. This is why he created us. This is why he has set his gaze towards us. He adores you. He's crazy about you. He wants us to live like people who are loved outrageously. God wants us to understand, receive and express this radical, out of this world type of love. God's love is so awesome that all the poets throughout history could barely describe it. God will love us all the days of our life because that is who he is. He doesn't know how to be any different towards you.

God's love comes to set us free from ourselves and to set us free from how we see ourselves. His love comes to set us free from rejection, shame, low self-esteem, despair and from self-abuse. When God looks at us, he sees someone who he loves outrageously. God has so much to say to us and so many places to take us in his heart. But we can't go there unless we allow him to love us completely. His love for us will break every barrier and crush every wall that we've built. **God's love is the most power force that has ever touched the human heart.** So allow yourself to be loved.

I hope your level of understanding will one day reach God's level of love for you. When you finally believe in God's unconditional love and receive it into your heart, it will change you in every facet of your expression towards him and others. The words written on the _BY GOD'S GRACE_ bookmarker will help you get a better understanding of how much God loves you.

BY GOD'S GRACE

I am dearly loved and have been chosen by God.
He has called me to be compassionate, forgiving and to reflect
the love of Christ to this hurting world. Colossians 3:12; Eph. 4:32
By God's grace every sin of mine has been forgiven.
I am free from the condemning voice of the enemy. I am God's holy
creation and I stand blameless in his sight. Romans 5:1, 6:1-6
God adopted me as his child because he loves me.
He has placed his seal upon me. I am a fellow citizen of Heaven
and a member of God's household. Ephesians 1:4 & 13, 2:19
God has enlightened my heart, given me wisdom and understanding
that I might know him completely. Ephesians 1:8 & 17
I have been made alive through Jesus Christ. I have God's mighty
power
and strength working in my inner being. Ephesians 1:18, 2:5 & 6
I have direct access to God through his Holy Spirit.
I can approach him with freedom and confidence. Ephesians 2:18, 3:12
I have been given salvation, love, peace and divine truth.
They are like an impenetrable suit of armor I wear
to protect me from this dark world. Ephesians 6:14
I have been redeemed and forgiven of all my sins. The debt against me
was canceled, removed, blotted out and forgotten forever. Col. 1:14
I have the right to come boldly before the throne of God
to find mercy and grace in my time of need. Hebrews 4:16
I have been given the mind of Christ. My mind is full of patience,
kindness, gentleness and self control. I will show the world the love of
Christ through my peaceful attitude and gentle actions. Galatians 5:22
I have the life of God inside of me and I will walk
in that new revelation everyday. Romans 6:4
God has done a great work in me, so that I can accomplish
his good and perfect will, which is my destiny. Philippians 2:13
I have been given the grace to live a life that is pleasing to the Lord,
bearing fruit in every good work, growing in the knowledge of God
and being strengthened with all power according to his glorious might.
Colossians 1:10 & 11
I have been rescued from the pit of despair
and brought into the kingdom of light. Colossians 1:13
I have been appointed by God to serve. He has ordered my steps and
supernaturally positioned me to accomplish mighty things. I Tim 1:12

compiled by Eric Johnson

Your comprehension of God's love is directly proportional to your hunger for his love. Dear saints of God, if we would just hunger and then comprehend how much God loves us, it would transform the core of our spirit and radically impact the world we live in. It would change the intensity and focus of your passion. It will change the way you think, your attitude, self-image and the words that come out of your mouth. It will affect how much you smile, what you read, what you look at and how you interpret life. God's love completely and totally transforms people. There is no area of your character that God's love will not influence.

If God had a mountain of diamonds, rubies, emeralds, gold and silver; he would cast them all away if you walked up to him. You are his creation, he treasures you. He calls you his friend. He adores you and cherishes you. You were created for his pleasure and glory. **You were purchased by sinless, holy, perfect, divine blood...God's blood.** A very high price was paid so that you could be reconciled to him. He adopted you into his family so that you now have legal citizenship in Heaven.

Nothing can ever separate you from the love of God! Romans 8:39

*I will protect them and bless them and fill them with my love,
they will be great because of me, says the Lord. I will love
them forever and be kind to them always. Psalm 89:24 & 28*

*God's love is so great toward us that he treats us
like we are his very own children. I John 3:1*

*Even while people were enjoying their sinful nature, God demonstrated
his great love towards us by sending Christ to die for us. Romans 5:8*

*God showed us how much he loved us by sending his only Son into
the world so that we might have eternal life through him. This is real,
pure, perfect, unmerited love. The way the world loves is not even
comparable to the way God loves us, because he sent his Son
as a sacrifice to take away our sins. I John 4:9-10*

*For God so loved the world that he gave his only Son to die for us,
so that everyone who believes in him will not perish but have eternal
life to enjoy everyday. God did not send his son into the world to
condemn people, but so that people could be saved
by Christ's message, actions and sacrifice. John 3:16 & 17*

Do you see the connection between God's love and the sacrifice of Jesus for our sins? God wants us to do four things with his love.

- God wants us to READ about his love in the bible…by meditating on it and opening our heart to the Holy Spirit's leading. When you allow God's word into your mind you allow God's love in your heart.
- God wants us to UNDERSTAND his love…by hungering for more of him and asking for wisdom.
- God wants us to RECEIVE his love…by letting go of hurt, pain, confusion, religion and control.
- God wants us to REFLECT his love to others…by showing genuine compassion and appreciation towards them.

STORY – A Day At the Beach With God

One time we went on a weekend trip to Lake Michigan. I asked God for good weather on this one particular day that we were going to go to the beach. But unfortunately the forecast called for thunderstorms and the dark clouds were already rolling in. We contemplated going home early that day because the weather looked so lousy and the weather report was so dismal. Then my daughter said, "But what about our day at the beach?" I realized at that moment how important to her that day at the lake was. So we decided to continue, as planned to Lake Michigan. I started to pray to God.

Lord this is just between you and me. It's just one of those things I need to see right now. Is it critical? NO. Is it a necessity? NO. It's just something my family would love. I just need to know Lord that you would change a weather front coming in for your children that you love.

The weather looked so bad that many people were leaving the beach as we were walking down to it. When we got down to the beach, a mysterious opening began to develop in the dark sky and it headed towards us. Clear blue sky stayed over us the entire day. I had prayed for God to bless us with great weather and he did. Guess what, the water was unusually warm that day also. PRAISE THE LORD! All day my wife and I kept commenting on how beautiful the weather was and how great God is.

I thought to myself, "God did you do this for me? God do you love me that much that you changed the air pressure, temperature and all the necessary climate conditions for us to have a great day at the beach?" I felt God in my spirit say, "You wouldn't ask that question if you understood the depth of my love for you."

Just as an earthly father would give good gifts to his children,
how much more does your heavenly Father love and care for you.
Matthew 11:17

I love that part where God says, *"how much more."* That's the part God wants us to completely comprehend. He wants us to know *how much more* he loves us, than anything else in all his creation. He wants us to realize *how much more* he has done and will do than any earthly father ever could.

Many times it seems like it's hard to fully understand and receive God's love. Receiving God's love may be just as simple as to STOP REJECTING IT. For some people it's hard for them to feel love. Maybe it has something to do with the way they were raised. Maybe the words I LOVE YOU weren't really said in the home where you grew up. I challenge you to stop rejecting God and receive his love in a completely new and extraordinary way.

ARE YOU ASHAMED OF JESUS CHRIST?

Some people feel that God is a very personal and private subject and they should just speak to God when they are alone with him. They rarely mention the name of Jesus to anyone, not even to their family members or others who are close to them. They let other people believe what they want to believe so they don't offend anyone. They believe everyone needs to find God in their own way, by themselves. The subject of God or Jesus rarely comes out of their mouth because their faith is a very private subject. This type of thinking does not align with the truth from God's word. **The good news of the gospel message is not a private subject.** Mankind being reconciled to God is GOOD NEWS and we're supposed to share that GOOD NEWS with everyone! **God in you is supposed to be attracting others to God through you.** Jesus said, *"Come follow me and I will make you fishers of men" (Matthew 4:19).* Your actions will always follow your beliefs. If you don't ever confess Jesus as Lord publicly, then what does that say about your faith in him? Here are the words of Jesus:

If you confess me to people, then I will confess you before my Father in Heaven. If you do not confess me before others, then I will not confess you before my Father. Matthew 10:32

This is the Apostle Paul speaking:

I am not ashamed of the gospel of Christ, because it reveals the truth about the life transforming power of God's salvation for anyone who will believe. Romans 1:16

Holy Spirit filled, born-again, fire-baptized children of God are not ashamed or embarrassed about telling people what the Lord Jesus has done for them. The Holy Spirit doesn't want you to be quiet, backward and timid. He wants you to continually speak the glories of God out of your mouth. **The Holy Spirits mission is to establish God's kingdom *in us*, so that others may see, understand and experience God also. If you're not an active participant in this process, then you're missing out on a huge part of your divine purpose.**

You are my children, I created you to bring me glory. Isaiah 43:7
Everything you think, say and do should glorify God. Romans 6:13

The Holy Spirit does not teach us to be a loud mouth or arrogant and preach down to people. He doesn't teach us to judge, criticize or condemn. That's not his way. That's not the Holy Ghost boldness I'm talking about. The Holy Spirit speaks the truth in love. He doesn't bother getting into arguments with people because he always speaks the truth about God. He speaks the truth about you and he speaks the truth about every other subject in life. **He's not afraid to confront people and you shouldn't be afraid either, because he lives in you. Let the Holy Spirit pull open that jaw you've wired shut and he will amaze you with what comes out of you.**

COMMUNICATION AND RELATIONSHIPS

My wife and I will be talking and I will be responding back to her. It seems like we're having a good conversation, at least from my perspective (a man's perspective). Then she will say to me, "You're not listening to me." I'm thinking in my head, "What is she talking about?" I am right here having a conversation with her. A few sentences later she will say it again, "You're not listening to me." I don't understand, I'm sitting right next to her, speaking to her and trying to solve all her problems. But again she will say, "You're not listening to me again."

My point is this, people have trouble communicating even when their standing right next to each other face to face. How are we going to communicate effectively with a supernatural being like God, whom we can't see, hear or touch? I've heard a lot of people say, "I don't feel like God hears me when I pray." Maybe you need to change your approach. Have you ever tried being still and listening to God? Maybe he's trying to speak to you, but you're not listening. Maybe he's already heard you and now he's trying to respond to you. **Sometimes our prayer life is like a tornado. It touches the ground for only a minute and then it's gone.** People spend a lot of time telling God about all their worries and fears, then they beg him for everything on their list…AND THEN IT'S OVER! That's all the time they have for him until their next crisis. Soon after that, their so-called prayer time becomes even less and less. They become disillusioned with a God that never seems to hear or answer their requests. Christian soldier, we need to slow down. We need to be still and know that the Lord is God. Great relationships have great two way communication. Great communication is not only comprised of good speaking skills but also great listening skills. God is already an excellent communicator, so it's you and I that need to listen with our heart, soul and spirit.

My sheep hear my voice, they feel the security
of my presence and they follow me. John 10:27
Call to me and I will answer you and show
you great and mighty things. Jeremiah 33:3

How much time do you spend just simply waiting and listening for God to speak to you in your spirit? What kind of relationship are you going to have with him, if you're the one doing all the talking all the time? Can you imagine how exhausting it must be for God; with everyone telling him what they want, how they want things to happen and what their opinion is on every subject. Many people yell at him because their mad and frustrated. Doesn't that sound similar to how Jesus was treated? **All God ever wanted to do was save us, heal us, bless us and show us how to be close to him forever.**

Do you know how big God's complaint department is? Is your relationship with God like a genie in a lamp, who's there to grant your request, but never seems to ever respond to you? Maybe that's why people feel so distant from God. He's trying to teach them about his character and how to connect with him. Many people just never seem to be able to find the time to experience the most important relationship they will ever encounter.

We are the one's who hinder God from flooding into our lives,
because we don't surrender <u>ALL</u> the areas of our life to him.

God says to us in his word:
I will stick closer than a brother. Proverbs 18:24
I will never leave you or forsake you. Hebrews 13:5
We were all distant from God, but now we have been brought close to
him, because of the atonement of the Lord Jesus Christ. Ephesians 2:13

I don't know how close you want to be to God, but I do know God wants to be close to you. He has repeated himself many times regarding this intimacy in the bible. God said a number of times in the Old Testament that he is a jealous God. This shows us that God has feelings also. God can be angered, outraged and lonely. He is also loving, patient and compassionate. When we turn our backs on God...he hurts inside... because his creation has rejected him.

A lot of times I'll find myself falling into a very busy life style. When I realize that I've been neglecting that important time with God, I'll find a quiet place where I can focus on him. I feel bad sometimes to even come before him and ask for his presence to surround me, because I've been so busy with all the stuff that life has thrown at me. I know that God is always with me... but sometimes I'm not always with him.

One time I said, "Lord...what right do I have to come to you and expect you to just come flooding in and show up at my front door? Just because I am now ready to speak to you. What right do I have to come before you just because I've finally found few minutes out of the day to connect with you. That doesn't really seem fair to you. You have always been so very patient with me. If you're there Lord..."

Right then God stopped me in the middle of my prayer and said to me, "If I'm there, you ask. I have always been here inside of you. I'm always patiently waiting for you and me to celebrate life together. Don't you know that I go before you, to lead you into your day? I walk behind you, to catch you when you fall. I'm above you, watching over you like a shepherd watches over their sheep. I walk beside you to comfort you and encourage you like a friend. I am beneath you to lift you up throughout your day. I told you that I would never leave you or forsake you. When I said I will stick closer than a brother...I MEANT IT. Believe this...I am here and I am listening, but I have something important to say to you first:

I LOVE YOU! I LOVE YOU! I LOVE YOU!
I LOVE YOU! I LOVE YOU! I LOVE YOU!
I LOVE YOU! I LOVE YOU! I LOVE YOU!"

Do you understand why I believe the way I do? This book is filled with my personal experiences with God and all the many ways he has revealed himself to me. I wrote this book to let you know that God is just as passionate about you. He's ready to reveal himself to you in many new and extraordinary ways.

I LOVE HIM BECAUSE HE FIRST LOVED ME
*Love the Lord with all of your heart, with all your soul,
with all your mind and with all your strength. Mark 12:30*

---

*God wants us to love him wholeheartedly, without
any reservations, because that's how he loves us.
The love that we give to God originated from him.*

I used to love God in the same way I love chocolate cake. But now all these many years later, I love him so much more. The love I have for God now comes in a different container. It shines a little brighter than I ever thought it would. You see before I was willing to learn about God, but I wasn't willing to change that much. After a few years of learning about how much he really loves me, I was willing to change, but my growth was very slow. After a few more years of serving God, reading his word and having greater revelations of him through supernatural experiences, I finally reached the point in my life where I was willing to grow at any cost. Have you ever felt this way about God? **I'm sure you love God in your own way, but we need to love God his way.**

With ALL of our heart. (Passion and will)
With ALL of our soul. (Personality and attitude)
With ALL of our mind. (Thoughts and consciousness)
With ALL of our strength. (Time, money, energy and actions)
(Matthew 22:37, Mark 12:30 & Luke 10:27)

True love means sacrificing something for someone else. **When I began to meditate on the tremendous sacrifice that Jesus made for me, it changed how I responded to God.** When I realized that everything he suffered through was because he loved me, then I began to love differently. It's a love that is out of this world, because it's not from this world. Jesus taught this lesson to his disciples.

*Two men owed money to a certain moneylender. One owed him
five hundred silver coins and the other fifty. Neither of them had
the money to pay him back, so the moneylender cancelled the
debts that both men owed. Now which man will love the lender
more? Simon replied, "I suppose the one who had the bigger debt
cancelled." Jesus said, "You are right." Then he turned toward
the woman and said to Simon, "Do you see this woman? When I
came into your house, you did not give me any water for my feet,
but she has wet my feet with her tears and wiped them with her
hair. You did not give me a kiss, but this woman, from the time I*

entered, has not stopped kissing my feet. You did not put oil on
my head, but she has poured perfume all over my feet. I tell you,
her many sins have been forgiven for she loved much."
Luke 7:41-47

This woman's entire body became a worship vessel. She knew what she had been forgiven of and she loved God with all she had within her. When you begin to understand what you have been forgiven of and the price that was paid for you, then you'll begin to love with intensity and passion. Can you imagine how sad God must feel when we don't love him back? **If you're too busy for God then you're just too busy. Take some time to discover God's love and it will stretch the limits of your human emotions.** God promises us that if we will put forth any effort at all, he will reveal himself to us in a way we can understand.

Jesus said, "If anyone loves me, they will obey my
teachings and my Father will come down from Heaven
and make his home in their heart." John 14:23

When we try to love people without the help of the Holy Spirit it becomes a conditional, fragile, limited, imperfect love. When we love people with the love that comes from God, it's a perfect love. It's a love that perseveres and hopes for the best in others. It's not a jealous love, it's not easily angered. The distance between God's love and the world's love is an entire universe apart. But if you'll surrender your heart to him, his love will travel from the edge of the universe to you in just a fraction of a second and fill your heart completely. **The heart of God is the only place you can truly find rest for your soul.** The world's love is driven by the flesh, but God's love came down from Heaven and walked among us through the Lord Jesus Christ. Don't miss out on the most awesome love you'll ever experience. Desire it, embrace it and never let go of God's perfect, unconditional, out of this world, mind blowing, heart healing love.

CHAPTER 6

THE ENEMY'S CAMP
by Eric Johnson

The night was black and cool as we crept through the forest.
We knew our enemies were somewhere out there in the dark.
It had been quite a struggle to get to this point.
It was only because we trusted in God that we made it this far.
My comrades were shoulder to shoulder with me.
We crept through the tall grass with a mysterious silence that was with
us. I could feel the presence of God all around. A battle was imminent.

We crept up to the edge of a clearing and I saw hundreds of tents
in front of us. We cautiously approached the enemy's camp.
My heart was beating so loud I thought it was going to give our
position away. I couldn't see anyone around, no guards and no horses.
Was this possibly a trap? Was the surprise attack going to be on us?
I knew this was no place for doubt or fear.

We waited in silence. I could feel God's presence all around us.
His words came to me, "NOT BY MIGHT, NOT BY POWER,
BUT BY MY SPIRIT SAYS THE LORD."
I took my first step into the enemy's camp and then another.
We began our slow steady trot through the camp.
We zigzagged through the tents like a silent breeze.

Suddenly out of the corner of my eye, I saw someone kneeling
by a tent. My sword was ready as I approached them.
This person had a cloak covering them.
I saw a chain around their wrists and knew it was a prisoner.
I pushed back the hood from the prisoner and
looked with amazement into the face of MY LOVED ONE!
Their eyes widened and a smile came over them
as hope leaped back into their spirit.
I held out my hand and said, "THE LORD IS WITH US."
They grabbed my arm and I lifted them up.

At that moment something burst from the tent.
It was large and deformed with a horrible face.
It let out a screech that warned the entire camp
and they began to pour out among us.
I let out a war cry I didn't know I had in me.
THE TIME FOR BATTLE HAS COME!
I raised my sword and swung it to the ground,
severing the chains that bound my loved one tightly.

With a powerful lunge the demon knocked both of us down.
The demon leaped on top of me. He was very heavy like a large beast.
His hand went to my throat and his other hand went to the top of my
head. He said, "NOW I WILL HAVE YOUR MIND!"
There was no escaping his clutches.
I could see the heated battles taking place all around me.
It was fierce and to the death. Was this the end of mine?

Then something long and sharp came out of the demon's belly.
I recognized it to be my own sword.
The demon let out a horrible shriek and crumbled to dust.
The sword was held fast in the hands of MY LOVED ONE!
They killed the enemy that had bound them for so many years.
The look of VICTORY was all over their face.
They looked straight at me and said, "I'M FREE!"

At that moment something hit the ground
with a tremendous force right where we were standing.
It shook the entire camp. It was as though
THE FIST OF GOD hit the center of the enemy's camp.
We grabbed hands and ran. Our enemies were running frantic now.
As we swung our weapons we hit our mark and brought the forces of
evil down. Everywhere evil ran it was met by God's warriors
and the SWORD OF HIS SPIRIT.
The earth continued to shake violently, many demons
were swallowed up by it and soon they all had perished.
We looked at each other in amazement at what had just happened.
Many husbands, wives and children had been sent free that day.
We shouted with all we had within us. We danced on the enemy's
camp that day and gave praises to the Lord.
What the enemy had stolen, WE HAD TAKEN BACK!

Does this sound scary or weird to you? Does it sound like a science-fiction fantasy tale? This story is far from science-fiction. It is actually a true story happening in the homes of millions of families around the world. It's a supernatural battle for the souls of people that has been happening since the beginning of time.

The Devil doesn't expect much from a generation of wimpy, watered down, lukewarm, spineless Christians in our churches today. Does this description of the modern day Christian community upset you? THEN GOOD! Because that's what the devil thinks of you! Now get mad at him and fight back. Fight for what is dear to your heart. Fight for yourself and fight for your family, friends and your community.

We've all seen those pitiful movies where a group of teens go to a dark wooded campground resort for the weekend. There is usually a crazy killer in the movie that likes to stalk campgrounds. When the killer finally corners someone and is about to attack, a friend of theirs hits the maniac killer in the head with a lamp. When the killer falls to the ground, the two teenagers run to the cabin right next door and hide, hoping that he doesn't come and attack again. Their full-proof plan of simply running and hiding doesn't work. It doesn't work in the life of the Christian either. Are you running and hiding from the devil? Are you waiting and hoping that he doesn't attack you or your family? Let me say this as plain as I can. SATAN IS OUT TO KILL YOU, STEAL FROM YOU and DESTROY YOUR LIFE! (John 10:10) He is dead serious about his vial plan for your life and you should be just as serious in your efforts to stop him.

What if someone came into your house and took a loved one of yours and drug them down the street. Would you sit there with the TV remote in your hand and say, "WOW, that's awful? I really wish they wouldn't have done that!" To sit there and do nothing would be ludicrous! If you're like me, you would grab the nearest heavy object in the room and meet them up the road, then you would turn that evil person into hamburger. **Yet we sit in our homes and entertain ourselves, while bibles go unread and prayerless people die spiritually.** The Devil is taking our loved ones, family members and friends and dragging them down the street. Won't you rise up with me today Christian soldier and say, NO MORE!

God has given Christians the resources, power, weapons, courage and authority to charge into the enemy's territory and take back what's been stolen from them. These include family members, friends, co-workers and our fellow brothers and sisters in Christ. It not only includes people, but it also includes anything else the enemy has stolen from you, your peace of mind, your joy, self-control, your love and patience. Maybe you've surrender some of these attributes because of difficult circumstances in your life, but you need that joy, peace, patience and self-control.

One time my daughter came bursting into the house and said, "Dad, my wallet has been stolen out of my car! You'd better check your car." Sure enough, there was my wallet on the front seat of my car. Everything that was in my wallet was on the floor of my car and the money was gone. I have a problem of never being able to find my wallet, cell phone or keys. So my solution to that problem was to just leave them in my car. We used to live in a pretty safe neighborhood, so I would sometimes leave the car unlocked. Now I realize that trusting everyone on the planet was a really bad idea. The police officer said, "You were just begging for someone to rip you off. You're a very easy person to steal from." No, I wasn't prepared to be visited by a thief and the police officer was right. I've made the necessary adjustment so people cannot steal from me so easily.

Even though the enemy's plan is to steal from us, a lot of times we just go ahead and give him our peace and surrender our joy to him. Then we're left with fear, frustration and anxiety. Don't ever just hand over to the enemy what God has given you. **Many times we make it so easy for him to rob us through our bad attitude and reckless words.**

There is a sentence in _THE ENEMY'S CAMP_ that says the fist of God struck the center of the enemy's camp. God gets mad when he knows his people are being attacked, bound and taken captive. God will fight for us! He's just looking for some Christians who will break out of that shell of mediocrity, be brave, open their mouths and use their faith-filled words to release the captives and heal broken hearts. Is any army or enemy you encounter greater than God?

King Aram secretly surrounded the city of Dothan where Elisha was. The next morning Elisha's servant saw the vast army that had surrounded them and he said, "Master what are we going to do?" "Don't be afraid", the prophet said, "Those who are with us...are more than those who are with them." Then Elisha prayed, "Oh Lord, open his eyes so he may see." Then the LORD opened the servant's eyes and he looked and saw the hills full of horses and chariots of fire. God had assembled his army all around Elisha. II Kings 6:13-17

A SOLDIER'S PRAYER POWER

Do you have enough prayer power under your belt so when you cry out to God, his fist strikes the center of your enemy's camp? I want the Devil to fear ME. Not ME the father, or ME the husband, or ME the son or ME the architect. I want him to fear ME and CHRIST together, ME the prayer warrior. I want him to fear ME the Holy Ghost filled, blood bought child of God. The devil fears what Christ's blood accomplished for every Christian. When we begin to tell the enemy about the power of Jesus blood, then a shaking begins right under his feet.

The bible describes our walk of faith using words like; war, fight, wrestling, battle, soldier, spiritual warfare and spiritual weapons. The bible describes our Christian attributes and character as a spiritual suit of armor in Ephesians 6:11. We need that for our protection and survival.

Unfortunately the modern day Christian community lives far below their position and authority that Christ has secured for them. We need to *wake up* and get out of the barracks! We have been resting, eating and entertaining ourselves for far too long. The fight is out on the battlefield. The fight is on our knees in prayer. The fight is in that unread bible you own. We have an enemy that is out to get us. He is the common enemy to all mankind and his name is Satan.

I've heard a lot of people say there is no devil, but that's exactly how the devil wants you to think. In any branch of the military it's important when they go out to battle to be completely camouflaged so they can remain unseen by their adversary. The alcoholic father is not the enemy. The adulteress spouse is not the enemy. The drug attic son-in-law is not the enemy. **THE DEVIL IS YOUR ENEMY! He's a very real, spiritual being that influences people to surrender to his philosophies and temptations. He has kidnapped the human race, diminished our worth, perverted our relationships and destroyed families throughout the ages. His successful plan has gone unchecked by the Christian community for far too long.** He will deceive anyone who will listen to him.

Evil abounds when Christian people do nothing and we have done nothing long enough! The enemy is on the loose, building strongholds in people's minds that cannot be torn down by self-help books or any natural means.

Many modern day Christians are like lazy soldiers that have gotten very comfortable living in their barracks where they can eat, rest and entertain themselves. But the war is on the battlefield. Our guns are accurate but have never been fired. The ammunition is powerful but it has collected dust for years. Our armor cannot be pierced, but we have to put it on first before it can protect us. Are you ready to take back what the enemy has stolen from you? That's why the Holy Spirit prompted me to write _The Enemy's Camp_, to remind Christians what the church is capable of. To accomplish this you have to be sick and tired of being discouraged, depressed, unhealthy, worried and fearful. You have to hate what the Devil loves and love what he hates. You have to become his enemy rather than his ally. Don't give the enemy any help throughout the day through your thoughts, attitude and words.

Prepare yourself for action Christian soldier. We're in this together. It's easier to charge into battle when we are united together with brothers and sisters in Christ. Your family and friend's souls are worth fighting for. **Let's stop wasting our time fighting against each other and start fighting for each other.** Satan is the prince of darkness and he accomplishes most of his work hidden in the dark. But the light exposes what's in the dark and we are the children of light. Matt. 5:14

Christians are called to stand firm, fight the good fight, run the race and be diligent. We fight when we fall to our knees and cry out to God. We swing our swords when we allow the Holy Spirit to direct our prayers. We sharpen our weapons and refine our aim when we read God's word. That way we can be more effective in battle. The Holy Spirit has laid out a battle plan so we can know exactly _what_, _how_ and _who_ to pray for. You need to guard your thought life Christian soldier, as if you were wearing a supernatural titanium helmet. Ephesians 6:17

Temptation begins in the mind not the body. The body will do whatever the mind tells it to do. There are many silent battles that rage in our thought life because the world is trying to capture our attention at every turn. The enemy whispers in our ears; YOU want this, YOU need this, YOU should do this, YOU deserve this. The enemy and the world's philosophy is always SELF-centered. The Christian mind should be focused on God and his agenda. **Did you know you can't be tempted by anything you refuse to think about? That's an awesome truth to extinguished Satan's advances.**

With your help Lord, I will charge forward into my enemy's camp and leap over the wall they've built. Psalm 18:29

You Lord, will make my enemies turn their backs and run for their lives. Psalm 18:4

Even if ten thousand of my enemies rise up against me, my fear is in the Lord. Psalm 3:6

COME

According to Jesus' own words he had the power to call down twelve legions of angels to save him from the people who were crucifying him (Matthew 26:53). A legion according to the Roman army was six thousand men. Twelve legions of angels would be 72,000 angels. Do you realize that one angel killed 185,000 men in the Assyrian army?

That night the angel of the Lord went out and put to death a hundred and eighty-five thousand men in the Assyrian camp. When the people got up the next morning their enemy's dead bodies were everywhere!
II Kings 19:35

Now let's multiply those two figures together (72,000 angels x 185,000 people) for a total of thirteen billion, three hundred and twenty million (13,320,000,000). That means while Jesus was hanging on the cross, suffering, dieing, being ridiculed, scoffed and laughed at, he could have called down from Heaven enough angels to kill 13 billion, 320 million people. All that he had to do was say…"COME." But he didn't. He was a man who was passionate about us. He was a man with a mission, determined and committed to loving us to the very end. He didn't say, "COME and take vengeance for me Lord upon my enemies. COME with your warring angels that can defeat all the armies of this world." No, he didn't say that. He said, "Father…forgive them…for they know not what they do." And then finally at the very end of his life, he said, "It is finished!"

The power of the Most High was deposited in you when you became a born-again, Holy Spirit filled Christian. It's the most phenomenal force that has ever touched a human being. God's spirit, power and anointing is in you. So it's time to wake up sleepy Christian soldier and get out of the barracks. We have a supernatural arsenal of weapons that are razor sharp, explosive and effective. We have warring angels that are ready to be dispatched at the sound of our prayers. Angels that are waiting for us to say, "COME…and fight for me! COME…with all your weapons of power! COME…and let's charge forward together LIKE A MIGHTY ARMY!

In Joshua 6:1 - God brought down the great walls of Jericho with a SHOUT.
In Exodus 17 - Moses fought and destroyed the Amalekites by LIFTING HIS HANDS up to God.
In Samuel 17 - David brought down Goliath with a SMALL STONE.

In Judges 7 - Gideon defeated and army of 135,000 with only 300 MEN. In Judges 15 - Samson struck down a thousand of his enemies with a piece of BONE.

In II Chronicles 20 – Jehoshaphat annihilated three enormous armies that joined forces against him by sending out only MUSICIANS AND WORSHIPPERS.

God used ordinary people with what seemed to be foolish tactics to win these supernatural battles. Why? To teach plain old ordinary YOU, that YOU AND GOD can do the same thing. I used to tell God, "How can you use me Lord? I'm just a big pile of nothing!" God spoke to me immediately after I said those words and he said to me in my spirit,

"Have you seen what I've created out of nothing?
I created the universe, the stars, the earth and everything on it.
I specialize in nothing and make something special out of it."

Make a resolution that you want to be one of those simple ordinary people who God uses to do extraordinary things. Make this declaration to God:

Here I am God. You can use me today for any purpose you choose.
I make my spirit, mind and body available to glorify you right now.

Maybe you think you're just an ordinary person and you don't have any special skills or abilities that are great enough for God to use. You're not an eloquent speaker. You don't have a charismatic personality. You have zero confidence. You live in fear most of the time. You're not comfortable speaking in front of people. You're not that smart. You think to yourself, "How could God ever use a person like me?" THEN CONGRATULATIONS! You are the perfect candidate for God to glorify himself through.

God really isn't interested in your professional resume. After all, God used a donkey to talk to Balaam and teach him about humility (Numbers 22). God has already anointed you to do everything he's commanded you to do. What God is seeking is your *availability*. Are you willing to go to a place called Nineveh (Jonah 3:2) all the way across an ocean? Or are you willing to even go to your neighbor's front door step with a plate of cookies? You see whether it's Nineveh or your neighbor's front porch, both of these decisions require your step of faith and obedience.

If you'll make yourself AVAILABLE to him,
he'll glorify himself in everything you do.
If you'll give him your LIFE, he'll give you ETERNAL LIFE.
If you'll give him YOUR TIME, ENERGY AND RESOURCES then
God will give you HIS TIME, ENERGY AND RESOURCES.

---

*I don't really have too much to give God...just myself. But if I
will give him ALL OF ME, then he will give me ALL OF HIM.
So far, that has been a mind blowing journey. God operates
in the little things we have and do and a little in God's hand
is enough to do the GREAT THINGS only he can do.*

Maybe you don't really see any specific spiritual battles that you
need to fight. That type of thinking leads me to this question: Are you
praying for and witnessing to your unsaved neighbors? God has placed
you and your neighbors next to each other so you can practice living life
together and so you can speak the truth to them in love. You may not
even realize it but you're right in the middle of the battlefield. Your
neighbors are worth your time, energy and resources. God didn't
suggest for us to love them if we get a chance. He commanded us to
love them.

*Love your neighbor with the perfect love that God
has planted in your spirit. Matthew 22:39*

The heart of spiritual warfare is Christian's praying for souls and
speaking the gospel of Christ crucified. There are people all around you
that you come in contact with everyday. They are worth fighting for!
The war is raging around us. Do whatever it is that the Spirit of God is
telling you to do. Show them plenty of God's love, grace and mercy
until they finally see God through you. God's given you a supernatural
assignment. If you're not at your post or position then your neighbor
could lose out, be spiritually blinded or eternally lost. Your prayers are
vital in this battle. **What you *do* and what you *don't do* will have
supernatural and eternal repercussions. What you *say* and what you
don't say will determine if God's power is released on this earth.**
Let's engage the enemy together. We need to cover each others backs as
we sweep through the enemy's camp. Won't you join your comrades
today in the fight of a lifetime?

SPIRITUAL VISION – Angels And Axes

In church one Sunday night my wife was at the altar praying with all her heart because she had been fighting some difficult battles with the enemy. Absent of peace, she frequently became angry, down cast and confused. While laying her head down on the steps of the altar she cried out to God and surrendered it all to him.

God opened up this spiritual window and I began to see these large chains shackled to her wrists. At the other end of each chain was a heavy weight. As people around her began praying over her, I saw an angel step up to her. He had a large battle ax in his hands. WOW! THIS WAS AWESOME! I knew something extraordinary was about to happen. He swung it high into the air and brought the blade down right next to her wrist, severing the chain. Then he severed the chain on her other hand. There was something in the supernatural realm that had her bound, defeated, discouraged and depressed, but now she had just been completely released of it all. Months later I found out she was severely addicted to prescription drugs. Her addiction of seventy vicodin a day almost killed her.

Angels were responding to our prayers and demonic strongholds were being broken that night. The Lord was bringing things to a turning point in her life. My wife really didn't even know how to get better on her own. It wasn't within her power to just stop taking the pills because she was so completely and thoroughly addicted. All she knew to do was to cry out to God. It was up to us to surround her with prayer and the truth of God's word. The addiction had to be broken in the spiritual realm first. Fortunately, she asked for help from the only person that could truly save her and that was the Lord Jesus Christ.

A GOD OF PROTECTION

*God has encircled the battle arena with his arms
and the war is being fought directly in front of him.*

There is a story in the bible about a teenage boy named David, who killed a giant man named Goliath by using only a sling and a small stone. I believe when Goliath fell to the ground he was dead. But David still took Goliath's sword and cut off his head. I don't know if a lot of people grasp the significance of that act. David not only defeated Goliath with a small stone, but <u>he used the enemy's own sword on Goliath's throat.</u> From a battle stand point that is not only humiliating, but look at what that says to believers and the enemy's of God.

*Every sword your enemies sharpen to bring you harm…
will be used on their own throat.*

<u>God says it this way:</u>

*Your enemy will fall into the pit that they dug for you. Psalm 57:6
The Lord laughs at the wicked, for he knows their days are numbered.
Psalm 37:13*

*Five of you will chase a hundred and a hundred of you will chase ten
thousand and all your enemies will fall by the sword before you.
Leviticus 26:8*

*The Lord will command his angels to guard you in all your ways,
they will lift you up in their hands so that no harm will come to you.
Psalm 91:11 & 12*

Do you think the Philistines feared that little shepherd boy as they ran for their lives across the country side? I believe they feared the Lord God Almighty that David spoke of just before the battle. The bible says, *"The fear of the Lord is the beginning of wisdom" (Psalm 111:10).* I think the Philistines gained a tremendous amount of wisdom that day. From that point on, the Philistines would be fearful about every shepherd boy they came across and wonder, "Does he serve the same God that David serves?" Since God has control over everything then your enemies will have to fear everything under his control. Even little shepherd boys who run at them with stones. NOW THAT'S INTIMIDATING!

*The LORD shall cause your enemies that rise up against you, to be
smitten before your eyes. They shall charge out against you in one
direction but will flee before you in seven different directions.
Deuteronomy 28:7*

I LOVE THAT VERSE! I always have this mental image of my enemies charging out against me to destroy me, screaming with their horrible war cry. Then a few seconds later they're running for their lives away from me in seven different directions. They're stumbling over each other, whaling, screaming and running for their lives. At first they couldn't get at me fast enough, then they couldn't get away from me fast enough. The bible says; *A thousand may fall at your right side and ten thousand at your left, BUT NO HARM SHALL COME TO YOU (Psalm 91:7).* WOW! Why will no harm come to us, because we are his chosen, precious and highly favored children. God's hand of protection covers us completely.

How else could Gideon's army of three hundred defeat one hundred and thirty thousand Philistines? That's a 129,700 man advantage. How did the Israelites kill the entire Egyptian army when they had no swords, spears, or mighty horse drawn chariots? How does a shepherd boy kill a lion, a bear or even a fully armored giant? BECAUSE GOD FIGHTS FOR HIS CHILDREN! These battles were not only happening in the natural realm but they were happening in the supernatural realm and God has control over both arenas. So trust in God because he can shake the land your enemies walk on.

When Jesus stood before Pilate to be judged, Pilate reminded Jesus that he had the power to have him executed. Jesus calmly reminded Pilate, *"You have no power over me, only that which has been given to you by my Father"(John 19:11).* WOW! That's AWESOME! Shouldn't we be that secure in our relationship with God? Shouldn't we be that confident in God's ability to protect us? **Do you sleep peacefully at night knowing that your father is the king of the universe? Because of your new birth, you can have that exact same relationship with God that Jesus has. The fullness of God lives in you. You are united with him without exclusion. God operates within you with no limitations.** Unfortunately your thoughts, attitude and flesh can hinder what's in your spirit from ever being released. People search for many things in this life but the discovery of God's complete nature in you...is the greatest treasure you could ever find.

STORY - A God Of Protection

When I was a teenager, I had an ex-girlfriend that had told some lies about me to her ex-boyfriend. She was trying to get her ex-boyfriend and some of his buddies mad at me. I know this because she called me immediately and said, "Eric, don't go out of your house!" She knew she had gone too far.

I met the boys about an hour later at my front door. It may have been stupid to go out of the house but I had done nothing wrong. When I went outside, I made sure my back was up against the car, so they would have to attack me from the front. After about five minutes of heated discussion about the lies my ex-girlfriend had told them, my dad stepped out of the house. He asked, "Is everything okay?" I told him yes and he went into the garage. The boys left after I calmly diffused their anger towards me.

That evening I told my dad those boys had actually come over to beat me up. My dad said, "I kind of sensed something wasn't right about the situation. That's why I went out to the garage and got a lead pipe and stood there with it until they left."

Whoever tries to harm one of my children, who calls me Father, then believe me, it would be better for them to go jump in the ocean with an anchor tied around their neck. Matthew 18:6

If you make the Most High your shelter and refuge, then no evil will conquer you. No calamity will come to your house, because the angels of the Lord have you completely surrounded. They will lift you up in their arms and shield you from harm. Psalm 91:9-12

The Lord is faithful, he will make you strong and guard you from every evil attack. II Thessalonians. 3:3

I know what these scriptures mean to me.
God's in the garage…with the lead pipe!

I could imagine God saying, "You've come onto my property, TO HURT MY CHILD!" It's a supernatural protection that transcends into the natural realm. After all, we are fighting these spiritual battles in an arena surrounded by God's own arms. If something does come against you, it could be an opportunity to refine your faith or prepare you for something even greater in the future. Just remember, the battle is going to be fought in the palm of God's own hand.

My wife used to have this terrible fear come over her when we drove by a semi-truck on the highway. The noise, size and shaking made her freak out. She would always scream at me to get away from along-side those huge trucks. It was so severe you could definitely call it a phobia.

One time we came up beside a semi-truck on the highway. It was shaking, it was loud and it was big. After we got past the truck, I noticed my wife didn't freak out like she had always done before. When I looked over at her she had a little smile on her face. I said, "What happened, why didn't you panic this time?" She said, "I decided that my God is much bigger than a semi-truck and he'll protect me along side anything."

Fear can be a good or bad thing, depending on how you channel it. Fear can keep you from harm. Fear of speaking in front of other people can be used to make you sharp and alert. You can even channel fear into giving you more faith. Now every time we drive by a semi-truck, my wife is reminded of HOW BIG GOD IS. Instead of fear controlling her and abusing her, she now uses fear to remind her that God is bigger than a semi-truck or any other problem she may encounter.

THE MASTER'S PLAN

In the spiritual realm, before the earth was created, the spiritual realm consisted of God, his angels, the Holy Spirit and Jesus. Lucifer was one of these angels. He rose to the stature of leader of praise and was beautiful. His prominence and grandeur became evil when he wanted to be exalted to a higher level than God. The Lord had to cast Satan down from Heaven because he wanted to be greater than God. Satan used this same temptation to deceive Eve in The Garden Of Eden. He told her, *"You will be like God". Genesis 3:5*

This same spirit is in people today. Everyone wants to be the master of their own destiny. They want to control their life. They ignore God because, if he's real, then they would have to be in submission to him and be accountable to him. Submission, humility, obedience and surrender are character traits that the world laughs at. They will not bow down to anyone. People have become arrogant, prideful, selfish and rebellious...God haters. They hate a God that they really know nothing about.

We know that God is represented by light and Satan is represented by darkness. *God is light and in him there is no darkness (I John 1:5).* Anywhere God is there is a lot of light. In the book of Genesis it says, *"In the beginning there was darkness."* Look what God did in the middle of where Satan was. God said, "LET THERE BE LIGHT!" (Genesis 1:3) Then he created the earth, the animals and mankind. God did all this in an area that was previously empty and dark (Satan's area). God presented a challenge to Satan. You see God has his angels to glorify him, just as Satan has demons (fallen angels) that serve him. So God created a brand new being, called the human race. God said that he created us just a little lower than the angels and in a similar way we are spiritual beings. God created a flourishing, beautiful garden for man. When God saw that man was lonely and needed a soul mate, he created a wife for Adam. God loved his creation and he wanted them to love him back, but he didn't want them to be robotic in nature. He gave them a free will to choose. That way he would know for sure if mankind would really love him back.

THE CHALLENGE
*God created a human race that would hopefully choose
to love him back and hate evil and eventually destroy the works
of the Devil in an area that was previously void and dark.*

That's one of our grand purposes in life. God is God; he could have destroyed the Devil with a snap of his fingers. So why didn't he? The angels could have overpowered the demons and it would have been a short battle and a long victory celebration. But God thinks much deeper than we do. His ways are not like ours.

God created the human race to destroy the works
of the Devil and anything that he's involved in!

Jesus was also sent to destroy the works of the Devil (I John 3:8). You see when you get beat up by the playground bully, IT'S EXPECTED! But when you get beat up by the wimpy nerd with glasses whose half your size, IT'S HUMILIATING. God created us as a spirit being with flesh and bones and a completely free will to choose, so that one day we would choose him.

God pointed at us and said to Satan, "That's who I will use
to defeat you!" It has been a battle ever since that day.

Ever since that day, God and Satan have been fighting *for us* and fighting *through us*. **God gave mankind dominion over the earth (Genesis 1:26 & 28) and Satan has tricked people into surrendering their power to him through ignorance, deception and temptation.** God is interested in winning battles supernaturally. Read the story of David and Goliath, that was a supernatural battle and victory. No boy could beat a giant, it was laughable, but God had the last laugh. How could the Israelites beat the Egyptian army the way they did? How could the walls of Jericho fall by a shout from God's people? How could Gideon's army of 300 defeat an army of 130,000? Because when we allow God to influence our thoughts and behavior, then God's power can be released from within us.

God and Satan both need willing people to operate through. God and Satan both need a person to work through. God had to figure out a way to exert his mighty power on earth through his spirit. He needs people who will surrender to his voice. Satan also needs people to surrender to his temptations (lies) so he can influence them and destroy them.

When the prophets in the Old Testament listened with their hearts to the voice of God, they began to write down what God was speaking to them. They even wrote down things that were going to happen in the future and they were one hundred percent accurate about those predictions. When the Virgin Mary listened to the voice of God she said, *"According to your word...be it unto me" (Luke 1:38)*. She received that word God had spoken to her and it became a seed in her womb. After thousands of years a young woman had finally listen to God's voice, believed it and received it. **God had figured out how to exert his power once again on the earth. He pierced through the Virgin Mary's spirit and into her womb and planted a seed (himself) there. The power of God was going to show up on earth in a significantly life altering way through the man Jesus Christ.**

God wants you to overcome the big, nasty, lying, wicked, evil Devil. This is a major part of his plan for you. God could easily squash the Devil like a bug, but he wants us to do it through the power of the blood of the Lord Jesus Christ. You might ask, "If this is really a battle between good and evil, Satan and God, why doesn't the Devil use his power to just wipe us out?" Well technically Satan has no power. It's been stripped from him. Satan has been made a spectacle of through the Lord Jesus Christ (Colossians 2:15). **Satan does not have all this demonic power to blast at you with his evil ray gun. The only power Satan has is the power you give him. He twists God's truth through**

lies and deception and if you'll surrender to those thoughts then he can influence your life (Ephesians 6:11). Satan needs your cooperation to destroy you and many people have surrender to his putrid melody. Satan doesn't have the power to make you fail, you fail by being deceived by his lies. The battle of truth between you and Satan takes place in your mind. One of our primary objectives as Christians is to destroy the works of the enemy and that is done by saturating our minds with the truth about God and us.

Remember when God told Satan, *"Have you considered my servant Job?" (Job 1:8)* That was a challenge to all the forces of darkness. LET'S FIGHT, IT'S ON, LET'S THROW DOWN, but it will be through the people that I've created. We'll fight through these people who have THE FREE WILL OF CHOICE to do whatever they want to do. We will see who they love the most. Do you love God or the things of this world? Do you love light or do you love darkness? All Heaven is standing by and anxiously waiting for your choice.

If anyone loves the physical and emotional pleasures of this world more than God, then their heart will grow cold and distant to him. I John 2:5

You might be thinking that sounds scary and dangerous going after the Devil. He's bigger, stronger, smarter and more powerful than me. Besides that, if I make him angry he's liable to really unleash his forces after me and my family.

Newsflash! He's already after you and your family.
He's out to KILL, STEAL and DESTROY you and them. John 10:10

But here is some awesome news God has
promised us regarding attacks from the enemy.

*Greater is he (Jesus' Spirit) that is in you,
than he (Satan) that is in the world. I John 5:4*

*Trust in the Lord and he will strengthen you and protect you
from satanic attacks of every kind. II Thessalonians 3:3*

*No evil forces will be able to strike you down. No plague
shall find its way into your home. God will send his warring
angels to protect you from evil. Psalm 91:10 & 11*

*God has given you power to tread on serpents, scorpions and over all
the power of the enemy. Nothing shall in any way harm you. Luke 10:9*

*If God is for us, then who is able to stand up
against God and us united together? Romans 8:31*

*The Lord saves the righteous because they trust in him, he helps
them and delivers them from the plots of evil men. Psalm 37:39-40*

*God will keep me safe and the evil one cannot touch me. I John 4:18
Through faith we are shielded by God's power. I Peter 1:5*

*Be strong in the Lord's mighty power. Put on the full armor of God,
so when evil comes, you will be able to stand against
the devil's schemes. Our struggle is not against flesh and blood,
but against rulers and authorities of this dark world and against
all the forces of evil in the spirit realm. Ephesians 6:10-12*

In these verses, God lets us know how much power we have over the supernatural forces of the enemy. **God has given us many spiritual weapons to overcome these forces. These consist of prayer, praise, fasting, communion, believing, trusting, loving renewing our mind by reading God's word and speaking out those promises he gave us. So don't be afraid to use them. They are more powerful than anything on earth you've ever experienced.** God reminds us that nothing will remove us from his hand of protection (John 10:28). His protection surrounds us constantly. He doesn't take a vacation or a day off from loving and protecting his children.

Whatever mess you're in right now, God has a way out of it. Your problem or situation is not bigger than God. The devil is wise and cunning, but God is in you and he's greater than your enemy. After reading the bible from cover to cover, I realized that God specializes in surprise endings. Don't give up, stand firm and see the salvation of the Lord Jesus Christ. Make the necessary changes in your life to accomplish your God given destiny. God has given us power and authority that needs to be spoken and released through our faith-filled words. He wants you with him in the victory circle at the end of this journey.

CHAPTER 7

THE BATTLE IS THE LORDS

God revealed to me one Sunday morning what was actually happening during this time of corporate worship together with my brothers and sisters in Christ all around me.

The Battle Is The Lord's
by Eric Johnson

As I pushed the church doors open that Sunday morning, I saw many sad faces. I could tell some people were hiding deep hurts in their lives. These scars and pains from the past left them defeated. Some weren't even sure what God's love felt like anymore. Many people looked discouraged and depressed. Their smiles seemed empty and they appeared to have lost all hope.

As the worship service began, a Spirit swept over us that I had not felt in a long time. As we praised the Lord and worshiped Christ the King, I felt an incredible freedom like never before. We began to get lost in worship and a deep ministering presence came over me. A deep refreshing spirit began to overwhelm all of us. I felt something being torn from within me.

At that moment I opened my eyes and saw a dark shadow come out of me. This spirit wandered to the back of the sanctuary. As others continued in worship, similar dark spirits leaped out of them and retreated to the same place. The dark demons at the back of the sanctuary formed a powerful chain of evil. Once again I closed my eyes and praised our savior Jesus Christ for delivering us from these spirits. Then I heard Jesus say in an audible voice, "I'M NOT FINISHED YET."

Suddenly I felt something in my hand. It was a long sword. Then I realized I had a complete set of body armor on. The armor covered my feet, waist and chest and included a helmet and a shield. I looked around me and saw the young and old, each with their own armor and weapons. Our Pastor stepped down from the pulpit also fully equipped.

It was then I noticed the angels above us, hundreds of them with spears and many on horseback. An entire army of God's angels had gathered for the battle. It was an awesome sight. We all drew our swords and with a thundering shout, that must have shaken the foundations of Hell, we charged forward down the church aisles towards our enemies.

Our Pastor swung his sword and struck the first blow. I saw many demons fall with one swing. THEN I SAW HIM! It was the demon that haunted me for years! He told me I was worthless and kept me bound in fear and guilt. He shot flaming arrows at me, but my shield extinguished them all. I swung my sword and as the word of God touched him, he let out a loud shriek and was gone. I saw the older saints charge the enemy with great power and a fresh confidence in the Lord Jesus Christ.

We battled for our souls that day. Demons screamed as they fell to the power of Christ's blood. You could see fear in their eyes as they knew they were going to fall to THE MASTER that day. The last thing the enemy heard was our victory cry as they were struck down and destroyed. Finally, every last dark force had fled the house of God.

Jesus took the keys from Satan that day. He freed us from many bondages in our lives. It had been so many years since we had felt such peace and freedom. The joy of the Lord came down into our hearts. People were laughing, dancing and praising God. GOD LEAD US THROUGH THE BATTLE AND TO VICTORY THAT DAY.

OBJECT LESSON - Rat Traps

When I was a children's pastor I did this one object lesson that always made a big impact on kids. What you do is go and buy about eight large rat traps, the type with the metal springs that slap together really loud. Place the eight traps randomly on the floor in front of the kids and set all the traps. Let some of the traps slip shut so they make a loud WHACK! That will get their attention. Have a brave child take their shoes off and step up to the front. Tell them to close their eyes. Now hold their hand and guide them through the maze of traps, always keeping their toes safe from danger. This is a great object lesson about trust.

(SAFETY NOTE: This object lesson needs to be performed on a stage, a safe distance from children. Please disengage the springs on all the traps.)

Most Christians don't recognize the enemy's traps and take heaping spoonfuls of his lies into their mouth and into their mind. Their excuse is, "I can't help it, that's just the way I am" or "I have to vent and let it out or else I'll blowup. I'm only human!" These are all just excuses for not walking in the truth of who they are IN CHRIST. When a Christian sins it should no longer seem natural at all. It should be an unnatural feeling of restlessness in their soul, even painful, like a splinter in their finger. **Christians have been freed from the indwelling nature of sin, but they do sometimes choose to surrender to the exterior power and temptation of sin. When Christians sin, the power of the Holy Spirit should come sweeping in like a flood, letting the Christian know that's not what they were designed for.** If your a born-again Christian, you have been freed from sin because your old sin nature is gone, don't make yourself a slave to sin once again (Romans 6:16). Christ died for our sins. We need to walk in that freedom from condemnation that Christ earned for us.

IS THE ENEMY AWARE THAT YOU ARE HIS ADVERSARY?

I've been a minister for the Lord Jesus Christ for sometime now and I've heard countless prayer requests like these:

My kids aren't serving the Lord.
I'm sad more than I'm happy.
I live in a state of depression.
I deal with a lot of fear in my life.
I'm frustrated most of the time.
I'm anxious about everything in life.
I don't think God listens to me anymore.

The Devil hurt me again.
My spouse left me.
The people at work are against me.
I'm tired and dry in my spirit.
I don't feel like God loves me.

Christians many times sit around waiting for the enemy's next punch without even putting up their fists to protect themselves. **The devil laughs at our weak prayerless lives. He doesn't even flinch at our stale, spiritless, once a week church services.** Christians love movie theaters, sporting events, vacationing and sleeping in on Sunday mornings more than they love the house of God. Christians who don't know their true identity IN CHRIST or what they possess in their new spirit, don't scare the enemy. That's why many Christians walk around discouraged, depressed, defeated, frustrated, anxious and fearful. These are not the fruits of their new born-again spirit. This type of fruit comes from carnal thinking and being lead by emotions.

When you tap into the power, authority and the blood of Jesus, that's when God's fist hits the center of your enemy's camp? The enemy recognizes and obeys that kind of prayer power. We call it a fight, but actually it isn't a fight at all. The enemy has to obey the authority Jesus earned for us. Jesus confronted a demon possessed man in Matthew 8:31 and the demon asked Jesus, *"What will you do to us?"* The demon didn't try to fight with Jesus. Jesus had authority and he was about to speak it over them and they were going to have to obey what he commanded.

Jesus said, "All authority and power has been given to me."
Matthew 28:18

That means all power and authority has been given to you as well. Many Christians don't believe that statement, that's why their not releasing the power of God into their lives. If you're a born-again Christian then you have the exact same power and authority Jesus has (I John 4:17, Ephesians 1:19 & 20). Whether on not your releasing it into this physical world is based on your knowledge of what God has deposited in you. As you read God's word and begin to understand all the tremendous spiritual gifts he has placed in you, only then will you be able to release them into this physical world and enjoy them.

Reading God's word is an awesome thing to do, but a proper interpretation of God's word is even more important. God wants you to enjoy the new life that's in you. **Your spirit is full of power, anointing, blessings, healing, forgiveness, joy, faith and love. It's all inside of you waiting for you to release it and enjoy it right now.**

So many Christians are living way below their level of anointing, their always waiting for God to anoint them more. Christians are always waiting for God to bless them and heal them. **Christians don't have a faith problem or a love problem, they have a knowledge problem. If we truly understood the authority we have inside of us we would have revival every night of the week. Revival wouldn't have to scheduled ever again. Your spirit is always in revival. Your spirit is always praising God. Your spirit is completely forgiven. Your spirit is ready to release healing right now.** Your body might not feel empowered but who cares, it's going to have to learn that you are more than just a physical being. Your mind may not even be in agreement with these truths, but it will learn as you allow the Holy Spirit to teach you.

Remember when Jesus confronted the one demon who had possessed a boy since birth. This demon had tried to kill the boy by throwing him into a fire and he even tried to drown him by throwing him into a lake. Jesus said to this boy, "BE CLEAN". Two words...that's it...TWO WORDS!

But this demon was extremely powerful.......................BE CLEAN!
But this demon threw the boy into a fire.......................BE CLEAN!
But this demon had complete control over his mind.........BE CLEAN!
The disciples couldn't even cast out this demonic spirit.....BE CLEAN!

Now that's demonstrating power with authority! **All spiritual forces are in submission to us through the name of Jesus! Jesus Christ has fought for and earned that power and authority for us!** We need to fully comprehend this phenomenal reality, never doubt it and then release it. It's just one of the many phenomenal truths we possess by being a born-again Christian.

Jesus said, "Anyone who believes in me, they will do the same works that I've been doing and they will do even greater works than I have done, because I go to the Father on their behalf. John 14:12

Jesus said "Ask God for whatever you need and you will have it, because you asked using the authority of my name." John 16:23

If you're a parent, have you ever had to yell or scream at your defiant teenager to get them to clean their room, take out the trash or do some other chores around the house? Usually, you have to negotiate with them if they're argumentative. There is usually an exchange back and forth about what they think a clean room is and what your vision of a clean room is. Can you imagine walking by your teenager's room and saying two words, "BE CLEAN" and immediately they jump up and start cleaning. They simply obeyed what you said; NOW THAT'S AUTHORITY! That's the authority Jesus possessed, spoke and demonstrated. That's the authority we have as well! Christ earned it for us and then he gave it to us.

The reason most Christians aren't using their authority is because they don't believe they really possess it. They don't believe God would ever use someone like them. They believe that kind of power is reserved for all the important people at church; pastors, deacons and elders. They feel like they've failed God too many times for him to trust them with that kind of power. **God trusted you with all his power...the moment you trusted him with all your heart.**

Jesus would have been unjust to tell us to go a do the same miraculous things he did, if he had not given us the power to do them. Christ was not lacking in spiritual authority and neither do any born-again Christians.

The enemy tries to keep you from realizing that you have the authority to dismiss him, cast him out and crush his head. Keeping you distracted and busy is one of the most effective tactics he uses. Recognizing the enemy's strategies and traps is critical to walking in the abundant life and power that Jesus has established for us. Christians sometimes feel they are powerless in making changes around them, but that couldn't be further from the truth. **Born-again, blood-bought, holy spirit energized saints of God have the identical power on the inside of them that raised Christ from the dead (Ephesians 1:19 & 20).**

The Lord Jesus worked in them and confirmed the truth about his word through miraculous signs and wonders. Mark 16:20

We have complete access to a tremendous amount of power that the Lord Jesus Christ has earned for us and it's all right here in us. It's not out there in Heaven waiting to be dispensed by God. We don't have to pray for this power to come and be in us. Christians need to understand that all of God's power is in their born-again spirit. Don't let it go to waste! According to the word of God, here are some tremendous weapons we have in our arsenal.

Speak positive faith-filled words over our situation and each other.
Dismiss negative thoughts from our mind.
If all things are possible for those who believe,
then we need to pray for the impossible. Mark 9:23
Love people with the supernatural love of the Lord.
Be thankful in every good work as if you're accomplishing it for God.
Continually have a praise on your lips that penetrates Heaven.
To believe God with such tenacity in our mind
that it overcomes our doubts, fears, flesh and logic.

Anything that comes blasting out of your spirit that was ignited by the Holy Spirit, is filled with God's anointing, power and wisdom.

When you walk around throughout the day, does the enemy hear your footsteps? Does the ground shake as you go on your spiritual walk, as if you have one hundred pound shoes on? We Christians should make the devil nervous every morning when we rise out of bed. GET MAD

AT THE DEVIL! Let's put on our 100 pound spiritual shoes and let him know we're on the move.

Be angry and sin not. Let not the sun go down on your wrath. Neither give place to the devil. Ephesians 4: 26 & 27

Be angry and sin not. - There's a righteous anger that is not sinful. God wants us to be angry and hate the devil and his evil.

Let not the sun go down on your wrath. - Don't let your anger ever fall asleep. Keep that anger towards unrighteousness and evil stirred up on the inside of you. If you truly love someone then you will have anger and wrath against anything that comes against them.

Neither give place to the devil. - Don't ever become lukewarm or neutral in your attitude towards the devil, if you do then you will allow him the opportunity to influence your thoughts, philosophies, ideas and inevitably your life.

Draw a battle line in the sand. Go and get some wooden stakes and write scriptures on them. Then drive them into the ground around your house. Tell the devil, "You've gone far but no further! You will not cross this line!" Let the enemy know:

> He's NOT going to have your mind.
> He's NOT going to abuse your body.
> He's NOT going to control your mouth.
> He's NOT allowed in your house.
> He's NOT going to destroy your family.

Now that's something the angels in Heaven, who have been waiting for you to open your mouth, can respond to. Jesus said, "*My house shall be called a house of prayer*" *(Matthew 21:13)*. Is your house continually filled with positive, uplifting, encouraging, faith-filled words, prayer and praise?

STORY - Do Demons Look At Your Neighbor's House And Say?

Look at that house over there. Hey our demonic brothers are fleeing from that house. I thought we possessed that home and everyone in it. That house had an alcoholic father living there, his wife was depressed and suicidal and all their kids were rebellious and destructive. We owned that house...WHAT HAPPENED!

Hey look at that, there are angels at the four corners of their property. But no one in that house is a Christian, what happened? Wait listen to that, there are prayers going up on their behalf from their neighbors. I don't understand what is being said, but I can't refuse the power of THAT NAME! There is no way to get into their house. It is completely covered in his protective power. According to *that name,* we have to surrender that home, at least until we're invited back again. Let's get out of here! Let's go find a house that has no power or authority surrounding it.

This is not a made up story. I'm sure you know people who are in similar situations. **Your prayer life is how God's presence, love and power is going to touch this planet. Don't ever underestimate the power of prayer. Just as God's spirit has changed you, your prayers can change this world. Your mouth changes the world every time you speak.** Here is a scripture from God spoken through his prophet Isaiah:

Is my ear too dull to hear your prayer?
Are my arms to short to reach down and touch your life? Isaiah 59:1
I tell you the truth, even before you speak, I have already
heard, answered you and touched you. Isaiah 65:24

The message of the bible is that God loves us and he speaks to us constantly. He desires to have a relationship with us and he wants to hear from us. He has everything you need to complete you and live a life that is abundantly overflowing with him (II Peter 1:3). When God touches us, he completely heals everything about us, physically, mentally, emotionally and spiritually. He heals our soul and he even heals the ground that we walk on (II Chronicles 7:14). Go to the nearest window, open it and yell:

You're not allowed in my house any more Devil!

Hopefully your neighbors aren't outside the window when you yell this, but even if they are…SO WHAT! You're on a mission. Your actions in the natural realm will cause a supernatural campaign to begin on your behalf. That's what Christians and churches are lacking, PUTTING THEIR FAITH INTO ACTION! Giving their faith substance and making it clearly evident for all to see. Hebrews 11:1

The bible tells us that all authority has been given to Christ Jesus. It tells us that we are more than conquers. Jesus tells us, *"Do not be afraid of the world, for I have overcome the world" (John 16:33).* He tells us this so we'll start acting like overcomers. We need to pull out those dusty and rusty spiritual weapons and use them. The bible gives us hundreds of scriptures that give us position, boldness, wisdom, freedom, rest, power and authority to conquer all the works of the enemy. These include; overcoming the world, destroying strongholds, casting out demons, sharing the gospel message, healing the broken hearted, lifting burdens off people, breaking lifelong bondages and commanding healing to manifest. **God has supernaturally equipped us to be ministers of reconciliation. II Corinthians 5:18**

It's time to lay aside our mundane religious activities and do the things Christ commanded us to do. He wouldn't have TOLD us to do them if he had not EQUIPPED us to do them. If you're IN CHRIST, born-again and spirit-filled, then regardless of how you feel... God has equipped you in your spirit to go and do these things.

I remember the first time I prayed for someone, I laid hands on them and they received their healing right there in front of me! It was unbelievable, marvelous, phenomenal and exhilarating, all at the same time. It was also humbling and overwhelming. I knew I was right where I needed to be, right in the middle of God's work. I've been a husband, a father and an architect. I'm also an inventor, a carpenter, an engineer and a wood/metal fabricator. I've done a lot of things that were great in life, but I had never been a channel for God to work through until that moment. That moment in my life trumped everything I had ever accomplished. God's miracle working power manifested itself in someone's life and I was the channel for that power to flow through. I don't think I could possibly describe that experience to you with words. You're going to have to get an experience with the word of God for yourself to understand it.

When you know you are doing exactly what God wants you to do...then there is no other thing you could possibly do with your life that would be more satisfying.

SPIRITUAL VISION - Surrounded By Angels

One time, during praise and worship at my church, I found myself just getting lost in worship. Just then, it was as though a curtain had been drawn back and I could see into the supernatural world. I saw a dark shadowy figure right next to me and I knew it was some kind of demonic being. I hadn't been going through any kind of trials or temptations lately. So what was this all about?

Then an angelic figure came down in front of me and the demonic figure leaped toward the angel and they fought, right there in front of me. The angel had a spear or staff that they were both wrestling with. Then the angel looked RIGHT AT ME! I remember it so vividly. He looked right into my eyes, like he was about to say something, but he didn't. Then he quickly left taking the demon with him. Immediately two other angels came and stood on each side of me. They continually looked around every where, like they were expecting others to come. Then this supernatural vision was gone…it was over…or maybe it had only just begun.

WOW! What had just happened! This isn't something that happens to people often. It's not something you can share with everyone. I didn't want to be classified as weird or spiritually out in space. But I couldn't deny what was just revealed to me. I've shared this story with a few people I knew I could trust and do you know what these spirit-filled people said to me? They said they had many similar experiences also and then they began sharing the details with me. So I know there are many others out there just like me, who have experienced these brief visions into the supernatural world. God wants to speak to us. He wants to reveal things to us. The question is….are you ready for that kind of information?

Because you have made the Lord your resting place, no evil will overcome you, neither will any plague come to your house. For the angels of the Lord will stand guard over you. They will surround you in every direction so that nothing will harm you. Psalm 91:9-13

The angels of the Lord stand guard over the children of God and protect them. Psalm 34:7

For some reason, God had allowed me to see what was happening in the spiritual realm. Wow! Awesome! Thank you Lord! A spiritual battle in my life had just taken place and God allowed me to see it vividly in another dimension. I could have just dismissed the whole event as silly and that I was just making it all up in my head. I could have been embarrassment about it and never told anyone. But I knew it was God showing me he was protecting me and I am truly thankful for that. Can God trust you with that kind of information? Do you want more of God's supernatural gifts operating in your life? **Are you so connected to this physical world through your five senses that you can't leave it for a moment and operate in faith? Are you afraid God will have you do something weird or say something embarrassing? Are you so concerned about what other people think**

that faith has a hard time breaking through your emotional barrier?

God has already given every born-again Christian his power, his spirit, his faith, his continual presence, his anointing and his blessings. We have God's complete fullness and power on the inside of us (Ephesians 3:19 & 20). We just need to understand all those awesome truths that are present in our born-again spirit, come into agreement with that truth in our minds and finally operate by those laws of faith through our words, attitude, emotions and actions.

God knew I would understand and take that experience seriously. That's why I'm writing this book, to encourage you that you can know beyond any doubt that God wants to meet with you everyday and be an active participant in everything you do. God speaks to people all the time. God is pursuing after you! Don't ignore his prompting when he speaks to you. Don't say, "That's not real, that's just me making up stuff in my head. God would never share something like that with me."

God is not a made up fairy tale.
He's real and wants to be the most important part of your life.
Allow God to reveal himself to you in a greater way today.

Don't ever under estimate the power of prayer, praise, worship, bible reading and meditating on scriptures. Apply the word of God to your life in everyday situations. Pray in your prayer closet and together in groups. Intercede for each other in prayer and lay hands on one another. Take and receive communion and anoint one another with oil. Step out in faith and speak what the Holy Spirit wants you to say. These are all SPIRITUAL POINTS OF CONTACT that literally pierce into the spiritual realm around us. Every natural action the bible gives us to do, creates a ripple effect in the spiritual realm. When these two realms collide, then that's when God's glory manifests itself before us. All these spiritual actions in the physical realm have tremendous supernatural implications in the spirit realm. Your prayers may seem like your only throwing a stone in a pond, then it disappears and is gone, but the ripple effect can reach all the way across the pond and touch every edge of shore along the waters edge. **Your prayers can reach all the way across Heaven and touch every situation in your life. Your stone throw of a prayer causes mighty waves to spill over from the supernatural realm and flood into this physical world.**

This is not "PATTY CAKE CHRISTIANITY". We are surrounded by a real spiritual war, where battles are fought and prisoners are being taken and held captive. The battle lines have been draw by God, his angels, Satan and his demons. Soldiers are being trained and positioned. Are you ready for the fight of your life? Let's get serious about proclaiming the gospel message of the Lord Jesus Christ, saving the lost and setting captives free through the blood of Jesus.

The demons are completely united in their evil mission. They use their tactics effectively and they work together to accomplish them. Remember in Matthew 5:10 when a demon told Jesus, *"We are a legion of demons and there are many of us."* **God's power can be neutralized by Christians who are argumentative, offended and divided. We need to stop bickering and battling between churches, church members and denominations and we need to unite together like a mighty army does.**

How would you like to be charging toward the battle with your comrades, ready to fight, ready to defeat the enemy and tear down strongholds; you're approaching the battle line swiftly; you can see into your enemy's eyes and you're ready to strike. Then you notice most of your war party has stopped charging forward or maybe even worse, RETREATED! What about the battle! Instead your comrades have picked up the TV remote and will now spend the next four hours mindlessly channel surfing for something to watch. **Folks, we spend an enormous amount of time entertaining ourselves. We pamper our flesh with everything the world has to offer by over-eating, over-sleeping and over-indulging in every aspect of our lives.**

Can you imagine how many thousands of hours we've spent watching TV, but our prayer lives can be measured in minutes. We need to understand that this war we're in the middle of is very real and we need to take it seriously. The times are desperate and critical, we need to sharpen our weapons with the word of God, put on our supernatural armor and listen to the Holy Spirit's voice so we can improve our aim. The language of the world is cursing, complaining, gossiping and bickering. People have become overworked, frustrated, hateful, arrogant and selfish. If people would just reach out to God and take hold of this peace he has to offer them, then they would be able to finally rest.

During World War II, sixty German soldiers surrendered to one American soldier. The Germans were tired, hungry and they had little ammunition. One American soldier crept behind enemy lines and into the German trenches and began shooting them one by one until they surrendered. Sixty German soldiers surrendered to one man, his name was Audie Murphy. He was the most decorated U.S. combat soldier of World War II. Among his thirty three awards and decorations was the Medal of Honor, the highest military award for bravery that can be given to any individual in the United States of America. Hollywood was so impressed by his heroic efforts that they made many movies (which he starred in) about his many heroic battlefield experiences.

Doesn't the church do the same thing? They throw down their weapons and give up. Their bayonets are never thrust forward and bullets stay in guns that are never fired. **They are spiritually starving because they never eat the bread of God's word. They don't take up the full armor of God to protect themselves and they become seriously vulnerable, captured by the enemy or even fatally wounded. The enemy has hypnotized people into thinking that their faith in God is not that important. They've been lead to believe that it should be pursued occasionally like a hobby they're slightly interested in.** If this is the way you think then you've been deceived. You've been captured by the enemy. He has tricked you into walking right into his invisible spiritual prison. Has the enemy lulled you into a supernatural sleep so that you've become lazy and ineffective in resisting him?

The weapons that we fight with have divine power to demolish supernatural strongholds. We can demolish everything that's against the truth of God, and take every thought captive and make it surrender to that truth. II Corinthians 10:3-5

THE BATTLE FOR YOUR MIND
... we have the mind of Christ. I Corinthians 2:16

What are you filling your mind with, the things of God or with everything this world has to offer? Something is going to capture your attention. Our minds aren't programmed to just remain idle. Try to shut your mind down for just one minute and think of nothing. Try really hard and see if you can think of absolutely nothing for one full minute. It's much more difficult than you think. Thoughts seem to just drift into your head from everywhere. Even when you're asleep your mind doesn't rest, thoughts continually fill your subconscious. That's why we should never let down our guard. Just as a soldier would put on a steel helmet to protect their head during a battle, we are to protect our thought life from the world and the enemy by saturating it with God's truth.

Shield yourself with God's supernatural impenetrable armor
so you can deflect the lies and deceptions from the enemy
that try to infiltrate your mind. Ephesians 6:11 & 16

The battlefield is in your mind. I'm not saying it's all in an imaginary realm in your head and not real. It's a very real supernatural battle that's taking place all around us. **Your thoughts about life, priorities, other people, yourself, sin, Heaven, your savior, God, love, forgiveness, your purpose, salvation and evil; will determine how hard you fight in this battle.** What we think about and meditate on influences our beliefs and actions.

The Devil pursues our thought life relentlessly. He generously offers negative, selfish, prideful, lustful, evil thinking to everyone who will listen. **Just give him one minute of your thought life and he will destroy you.** He even gives Christians plenty of opportunities to be self-righteous, unforgiving, hateful, condemning and judgmental. He loves for people to cover themselves with a robe of self-righteousness. He offers wrong twisted thinking to everyone and when people nurse these thoughts long enough they will act on them. We can't stop these evil thoughts from coming into our mind. Satan will never stop whispering into your ear and twisting the truth. But what we do with those thoughts is what is so vitally important. Don't feed and nurture those evil thoughts with your valuable time and energy.

Entertaining sin is like putting a needle next to a magnet. The closer you put the needle to the magnet the stronger the force is between the two. There is a thin area between the magnet and the needle that I'm going to call the COLLAPSE ZONE. That's the area where the metal you're holding jumps to the magnet beyond your control. That's how sin works. It will capture your complete attention if you allow it. Don't try to get as close as you can to sin without falling into it. Soon you'll be in the COLLAPSE ZONE. Don't wander down that path in your thought life. Don't surrender your mind to it, because sin will take you places you never wanted to go.

Each person is tempted (when they're dragged away and enticed in their thought life) *by their own evil desires* (the power of sin). *Then after the desire has conceived, it gives birth to sin and sin when it is full-grown gives birth to death. James 1:14 & 15*

The devil knows if he can control your thought life your emotions and actions will soon follow. Most well seasoned Christians know they're not allowed to meditate on every thought they have. We are supposed to take every thought captive to the obedience of Christ.

Prepare your minds for action. I Peter 1:13

We prepare our minds when we read, learn,
understand and meditate on the truth in God's word.

When they refused to retain God in their knowledge, God gave them over to a reprobate mind (a mind that continually surrenders to evil thoughts) *and they began doing things that should have never been done before the eyes of God. Romans 1:28*

Be particular of the thoughts you think. Our thought life needs to come into alignment with the word of God all throughout the day. Allow the Holy Spirit to filter and influence your thought life. The bible says that we have the mind of Christ (I Corinthians 2:16). Jesus was perfect and we will never be perfect in our actions, but we should at least be headed in that general direction, not the opposite direction. **In God's eyes he already sees us as perfect, holy and righteous. IS GOD BLIND? No, he's looking at our *new nature*. He's looking at our born-again spirit within us.** You can't see it, but you can learn about it in the bible. Our new nature gives us a new identity, new purpose, new desires and a new destiny. As we renew our mind our thoughts and actions will begin change and align with our new identity.

A crowd soon gathered around Jesus, because they wanted to see for themselves what had happened. They saw the man who had been possessed by demons sitting quietly at Jesus' feet, clothed and in his right mind. Then those who had seen what happened told the others how the demon possessed man had been healed. Luke 8:35-36

Was the demon healed? No! Was the demon cleansed? No! The man was cleansed and healed. The demon was cast out. We need to cast out some of those thoughts and imaginations we have in our minds and we need to replace them with the truth of God's word. **Some of the thoughts we have aren't worth two seconds of our time, yet we entertain them for hours, days, weeks and even years.**

Reading about Jesus' life and character, his teachings, the miracles he did, what he said and why he said it, gives us a bench mark for truth in our lives. You can't stop a garden from getting weeds in it, but you can pull the weeds up and water the good plants. It's the same with your mind. Don't let the weeds take over and choke out what God is trying to accomplish in your life.

Christians must have a daily intake of the word of God. That's how you fill your mind with the right thoughts about God's nature and your new nature. If you will fill your mind with the truth, then when a lie comes to you, you can easily recognize it and dismiss it. I love that scripture in Hebrews 4:12 that says, *"The word of God judges the thoughts and attitudes of our heart."* The world is full of evil, restlessness and lies, but God's word is full of life, love, peace and truth. By reading the truth of God's word we can recognize the traps the enemy has placed before us.

Is your mind a continual haven for jealousy and angry thoughts?
Do you secretly robe yourself in a judgmental spirit of pride?
Are lust and debauchery playmates in your imagination?

Jesus called people hypocrites who looked righteous by their actions, but their thought lives, motives and hearts were far from God. Jesus knew the motives within their hearts. **God wants us reading his word because a proper interpretation of the truth transforms our minds (Romans 12:2). You see *what* you do is important, but *why* you do what you do is even more important. When we intertwine the truth of God's word around our spirit, it changes the WHO, WHAT and WHY in us. The truth changes us at the core of our being. The truth changes the reason for everything we do in life.**

The TRUTH always changes people and reveals to them everything they need to know about living an abundant, thriving, supernatural life. The truth of God's word brings us to a phenomenal revelation and realization of who we are IN CHRIST. We are born-again, blood-bought, fire-baptized, fully armored, outrageously loved, spirit-filled, completely and thoroughly forgiven children of the KING.

TRANSFORMED BY TRUTH

I am an ambassador for Christ. II Corinthians 5:20
I am the apple of God's eye. Zechariah 2:8
I am clay in the potter's hands. Jeremiah 18:6
I have redeemed you, I have called you by name
and you are mine. Isaiah 43:1
I am alive in Christ and complete in him. Colossians 2:10 & 13
I have been chosen by God, he has called me out of
darkness and into his wonderful light. I Peter 2:9
I am a conqueror in Christ Jesus and can never
be separated by the love of God. Romans 8:37
I have been brought close to God and quickened in my spirit. I Ptr. 3:18
I have been lavished with wisdom and understanding
about God's grace towards me. Ephesians 1:7 & 8
I have continual access to God because I am his child. Ephesians 2:19
I am inseparable from God's love. Romans 8:35
I am a light in this dark world. Acts 13:47
I am shielded by God's power. I Peter 1:5
I am God's handiwork. Ephesians 2:10
I have been searched for, sought after and found by God. Luke 19:10
It was God's pleasure to adopt me as his child. Ephesians 1:5
I am a brand new creation in Christ,
the old me is gone and the new supernatural me
is here to stay forever. II Corinthians 5:17
I have been purged from all guilt and condemnation. Rom 8:1,Heb 9:14
I please God and he delights and rejoices in me. Psalm 149:4
My faith can move mountains. Mark 11:22
I am completely surrounded, filled and
overwhelmed by the love of God. John 3:16
I can never be alone or forsaken by God,
because he lives inside me. Hebrews 13:5
The creator of the universe listens to me. I John 5:14
I have God's complete protection covering me. Psalm 91:14
My spirit is a temple where God lives. I Corinthians 3:16
I shine the light of God's glory as I express Christ's
truth in my words and actions. II Corinthians 3:18

compiled by Eric Johnson

This information is adapted from the I AM bookmarker found in
The God Still Speaks To Us Collection.

If you allow the truth about you to transform your mind it will reveal to you <u>WHO</u> you are in Christ. It will change <u>WHAT</u> the Holy spirit does through you and it will reveal to you at the core of your heart <u>WHY</u> God loves you so much.

This war between God and Satan, Heaven and Hell, angels and demons, truth and deception, good and evil, darkness and light will be fought in the spirit realm, which is manipulated by our belief system.

The bible tells us to:

Cast down imaginations and everything that sets itself up against God's true nature. II Corinthians 10:5

We have the mind of Christ and we need to focus our minds on heavenly truths...not on worldly cares. Colossians 3:2

God will keep you in perfect peace when your mind is focused on him. Isaiah 26:3

Those who live according to the sinful nature have their minds set on what their old nature desired. But those who live according to spiritual truth think about what God has deposited in their new born-again spirit. The mind focused on sin will inevitably bring destruction and depression into your life, but the mind influenced by the Spirit is full of LIFE, TRUTH and PEACE. The sinful mind is in direct opposition to God. It does not submit to God's nature. Romans 8:5-8

Love the Lord with all your heart, with all your soul and with all your mind. Matthew 22:37

Look at what happened in the story about David and Bathsheba in the Old Testament Book of II Samuel 11. David looked and saw a beautiful woman. Then he turned back a second time to look at her more intently. This time his thoughts turned to lust and desire. Then he had to have her for himself and he sinned against God. He ended up committing adultery, lying, stealing and finally murdering the woman's husband Uriah. His initial sinful thoughts took him much further than he ever planned on going. Looking at a beautiful woman is not a sin, however, if you allow the enemy to pervert your thoughts, that's when people surrender to the external power of sin as it's mixed with their carnal desires.

The word perversion means to use something for a different purpose than it was originally designed for. I'm a carpenter, but if I take a screwdriver and use it as a pry-bar or a chisel, then I have perverted that tool. I'm not using it for the purpose it was originally designed for, I'm misusing it. I took that tool and used it outside of the boundaries which the creator designed it for.

God makes the floors of Heaven out of precious gold. He gave gold to the human race to use, fabricate and enjoy. We see its beauty and fashion jewelry and other marvelous things from it. What have people done throughout the ages for gold? They have fought and cheated others out of it, stolen it and even murdered for it. People have killed other people over a piece of ore found in the dirt. See how we pervert God's goodness. He gave us gold to enjoy, but we pervert it and people have broken many of God's laws to possess it. The gold isn't evil; it's the perverted desire for it that's evil.

Eating the apple from the tree in the Garden of Eden really wasn't all that bad a thing to do. I mean all Adam and Eve did was have a snack. But it was their disobedience that was so horrific. They went against their creator's words. They set themselves against God's truth and his perfect design of things. When people go against what God commands them to do they are on dangerous ground. If people would simply eat a piece of fruit to disobey God, then they will cheat on their taxes, steal when no one is looking, kill for gold, steal another person spouse or whatever else they desire. It's that spirit of sin in people that's so ugly to God. **Satan's message to the world is to take what God has created and pervert it, take it outside of the boundaries which God created specifically for it. Fortunately for mankind, Jesus will crucify that spirit of sin in them if they will let him. Lay your sin before him, surrender it to him and walk away from it completely free from your *old nature.***

If you're a born-again Christian you are a brand new creation IN CHRIST. Your actions and thoughts are in the process of being renewed daily as you read the bible and listen to the Holy Spirit. You have a new, alive, divine spirit in you. Your spirit leaps when you think of the goodness of God and when you read the truth found in his word. The bible is not only God's road map that leads us to salvation and Heaven, but it also shows us God's nature at its deepest level.

One time I was driving down a road that I normally don't travel. It was a beautiful, sunny, autumn, October day in Michigan. The trees were absolutely gorgeous and the leaves were slowly falling to the ground. The colors were magnificent, bright red with vibrant oranges and yellows. The sun illuminated the colors in every leaf. This entire view of the beauty of God's creation just overwhelmed me. I just started crying when I realized how God has perfectly designed everything. **When God looks at us he says, "I made them, they're mine. I created them specifically for me." The only way you will ever find purpose and meaning in this life is to make a connection with your designer and creator. God designed people and this earth for his pleasure, glory and companionship.**

Satan is all about perverting what God created. Satan lies to us about our character, identity, forgiveness, Heaven, our destiny and purpose. He tries to steal our time and keep us so busy that we never have the opportunity to discover God in his complete dimension.

Christians need to guard their minds against the devil's schemes, because any of us are capable of any kind of sin at anytime. Our first line of defense is our thought life. If we allow the lies of the enemy to penetrate into our mind, the chances of stopping him will significantly decrease.

STORY - A Bag Full Of Candy Bars

A woman had a severe fetish for chocolate candy bars and many times she would eat an entire bag at one sitting. One day she vowed to stop and never eat those candy bars ever again. While watching TV that same day she saw an advertisement for them. The commercial made them look so good. She was beginning to get hungry so she went to the refrigerator and noticed she was getting low on milk, so she went to the store to get some. Wouldn't you know it, there were some chocolate candy bars on an end cap right in front of her, and they were ON SALE! She felt that desire for them come over her and had to force herself to walk away. As she was getting some milk she saw a little boy eating a chocolate candy bar. She backed away from him and went down another aisle. At the end of that aisle was a nice old lady who had individually cut sample pieces of a new brand of dark chocolate candy bars. The woman handed her a sample and she could smell them and saw how good they looked. She rudely refused the sample and thought, "I've got to get out of this store." As she was checking out, there they were again right in front of her. She bought the milk and a whole bag of candy bars, then she ate the entire bag out in the car and drank the milk right out of the jug.

Our five senses are our worst enemy when it comes to temptation. Immediately our receptors process the information in our minds and command us to react. Throughout this story there were five times where the woman was tempted. The temptation came when she saw, smelled and meditated on those candy bars. The battle line in her mind had been penetrated. She positioned herself to fail by going to the market. Another bad strategy was telling herself over and over,

> "Don't think about those candy bars...
> don't think about those candy bars...
> don't think about those candy bars,"

...was essentially forcing her to think about candy bars ALL THE TIME. She had the best intentions, but she didn't have a battle plan in place when the temptation came.

Did you know it's impossible to be tempted by something if you refuse to think about it? Christians are not allowed to meditate on every thought they have. Christians need to eject some of the thoughts they're thinking. Some of those thoughts don't belong anywhere near your precious mind.

WE'VE GOT THE ENEMY'S PLAYBOOK

Satan's battle plan in this war is to destroy us (God's creation). Specifically it is to draw us away from God's word (which is the truth about his nature), thwart God's purpose in our lives and to deny God his rightful glory and honor. The enemy creeps in so slow it doesn't even seem like he's involved in your life. He always wants to remain camouflaged and concealed so most of the world believes that he doesn't even exist. When that happens he can manipulate and influence people's lives freely without suspicion or resistance.

> *Satan leads the whole world astray. Revelation 12:9*
> *The whole world has allowed themselves to be*
> *influenced and controlled by the evil one. I John 5:19*

> *Satan hates the truth and there is never any truth associated with*
> *the words he speaks. When he lies he is consistent with his*
> *character, because he is the father of lies. John 8:44*

He's a liar, a deceiver, he's crafty. He's a seducer and a master debater. He only wants to give you the desires of your heart. YES, THE EVIL DESIRES! Satan's been deceiving people since the beginning of time and he's a master at it. **He can get a person to rationalize just about any of their actions.** If Adam and Eve were deceived in a perfect garden, then you know the enemy has a whole arsenal of resources in this fallen world.

Satan is not afraid of you at all. In fact he laughs at you and your feeble religious attempts to overcome him. Soon you'll become disillusioned and wonder why does God seem to be so far away? Are fear and frustration your constant companions throughout the day? God has given us a list of the things that Satan really fears.

WHAT DOES SATAN GET?

He gets <u>nervous</u> when we read our bibles.

He gets <u>mad</u> when we start believing and speaking the truth of God's word.

He gets <u>evicted</u> when we are filled with the Holy Spirit.

He gets <u>anxious</u> when our desires align with God's will.

He gets <u>tortured</u> when we praise and worship our Lord.

He gets <u>frightened</u> when we share our testimony with others.

He gets <u>defeated</u> when we talk about the blood of Jesus.

He gets <u>depressed</u> when we know the joy of the Lord is our strength.

Won't you join me in giving Satan what he deserves? Send him a special delivery package today, straight from you to him, so that he finally gets what's coming to him.

Dear Satan

Just a quick note to let you know, I will not accept anymore of your lies…because I have heard the truth. There will be no more walking in darkness…for I have seen a great light. I no longer entertain spirits that are evil; the spirit in me now brings me eternal life, peace and hope. What I use to laugh at and enjoy, I now have repented of. My cursing has changed into a song of salvation. My mind used to be a dumping ground for you, but now it's a thriving garden that glorifies God. You've had your last dance with me because I have found someone else, his name is Jesus Christ the Messiah. He's my King and my Lord.

DISTRACTED CHRISTIANS

Distracting Christians is one of the enemy's prime objectives. Satan is clever at twisting your thoughts, zapping your energy and stealing your time. He uses every means necessary in this world to accomplish this. You see if a Christian person is busy reading a magazine, then they're not reading God's word. If a saint of God is watching TV, then they're not connecting with God's love at a deeper level. If a born-again believer is spending the entire evening browsing the internet, then they're not forming a close, supernatural bond between them and their creator. None of these activities are evil or sinful but when they continually consume our time and there is nothing left for God at the end of the day, then we need to reprioritize our life. God has given us a beautiful gift of one thousand four hundred and forty minutes in a day. Let's use them like they are our last minutes here on earth.

If you're to busy for God...then you're just too busy.

I knew a person who loved to play softball so much that he played it four days a week on different leagues. He played from 6:00 PM to 11:30 PM at night. He loved it so much, it was all he thought about or talked about. I'm not saying a Christian can't love softball, sports, hobbies or other activities. God has given us many abilities to glorify him with and we can glorify God in all these activities...but are we? When these things supersede our passion for God then we can position ourselves for a long distance relationship. Does God come in third or eighth place at the end of your day? Does he come in last place everyday? God says in his word:

My people have forsaken me for so many days and I miss them deeply.
Jeremiah 2:32

Anything you schedule into your life in place of time with God can distract you from the most important encounter you could ever have with him. That meeting with God could be the very day he reveals how valuable you are to him or how treasured you are. That time with God could change your direction and purpose for the rest of your life.

What if I told you to list five people who you could meet with, regardless of how important, powerful or famous they were? I will arrange it so you could meet with any five people of your choice. Would God's name be on that list? Shouldn't a personal one on one meeting with God be more important than anything or anyone else? Would his name be in all five slots on your list? The great thing is, I don't need to schedule a meeting with you and God. He's always pursuing after us relentlessly and whispering into our ear, *"Here I am, I stand at the door and knock. If anyone opens the door, then I will come in and be with them" (Revelations 3:20).* God is always patiently waiting for us to fellowship with him.

I suggest beginning your day with God. Your day will take on a new direction, with greater joy, purpose and passion. Even if nothing else significant happens that day, you began your day in the best way you could, by pursuing and glorifying God. I don't know what God specifically has planned for you for the rest of your life; but if you will spend time with God and glorify him in everything you do, then that would fulfill your purpose. Here are two different prayers, which one do you want to pray?

THE MORNING PRAYER:

Good morning Lord! I love you and I know that you love me. I'm excited about celebrating life together with you today. I can't wait to understand your nature at a deeper level. I would just like to take a moment to exalt your name Lord. Accept my worship and praise as a genuine thanksgiving offering from my heart. Today I would like to invite you into every area of my life. Teach me, direct me and guide me. I want your Holy Spirit to refine my attitude, guard my words and saturate my thoughts. May the light of Christ shine from within me. In Jesus name…Amen.

LATE EVENING PRAYER:

Lord I'm sorry, I failed today. I sinned in my thoughts, words and deeds. Anger and unrest were my constant companions today. Strife met me at every crossroad. I needed your peace but I was to busy to release it and enjoy it. I'm sorry Lord.

Which prayer do you want to say each and everyday? We need to start the day out right. We can get extremely busy so quickly. The acronym for busy is:

Being   Under   Satan's   Yoke.

Let's examine what happens to our busy minds as they are bombarded all week long by this fast paced world we live in. Let's take a look at what a busy mind does during a regular Sunday morning worship service. During worship service many people are thinking about what restaurant they are going to eat at after church. During worship service they're supposed to be thinking of the goodness of God. Instead they're thinking about the goodness of that prime rib or the seafood buffet they will soon be enjoying when they get out of church. Worshiping God is not about singing three songs on Sunday morning and going home and it's over. It's a complete life style change, similar to how we love and forgive people. It's apart of who we are. The desire to continuously worship God is deep within our new nature.

People's minds have become so busy that they can't worship God from their spirit. This is because we have entirely too many spectators (busy, carnal and distracted minds) in our churches today. Many people are looking around to see what everyone else is doing, or what they're wearing. Many Christians are distracted by who is with whom or who walked in late and who's leaving early. Get your eyes off other people and focus on the one you're supposed to be worshiping. If you're not interested in praising God on Sunday during worship service, then more than likely you're not praising and glorifying God throughout the week either.

Many people are distracted and pre-occupied with everything this life has to offer. Satan will always try to capitalize on those attributes within us. Satan wants us to be distracted during worship service with all the details of life that don't really matter. If you are distracted by people during worship service then I can solve that problem for you. Move to the front row or maybe just close your eyes during the worship service. You might say, I'm just not comfortable in the front row. Well, worship isn't about you and how comfortable you are. It's about God and how worthy he is of our praise. You might say, "Well my family has always sat on the right side, fourteen rows from the front for the past fifteen years." Here is some wisdom for you. You're at church; they're all your brothers and sisters IN CHRIST. Besides, God might be trying to grow you out of that fourteenth row on the right to a new level in your faith. You could be one row away from a break-through in your life. It's time to move forward.

Be open to the Holy Spirits prompting on <u>where to sit in church.</u>
Be open to the Holy Spirits leading on <u>how to worship.</u>
Be open to the Holy Spirits direction on <u>how to pray</u>.
Be open to the Holy Spirit on <u>when to give</u> out of your abundance.
Be open to the Holy Spirit on <u>how to treat people</u>.
Be open to the Holy Spirit about <u>what to think, say and do.</u>

The Spirit of God lives on the inside of you. He always has the right answers to every question that confronts you in life. Listen to his voice from within you. He wants to slow your life down so you're not so busy and distracted. Even if this book is keeping you from spending time with God, then put it down and go to him, seek his face, let him reveal his nature to you in a deeper way. Make sure you do come back and continue reading because this book has information in it God wants people to know. I'm not interested in writing a book just so I can say that I'm a published author. I didn't sit down to even write a book, I just started writing down everything that God has done in my life and eventually it filled all these pages.

All of us should be able to write a book on how faithful God is and about his unwavering love for us. We should be able to fill the pages with the miracles God has done for us, the hope that we have in him and the people he has saved in our families and neighborhoods. The only way we are ever going to fill and entire book with all that information is by clearly understanding what Christ has accomplished for us and submitting to what he wants to do through us. **Lay down that busy, distracted, whirlwind life of yours. Set aside some time for the most important relationship in your life…YOU AND GOD.**

DOUBTING GOD'S WORD

Reading God's word gives us great insight about the Devil's lies, traps and agenda. Can you imagine having the opposing teams secret play book in front of you? You could find out the plays they're going to try to run and immediately counter act them. When you have the enemies play book you can run circles around them. Remember the Devil knows God's play book also. He knows what God has spoken. He hates it, he twists it and he wants you to doubt it. The devil even tried to twist the truth when he was talking to Jesus (Matthew 4). The good thing is God's plays trump the enemy's plays. God's play book (THE BIBLE) defeats the enemy every single time and Satan knows it. Satan's plan is to keep us so busy that we never have time to read the bible. He doesn't want you to understand the truth, believe God's word and speak it out of your mouth. **Satan is continually trying to deceive people about the truth in God's word and he's been very successful at his mission.**

A huge lie in THE ENEMY'S PLAY BOOK would say, "GET THEM TO DOUBT GOD'S WORD!" Satan has many tools in his arsenal to use against us and DOUBTING GOD'S WORD is one of the most destructive tools he uses. These are some lies about the bible that the enemy has planted in people's minds. I have heard all these deceptions when discussing the bible with others.

Satan's Deceptions About The Bible:

Is that really what that means? Did God mean exactly that?
There are many different opinions and viewpoints about the bible.
Christians can't even agree with each other about the bible,
look at all the different denominations there are.
The Bible was for the people who lived thousands of years ago.
We live in a completely different time and culture today.
You'll drive yourself crazy trying to follow that book.
The Bible is simply man's opinion of God and
therefore the information in it could be wrong.
There are many contradictions and flaws in it.
It's a great piece of literature, but that's all it is.

Satan doesn't want you anywhere near the bible and investigating
the truth. He certainly doesn't want you reading, believing, speaking,
shouting and standing on the promises in God's word. He knows those
deceptions will deter people from seeking the truth. **If the enemy can
steal God's word from your heart, then he can completely
neutralize you (Mathew 13:4). He fights so hard against it, because
it reveals his battle plan, his weaknesses and his destruction. God
wants us to READ, UNDERSTAND, BELIEVE, SPEAK, SHOUT,
SING, PRAY, HOPE IN and MEDITATE ON his truth. Satan
wants us to doubt, second guess and question God's word.** Because
if we do, then we'll doubt God's love, complete forgiveness, eternal
salvation, power, peace, anointing and healing. All these things were
accomplished for us on the cross through the Lord Jesus Christ. If Satan
can get you to doubt any of it, then you won't walk in the fullness of
what Jesus accomplished.

- If we doubt God's word, then we won't fight against our invading
  enemy, because we will feel ineffective.
- If we doubt God's word, we won't be able to pull down the
  strongholds of the enemy, because we really don't believe that we
  can.
- If we doubt God's word, we won't rise up against our enemy *in the
  name of Jesus*, because we don't understand the authority behind
  that name.

Do you see why the enemy tries to inject his lies into our mind? If
we believe him, then his evil can run wild and unchecked.

*Don't just depend on the daily bread you eat to nourish yourself,
but read from the word of God everyday to feed your spirit. Matt. 4:4*

*The bread that came down from Heaven is he who gave his life as a
ransom for the world. The disciples said, "Lord give us this bread",
and Jesus said to them, "I AM THE BREAD OF LIFE, anyone
who comes to me shall never hunger and anyone who believes
in me shall never thirst." John 6:33-35*

*Job said to God: Your words, your truth and your instructions
are more important than my daily bread. Job 23:12*

How's your spiritual diet? Are you eating the bread of life every chance you get? Are you eating three square meals a day? We need to feed our minds with the truth about our spirit just as much as we feed our body.

DIVIDE AND CONQUER:
Meditating on our differences divides us…celebrating our uniqueness unites us.

Another major strategy in THE ENEMY'S PLAY BOOK would explain how to divide and conquer people. Satan's main strategy of divide and conquer has never changed because we've always allowed it to be so destructive. Satan divides husbands and wives, brothers and sisters, bosses from employees, employees from companies, church members from church members and churches from pastors. We allow this strategy to be so easy for him to administer and it's very effective. He separated Adam and Eve from God in the Garden of Eden. He divides entire communities, countries and nations. Satan just puts a little plate of offense in front of us, with a little resentment on the side and a little unforgiveness sprinkled on top. Then we gobble it up and have a stomach ache for a month, a year or even worse…A LIFETIME! It all depends on how long you keep reordering that plate of bitterness. We need to push that plate aside and say, "NO THANKS!

God's great love is how we combat the DIVIDE AND CONQUER tactics of the enemy. So don't get upset or offended by people who don't know how to love others like you do. You have a tremendous advantage over them. Your heart has been touched by God and filled with his spirit. People, who aren't born-again, need to see, hear and feel God's love through the anointing you have radiating from you. They'll know you're different from everyone else they've ever met. God's love is designed to melt away the cold hard heart. His love can melt the heart of your greatest enemy. God's love hopes for the best in people. His love removes the dividing walls between people. Expressing God's love is what brings unity and peace to our communities.

You can love and forgive people to a certain degree, by operating in the physical realm where your five senses and emotions are accentuated. You may be able to forgive people for some minor offenses under you own power and will. **However, to love and forgive the way Jesus did, is going to require you to reach down into your spirit and draw the power of God out of the core of your *new nature*.** Peter proudly boasted to Jesus, "I could forgive others up to seven times a day." But Jesus told Peter, "No, how about up to seventy times seven a day." That's 490 times in one day! In Peter's emotional realm he could find it within himself to forgive up to seven times a day, but **Jesus wanted him to reach deep down into the core of his nature and forgive based on the divine power that's in him. Peter operated in the flesh quite often, so Jesus was trying to teach him how to be dominated by spiritual truths. The power in your spirit is unlimited in its ability to love and forgive.** The divide and conquer tactics of the enemy will have very little effect on you when we love and forgive others this way.

IDENTIFY YOUR ENEMY BEFORE YOU SHOOT
Let me give you a hint…it's SATAN.

<u>Your enemy is not:</u>

Your challenging family member.	A defiant co-worker.
Your frustrating neighbor.	The erratic driver in front of you.
A sales clerk with a bad attitude.	A strange church member.
Your pastor that you disagree with.	Your angry boss.

To kill a tree you need to put an axe to the root…not the fruit.

Although people do allow themselves to be used by Satan, he alone is the root cause of the attack. **Satan likes to work behind the scenes so we spend our time fighting against each other rather than fighting for each other.** Remember our fight is not against flesh and blood (each other) but against rulers and principalities of the enemy. Ephesians 6:12

All of Satan's tactics are designed to make you ineffective in releasing the kingdom of God from your spirit. If you're a born-again Christian, Satan has lost the first and major battle for your spirit. He is furious about that. HE HATES THAT! The second battle is for your mind and body. He can immobilize Christians through fear, intimidation, guilt, doubt, condemnation, depression, embarrassment, hate, unforgiveness and ignorance. If you're a Christian, then he's lost the battle for your spirit, but he certainly doesn't want to lose any other souls through your testimony, influence and prayers. He can no longer take your eternal home in Heaven away from you. But he can snatch that eternal life from within you that God wants you to experience here on earth. **Satan can keep you so busy, distracted, confused and divided that the eternal life that's in your spirit never bubbles over into the natural realm.**

Satan wants to rob you of your position, authority and power earned for you through Jesus Christ. Can he actually steal it from you? NO! But people do surrender their God given gifts to the enemy through doubt, fear, confusion and insecurity. Does God's love, power, authority and anointing lay dormant inside of you, undiscovered and never used?

As for me, I finally said enough is enough. I'm going forward IN CHRIST. I'm charging into the enemy's camp and taking back everything I've surrendered to him. Knowing the enemy's game plan will help you to extinguish any attempts he makes to gain ground and establish a foothold in your thought life. Understanding your enemy and his battle plan, will keep you focused on fighting him instead of fighting against each other. The enemy will bring a thought to your mind like:

You don't deserve to be spoken to that way by them.
Lash out at them.
Go tell someone else what that person said about you.
No one likes you.
Everyone is against you.
They're not worth your time and energy
and their certainly not worthy of your love.

Satan loves for us to retaliate against the offender to gain short term satisfaction. He's in the NOW business. He wants you to have your satisfaction NOW! He wants you to have your revenge NOW! He doesn't want you to think about the future consequences or repercussions for your thoughts, words and actions. Christians are always supposed to be heavenly minded long-term thinkers (Colossians 3:2). We are to look at the world through spiritual eye glasses. Always contemplate to yourself; if I say that, fall into that, join that, then what's it going to cost me later? Satan wants you to be self-centered, self-righteous, easily offended and to start judging everybody around you. He wants to slowly puff you up so you become a prideful haughty person. Those are the characteristics Satan had just before he was cast down from Heaven. If you're a born-again Christian, you are saved and on your way to Heaven. The enemy can't do anything about that, but don't let him immobilize you and make you ineffective for the kingdom of God right now while you're here on this earth.

Do not let any unwholesome talk come out of your mouth because an encouraging word may be desperately needed by that person. Positive faith-filled words are like medicine to the soul, so be a people builder and you will never have an unproductive day. Negative thoughts and words grieve the Holy Spirit that's in you. You have been sealed and set apart for righteous deeds. So get rid of that fighting spirit full of bitterness, rage, anger and every form of strife. Be kind and compassionate to one another, forgiving each other, just as through Christ, God forgave you. Ephesians 4:29-32

This is heavenly minded thinking.
This is others-centered thinking.
This is long-term thinking.
This is Christ-centered thinking.

If you're interested in extinguishing Satan's plan then never behave in a way that is contrary to Ephesians 4:29-32. Can you imagine the bountiful harvest you would have if you obeyed and applied that scripture to your life?

In Ephesians 6:10-20, the Apostle Paul tells us to *stand firm* four times. He tells us to pray always and to speak the word of God boldly. **When God sees that we are aligning ourselves with the truth of his word, then he gets excited. He knows we're about to experience the riches of his glory that he deposited in us and it will be unforgettable...because it's something that came from him. Ephesians 1:18**

Anyone who hungers and thirsts after righteousness will be filled.
Matthew 5:6

God is already in you, but we need to connect with God through a greater understanding of everything he has placed in us. Let me explain it this way. There are married couples out there who are completely disconnected from each other. They're supposed to be married, one flesh, one mind, one purpose with common desires. But you don't see that in their marriage. They're not connected or united in God's love. They have no common goals or dreams that they share with each other. They simply co-exist together. There might be a marriage license in their filing cabinet, but unconditional love is certainly not propelling their actions. They have totally disconnected themselves from each other. Any love or passion they had for each other dissipated a long time ago.

Are you connected with Christ or is your life disconnected from him? When you got saved the marriage license was written up, but how's your relationship with Jesus? Have you let the cares and distractions of this world come in and quench the fire? Has busyness stolen a lot from your relationship with him? START FRESH AND NEW TODAY! Understand that marriage between Christ and you by researching the bible and understanding his *true nature and your new nature.* Renew your mind with Christ's thoughts, his deep love for you and everything he has done for you. Let God heal your hurting heart. Make a declaration today that you'll begin a new, fervent, passionate, prayer life with open communication between you and God. Not so God will love you and bless you more, but so you'll understand his *true nature* and the *new nature* he's deposited in you. **Tell God that everywhere you go you want him right there with you; speaking to you in your spirit, prompting you with words and actions that glorify him.** He desires that with you and if you desire to know him better… THEN YOU WILL.

RELIGION

STORY – Sunday Morning Cynic

Many Sunday morning church families start out something like this. You get out of bed and the first thing you moan is, "I've got to go to church today." Then you get up and start getting ready. You think to yourself, "What am I going to wear? What are we going to eat after church? I hope brother and sister so-and-so aren't there this morning. THEY BUG ME! I hope that new person isn't there again, last week they sat in MY SEAT!" As you drive to church, you fight all the way there.

Next you think, "Ok, I'll walk through the doors and keep a smile on my face like everything is fine in my life. I don't need anything these people have. Where's the pastor? He'd better shake my hand or look at me and acknowledge me in some way. Last week my spouse gave money to this church. I should have a say in how things are ran around here."

When the praise music begins you think to yourself, "I AM NOT SINGING THIS SONG AND I AM CERTAINLY NOT GOING TO RAISE MY HANDS! This music is kind of slow for me, I like my music better. I don't like that song, it's too fast. Do they have to sing that one over and over like that? These people are too emotional for me. I forgot my earplugs, those worked really well last week. He'd better not preach long, ten minutes would be just fine with me. Why is my spouse giving me that look? I'm a good person compared to a lot of other people I know."

"How do I get out of here without shaking anyone's hand and acting like I care about them?" On the way home from church they say, "You know, the pastor didn't even come and find me to shake my hand!"

This is not a fictional story I've made up. I've heard all these many complaints from people. Church...why do we do the things we do? I guess there are as many different reasons as there are people. We should be doing the right things for the right reasons. How many times does this story *Sunday Morning Cynic,* happen at churches all over the world? I think that sometimes God must look at us, hang his head and sigh. I believe God wants to shake us and say, "WAKE UP! **Salvation is so much more than just going to church and trying to act like a Christian. I've deposited my presence and power in your born-again spirit. Stop trying to relate to me using your five senses and emotions. I'm a spiritual being, use your spirit to perceive and commune with me.**"

The one who received the seed that fell among the thorns is like a person who hears the word of God, but the worries and cares of this life and the deceitfulness of wealth, choke it out and make it unfruitful.
Matthew 13:22

When will people get tired of going through stale, dry, religious motions which have no point to them? Religion has no direct connection to the power of the gospel message.

They are darkened in their understanding and separated from the life of God because of the ignorance that's in them and they continually harden their hearts towards God. Ephesians 4:18

Many people honor me with their lips,
but their hearts are far from me. Matthew 15:8
They have a form of godliness but deny the truth,
power and the authority of the living God. II Timothy 3:5

Religion is about people trying to reach God through works,
rituals, their own goodness or behavior modifications.
Christianity is about God reaching out to people
through the sacrifice of his Son Jesus Christ.

You can put on a show for God, but he's not the least bit entertained by it. Many of the Pharisees that Jesus talked to in the gospels were a stiff necked, arrogant, prideful, haughty, sinful group of religious, self-righteous people. They got that way by misinterpreting scripture in the bible. They used God's holy word like a sledge hammer to beat people down. They used God's holy word to separate the so-called good people from the bad.

Religion is fake; it's not based on truth. Religious people believe that if they will just do enough for God then he will love them, he will accept them and he will fellowship with them. Religious people have their ritualistic, traditional duties that they perform to gain or maintain God's love, acceptance, forgiveness and favor. But the truth is Christ has already earned all this for us through his blood. Religious people are constantly trying to please God and maintain their right standing before him through their so-called *flawless performance.* Religion is like a balloon people inflate with their actions and works, or their own goodness and righteousness; this eventually reaches a point were it just explodes. You can only maintain that pace for so long then eventually you'll be frustrated, discouraged and burnt out. Religious people have been blinded by confused religious teachers. Religion positions people against each other. Trying to be or proclaiming that you're better than other people is a complete waste of time.

Religious people focus so much on *actions* that many times they forget about the phenomenal *transformation* that has taken place in their spirit. **The spirit of God that lives in every born-again Christian should be radically influencing our thoughts and motivating our actions.** The unsaved are not sinners because they sin. Their actions are a fruit of their nature. Unbelievers are sinners because of their inbred nature to sin. This is where confused religious people waste a lot of their time fighting against sin. Remember, Jesus has already fought sin and he won (Colossians 2:15). That truth should be saturating your life in an amazing way. We can only see a person's actions; we can't see their nature or spirit. **When a person becomes born-again in their spirit, they are made righteous before God. It's a character attribute of their new spirit. Whether or not righteous actions come flowing out of them is determined by having a clear revelation of who they are now that Christ is living in them.** This happens by reading about your new identity (in the bible), interpreting that information correctly, believing that truth about yourself and then surrendering to the Holy Spirit as he prompts you to release the glory of God into this world. The Holy Spirit's job is to establish us IN CHRIST.

People are sinners by birth and they can also become righteous by birth. The confusing part is Christians still sin and a person who is not born-again can display very righteous actions. **You can waste a lot of time trying to get people to change their actions. Churches have been doing that for thousands of years. We need to teach Christians that they have been made righteous (Ephesians 4:24). We are in complete right standing before God because of Christ's actions at the cross (I Peter 3:18).** Most Christians don't believe that God is at peace with them, therefore they always feel they have to be doing something to please him. When God looks at us, he sees Christ's righteousness all over us. Christians can't see it because it's in their spirit, but they can read that truth about themselves in God's word and begin to believe it in a greater way. As you begin to believe that truth then God's righteousness will shine from within you like the mid-day sun (Matthew 13:43). Our actions are extremely important and as we learn about what God has deposited in our new born-again spirit, then our actions will come into alignment with all these truths with in us.

Jesus said to the chief priest and the elders, "I tell you the truth, the tax collectors and the prostitutes are entering the kingdom of God ahead of you. John The Baptist came to show you THE WAY of righteousness and you did not believe him, but the tax collectors and prostitutes did. Why didn't you repent and believe. Matthew 21:31 & 32

Prostitutes are entering the kingdom of Heaven before
the religious chief priest! Tax collectors are righteous and
justified before God and the elders of the priesthood are not!

If you wanted to incite a riot then that's how you would do it. If you wanted the religious leaders to kill you, then that's what you would say to them. Jesus wasn't even gossiping behind their backs. It wasn't second hand information that they could have taken out of context. Jesus said it right to their faces. He told them the truth and if they would have listened to him, they would have been set free from their religious philosophies and duties. **Jesus was letting people know that *peace* between them and God was going to be obtained through *his* actions. He was letting them know that the *barrier of sin* between them and God was going to be broken down by *his atonement for us* (Ephesians 2:14). He was trying to teach them that they can be righteous before God without even lifting a finger. We are made righteous by Christ's actions (Romans 5:19). We have the righteousness of Christ covering us and we didn't even have to try to be righteous in our actions to gain it. It's something Christians** possess in their spirit by being **IN CHRIST (II Corinth. 5:21). The righteousness of Christ was imputed to us (Rom. 4:24).**

This was really hard for the religious Jews to accept. They spent their entire lives trying to please God through THE LAW. That was a huge mistake on their part; no one could ever keep all those laws. That was God's point. *You can't obtain righteousness through THE LAW (I Timothy 1:9, Galatians 2:21).* Many Jewish people were confused about this New Covenant Jesus was ushering in full of mercy, love and grace.

No one sews a new patch of un-shrunk cloth on an old garment. Otherwise, the new piece will pull away from the old making the tear worse. No one pours new wine into an old wineskin. Otherwise the wine will burst the skin and both the wine and the wineskin will be ruined.
Mark 2:21 & 22

Jesus was talking about the New Covenant that was going to be secured through his blood. You can't mix the Old Covenant principles (The Law) with this New Covenant of grace and mercy. **Jesus was letting them know, "It's not about *your* actions it's about *my* actions for you. Righteousness, holiness, perfection, acceptance and salvation are obtained through Christ and the only thing people needed to do to have all that was to receive Jesus as their Lord and savior.** The Pharisees just couldn't grasp this concept. They were going to have to completely turn their backs on all their religious philosophies. This New Covenant was too good to be true! This New Covenant was going to shake the church's religious foundations and rip the dividing curtain from the ceiling. Matthew 27:51

<u>God established a new covenant (through Jesus)</u>
<u>that eradicated performance and works-based acceptance.</u>

God established a <u>better</u> covenant between him and mankind. Heb. 7:22
This <u>superior</u> covenant was going to <u>sanctify us.</u> Hebrews 8:6 & 10:10
This <u>New</u> Covenant was going to <u>perfect our spirit forever</u>. Hebrews 8:8,10:14
This covenant was <u>sealed</u> in God's blood. Hebrews 9:14
This <u>New</u> Covenant was going to allow us to have <u>intimacy</u> with God. Hebrews 8:11
It <u>purged</u> our sin and gave us a <u>clean</u> conscience to serve the living God. Hebrews 1:3, 9:14
This <u>New</u> Covenant was going to make us righteous, acceptable, pure and perfect before God. Hebrews 10:1 & 14

You can't mix this new covenant with the old covenant. Hebrews 8:13, 10:1 & 9, Mark 2:21-23

Many Christians today try to blend the performance-based old covenant with God's new covenant, but Jesus said it's impossible to approach God through the old covenant. Christ's atonement is a completely free gift that we accept by way of God's grace. God is responding to us by grace because his wrath has been appeased through the blood of Christ. The Pharisees must have been thinking, "But nothing is free in this world, especially from a holy, righteous, perfect God, he has very high standards and we need to meet those standards." **Putting all your faith and trust in the Lord Jesus Christ was all that God required. NOW THAT'S THE GOSPEL MESSAGE! If you try to add anything to what Jesus did for you, then you can't have what he alone accomplished for you.** It would no longer be a free gift wrapped in God's grace (Galatians 2:21).

Many good Christian people today would agree with me that we're no longer under THE LAW (Romans 6:14) and we don't need to follow the Old Testament laws to be accepted or justified before God. Most Christians are in agreement that it is by grace that we are saved and not of works (Ephesians 2:8). Yet these same Christians have inadvertently substituted a different kind of law in its place. The Old Testament laws are gone, but now they've replaced them with New Testament laws. Unfortunately many Christians work, sweat and toil under these New Testament laws, just like the Old Testament Jews did. Here's just one example of these new laws they live under:

You need to attend church because that pleases God.

Christian shouldn't *have to go* to church; they *get to go* to church. It's something they should want to do. It should be a desire that's comes from their new born-again spirit. Your church attendance doesn't please God. Being the church, is what pleases God. You being IN CHRIST is what pleases him. Going to church is a smart thing to do if you're being taught the truth that sets people free. At church you get to learn about God, his divine character attributes, his unconditional love and discover new truths in his word together. I've had some mind blowing supernatural experiences with my brothers and sisters at church that I'll never forget. Here's the truth: God is already pleased with you. He's pleased with you because you accepted Christ's atonement for your sins. He is pleased with you because his Spirit lives in you. He is pleased with you because of Christ's actions.

There is now peace between God and mankind
through the blood of Christ Jesus. Colossians 1:20

You are not walking in more favor because you attend church. God has not marked your file folder with a smiley face because you never missed a Sunday service. If you're trying to gain something from God based on your church attendance, then you've just crossed over into legalistic religious duty. *Why* we do what we do is so much more important than *what* we are doing.

Here is another New Testament law that Christians live under:
God will bless you as you become
more and more holy and righteous in your actions.

God doesn't bless us because we pray to him more. The bible says that we are (present tense) blessed with ALL of God's blessing in the spirit realm (Ephesians 1:3). All of God's blessings are in our spirit. God has already commanded the blessing to be deposited in his children. **As soon as our mind realizes they're there, then we can have them. We can release them into this physical world through our positive faith-filled words and actions.**

Blessed are those whose iniquities are forgiven and whose sins are covered. Blessed is the person who the Lord will not impute sin.
Romans 4:7 & 8

If your sins are forgiven (and they are) and God is no longer imputing sin to you or charging sin to your account (and he isn't), then you're blessed beyond measure! The blessings of having Jesus Christ as your savior are unlimited. We are blessed because we are children of God. Not because we tithe every week, pray for 15 minutes a day, sit in the front row at church or try our best to be as sinless as possible.

I love Jesus and I love being surrounded by other believers. I'm not trying to teach anyone to stay at home and not go to church. I'm trying to teach you to not obtain righteousness (right standing before God) by your church attendance or any of your other actions. **You are not accepted by God because of your flawless performance. You are accepted by God because of Christ's flawless performance.** God is not withholding from you because you are not living up to his standard. You could never live up to his standard, that's why we needed a savior. This concept that is saturated with God's grace will totally deflate the religious person's self-righteousness, because there won't be anything left for *them to do* to be in right relationship with God, except to just trust in Christ's atonement and God's grace (Romans 3:24). The only way to truly be righteous before God is to accept what the Lord Jesus Christ did for you, not by conforming to any Old or New Testament laws or any performance-based church doctrines.

The Old Testament laws are still around today, they've just been rewritten by confused New Testament believers. Here are some additional New Testament laws that religious people live by today:

You need to spend a certain amount of time in prayer before God will respond to you. James 5:15

You need to have no sin in your life before God will answer your prayers. Hebrews 8:12

You need to follow God's biblical teachings to stay in God's favor. Philippians 3:9

God's acceptance of you is based on your sinlessness. Ephesians 1:6

You need to be holy so God will continue to love you and bless you. Colossians1:22; Ephesians 4:24

You need to improve your actions so God will continue to fellowship with you. Hebrews 13:5

God loves you when you perform well and he's angry at you when you disappoint him. Colossians 1:22

We must perform at God's higher standard to be accepted by him, to enjoy fellowship with him and have peace with him. Romans 5:1

The church wants people to improve their performance so God will love them, bless them and accept them. But God says over and over throughout his word, that because of Christ we are: accepted by God (Ephesians 1:6), we are loved (Romans 5:8), we are reconciled to God (Colossians 1:21), favored and blessed (Ephesians 1:3), cleansed and anointed, healed and made whole (Colossians 2:9 & 10). Our new spirit was made holy (Colossians 1:22) and righteous and then it was sanctified (Hebrews 10:10) and sealed (Ephesians 1:13). We stand guiltless and blameless before God (Colossians 1:22), because our old sin nature has been removed (Romans 6:6). If you'll read all those scripture references you'll notice that they don't have anything to do with your awesome performance or virtues. They were acquired independent of you through Christ. These are the attributes of the new you, because of what took place in your new born-again spirit. WOW! That just removed all the effort of *becoming* a Christian, *being* a Christian and *remaining* a Christian from you! Maybe now you can relax and love God for all that he's deposited in you. The New Testament message to sinners, religious people and born-again Christians is this:

SALVATION is by God's grace…not your works and deeds.
LOVE came by way of the cross of Christ…
not through your flawless performance.
PEACE between God and mankind was made
through Christ's blood, not your actions.
You are made RIGHTEOUS through Jesus Christ...
not through your own righteousness, goodness or works.

Being religious is a full time job. Trying to maintain some kind of righteousness through your works and deeds is exhausting. **The way religion is being practice in today's modern churches is a sin! Religious people focus on everything they're doing for God instead of everything he's done for them.** Don't lose your focus. Don't let the truth of God's grace slip through your fingers.

I actually heard a pastor say that he began to remind God of a few things when he was praying for the salvation of his kids. He brought it to God's attention that; he was a pastor that preaches the gospel message and that he had dedicated his life to God and that he has served God for such a long time. He was trying to get God to respond to him based on everything he's done for God. Once again, God's response to us based on everything Christ has done for us. That's true bible grace. This pastor kept saying the words I've done this and I've done that. I knew he had just stepped out from under God's grace. You know what; I've also done the exact same thing many times. Since then, God has taught me many things about his grace. Now I make sure I mix God's grace with every prayer that leaves my mouth.

People of faith can be lured into a *self-righteous* mindset if they're not careful. Anyone of us can fall into performance-based salvation and acceptance at any time. Legalism can sneak up on pastors, ministers and Christians, so be aware of it. Any Christian can allow themselves to get puffed up, or what the bible calls haughty, when they use the bible as a set of rules and conditions for others to conform to so God will save them accept them and love them. Our religious concepts always get in the way of what God wants to do through us, for us and in us.

You religious hypocrites! You are like a whitewashed tomb that looks clean on the outside, but on the inside there is nothing but rotting flesh and bones. On the outside you appear to be righteous, but on the inside you are full of hypocrisy, selfishness and wickedness. Matthew 23:27

Jesus said, *"You load people down with religious laws that no one should have to carry" (Luke 11:46)*. The Pharisees enjoyed their religious rituals and they looked holy because of their long flowing robes, tall hats and decorative tassels. But Jesus told them, *"You are like a white washed tomb."* Jesus was able to look beyond their outward appearance, positions and titles and see right into their hearts. When Jesus told them what he saw they hated him for it and keep trying to justify themselves. They could have believed the truth of their Messiah's words and received him as their savior; but instead they burned with jealousy, anger, hatred, offense and all kinds of putrid self-righteous evil. They were ready to do anything to silence him, even murder him. They hated him so much they decided that killing him would be too simple and swift. They wanted him to be tortured to death through crucifixion.

Many churches today seem to be a place where people show others the best of who they are. People hide their wicked flesh with suits, ties and dresses. They cover up their depression and pain with a mask of makeup or a brushed on smile. Their thought lives are covered with a fancy hairdo or a decorative hat. They perfume themselves down to mask any residual stench of sin. Now I know these words are kind of harsh, but we would be better off to testify about the worst of who we were. We look so prim and proper that no one would ever think we were ever a sinner. **Churches are not museums for the perfect people; they're hospitals for hurting people.** What I'm saying is this, just be real and truthful about yourself. Don't forget to share your testimony with people. Make sure you tell people not to let your outward appearance fool them. You were a sinner, a child of darkness, a child of wrath and disobedience (Ephesians 2:2 & 3), but now you've been saved by faith in God's grace.

You have a completely new nature in your spirit. Your soul and mind are being renewed daily as you read in God's word about those changes that have taken place in your spirit. That's one of the reasons a born-again Christian is supposed to attend church, to learn about what happened to them the moment they accepted Christ as Lord.

Churches have failed miserable when it comes to teaching people about their new born-again spirit. Doesn't it make sense that we should teach born-again Christians about their new born-again spirit? Many churches skip over that part (because of ignorance) and go straight to trying to change a person's actions, which causes Christians to struggle much more in their faith.

There are a lot of Christians out there trying to act holy, righteous and sanctified in their physical actions, but Christians should do these things because of the change that has taken place in their spirit. Don't promote your holy actions; promote the Holy Spirit and then he will propel your actions to even greater levels. Our spirit is one hundred percent holy, righteous, anointed and sanctified. God tells us in the bible to, *"Be holy because I am holy" (I Peter 1:16).* This scripture is not referring to the contrast between God's holiness and our holy actions. It's a comparison between God's nature and the spirit he's placed in us. You know what…THEY'RE IDENTICAL! **God's Holy Spirit in you will prompt you to desire holiness in your actions. I guarantee you will never be as holy as God in your thoughts, attitude and actions. But you are just as holy as God *in your spirit right now,* because he lives in you. So go and be holy on the outside (in your thoughts, words and actions) because you are holy on the inside (in your spirit).**

We have been made holy through the blood of Jesus. Hebrews 13:12
We have been made holy through the sacrifice of the body of Jesus Christ. Hebrews 10:10
Through Jesus Christ we have been made righteous. Romans 5:19
God himself has anointed us. II Corinthians 1:21
We have an anointing from the Holy One. II Corinthians 1:21
We are sanctified by faith in Jesus. Acts 26:18
We are sanctified in our spirit. Romans 16:15
We are sanctified by Christ's blood. Hebrews 10:29

Have you ever thought of yourself as being HOLY, ANOINTED and SANCTIFIED? If you're anything like me…probably not. Actually I've never thought of myself as being holy, anointed or sanctified, because I know me better than anyone. I know how many times I fail in a day. But that was my problem; I was focused on my actions and virtues. I was focused on my outward performance, but God is interested in changing us from the inside first. **Until you understand that you are holy, righteous, anointed and sanctified *in your spirit* then your actions will always wavier based on your day to day circumstances. When your mind and body surrenders to what's true about you in your spirit, then your thoughts, words and actions truly become Christ-like.** That's how the fruit that's in your spirit: love, joy, peace, patience, kindness, gentleness, goodness and faithfulness is going to come out of you. Galatians 5:22

Unfortunately many Christians believe the bible is a set of rules for them to follow to gain God's favor, acceptance and to maintain their salvation. It's so much easier to be a Christian knowing that it really doesn't have anything to do with your great virtues or awesome performance. The truth is, the bible reveals God's nature and our destiny to us. Those performance based scriptures like, *"Love your neighbor as yourself" (Matthew 19:19),* reveal to us what's in our spirit. Your future actions will soon be Christ-like because of what's been deposited in your spirit. You will soon love your neighbor with passion and deeds, because that's the love that's growing out of your new born-again spirit. Not because of a rule God gave you to follow in Matthew 19:19, but because **unconditional love is a bi-product of the spirit that's in you (Galatians 5:22). A supernatural revelation will erupt from your spirit when you properly interpret scriptures; this is when the truth will set you free. This is the difference between religious duties and the life giving spirit that's in us. Our quickened spirit prompts us to love, give and serve others. Rules and regulations confine people, but the truth about our new nature sets us free from religion and allows us to run towards our divine destiny.**

People have serious issues and they need to address those problems with help from mature brothers and sisters in Christ. Most new people that visit a local church would not be able to live up to the perfect standard the church has on display. That's why I like to see pastors who dress down a bit. They're plain ordinary people just like you and me. They were sinners saved by God's grace, with a message of salvation that we should all be testifying about.

No matter how much you scrub and clean a coffin, it still has decaying bones and rotting flesh on the inside. People are not fooling God. God's interested in changing people from the inside. It's uncomfortable to take a close inward look at yourself. In fact, we need the Holy Spirit's help to uproot the deep things in our heart that go against God and his truth.

Woe to you, teachers of the law and Pharisees, you hypocrites! You look clean on the outside but inside you're full of greed and self-indulgence. Blind Pharisee! Let God clean your spirit first, then everything that comes out of you will be clean. Matt. 23:25 & 26

You can look like a Christian on the outside, but God can see right into your heart. Why bother putting on a show for people. Do you care more about what people think than what God thinks? Maybe no one explained to you what happened at your born-again salvation experience. Since then you've failed God so many times you figured what's the point in trying anymore?

If we claim to be sinless, we're only deceiving ourselves and the truth is not in us. If we confess our sins, he is faithful and just and will forgive our sins and purify us from ALL UNRIGHTEOUSNESS (in our spirit). If we proclaim that we have no sin, we make God out to be a liar and his word has no place in our hearts. I John 1:8-10

Let today be your *turn around day*, the day you turn from your old way of thinking and rejoice in the freedom of your new way of living. Ask God to give you a hunger that will drive out those religious cobwebs in your mind. Draw closer to God and into a life that is free from religious duties, conditional love and judging others .

Catch the Devil off guard today. Make him nervous by praying and giving thanks to God. Give the enemy a headache today and start praising the Lord with a song from your heart. We've been down for too long saints of God. Let the Devil be discourage and depressed from here on out. It's time for him to have a BAD DAY! Rise up Christian soldiers, take up your weapons saints of God and let's charge forward together in the name of the Lord Jesus Christ.

ARE YOU ON THE ENDANGERED SPECIES LIST?

You see dear brothers and sisters in Christ, when it comes to spiritual warfare; we've only scratched the surface. There is an endangered species in the church today. It's the children of God who know what they possess by being IN CHRIST and how to use the power, weapons and authority that have been deposited in them.

Endangered species #1 - Disciplined Bible Reader:

You can find them just about anywhere. At home, work, waiting rooms, standing in line at the grocery store and in their cars. Usually they are very quiet, but sometimes you might find them reading and laughing, reading and praying or even reading God's word and crying. The more they read the more they want to read. It's like God's word is the bread that they nourishment themselves with. They just can't get enough of his truth. They continuously study about this awesome God their so deeply in love with.

Endangered species #2 - Prayer Warrior:

You may have not seen this species around very often. They tend to stay to themselves and God. Most of the time, they pray in quiet places but they're certainly not afraid to pray in public places either. If you look closely for them, your chances of seeing them are good, because they engage in powerful prayer every day. Your chances of hearing them are also good because they continually cry out to God. They might cry out to God or shout towards the high Heavens depending on how the Holy Spirit leads them. They're completely harmless to people, unless they are praying specifically for you. Then be ready for something to happen in your life. Even though this species is rare, they are not bashful, fearful or embarrassed. So keep your eyes and ears open and you might stumble across this extremely endangered species.

Endangered species #3 - Praise Warrior:

This species is usually heard before they're seen. They can be heard just about any place they go. They continually sing praises to God. Sometimes you might hear just one word blast out of their mouth like, "JESUS!" or, "MASTER!" or "SAVIOR!" They never run out of reasons to praise God. If you hear them in the distance, approach them very slowly. Try not to disturb them, but if you do, they will not harm you because they are peaceful creatures, very gentle and loving. They are always joyful and positive. Don't be afraid of them, they're not dangerous, at least not to you.

Is there any chance of your household stumbling across you in your prayer closet and hearing you crying out to God? Is there any chance of them seeing you reading your bible more than you watch TV? Would your household be utterly shocked if they heard you praising God? I hope these questions raise a red flag, challenge you to discipline yourself and grow under God's grace.

A LETTER FROM SATAN
Every Christian should have one of these letters in their possession.

I thought I'd write you a letter, just to let you know how much I miss you. I've always enjoyed spending time with you, but lately you have drastically changed. I'm very confused because you've been ignoring me constantly. This is why I've written this letter to you.

One thing I've noticed that is different about you is the words you speak. We used to have some great laughs talking about people, cursing at your friends and putting down co-workers and your boss. Lately your words have changed drastically. Why do you speak positive encouraging words? That's no where near as much fun as bashing people. You used to say whatever I whispered in your ear. You always loved listening to my putrid melody. I was your soul source of information and entertainment. You used to latch on to every thought I whispered to you. Lately, it's like you're speaking a different language! I don't seem to have any influence over you anymore.

Another concern I have about our relationship is what you're filling your mind with lately. It goes against everything I've ever taught you. You know what book I'm talking about, THAT BIBLE BOOK. It's a scary piece of man-made literature AND THAT'S ALL IT IS! I've told you many times the bible is just man's opinion of a fairytale God. It's so full of contradictions and mistakes. I'm warning you to stay away from that book, it will really confuse you. There is no way you and I are going to hang out together if you keep reading, believing and worst of all quoting that book all the time. Besides, do you know how much TV you're missing out on when you spend time reading the bible?

I'm confused about our relationship. Every time I try to talk to you, you turn away from me. Every thought I give you, you completely ignore. Every temptation I place before you, you immediately reject it. What's up with that! You never did that before! How are you and I going to have a relationship if you're going to act like this! I've always told you you're not going to have any fun without me around!

I'm getting tired of hanging around you. Lately you've been so unpredictable. I'm so uncomfortable just being in the same room with you. You're not the same person you used to be. I give up. I'm out of here…at least for now.

CHAPTER 8

GOD'S WILL AND WISDOM FOR YOUR LIFE

I've had some people say, "You actually think you know what God thinks?" My answer is…most definitely YES! The bible says that God has given me the mind of Christ (I Corinthians 2:16). The more I love and seek him, the more I understand God's nature, my new nature and our destiny together. When God planted his Holy Spirit in me, he gave me a teacher that is constantly with me, encouraging me and helping me understand my new born-again spirit.

Our wisdom does not originate from this world. The people who reject God and are perishing don't understand heavenly truths. We speak of God's secret wisdom, a wisdom that has been hidden and that God destined for us. The bible says, "No eye has seen, no ear has heard and no mind has conceived what God has prepared for those who love him," but God has revealed it to us by his Spirit. The Holy Spirit teaches us everything we need to know about God's nature. No one knows the thoughts of God except the Spirit of God and his Spirit lives in us. God wants us to understand what he has deposited in our spirit.
I Corinthians 2:6,7,9,10,12

God is always ready to give out knowledge and understanding about his divine nature. God loves when we seek to know him intimately. When you humble yourself before God and submit to the truth of his word, then he'll pour his wisdom into you. God can make you wise in one quick supernatural flash of time. Get ready to be flooded with a tidal wave of information. Be ready to be completely overwhelmed with supernatural wisdom from the most high. The bible says:

If anyone lacks wisdom, don't be afraid to come to God
who gives generously to everyone without ridiculing them.
He will surely give you wisdom when you ask for it. James 1:5

God helps people to understand him when they seek the truth about him. He can make you wise with just one quick flash of supernatural power that goes straight to your tiny brain. God's truth frees up our mind to understand things like never before. Anyone can know God's will and their purpose by seeking God, reading his word and asking for wisdom. God's will is written in his word. It's just up to us to read it, believe it and receive it.

WISDOM ABOUT GOD'S WILL

Every Christian wants to know what God's will is for their life. What does God want me to do? What does he desire of me? Here is a simple scripture that will keep you in God's will.

Be joyful always, pray continually and give thanks in all circumstances, for this is God's will for you in Christ Jesus. I Thessalonians 5:16-18

See how easy it is to know God's will. When we spend our time being joyful always, praying continually and giving thanks in all circumstances, then we won't have time to grumble, complain, be offended and negative. Those things put out the Spirit's fire. Read God's word and you'll know God's will. God's will is directly connected to his character, his grace, his love and his forgiveness.

When YOUR character is becoming like Christ's character on a daily basis...then you're in God's will.

Jesus said, "I tell you the truth, the Son can do nothing by himself. He can only do what he sees his Father doing, because whatever the Father does, the Son does also." John 5:19

The Lord looks down from Heaven and searches the earth to see if there are any who are wise and want to please him. Psalm 14:2

Be passionate, children of God, when you offer yourselves as a living sacrifice, holy and pleasing to him. This is your spiritual act of worship. Do not conform any longer to your old pattern of thinking, but transform your mind by reading about God's character and the truth about your new nature. Then you will clearly know the will of God. Romans 12:1 & 2

WISDOM - GOD IS REAL

No, I've never actually seen God, but I have seen all his creation. I've never actually walked with Jesus or touched his hand. But I have seen the life transforming power of Jesus Christ in my life and many others as well. I don't know what the Holy Spirit looks likes, but I sense this direct connection with him. Many people have told me, "There is NO GOD!" But the truth is they simply don't know God. They've never been properly introduced. They've never experienced his overwhelming presence and love. In a way they're right, there is no God, in their own spirit. Their spirit is dead to him. A born-again Christian's spirit has been touched by God. Their spirit that was once dead is now alive and sensitive to him.

Many lost souls have determined that everything in life can be explained through coincidence, accident or just the natural circle of life. They view everything through "THERE IS NO GOD" gray colored glasses. I want you to tell your unsaved friends, family and co-workers something they may have not heard before. God is speaking to them just as much as he speaks to Christians. God doesn't hate them because they reject him.

God did not send his Son into the world to condemn the world, but to SAVE THE WORLD through Christ's payment for their sins. John 3:17

The Pharisees asked Jesus' disciples, "Why is your teacher having dinner with tax collectors and sinners?" Jesus heard their comments and said, "Who is it that goes to the doctor, the healthy or the sick? But let the whole world know that I have come to save the lost."
Matthew 9:11-13

I gave up doubting God the moment he introduced himself to me. The more I seek him the more evidence I've seen through his manifestations in my life. Now I view life through my, "THERE IS DEFINITELY A GOD", crystal clear glasses. He has never forsaken me. God has continually manifested himself in my life as I got desperate in seeking him. I have seen a mountain of evidence that God is real, because he has removed many of the mountain sized obstacles in my life. **Remember a person with an argument has nothing over a person with an experience.** The bible says, *"Seek him and YOU WILL find him" (Matthew 7:7).* It doesn't say you *could* find him as long as God's having a good day or you *may* find him if you're lucky. God promises, "YOU WILL FIND ME." That's what he's all about.

You're as close to God as you want to be.

If anyone hungers and thirsts after my righteousness then I will fill them with my spirit. Matthew 5:6

The choice is completely up to you. You can draw close to God or turn and run as fast as you can away from him. God is not going to reveal himself to the proud taunts of an arrogant person. God has already made his choice about us, HE LOVES US ALL! He's pursuing after us. If you want to hear from God, then humble yourself before him, seek him and you will find him.

WISDOM ABOUT EXPECTATION

Expectation is a powerful thing. Someone once put a sign up as you entered through the sanctuary doors at our church and it read:

> Come in with a spirit of expectation, strongholds are
> going to be broken and miracles are going to happen!

What a powerful proclamation to make just before entering the tabernacle. After all, why even enter into the sanctuary, if we really don't expect God to actually do anything in people's hearts and lives. **Attending church just for the sake of attending is just another sandbag in the foundation of religious duties.** Religion is a lot of work and a complete waste of your life.

In Matthew 13:58 it says that Jesus could not do many miracles in his own home town because of their lack of faith or unbelief. Isn't that an awful way to be remembered in the bible? Is your hometown or household a place where Jesus can operate freely and influence others? I hope these questions begin to prick your heart:

Will it be MY HOUSEHOLD where Jesus could not do many miracles...because of my lack of faith?
Will it be MY HOUSEHOLD and family members that could not be healed...because of my unbelief?
Will it be MY HOUSEHOLD where strongholds and addictions could not be broken...because I had questions and doubts?
Will it be MY HOUSEHOLD where God could not release his power... because I was too busy, distracted and overwhelmed?
Will it be MY HOUSEHOLD that God could not use as a supernatural channel...because of anger, unforgiveness and strife?

How do you want your household remembered? I want my faith to change history and make its mark on my household and my future generations forever.

Unless you allow God to build your house...in the end...
all of your efforts will be in vain. Psalm 127:1

Faith-filled expectation channels God's power into your situation. Not an arrogant or demanding type of expectation where we twist God's arm. The expectation I'm talking about is birthed between hope and humility. What I'm talking about is a MY GOD CAN DO ALL THINGS or IS ANYTHING TOO HARD FOR THE LORD type of expectation. Expectation should shout from your spirit, "MY GOD IS THE GOD OF POSSIBILITIES."

All things are possible for those who believe. Mark 10:27

If we really believe this scripture is true, then we need to believe, hope, expect and pray FOR THE IMPOSSIBLE.

People have read that scripture so many times, that they can sometimes desensitize themselves to what the Holy Spirit is trying to teach them. One summer I wrote down ten miracles I needed from God in my daily planner. Then I wrote the dates in my planner as God answered each request. By the end of the summer I had put a date next to every miracle. God had answered every request that I had written down. That was the summer God showed himself mighty and strong, holy and righteous. He is my provider and healer. That summer I believed that NOTHING WAS TOO HARD FOR GOD. That summer I finally understood that ALL THINGS ARE POSSIBLE FOR THOSE WHO BELIEVE! I still have that list in my planner today and I still praise God for those miracles. **Expectation is an explosive attribute to mix with your faith.**

In Matthew 9:20, the woman with the issue of blood had an expectation building within her. She said to herself, *"If I could just touch Jesus, I know I would be healed."* Expectation drove this tired woman through a massive crowd of people. She physically couldn't push her way any closer to Jesus to touch him, but when she fell to the ground determination was still in her fingertips. She grasped the edge of his garment in such a way, that it COMMANDED THE ATTENTION OF HEAVEN! Expectation brought this woman to the feet of her savior, her healer and her miracle. When was the last time power left Heaven because of your expectation?

When we mix expectation with hope deep down in our spirit, then our faith erupts like a volcano into this physical world. It comes flowing out of us through our confident prayers and faith-filled actions.

---

*When you ask God for something be sure you really expect
him to answer. A doubtful mind is like a wave in the sea
driven and tossed by the wind. James 1:6*

One time, just before our Sunday night service, I was sitting next to my wife and I said to her, "I'm expecting God to do something incredible tonight. We need the presence of God to sweep over us like a nuclear explosion and blow us all into areas where we've never been with him before." My wife agreed with me and said, "Yes, I'm feeling that too." Guess what happened that night? We got what we expected. The life changing presence and power of God was so thick that we just loved on him all evening. So be a Christian with great expectations in Christ Jesus because:

WITH GOD…ALL THINGS ARE POSSIBLE!

WISDOM ABOUT FORGIVENESS
Love blossoms when an offense is forgiven. Proverbs 17:9

Forgiveness is an incredible gift to give to someone. It's always freely given by Christians who truly understand the debt of sin that they have been forgiven of. Forgiveness is a spectacular supernatural event. It's a huge opportunity for God to operate in your life and in someone else's life. Great things are accomplished for the kingdom of God, when genuine Christ-like forgiveness is released. **Don't miss out on those precious opportunities to forgive when they come your way. If you get swept away by an offense then forgiveness will drowned in your bitterness.**

Forgiveness is not something that is earned. Trust is earned. You can forgive someone but not trust them. Don't get these two issues confused. Forgiveness is a free gift we should joyfully bestow on others. Genuine forgiveness doesn't have conditions or regulations attached to it. If you've taken years to forgive someone because you were waiting to see some evidence of genuine change in them, then that's trust not forgiveness. Don't wait until people meet your requirements to forgive them. If you wait until you can trust someone to forgive them, then you've missed your opportunity to forgive that person back when they didn't deserve it. Don't ever lose sight of the fact that you didn't deserve God's forgiveness; it was extended to you as a gift. People, who understand the power of that gift, extend it freely to others. Forgiving others when they don't deserve it, mimics the forgiveness God gave us when we didn't deserve it. Those people you choose to forgive may for the first time understand God's love and forgiveness in a greater way

(Romans 5:8). Wouldn't it be great to know that someone you forgave, forgave someone else because you extended forgiveness to them. While Jesus was dying on the cross for all mankind, he said:

Father forgive them...for they know not what they do. Luke 23:34

Jesus forgave while hanging on a cruel, shameful, torturous cross that he didn't deserve. He could have called down twelve legions of angels to fight for him and avenge him of this terrible unjust punishment, but he didn't. Every drop of blood that was stripped from his body was the evidence of his love for us.

Let the power of the cross overflow from your spirit constantly. Born-again, spirit-filled Christians are attached to that cross of forgiveness. Forgiveness is stuck to us in a way that it cannot be removed. It is a part of us. **It's not just something we do; it's a character attribute of who we are. Christian soldiers, we are united together by God's forgiveness. Any Christian who limits forgiveness, doesn't have a genuine revelation of God's complete forgiveness towards them.** A clear comprehension of God's forgiving grace enables us to forgive others beyond our emotional offences.

Unforgiveness promotes you, satisfies your flesh and focuses on your emotional hang-ups. Forgiveness promotes God and glorifies him.

Though your sins be as red as blood...
Christ's blood shall make them white as snow. Isaiah 1:18

Can you imagine yourself being that clean from sin forever. Many Christians believe they are only clean for a short period of time and soon after they sin, their dirty rotten sinners all over again. They believe they are clean one day and filthy the next day when they fail. Saved one day and lost the next moment when they sin again. Eternally redeemed one day then eternally forsaken when they disappoint God. That's a sad way to interpret God's grace and Christ's sacrifice for you. I wish that every Christian had the awesome revelation of the true power of Christ's blood.

We sing about the blood of Jesus and we hear sermons about the power of the blood. However, many Christians remain confused about their individual acts of sin. Some people believe that you have to get every sin you've committed (which happen everyday and some you've don't even realize you've committed - James 4:17) under the blood of Jesus, similar to how the Old Testament Jews did under the Old Covenant using the blood of animals. But something is drastically different for New Testament saints. We live under a completely New Covenant between God and mankind. The Old Testament Covenant of *covering* sin was done with the blood of animals. The New Testament Covenant of *removing* sin was done by the blood of Christ. **The difference between the OLD and the NEW wasn't just the frequency of the blood being poured out for sin, but it reveals to us how God, once and for all, completely obliterated the sin issue between him and mankind. God's anger, wrath and condemnation towards sin was finally appeased when it was imputed to Christ.** God reveals the details of this New Covenant we get to enjoy in many scriptures.

> *I will separate my wrath from your sin nature*
> *as far as the east is from the west. Psalm 103:12*
> *I will be merciful towards their unrighteousness*
> *and remember their sins no more. Hebrews 8:12*
> *I will blot out your sins for my own sake*
> *and remember your sins no more. Isaiah 43:25*
> *God was in Christ, reconciling the world to himself,*
> *not imputing peoples sin against them. II Corinthians 5:19*
> *Sin is no longer and issue between God and you because*
> *he has forgiven us of all our sins. Colossians 2:13*

A person who chooses to have an unforgiving spirit doesn't have a clue of the *debt of sin* that they themselves have been forgiven (Luke 7:41-47). They are also completely oblivious to the extreme price that was paid for their forgiveness. That person has removed themselves from the kindergarten classroom of Christianity 101. They removed themselves from the basic fundamental teaching of God's message and Jesus' mission. The only reason Christians can even call themselves a Christian is because God forgave them by way of Christ's obedience, blood and atonement.

If your forgiveness from God was based on
your forgiveness toward others, would you be forgiven?

I believe there is a general misunderstanding when it comes to forgiving others. *Forgiving does not mean forgetting.* You may never be able to forget the offense. Christians need to release the pain associated with that offense to God. Surrender that hate, disappointment and anger to him. If you have truly extended a person forgiveness, grace and love; then the next time you see that person, the pain from that offense should be completely gone. Will the memory of that incident still be there?

Yes…maybe…I guess it depends on how thoroughly you've released the offender. I believe God can help you supernaturally forget the offense just like he did in Hebrews 8:12 & Isaiah 43:25

If you've only partially forgiven someone, then you don't understand the magnitude of the price that was paid for your sin by Christ. Through your own human effort you may be able to forgive someone for some minor infractions (up to seven times maybe). But Christ wants us to forgive from deep within our spirit up to 490 times in a day if necessary. Matthew 18:21 & 22

Christ had no sin. He was sent to the cross because of your sin. A completely innocent and sinless man was put to death because of you and then he forgave you while he was being tortured on the cross where your sin placed him. Jesus took the punishment for all our crimes and then forgave us for all our crimes and the crime of putting him on the cross. That's mind blowing forgiveness, grace and love! In Isaiah 52:14 it says that his face was torn and his body was marred more than any other man. I believe that means Jesus did not even look like a human being when they were done with him. **Jesus was holy, righteous and sinless and his blood was shed for unholy, unrighteous, sinful people so that they could become holy, righteous and sinless in their spirit just like him (I John 4:17).** He thoroughly and completely took care of all the sins of the world. We esteem his sacrifice by recognizing that God's wrath was appeased through the atonement of Christ. **Your sin was imputed to Christ! That's a monumental revelation that should be radically influencing our daily lives (II Corinthians 5:19). God is not mad at mankind anymore.** We confirm this spiritual reality when we extend forgiveness to others as well. Don't be mad at others because God is no longer mad at you. **When we accept this kind of forgiveness from God we lose our desire to withhold it from others.**

Don't look at forgiving people as something you have to do, as if it was going to hurt you to extend forgiveness to someone. Don't grind your teeth in the process of forgiving someone. For a Christian person, the act of forgiveness should feel very natural and even pleasant. Forgiving people is exciting. It's a reminder of the grace that God has freely extended to us. Forgiveness is a part of that living water that God pours into our vessel so that we can let it flow out of us and into others. **If you stop the flow of forgiveness then you'll stop the flow of God in your life.** Forgiving others is extremely beneficial to you and to them. There are monumental benefits for everyone.

The most important message the lost will ever hear is that they need to accept Christ as Lord and walk in God's complete forgiveness. That's the foundation of every person's salvation. Forgiveness is definitely something to celebrate. So be on the alert for people to forgive. When someone cuts you off in traffic roll down your window and yell, "I FORGIVE YOU!" **If you're a person who is easily offended then that's one of the first things God wants to change about you.** Forgiveness is an opportunity to shine the light of God's love to people. You will totally confuse people with this type of forgiveness and when they ask you about the joy that you have, you'll be able to point to the cross of Christ.

...who for the joy that was set before him endured the cross for us.
Hebrews 12:2

Christ was full of joy knowing that the crucifixion was in his future, because he could see us being reconciled to God through his sacrifice. Jesus knew we were going to be able to know God in the same way he knows him. His mission filled his heart with joy. Hebrews 8:11

Why are there many people who say they are Christians but have a difficult time forgiving others? I believe it happens, one sinful drop at a time. One little drop of water multiplied over and over thousands of times will eventually rot a whole house. One drop of offense, a drop of rage, two drops of anger, and a flood of bitterness, will soon lead to an ocean of unforgiveness. The bible says,

Anytime you have bitterness, envy and strife in your heart, then you'll have confusion, restlessness in your mind and every evil opportunity for the enemy to intervene in your life. James 3:16

My interpretation of that scripture is this:

Being mad at someone is a rotten way to end the day.
Being angry at someone is a terrible way to spend the week.
Holding on to resentment is a dysfunctional way to live your life.

If you've been angry at a family member, friend or co-worker for a long time or maybe even years; then according to James 3:16 you've had evil knocking at your door the entire time. Some days you may have even flung open the door and invited him right on in. **We invite the devil in when we have negative thoughts towards someone, we ask him to sit down and make himself comfortable when we meditate on the pain people have inflicted on us. This can lead to all kinds of**

hatred, offense, restlessness and no peace. That's not the life God had in store for you. Anger, resentment and frustration are not fruits of the Holy Spirit. Release those OLD habits, those OLD emotions, your OLD heart and that OLD rotten fruit to the Holy Spirit. The Holy Spirit has beaten your *old nature* to death (II Corinthians 5:17). He hated it and you should hate any of these old lingering habits or thoughts that try to influence and harm you.

I don't know if it is humanly possible to actually forget anything. Some memories we have are so vivid and hurtful, that we will probably never forget them. But we can forgive those people who caused those hurtful memories. **Forgiving someone releases the hurt, pain and offense that's inside of you. Forgiving is choosing to not be hurt anymore.** The memory may still be there in your mind, but don't let that pain re-enter into your emotional realm. When the memory of that incident comes back to you, just start thanking the Lord for your own forgiveness that he gave you. Let that memory be a reminder to you of the tremendous price that was paid for your forgiveness. One thing that helped me in this challenging area, is knowing that while I was a sinner, Christ died for me and God forgave me. **A person who does not forgive easily does not completely comprehend the debt of sin that God forgave them of (Luke 7:41-47). When we understand the tremendous sacrifice that was made for us, then we will be able to love and forgive the way God designed us to. Remember forgiveness is something that was freely extended to you by God and we should forgive others with the same love, passion and grace from our heart.**

If someone has offended me, hurt me or gossiped about me, then I know that I need to forgive them and the sooner I do it the better off I'll be. The next time I see that person, something in my spirit may rise up; like anger or resentment and I know those feelings shouldn't be in me. Here is something I do that gives me a confident smile on my face and joy in my heart. I envision a big sign across their body or on their forehead with red letters that say, FORGIVEN. The reason I get such joy out of that is because it's a reminder that those big red letters are FASTENED TO ME AS WELL. God sees the word FORGIVEN on us when he looks at us. I need to see that on the people that I've forgiven. Otherwise I can't wear that message on me. That's what God showed me one day. I hope you'll try that and be successful when it comes to forgiving people GOD'S WAY.

WISDOM ABOUT WORSHIP
God inhabits the praises of his people. Psalm 22:3

Shout for joy all the earth. Worship the Lord with gladness and come before him with a song. Know that the Lord is God. We are his creation, we are his people. Enter his presence with thanksgiving and praise. The Lord is good, his love endures forever and his faithfulness continues throughout all generations. Psalm 100:1-5

Worship is a time when we proclaim to God how worthy he is. It's the most selfless time in our lives. That time with God is a vital connection that we need and God desires. It's a time when the attention is taken off ourselves and given to God.

If you're worried about what you look like during worship, then you missed it. Worship isn't about YOU, what YOU like, what YOU want to hear or what YOU want to do. It's entirely about God. Authentic spirit-filled worship is our continued grateful response to God.

Worship is birthed from three characteristics; a humble heart, a surrendered soul and a submissive spirit. There is nothing God can't accomplish in that atmosphere.

Proper praise

To properly praise the Lord, you should lift up your hands above your head with your arms up high, like the letter "V". Next you may want to put all your weight on your right foot then slowly shift it to your left foot, this type of rocking motion pleases God. This is a very conservative way to worship him.

If you happen to be in a more charismatic service, you can try a helicopter spin with your arms stretched out wide. Please be aware that during this style of worship a number of people may distance themselves from you.

Doesn't this sound silly? You can't tell someone the proper way to praise God. It's like trying to read someone's mind. True worship comes from the Holy Spirit that's in us. The only way you cannot praise the Lord properly is to not surrender to the Holy Spirit while you're worshipping God. So much is accomplished during corporate praise and worship. **That's why we must come to a turning point in our lives where** what God thinks is far more important to us than what people think.

If you're worried about how you look during worship in front of your family, friends and everyone else (I guarantee that's not the Holy Spirit giving you those thoughts) then you'll always be intimidated, self-conscious and distracted when you try to worship God at church.

We must conquer those feelings of being embarrassed about God in front of others. That fear of embarrassment will stifle the Holy Spirit's movement in everything he's trying to accomplish through you. This is important because corporate worship is so powerful. **Being fearful, self-conscious and embarrassed will strangle the mountain moving praise that's in you.**

The more I read and learn about God, the more my song to him changes. Eventually as you become more and more sold out to God, you become less and less intimidated in front of people. Knowing *who* you're worshiping changes *how* you worship. What God thinks will begin to matter more to you than what people think. **Your love for God should release a song from your heart like nothing else you've ever sang before.** The Apostle Paul said:

Should I try to please people or God? Do I look like I'm trying to please people? If I were still trying to please people, I would not be able to serve the Lord effectively. Galatians 1:10

God has put a new song in my mouth. It's a song of praise for his unwavering goodness. Psalm 40:3

The time has come for God's people to worship the Lord from deep within their spirit. This kind of worship is like a sweet fragrance for him to enjoy. John 4:23 & 24

God is worthy of praise, glory, honor and thanksgiving. We are supposed to bless God all the time. Real worship is a continually state of rejoicing over who your Heavenly Father is. It's a time when your spirit and God's spirit dance together. If you allow yourself to be lead into authentic spirit-filled worship, it will be a moment you and God will never forget. For me, worship is sometimes a simple song like, "I Love You Lord", repeated over and over until my heart touches his heart. It's your voice God wants to hear. Your words and praise are music to his ears.

One time I was in my prayer room and I was playing the best praise and worship music I have. I got down on my knees and waited for God to show up. I waited and waited but I never really felt God step into the room. Finally the Holy Spirit said, "Shut the music off." I ignored that comment; after all it was my best praise and worship music. Then I felt that tugging again, "Shut the music off." I thought to myself, "But this was my favorite praise music. I always feel God's presence when I play this anointed music."

Finally, I obeyed his prompting and turned off the music. Then I got back down on my knees and waited. I was just reflecting on the goodness of God and began thanking him for the things he has done in my life. I know how much God loves me and it was time to show him how much I loved him. I felt the Holy Spirit leading me into my own song and I began to sing to God.

I believe it was *three words* that came out of my mouth and then I could not sing anymore because I was crying so hard. You see God entered the room on the third word. He just wanted to hear my voice...that's all. He just wanted to hear three words from my lips. He wanted to hear a song from my spirit being lifted up to him.

God wants to hear *your* song in *you*, come out of *your* mouth, for *his* ears to hear. Listening to praise and worship music is a great idea. I'm not trying to discourage anyone from doing that. **It blesses me to hear other people sing of God's goodness. But it blesses God when we sing of his goodness.** God wants to hear your own personal song to him. Many times during our regular worship service at church, I'm not even singing the same song that the rest of the congregation is singing. I'm singing a song that comes from my spirit to God. That means so much to him because it came from deep within me.

I've heard many people say they really can't sing that great. But that really doesn't matter to God. Just humble your heart to him, open your mouth and let out a love song to him. God doesn't need music or an orchestra behind your voice. So lift up your hands and surrender your mind, words and body to the Lord.

Being on key is not a requirement from God. Being sincere and surrendered captures God's attention. Your voice, regardless of how it may sound to you, is music to his ears.

God gave you your voice...now it's time to give it back to him. God doesn't care about how you sound. He's longing to hear genuine passion flow from your heart. Your voice is in perfect key and pitch when you're lifting up praises to the Lord. He just wants to hear *your* song...from *your* heart...come out of *your* mouth.

You see the best praise and worship music you own is deep down in your soul. We need to release that song that's in our spirit so it can break forth out of our mouth and shake things lose in this physical world. You're not just singing a song, you're releasing angels to go and perform, search out and intervene. You are joining with angels in a supernatural choir. They encircle around you and sing with you. They break forth in a song that opens up the Heavens. Comforting angels begin to minister to you. Warring angels begin to fight for you. There are angels with specific orders in their hands to protect you. Many major battles in the bible were fought using only musical instruments and a shout of praise.

So get your flesh out of the way and get your mind focused and under control. Point your heart in the direction of Heaven and don't stop worshiping until you see the face of God. In my case it only took three words to touch God's heart and for him to touch mine.

We need to let the Holy Spirit teach us how to worship God. **Once you've worshiped God, in spirit and in truth (John 4:24), you will never go back to your old religious style of worship again.** It will be an experience you and God will never forget.

Let everyone who has God's breath of life in them...praise the Lord.
Psalm 149:6

Going through the motions doesn't please you Lord,
a flawless performance means nothing to you. I really learned
how to worship you when my pride was shattered. My surrendered
heart is what you've always longed for. Isaiah 29:13

When the people were praising the Lord Jesus, the Pharisees asked Jesus to calm the crowd down, but Jesus said to them:

I tell you the truth...if they keep quiet...
the stones around me will cry out! Luke 19:40

We are uniquely designed to be worship vessels. That's one of the many ways God has designed us to connect with him. You would think that during worship God sits back and receives all the love, praise and honor he's due. But you see it's God's nature to give.

God inhabits, lives and operates through
the praises of his people. Psalm 22:3

God manifests himself in an atmosphere of people who are humbled, submissive and surrendered to him. I know I use those three words many times in this book, but that's where God lives. He lives in the city of HUMILITY, on the street of SUBMISSIVENESS and in the house of SURRENDER. If you want to see a manifestation of God you're going to have to go to his address. That's where he can minister to you in every way you need, because he knows you inside and out. He knows what makes you tick. God knows <u>what</u> you need, <u>why</u> you need it, <u>when</u> you need it and <u>how</u> much of it you need. You see he planted those needs inside of you when he designed you. They're inside your new Jesus DNA that unites you to God.

We need the Holy Spirit's burden lifting, soul fixing, doubt crushing presence and power. I can't tell you how many times God has exploded during praise and worship at my church and people just came out of their seats to the altar, fell on their faces and cried out to him. People were healed, lives were restored and faith was renewed. That's because God inhabits the praises of his people. That's where he lives, that's his address. That's the atmosphere were God releases himself into your life.

God wants us to completely surrender to him the praise he's worthy of. God will unlock the secret mysteries of Heaven for you when you praise him from your heart and not just from your lips. When we get to that point in worship, then every care and worry in this world will disappear. An exchange between Heaven and earth will take place, transformation takes place in your heart, your faith will be quicken, the anointing will flow and spiritual authority will be discovered at a new level.

Worship and prayer are actually very similar. Prayer is just loving God and worship is loving God with rhythm. **Worship and prayer should mainly be about telling God how much we love him. Ninety-five percent of your prayer life should actually be about loving and worshiping God.** True spirit-filled worship is actually a two way path of communication. We tell God how great and how wonderful he is and then he speaks to our soul and reveals his character to us in a profound way. He begins his supernatural work in us as we lift our hands and hearts to him.

Worship may begin with us singing to God, but it ends with God speaking to us, healing us and comforting us. Don't you dare let anything distract you during such an important time with God.

Surrender yourself to the Holy Spirit that's inside of you, then release that worship song to God that's in you. **Worship is an external reaction to the internal work of the Holy Spirit.** Let it burst forth externally from you and eternally to God's ears. Let the Holy Spirit lead you into this phenomenal spiritual experience. It will be a new style of mind blowing life changing worship. **Anything you let the Holy Spirit lead you into will be a moment with God you will never forget.**

God's true worshippers will be lead by the Holy Spirit as they worship him. John 4:23

You will never forget that type of worship for the rest of your life. Worship is like a runaway freight train coming out of your spirit. Begin to sing a song on the five strings of your heart, mind, soul, spirit and body. You may even let out a war cry at the end that will shake the spirit realm. You might say, "There's no reason to get all emotional and dramatic and let out a *war cry* at the end of my song." My answer to that is...DO IT ANYWAYS! **Do what the Holy Spirit is leading you to do; anything else is just religious calisthenics.**

Do not quench the Holy Spirit's fire. I Thessalonians 5:16-19
Do not resist the Holy Spirit's promptings. Do not ignore the Holy Spirit's voice. Do not turn from his counsel.

God created us as emotional beings. Do this little test. Put your thumb down on a hard surface and now hit it firmly with a hammer. Did you get emotional after that experience? Did you curl up on the floor and cry like a baby? God created us with emotions to experience all of the earth, each other and him using these emotions. God designed us to cry, laugh, be joyful, to sing and to love. The bible tells us we will sometimes be angry, discouraged, down cast and depressed. But it also says that our hope is in the Lord and joy comes in the morning.

God wants to hear an emotional praise from his emotional beings he created. Don't be lead by your emotions but let the Holy Spirit lead your emotions into a God glorifying song.
Let the Holy Spirit shake your worship to the core and then listen to the new song that comes flowing out of your mouth.

Sing to the Lord a new song from your inner spirit,
sing to the Lord all the earth. Psalm 96:1

STORY - You Can Worship Your Way Out Of Your Problems

One time my car was running very rough. It was coughing and sputtering along and it completely quit on me many times. I was only about ten minutes from home but my car was running so bad, it was just not going to make it. So I pulled into a parking lot. It kept stalling out on me many times there in the parking lot as I tried to idle and race the engine. After about 20 minutes of prayer and racing the engine I decided to try to continue home. I kept looking for a place to pull off the road just in case it completely died on me again. Then I remembered something my music minister said at church. He said,

"You can praise your way out of you problems."

I decided to *believe* and *do* just that. I let out a song in my car and just concentrated on the goodness of God. I let out a praise to the Lord because he is worthy of all glory and honor. I told him how much I loved him. Tears began rolling down my face, not only because I felt God all around me, but I had noticed that my car was running perfectly smooth now! How is that possible? It hasn't ran smooth in the past two hours! All of a sudden now there were no sputters, no jerking and no rough idle. I just pressed the gas and it went all the way home.

How did this happen? Is this a tremendous coincidence? Did God actually enter my carburetor, the ignition system and the internal combustion engine and fix it? The bible says, *"God inhabits the praises of his people."* God fixed me, my soul, my mind and YES my car during that time I was praising him.

God is in the repair business
and his specialty is everything that concerns us.

God doesn't have to diagnose your problem like an auto mechanic. He created you and he already knows you have issues. I've got things that need fixing on the inside of me. You might not even be aware of all the things that need to be repaired in you emotionally. **But when you come before God; broken, surrendered, hungry and desperate, then he begins to fill every square inch of your heart with his undeniable love, intrinsic nature and endless wisdom.** He begins to fill every area of your mind with the knowledge of his divine character attributes. This stirring or quickening is something we so desperately need from him. God repairs our soul, gives our mind a complete overhaul and quickens our spirit so we can perceive him instantly. He gives us a heart that chases after him. No one walks away from true, thankful, spirit-filled, heart wrenching worship…unchanged.

Let the Holy Spirit burst out of your spirit, mind and mouth in a song. Ask God to give you a radiant revelation of his nature as you worship him. The Holy Spirit blasting out of YOUR MOUTH with HIS SONG is one of the most power manifestations of God you will ever experience.

That new song coming out of you is going to shake the supernatural realm. **The Holy Spirit wants to tear you apart, he wants to break down your old way of thinking and with the new room he has created in your mind, he can fill it with himself, with God, with new thoughts and a new song. That new** song coming out of your heart is going to split this world wide open.

You see less of your old way of thinking and more of God's new way of living is a great combination. John 3:30

Worship turns worriers…into warriors.

You don't walk away from a worship service, it goes with you. Worship is not over when the music is turned off. It's in you…it's got you…and you can't escape it. You don't take a vacation from being a worshiper. Worship is more than something we do; it's a part of who we are. There's a supernatural presence that encircles worshipers (people who love God). It's an atmosphere where God's spirit can literally be felt everywhere we go. When we start worshiping like this, then prisons will be opened, strongholds will fall and chains will be severed from us and those around us. When you read the story of Paul and Silas in Acts 16:25-34, you'll begin to understand that **everything in the supernatural realm revolves around our actions, words, prayers and worship. Get alone with God, open your mouth and let an EARTH SHAKING, GOD GLORIFYING, HISTORY MAKING PRAISE come out of it. The Holy Spirit will cut you wide open during worship and release the power of God that's in you.** I've seen and experienced it many times.

<u>We need to spring out of bed with these words:</u>
Praise your name Lord! I bless your name God!
Thank you for another day, so I can let you know how precious you are
to me. I've accomplished the most important thing I can today,
when I seek your face and draw closer to you. PRAISE YOU LORD!

Worship turns complainers…into praisers.

Blood-bought, Holy Spirit filled, saints of God; we need to get excited, grateful and passionate when we worship the Lord. Corporate worship is so important because seeing other people who are bold and free when worshiping God, inspires you to be just as free. Let the Holy Spirit lead you into a completely new realm of worship so God can be glorified through you.

<u>WISDOM ABOUT YOUR DESTINY</u>

You have God's Holy Spirit in you and you were designed to produce good fruit. You have been set free from your *old dead spirit*. You need to walk in the *new spirit* you have in Christ. God does not want you to *blend* your new, born-again life IN CHRIST with your old habits (that were sinful) and your old thought patterns (that were sinful). The Apostle Paul said:

I have been crucified with Christ, it is no longer I that live,
but CHRIST LIVES IN ME. My new spirit-filled life IN CHRIST
that I now possess is extraordinary and it was purchased
by Christ's loving sacrifice for me. Galatians 2:20

Since we are born-again, Holy Spirit filled, new creations in Christ,
we can never be disconnected from God. He's living on the inside of us.
We are a temple for him to live in. We can make really bad choices
and turn from the direction he wants us to go, but he's still there
with us. He will never leave us or forsake us. Nothing will ever
separate us from the love of God. Hebrews 13:5, Romans 8:39

I used to think that if I didn't behave a certain way, then God would remove his presence from me and leave me until I started acting better, then he would come back and fellowship with me once again. I used to think if I followed and obeyed the scriptures in the bible, then God would love me and stay close to me. Then I realized that these behavioral scriptures are *my destiny*. This is where I am headed in the future. God loves me and I love him and that's why I do what it says to do in God's word. *"Those who love me will obey my commandments"* *(John 14:15)*. The truth is: God loves me whether I obey his commandments or not. He loved me even when I was a child of wrath and had an evil sin nature in me. My love for God is expressed to him by obeying his commandments, just as a husband would give flowers to his wife that he loves so very much. **Genuine love produces genuine actions because God's love transforms our heart.** If I don't obey his commandments that does not mean I don't love God. But it is an indicator of how much (or how little) I've been renewing my mind in God's word. **If we truly understood the complete nature of God, his tremendous love for us and that his entire wrath toward our sin was placed on Christ, then this would cause people to express their love for him with passion, commitment and obedience. Passion is a by-product of knowing intimately who it is that you're in love with.**

When I became a born-again Christian my spirit was transformed instantly, but my mind has to be renewed everyday (Romans 12:2, II Corinthians 4:16, Colossians 3:10). My thoughts, words and actions are in the process of changing. The commandments that we obey are not rules administered by God so he will accept us, love us and fellowship with us. God's word reveals his character, his nature and his other divine attributes to us. Born-again Christians have those same attributes inside their spirit. I do the things God wants me to do because I love him and my actions are a by-product of discovering the *new nature* that's in me. Serving the Lord pleases me in my new transformed spirit that he gave me. It's a part of my identity and will soon be apart of my destiny. My *old way* doesn't please me any more. My new heart gives me new desires.

Have you let the sun go down on your anger? Ephesians 4:26
Have you not forgiven people even though you have been completely forgiven of all your sins (past, present and future)? Colossians 3:13
Have you loved your neighbor regardless of how they treat you? Colossians 3:14
Have you paid anyone back wrong for wrong? I Thessalonians 5:15
Are you compassionate, kind and patient with everyone? Colossians 3:12
Does the peace of God rule in your heart? Colossians 3:15
Have you put on love which binds all these other characteristics together? Colossians 3:14
Have you let the word of God dwell in you richly? Colossians 3:16
Do you love your spouse like Christ loves the church? Ephesians 5:25 & 33, Titus 2:4

These are all character traits or actions that we are either walking in today, or will soon be walking in tomorrow or in the near future. As a Christian, your *actions* are always headed toward your *identity*. You're either doing all these today or you'll soon be doing them, because it pleases you to do them. You're not happy unless you're doing them. **The performance-based scriptures we find in the bible are not rules we must obey to be loved and accepted by God. They're attributes of being IN CHRIST. Living from the perspective of our *new identity* leads to; freedom, growth, fulfillment and peace.**

Don't just listen to God's word and then walk away unchanged by the truth and the power of the gospel, but meditate on it daily so that you will experience a profound manifestation of God's glory. James 1:22

Some days you may feel like God is far from you...but he isn't. He's right there in you. Chances are if you will just turn from the direction you've chosen, you'll find God right there behind you waiting with open arms. Sin tries to rob us of that close connection with God through guilt and condemnation. BUT IT CAN'T! YOU'RE IN CHRIST (Hebrews 10:2 & 22). You have a blood covering that extends out over you further than you deserve. Put this book down go before God and say:

I've been letting wrong thoughts control me. Lord you have taken care of all my sins at the cross of Christ. Sometimes I go my own way with my thoughts, flesh, attitude, emotions and mouth. But I want to align myself with the truth of your word. I want to live an abundant life IN CHRIST and to be directed by your perfect spirit that's inside of me. God fill that hunger deep within me. I humble myself in your service. In the precious name of Jesus Christ...AMEN.

WOW! AWESOME! Talk about opening the flood gates of Heaven! That kind of sincere prayer causes a shaking to take place in your spirit. It's that kind of humility that absorbs every drop of God's grace. Wisdom is released in that type of surrender. That's a prayer and attitude God desires from all of us.

CHAPTER 9

MY HOUSE WILL BE CALLED A HOUSE OF PRAYER

God is calling every member of his household back to the foundation of prayer, which launches every awesome manifestation of God's power in this world. Our response to his call is critical.

Space rockets have lots of thrust power to take off. Asteroids generate a lot of frictional power trying to enter the earth's atmosphere. Volcanoes can blast with a force of up to ten thousand pounds per square foot. But all of this power combined cannot match the power of a prayer whispered from the lips of a child of God. **God is longing to hear from us and see his power released through us.**

Story:

I remember one time I was praying for someone's marriage. I began swinging my arms and speaking loudly with a voice of authority and victory. It was a different type of prayer, that's why I still remember it today. Something swept over me that I could definitely feel all over my body and in my spirit. I remember thinking something had just happened in the spirit realm and I was confident things were going to be mended in their marriage. Later this was confirmed to be true.

Prayer is mankind's greatest privilege, but it has been diminished and underestimated by most in the Christian community. Unfortunately many Christian's don't have an intimate prayer life with God. People just don't take the time to talk to their creator. Most Christians can count on their fingers (on one hand) the minutes they spend in prayer a day. **It really isn't so much about the lack of time spent in prayer as it is the lack of passion for deep close communion with God.** Children of God, your heavenly Father longs to hear from you. Many times I'll be waiting for my wife to get home after she has been gone all day. I miss her when she's not around. I can sense in my spirit that I'm anxious and excited to see her face and listen to her voice. Why do I feel this way about her…because I love her. How many times has God stayed up late waiting for you to come home? He's staring at the door and waiting for you to walk in. God loves you, he's passionate about you and he's infatuated with you. His heart leaps when he hears your voice. He desperately wants to hear from you and he wants to spend time with you everyday.

There certainly seems to be a lot of prayer requests everywhere you turn. Pray for me. Pray for this and that. Lift me up in prayer. Pray for my family, pray for my children and their children. So why aren't there more miracles surrounding the Christian community? God's miraculous power should be everywhere you turn. Let's examine prayer a little closer.

Statement #1
There is no limit on what can be accomplished by praying people.

Now that's a nice statement to make. I believe what that statement says, but it's also an extremely general statement. So now let me be more specific.

Statement #2
There is no limit on what can be accomplished by a born-again, fire baptized, Holy Spirit sensitive, bible believing, grace centered, faith-filled, doubt crushing, flesh crucifying, thankful, Holy Ghost energized, mountain moving, disciplined and determined praying child of God.

The difference in those two statements could be the difference between a powerful, victorious, fervent prayer life and a dismal, dysfunctional, disillusioned prayer life. I believe this is why many people are praying but not a lot is being accomplished.

We need to make sure we're doing everything we can to position our prayers to be heard and then surrender the results of those prayers to God's grace and Christ's atonement.

Prayer is not only what we are called and commanded to do, but we should have a desire and passion to commune with God deep within our hearts. Here is a collection of verses from the bookmarker I have written called *PRAYER IS.*

PRAYER IS
by Eric Johnson

Prayer is talking to God.
Prayer is listening to God.
Prayer is seeking God.
Prayer connects you and God.
Prayer is learning from God.
Prayer is God changing us.
Prayer is God healing us.
Prayer touches God's heart.
Prayer is God touching our heart.
Prayer changes everything.
Prayer gives us God's plan.
Prayer gives us God's thoughts.
Prayer is receiving God's love.
Prayer releases God's power.
Prayer is fresh revelation from God.
Prayer sends out angels.
Prayer is climbing in the arms of God.
Prayer moves the hand of God.
Prayer breaks the yoke of bondage.
Prayer pulls down strongholds.
Prayer cast out demons.
Prayer saves souls.
Prayer changes your attitude.
Prayer humbles you.
Prayer is saturated with thanksgiving.
Prayer is how we love God.
Prayer changes you.
Prayer changes your future.
Prayer reveals God's mighty strength.
Prayer will give you rest on all sides.
Prayer strengthens you.
Prayer captures God's heart.
Prayer gives God control.
Prayer charges forward.
Prayer illuminates our path.
Prayer unites the children of God.

Folks, we haven't even begun to scratch the surface of spirit erupting, water walking, demon crushing, mountain moving, cancer killing, earth shaking, life transforming prayer. Everything God is going to accomplish through you is going to begin with you on your knees, humbly surrendered before him. Prayer is the most humbling thing you'll ever do. God loves when we bow down before him and surrender our lives, our goals and our dreams to him.

You know what God does to humble people? He exalts them (Luke 14:11). The word exalt means to rise in rank, status, character and to honor. It also means to increase in effectiveness or intensity. When God increases your intensity and effectiveness you and everyone else around you will notice the difference. The change in you will be undeniable. I want God's supernatural power to manifest itself in this physical world and it begins with us on our knees, humbly before him.

Our prayers show God that we don't have *all* the answers. It also shows God we don't have *any* answers. Our prayers reveal to God that we need him and he is worthy of the time we spend with him. Prayer is more than a physical position, it's a spiritual position. Prayer is God directing our hearts. God knows if you're praying selfish, self-centered prayers or if you're asking God to glorify himself through your situation. **Prayer reveals to God how much you really trust him, after all what good is faith without any real trust behind it.** When you trust someone you're usually putting something on the line that you could lose. It could be time, money, friendship, your immediate safety or even your life. My point is trust takes a chance. **Faith with no real trust behind it is just a religious show for others. Prayer let's God know you want him to impart the fullness of his character into your situation. Prayer is how our heart tells God that we want to be with him and know him completely.**

SCRIPTURES ON PRAYER

1. *We have complete confidence that God hears and answers our prayers when we seek his face. God will answer your request and desires when we seek him with all our heart. I John 5:14-15*

2. *Pray in your private secret place to the Lord and what he sees you do in private, will be rewarded openly for everyone to see. Matt 6:5-6*

3. *God would never tell a lie or change his mind regarding a promise he's given us. God will follow through with every promise he has made to us because truth flows from his nature. Has he ever promised and not carried it through? Numbers 23:19*

4. *If you abide in me and my words abide in you, then you can ask for whatever you desire and it shall be done for you. John 15:7*

5. *Confess your faults to each other then pray for each other expecting to be healed. A passionate prayer from a child of God has tremendous power. James 5:16*

CALLING OUT TO GOD IN JESUS NAME

1. *Jesus said, "The truth is, you can go directly to my Father and he will grant your request because you speak using the authority of my name." John 16:23*

2. *We have a great High Priest who has gone to Heaven, Jesus the Son of God. Let us cling to him and never stop trusting him. He understands our weaknesses because he faced all of the same temptations we do and he did not sin. So let us come boldly to the throne of our Father. There we will receive his mercy and we will find grace to help us when we need it. Hebrews 4:14-16*

3. *If two of you ask, touch and agree in prayer, then it shall be done for you by my Father in Heaven. Matthew 18:19*

4. *Jesus is able to save anyone who comes to God through him, because he is always speaking to his Father on our behalf. Hebrews 7:24-26*

5. *My dear children, I am writing this to you so that you will not sin, but if you do sin, there is someone who speaks to the Father in your defense. He is Jesus Christ, the one who pleases God completely. He is the perfect, righteous sacrifice for your imperfect, unrighteous sin nature. He takes away not only your sins but the sins of the whole world. I John 2:1-2*

6. *Christ died, but then he rose from the grave and he's at the right hand of God interceding for us. Romans 8:34*

7. *Jesus makes intercession for the saints according to the will of God. Romans 8:27*

8. *Through Jesus we have access by one Spirit to the Father. Eph. 2:18*

9. *I encourage you to pray for all people and every situation as the Holy Spirit leads you. God wishes that everyone would receive Christ as their savior. There is one mediator between God and mankind and he is Jesus Christ, he gave his life as a ransom for the entire world. I Timothy 2:1-6*

10. *Jesus said, "Anyone who believes in me, the works that you see me do, you will do also and you shall do even greater works than me; because I go to my Father. Whatever you ask in my name, I will do it, so that the Father may be glorified in the Son." John 14:12-14*

11. *Jesus said, "I have chosen you and ordained you to go and produce good fruit and God will help you do this by granting your request using the authority of my name." John 15:16*

12. *Call to me and I will answer you and show you great and mighty wonders, which are beyond your comprehension but not your imagination. Jeremiah 33:3*

13. *Before they cry out to me I will hear them. While they are still speaking I will answer them. Isaiah 65:24*

Why would all these scriptures be in the bible if God did not want to communicate with us? God's ear is pressed to our lips waiting for us to speak. We should always have an ear turned towards God because he is still speaking to people today. He is a master communicator, teacher, counselor, encourager and listener. I hope this dismisses any doubts you have because God wants to hear from you. Sometimes you might feel distant from God, but he's not distant from you.

Jesus said, "Everyone who <u>asks</u> receives, anyone who <u>seeks</u> will find me and anyone who <u>knocks</u> the door will be opened to them. If your child asked you for some bread, would you give them a stone? If your child asked you for a fish, would you give them a snake? If you then, being from this evil world, know how to give good gifts to your children, how much more will your father in Heaven give good gifts to those who ask him?" Matthew 7:7-11

STORY - My Humble Walk With God

One time I was walking into work at Chrysler Corporation's World Headquarters in Auburn Hills, Michigan. It was about a five minute walk from the parking lot to the front door. I had hurt my foot the previous day and I realized how bad it was when I started making the long walk. I started praying,

"Lord, I believe you can heal my foot right now. There is absolutely no reason for me to have this limp. Lord you know I serve you with all my heart. In the name of Jesus be healed."

I continued on my long walk into work, but my foot was not getting any better. I thought to myself, I'll just be patient because God doesn't operate in our time frame. I sat in my chair at work and got some relief for a while. When I got up and started to walk again the pain was still there. So I went and prayed over my foot again. I sat down and prayed, believed and I said," I'm tired of my foot hurting. God I'm a born-again Christian why aren't you healing me?" I stood up on my feet and suddenly I became frozen stiff with pain. I COULDN'T MOVE! There was incredible pain in my back and now I couldn't move EITHER OF MY LEGS!

What was going on here? I could not move a muscle!

I stood there for a while, because that's all I could do. Then I felt something begin to grow in my spirit. A warm tingling sensation started to radiate out into my body. Was God healing me? No, I still couldn't move. Then I realized God wasn't healing me, HE WAS TEACHING ME! I felt God in my spirit saying,

"Don't give me all the reasons you deserve to be healed. Don't give me a long list of things that you've done to persuade me to heal you. Don't try to convince me to do something that I already want to do and have done for you. Do you even comprehend who you're talking to? I see your heart. I know exactly WHO YOU ARE, but you don't know completely WHO I AM. I am about to teach you something you will never forget."

I began to realize that I was lacking a very powerful attribute in my request, it was *humility*. When I was asking God to heal me, I kept saying the word "I" continually. I shouted to God, "I've done this, I've done that, Lord I don't deserve." My focus was on me and my pain and not on what the Lord Jesus Christ had done for me and my pain over 2000 years ago. I Peter 2:24

While I was standing there frozen in pain, God gave me an accelerated course in HUMILITY 101. I realized that God does not owe me anything. **God is good to us because of who he is, not because of how great we are.** His grace and mercy extend out over us further than we deserve. He is the God that governs over the universe. He's the designer and creator of everything. I was talking to God like he was a friend of mine who just happened to have the ability to heal. I didn't come to him with confidence and security or with reverence and humility. I should have come to him with thanksgiving because of what Jesus accomplished on the cross for me. I was talking to God about my pain all morning; instead I should have been talking to my pain about my God. God knows what we need before we even open our mouth (Matthew 6:32). **God loves us and he never wants us sick and in pain.** That's why he sent Jesus to be the atoning sacrifice for us. Not so a few of us could be saved, healed and whole, but so *all of us* could be saved, healed and whole.

I knew God's healing power was completely available to me, but I was praying the wrong way, with the wrong motives and attitude. I forgot who I was talking to. I needed to humble myself before the mighty hand of God. I had positioned my prayer to fail because of the manner in which I released it to him. Telling God everything I was doing for him was not an effective way to tap into his power. Reminding myself about everything God's done for me and thanking him for it is a much better way to start out in prayer. So that's what I started doing. I learned that humility blended with thanksgiving is an awesome way to start out in prayer. **Seeking God's face and not just his hand will humble you right into a passionate and more effective conversation with him.** Maybe our prayers should be more like this:

Lord I'm not here to ask you for anything. I'm just here to listen to you and to be in your presence. I'm just here to worship you and glorify your name. I love you Lord. I'm not here to seek your hand of blessing; instead I'm here to seek your face and to hear from you. I'm here to commune with you. That's more important to me than anything. I'm blessed beyond measure because I'm your child. I'm not going to do without anything you want me to have. So right now, I lift up my positive faith-filled words and intertwine them with your grace. Is there anything I can do for you today Lord? I surrender my life to you and I desire to understand your character in a greater way. Lord, glorify yourself through me today.

That's a GOD-centered prayer not a ME-centered prayer. That's a FAITH-FILLED prayer not a PROBLEM-centered prayer. We can't forget who we're speaking to when we pray. Our God is the Lord of all creation. He is a universe maker and has set each star in place with his creative finger tip. He stretched forth his hands and said, "This is how large the universe will be." He fashioned a big beautiful earth for us to live on. He told the oceans you'll go this far and no further. He pushed the mountains up with the palms of his hands. God made all the beautiful animals and people.

In the book of Exodus, Moses began questioning God's wisdom and direction for his life and God told him, *"Who made man's mouth? WAS IT NOT ME!"* Once again we can't forget who we're talking to. God deserves all honor, reverence, glory and praise.

Now back to my hurt foot story. As I said earlier, I went from having a simple hurt foot to being completely immobilized with pain in both legs and my back. I COULD NOT MOVE! God had my complete attention. I knew I had messed up. I began thanking him for my salvation, his goodness and his grace. I thanked him for being patient with me as I learned more about him, his character attributes and his love. Then it happened at that very moment! I WAS HEALED from head to toe! IMMEDIATELY I WAS HEALED! God is gracious, merciful, patient, loving and all powerful! Tears began to roll down my face as I felt God all around me. **Little old insignificant me, had just connected with the universe creator. I knew I would never forget that moment or ever be the same again.**

God knows we have issues and fall short of the mark many times. He knows we are made from the dust of the ground. God knows how much we're able to comprehend with our little minds. But fortunately HE'S COMPLETELY IN LOVE WITH US, that's why he's so patient with us. God loves when we remain teachable and willing to grow under his grace.

HUMBLY BEFORE THE THRONE OF GRACE
*People who humble themselves before God,
truly understand his amazing grace. James 4:6*

> *Humility is not thinking
> less of yourself or thinking of
> yourself less. Humility abounds when
> we meditate on what God has done
> in us through the person of Christ.*

"Humility" is severely under rated in today's modern Christian world. It's a word that we use all the time but many Christians do not put deep enough actions behind that word. Many times in the bible when people experienced God or an angelic presence, they fell down or bowed down and hid their faces. They humbled themselves in the presence of God. The Holy Spirit is activated in our soul when we humble ourselves before God. Humility allows you to hear the Holy Spirit clearly and to be taught by him at a deeper level.

Humility is the supernatural key that unlocks everything you will ever receive from God. **Humility should be the prominent characteristic that leads us into prayer, praise and worship. You can't do any of those things without being humble. Try as you may, but you won't accomplish much without humility.** A humble heart is an atmosphere where God thrives. When we submit ourselves (body, mind and soul) to what the spirit of God wants, then God can flourish in that humility, surrender and submission.

Jesus told a story about two men who came to church. One had a self-righteous spirit of pride in him and the other humbled himself before the Lord. One man felt he was pretty successful at serving God and the other man felt he was a failure. Jesus told this story about people who placed their confidence in their righteousness virtues and holy actions.

Two men went to church to pray, one was a Pharisee and the other was a tax collector. The Pharisee stood up and prayed about himself: 'God, I thank you that I am not like other men, robbers, evildoers, adulterers, or even like that tax collector over there. I fast twice a week and give a tenth of all I get.' But the tax collector stood at a distance. He would not even look up to Heaven, he pointed to himself and said, 'God, have mercy on me, a sinner.' I tell you that this man, rather than the other, went home justified before God. Anyone who exalts themselves will be humbled and anyone who humbles themselves will be exalted. Luke 18:9-14

Remember the definition of exalt means to rise in rank, character or status; or to increase in effectiveness or intensity. Everyone who goes into prayer with a humble heart, sincere, surrendered, listening and teachable; they will walk away different, *exalted*. One drop of humility can release a tidal wave of revelation from God. Don't ever forget that everything you are in your new born-again spirit is because of what Jesus did for you.

HAVE YOU CONSIDERED MY SERVANT JOB?

Many of you know the story of the man named Job in the bible. He suffered through the death of his children and suffered in his flesh with open sores. He was tormented in his mind and suffered everyday. Near the end of his story Job let his words fly out of his mouth. He was angry and venting. His feelings and emotions were totally dominating him.

Job opens his mouth with useless talk, without knowledge he multiplies his words. Job 35:16

In chapter 37:5-7,10 & 20 God speaks to Job.

God's voice thunders in marvelous ways, he does great things beyond our understanding. He says to the snow, fall on the earth and to the rain, shower and be a mighty downpour, so that everyone will see his mighty power. The breath of God produces ice in the oceans. Should a man be told that God wants to speak? Would anyone ask to be swallowed up?

Job 38: 1-5, 8 & 9,11 & 12,16,18 & 19, 21, 31, 34

Then the LORD answered Job out of the storm, "Who is this that darkens my counsel with words without knowledge? Brace yourself and I will question you and you shall answer me. Where were you when I laid the earth's foundation? Tell me if you understand exactly how I did it. Who stretched a measuring line across it and marked off its dimensions? Surely you know! Who shut up the sea behind doors when it burst forth from the depths? Who made the clouds its garment and wrapped it in beauty. Who told the oceans you may come this far but no further. Here is where your mighty waves shall stop. Have you ever given orders to the morning sky or shown the dawn where it will rest? Have you journeyed to the springs of the sea or walked in the recesses of the deep? Have you measured the vast expanses of the universe? Tell me if you've done this. Can you spin the starry constellations with your fingertips? Can you raise your voice to the clouds and cover the earth with a flood of water? What is the way to the abode of light? And where does darkness reside? Surely you know, for you have lived so many years!"

Please read Job 39 where God continues to humble Job by revealing all the wonders of his awesome creation to him.

Job 40:1-14

Then the Lord said to Job. "Will the one who contends with the Almighty correct him? Let him who accuses God answer him!"

Here comes the part where Job is overwhelmed with humility.

Then Job answered the LORD, "I am unworthy...how can I reply to you? I put my hand over my mouth. I spoke words without wisdom but I will say no more." Then the Lord spoke to Job out of the storm, "Brace yourself like a man, I will question you and you shall answer me. Would you condemn me to justify yourself? Do you have an arm like Gods? Does your voice thunder like mine? Then adorn yourself with glory and splendor and clothe yourself in honor and majesty. Unleash the fury of your wrath on every proud arrogant person and crush the wicked where they stand. Then I will admit to you that you can save yourself."

Job 41:10, 11 & 34

"Who then is able to stand against me? Who has a claim against me that I must pay? Everything under Heaven belongs to me. I look down on all that are haughty; I am king over all that are proud."

Finally, in Job chapter 42:1-6, God has Job right where he wants him, humbled before him.

Job replied to the LORD, "I know that you can do all things, no plan of yours can be thwarted. You asked, 'Who is this that obscures my counsel without knowledge?' Surely I spoke of things I did not understand, things too wonderful for me to know. You said, 'Listen now, and I will speak, I will question you, and you shall answer me.' My ears have heard you and my eyes have seen you.

When we are humbled before God, it's like opening a gate to a dam. Humility opens the gateway between the supernatural world and the physical world. It all begins with us on our knees, humbly before the Lord and seeking his face. God is just waiting patiently for us to come to our senses. He's waiting for us to fully trust in him, surrender to him and humble ourselves before him. Then he can reveal his nature to us in a much deeper way. **God's spirit is in us and it contains his anointing, power, character, protection, provision, blessings, love, peace and much more. Humility releases those attributes from within our spirit. It will always be through humility that God completes his work in our mind, body and soul.**

HUMBLE PRAYER

Prayer is one of the most selfless things you can do. It demands sincerity, surrender and humility. All pride must leave when you pray. Prayer can be rendered completely worthless, dry and mundane when we do it with the wrong attitude, motives and spirit.

We must prepare ourselves to be HEARD BY God.
Then we must prepare ourselves to HEAR FROM God.
Finally we must prepare ourselves to RECEIVE FROM God.

Prayer is the spiritual surrender of your heart, mind and soul to God. It's only when we surrender to him that God can minister, change, strengthen and heal us. God loves when we pray to him. God told Solomon, "I'll give you anything you ask for." Solomon only asked God for wisdom to lead his people. God not only gave Solomon wisdom, but he gave him great riches and power beyond anyone else in the world. Solomon had the right spirit before he prayed. Solomon trusted God, that's how God knew he could trust Solomon.

When we trust God, then our prayers have powerful potential.
When we fully rely on that trust and speak out that trust,
then God's power is released through that trust.

Getting on your knees and bowing down before God, shows him you value the relationship between him and you. Prayer is the evidence to God that you love him. It displays to God that you need him and are completely dependent on his instruction, provision and counsel.

God knows we are only just beginning to understand who he is. God reveals who he is through his spirit that lives on the inside of us. The Holy Spirit can speak clearly to us when we humble and surrender ourselves to his leading.

HINDERED PRAYERS

So why isn't God answering your prayers? That's a question you'll have to ask him. It could be any number of things. I knew someone who has attended church their whole life say,

"God has never answered any of my prayers."

What a sad way to think of yourself and God. I would really take a closer look at my relationship with God if that was the case. That statement just blew me away. I couldn't even process that statement. Maybe they let a lifetime of confusion, pain and misunderstanding concerning sin, render them ineffective and distant from God.

God doesn't answer prayer because you are a member of a church. God doesn't answer prayer based on the amount of money you give to the church or based on everything you do for him. He doesn't answer you based on your glorious virtues or by how holy you try to be. **God has already answered all our prayers based on everything Christ has accomplished for us. The YES answer to all our prayers has been completed IN CHRIST.**

There are no unanswered prayers. God has answered all our prayers through the work of the Lord Jesus Christ.

- Your prayer may be <u>hindered</u> by you or the person you're praying for.
- You might not be praying <u>the right prayer</u> that God wants to answer. What I mean is, you might have your priorities mixed up when it comes to the prayer that is needed for a particular situation. Just because people ask for prayer for a particular situation doesn't mean that is the specific spiritual priority at that time for them. God may be trying to accomplish something completely different in that person's life. God is trying to direct your prayer through the Holy Spirit…if you'll let him.
- The answer might not be <u>what you expected</u>.
- What you call prayer…God may call <u>complaining.</u>
- Are you asking God to do something that he gave you the power and authority to do?
- The answer might not be in <u>the time frame</u> you desired.
- A <u>hardened heart</u> can hinder your prayer.
- Wondering whether God will actually do it causes unbelief and doubt to cancel out your faith.

God always answers prayers. It may not be in the form we envisioned, but if it aligns with his will; if we do not doubt, stand firm in our faith and thought life, then God will hear and answer because he said he would.

It's not only important to know that God WANTS to answer our prayers and that he CAN answer our prayers and that he DOES answer our prayers. But confident, bold, secure faith believes that God ALREADY HAS answered all our prayers through the atoning work of Jesus Christ.

The answer to your prayer is YES!

YES…my good and faithful servant!

YES…but there are some things in your life that are hindering your faith.

YES…be patent, I will unfold my master plan before you.

YES…right now, your prayer seems to be hindered by confusion, doubt and guilt.

It's not that God doesn't answer prayer, sometimes we just don't *like* the way in which he answers us or we don't *see* the way he's answered it. People are looking for an immediate YES ANSWER to what they're praying for. They want to be healed right now and they want a side-order of financial blessings. People want to see the evidence immediately in the natural realm. Some of the prayers God has answered for me, have taken years for me to see exactly what he was accomplishing. The answer was coming in a step by step process that God had to lead me through. Not because God is slow at answering prayers, but because I am slow at understanding him, trusting him and releasing my faith. Our vision is limited by the time frame in which we live. But God sees it all from beginning to end. There were critical steps that needed to take place before my desires could come about. It took years for me to see his plan and his power come together and unveil a wonderful work in my life.

God has answered many of my prayers instantly. PRAISE THE LORD! That's always phenomenal. **We need to believe, not doubt, praise and thank God during our prayer time with him, just as if he's already answered our prayer the moment we spoke. The YES answer to your prayer will never pierce from the spirit realm into this physical world until you actually believe the answer to your prayer is YES in your spirit. Otherwise prayer to you will always seem like God is flipping a coin to decide if he will grant your request or not. There's a lot of doubt and unbelief mixed in with** that type of prayer. **The YES answer to your prayer is not based on your accomplishments, virtues, performance, holiness or sinlessness. The YES answer to your prayer is based on Jesus Christ's accomplishments, virtues, performance, holiness and sinlessness.**

> *The answer to all of our prayers in God's promises is YES...*
> *through Christ Jesus our Lord. II Corinthians 1:20*

God answers our prayers immediately, but sometimes the manifestation of your prayer takes time, once again, not because God is slow but because we are. Sometimes we get frustrated and discouraged because we don't understand what God is doing. **Our job as Christians is to trust God, believe in his promises, stand firm on his word and to speak it out of our spirit.** His plan is not to harm us but for us to continue hoping for a victorious future. So leave the results up to God. **If you're anxious and worried after you've prayed, then you haven't left the results up to him. God wants us to pray and then have peace regarding his provision immediately after that.**

> *Don't be anxious, negative, depressed and fearful in your heart.*
> *Let your prayer be mixed with joy and thanksgiving. Allow God's*
> *peace to guard your heart and your mind as you trust in the*
> *finished work of the Lord Jesus Christ. Philippians 4:6-7*

This scripture tells us to not be anxious, to pray, be thankful and then look what happens next. We need to let the peace of God come flooding in regarding his provision. When God gives you peace and rest then we need to latch on to it like a life-preserver in a roaring ocean. **The language of trust is thanksgiving and praise, then our confidence in God will manifest itself in the peace we have after that.**

Do not confuse unanswered prayers or prayers
that seem to go unanswered with hindered prayers.

Our Prayers Can Be Hindered When:

- We have the wrong attitude, are selfish, angry, bitter and unforgiving.
- We don't listen to the Holy Spirit.
- We withhold God's love from others.
- When we harden our hearts towards God.
- Spouses don't love each other like Christ loves the church.
- When our actions don't align with the truth about who we are in our spirit.

- When we are constantly telling God what we have done for him, rather than recognizing what Christ has accomplished for us by way of the cross.
- When we don't understand that our prayers must always be saturated with God's grace.

God's grace towards us is independent of our virtues and accomplishments. God responds to us because it is his nature to do so and because of what Christ did for us at the cross. Our faith mixed with God's grace brings about a manifestation of God's power.

UNANSWERED PRAYERS don't exist. God answers our prayers. However, the answer may not always come in the form that we want. ANSWERED PRAYERS chase after people who align themselves with God's grace, truth and Christ's atonement. God's word promises us his salvation, healing, blessings and provision. So we need to saturate ourselves with God's truth in every way we know how. When we read his word we will know his will. His desires will become intertwined with our desires. When we listen to the Holy Spirit, then he can pray the perfect prayer through us.

Let the Holy Spirit lead and direct you when you pray. Jude 1:20

We don't always know what to pray for,
but the Holy Spirit will help us when we pray. Romans 8:26

When you're praying to God, try to do more listening than talking. Not many people are attune to this but the most important part of prayer is the listening part. Successful and effective prayer has a lot to do with listening to the Holy Spirit. Who has the most valuable information in the conversation between you and God? God does of course!

Jesus said, "Don't worry so much about your life! Why worry about having something to eat or wear? There is more to life than thinking about food, clothing and shelter all the time. Have you ever noticed that the birds don't plant or harvest and they don't have storehouses or barns. Doesn't God take care of them? Do you understand how much more valuable you are to God? Look how the wild flowers grow. They don't work hard to make their leaves, stems and pedals. But understand this, King Solomon with all his wealth wasn't as well clothed as one of these beautiful flowers. God gives such beauty to everything that grows in the fields, even though it is here today and gone tomorrow. How much more will he feed you, clothe you and take

care of you. Don't worry about what your going to eat, drink or wear.
People who don't trust God are always worrying about those things.
Your Father knows what you need before you even ask.
Put God first and all your needs will be supplied." Luke 12:22-31

Obviously God already knows what your needs are before you even ask. So why does he tell us to ask? Have you ever thought maybe he wants to see how mature your prayers have become since the last time you talked to him? **Is your prayer life like a sweet song of thanksgiving played on the strings of your heart, or is it more like an old broken record of begging and complaining? Are your prayers mixed with confidence and hope or are they polluted with confusion, doubt and frustration?** Let's examine the following verses in James 4.

What causes fights and quarrels among you? Don't they come from the desires that battle within you? You want something but don't get it. You're never satisfied or thankful for what you have and you still want more. You constantly quarrel and fight with each other. You do not have, because you do not seek the face of God. When you ask you do not receive because you ask with wrong motives, that you may spend what you get on more pleasures. You adulterous people, don't you know that friendship with the world is hatred toward God? Anyone who chooses to be an intimate friend with this world becomes an enemy of God. Don't you know that the Holy Spirit who lives in us, envies our attention intensely. James 4:1-5

You do not have because you do not ask <u>for the right things.</u>
You do not have because you do not ask <u>for my will to be done.</u>
You do not have because you do not search <u>for souls to be saved.</u>
You do not have because you do not <u>seek first the kingdom of Heaven,</u> then all these things will be added unto you. Matthew 6:33
You do not have because you ask <u>with selfish motives.</u> James 4
You do not have because you do not <u>treat your spouse right.</u> I Peter 3:7
You do not have because you do not <u>love each other deeply from your heart.</u> I Peter 4:8
You do not have because you've allowed a <u>root of bitterness</u> to separate your ear from my voice. Hebrews 12:15

I could continue the list, but basically when your life doesn't align with God's word, it won't align with his will either. Answered prayer is a supernatural law that God will not break. He is true to his word. The question is: ARE YOU BEING TRUE TO HIS WORD?

According to all the scriptures that I have read in the bible, GOD ANSWERS PRAYER! There is no debate on this subject. Whether or not you're enjoying the benefits of the life of God that's inside you is the real question. I hope you're beginning to understand that the truth is we stand in the way of our blessings. Our actions, thought life, words and attitude hinder and misdirect our prayers. We know this is true because God spends a lot of time in the bible telling us what to think about. He's constantly trying to influence us so we will speak confident, encouraging, faith-filled words. God's word tells us how we are to treat each other. Why would God spend so much time speaking to us regarding these subjects if they weren't so vitally important?

I can't see into a person's heart like God can, but through his Holy Spirit, he can reveal what could be hindering your prayer. There could be a whole host of things hindering our prayers because people are so complicated. The bottom line is a bad attitude, wrong thinking and lack of self-control can hinder our prayers. Whatever it is that's keeping you from being able to pray in the spirit with freedom and confidence, lay it at the CROSS OF CHRIST and walk away free from the condemning voice of the enemy.

Know this child of God, God chooses to use your prayer
to accomplish his kingdom's work. He shares his power
with us so he can be glorified through us.

Do you want God to answer your prayer so you will look really spiritual in front of people? Are you asking God for some sign to validate *your* ministry and prove to others that you're in right standing with him? Are you asking God to answer your prayer to prove to you or others that he's real? Only God knows why people pray the way the do.

Everyone's ways seem innocent to them, but their
motives are known by the LORD. Proverbs 16:2

Let's say that every time you pray to God, he responds to your prayer with a resounding YES! Then you stand there and wait for the miraculous provision to occur. While you looking up to Heaven for God to perform, he's looking at you. Why is he looking at you? Because his YES answer has already been deposited in us (II Peter 1:3) His answer to us is always YES (II Corinthians 1:20). So where's the manifestation? IT'S IN YOUR SPIRIT! God has already given us everything we need to live this life in victory and power. **Here are some things God deposited in our spirit the moment we became born-again; salvation, righteousness, acceptance, perfection, holiness, love, healing, anointing, power, faith, authority, revival, provision and** blessings. **This is an incredible inheritance that is ours to enjoy right now while were here on this earth!**

So where's all this great stuff at? If God's already giving me everything I need, then how come I'm not enjoying the benefits of it? WOW! I'm glad we've finally arrived at one of the most baffling questions in the Christian community.

God's divine power has been deposited in us, so that every need we have in life will be supplied. Our knowledge of this truth is critical to living a Godly life, a blessed life and a victorious life. II Peter 1:3

Faith is the bridge that spans the gap between your spirit and your world. Operating in the laws of faith that God has established is the way to release the power that's in you. **There are many laws of faith and this book has touched on a lot of them. Your spirit, mind, mouth, attitude, emotions and body can operate within these laws or not. That's a choice we make every time we think, speak and believe.** When it comes to your mind, proper understanding is critical for your faith to operate. Meditating on God's word is essential for the believer. Believing is one of the most powerful things you can do with your mind. All the laws of faith are launched through our beliefs. Our beliefs prompt our actions and words. When it comes to your mouth; speaking positive faith-filled words is absolutely essential to seeing a manifestation of God's power released from your spirit. Speaking at your problem is another law (shout if you have to). When it comes to your body; getting out of your sick bed and proclaiming the goodness of God is another law of faith. Moving that stiff aching joint and commanding it to be whole are two laws that work together to release faith from your spirit. Resisting the devil in your thoughts and actively fighting against him with your spirit are laws of faith. To draw that YES answer out of our spirit we must operate within the laws God has given us.

By now you may have concluded that with all these requirements in place, God will never answer your prayers! You attitude isn't pure enough and your actions aren't measuring up to God's standard of holiness. You fail God almost everyday, so why even bother praying anymore. Why would God ever answer one of your prayers?

God knows we are made from the dust on the ground (Psalm 103:14). We are foolish, immature and we make plenty of mistakes. Don't feel like you have to be perfect for God to answer your prayers. The YES answer to your prayer was established long before you came on the seen in this imperfect body of yours. It was secured for you when you weren't seeking God. The YES answer for your righteousness was sealed for you before you had any rotten actions. I can state for certain that none of us are perfect or will ever be perfect. God already knows that about us. He's not seeking out perfect people to bless, heal and answer. **God sees us as perfect, righteous, holy and sanctified in our born-again spirit. He accepts us because we accepted Christ.** He's pleased with us because he's pleased with Christ's redeeming work on the cross. This type of grace is something we must mix with our prayers. God's grace is a major principle to balance your prayers with.

Your bad attitude hinders you from praying to God. It doesn't hinder God's answer to you. His answer is YES towards us because he sees us in the spirit (John 4:24). God's YES response to us is based on our spiritual position we have IN CHRIST (John 10:28 & 29). Our faith-filled actions and words release that YES answer from our spirit. That's why a negative thought life will *never* produce a manifestation of God's glory (Romans 8:6). **Faith is our *positive response* to what God has already done by grace. So when I say that being selfish can hinder your prayer life, it's not because God hates selfish people and that he's not going to answer your prayer. It's because selfishness is *not a positive response* to what God has already done by grace. Being selfish in your thoughts and actions goes against what's true about you in your spirit. When your mind comes into agreement with what's true about you in your spirit, only then will you be able to draw the power of God out of your spirit and into your physical body or into this physical world (Philemon 1:6).** This is a principle that we must comprehend before we can release our power, faith, authority and the YES answer from our spirit.

It's not that God refuses to answer your prayer because you have sin in your life. **If sin was still an issue between God and you, then none of us would ever get our prayers answered.** God has already taken care of the sin issue between him and you through the sacrifice of his son. If you don't really believe that statement with all your heart, then you are not esteeming the value and the power of the blood of Jesus. **Sin hardens your heart towards God, not the other way around. Condemnation, confusion and worthlessness will creep into your mind and cause you to seek God less and less because of failure, guilt and shame. Sin can separate you from God (if you'll allow it to) but it cannot separate God from you. Jesus sacrifice made sure of that.** There is nothing separating you and God, that's the good news of the Gospel message! The only thing that could separate you and God is the guilt, condemnation and shame that the enemy gets you to focus on. This is an awesome truth for the believer and the unbeliever to start believing.

God's wrath and anger were poured out on Christ at the cross. Christ has already accepted all the guilt and condemnation from God because of your sin. Can you imagine if God could completely erase from your conscious all the guilt and shame of sin. Think about how free you would finally be! You weren't designed to carry the weight of sin. That was Christ's burden! **Stop trying to deal with sin! Christ has already completely and thoroughly dealt with the sins of the whole world (I John 2:2).** If you keep trying to deal with sin, then you are not esteeming the sacrifice that was made for you, you're devaluing the blood of Christ and ridiculing the atonement of his death.

New Testament saints who have been perfected and purged in their spirit, should have no more conscience of sins. Hebrews 10:1 & 2

I will be merciful towards their unrighteousness, and their sins and iniquities I will remember no more. Hebrews 8:12

So many Christians are completely oblivious to the New Covenant that was secured for them. **Continuing to deal with the sin issue of mankind is a trick from the enemy that the church has embraced.** This keeps people focused on their problems instead of the solution. Christ has already dealt with the sin issue between you and God once and for all. The enemy wants you to stay focused on sin, but God has repeatedly said that you are clean and free from the guilt of sin.

Our willingness to listen, learn, change and grow is what the Holy Spirit loves. God knows your heart and your intentions. We are all "IN THE PROCESS" of becoming Christ-like. Don't ever attack the process! Christians know their not supposed to be sinning. Screaming at the top of our lungs for them to stop sinning is not going to stop them. Don't attack people's sin issues. **Promote the new born-again spirit that's in them. Knowing who you are in your spirit, through the Holy Spirits promptings, is the only way to discover that you are a completely different person at the core of your being. Teach people what being born-again really means and God's grace will teach them to stop sinning. Titus 2:11 & 12**

If I come to the Lord with humility and thanksgiving, then my prayers will not be hindered. If I come to God with love, extend his love to others, forgive people and show them compassion and patience, then my prayers will not be hindered. If I come to the Lord with a confident hope, mixed with expectation, then my prayers will not be hindered. Not because God likes me more because of my improved performance or because I've raised my standard of holiness. But because all those characteristics are positive responses to what God has already done by grace.

DOUBT
*I challenge you to do something maybe you've never
done before and that is to have faith and do not doubt.*

---

*Doubting God's word will dissolve every ounce of faith you have.
We can step out in faith when we have fear, anxiety
and unanswered questions, but we cannot step out
in faith when we have doubt and unbelief.*

Satan persuaded Eve to doubt what God said. The enemy told her, *"You shall not surly die (Genesis 3:4)."* As soon as she chose to doubt what God said, she positioned herself for failure. Doubt drives a dagger through your heart of faith. **Unfortunately a lot of people don't really expect God to answer their prayers, that way they won't be disappointed when it doesn't happen. That's doubt and that's a pitiful way to live.** Our prayers need to be wrapped in hope and expectation not doubt and unbelief.

STORY - So Whose Report Are You Going To Believe?

One time there was this man at church who told me he got a bad report from the doctor. He said something was wrong with his heart and his blood test came back with bad results. The Holy Spirit immediately led me to pray for this man. So I prayed right at that moment with him. I prayed a healing prayer of faith over him; I commanded strength to come into his body and that supernatural peace would be released from his spirit. It was a powerful, anointed prayer. I could sense the Holy Spirit all around me. But as soon as I finished praying for this man he said, "Brother Eric the doctor said this about my liver and then he told me I had an irregular heart beat and my blood pressure is high and I was going to have to take all these pills for the rest of my life." He wanted to make sure I heard everything the doctor told him. But what about the words I just spoke over him!

It was as though I never even prayed for this person!

He didn't receive any of the words that I had just said. I realize he was afraid and worried about everything he had been told by the doctors. He certainly had been given a lot of bad news in the past week, but what about the good news? What about the positive healing words that I had just spoke over him? I wish he would have latched on to those words, believed and received his healing. God's mighty power was right there in front of us; poised and ready to be released through this man's faith. I could feel the power of God so strong in my spirit that it was bubbling up and over into my physical and emotional realm. The presence of God was all over the place when I was praying, but this man did not reach out and become a channel of faith so that healing could flow into his body. His mind was dominated by his emotions and the doctor's words, that's why his body didn't receive the healing it needed.

The truth is this person wasn't ready to be healed. He was so absorbed by what the doctors said that there was no room for God's word in his heart. The Holy Spirit was trying to fill him with new words from Heaven that he needed to hear and receive. The moment I finished my prayer, he started with the negative report the doctor had given him. **Negativity is not a positive response to what God has already done by grace. That's why this man could not release the YES answer to his healing out of his spirit.** He chose not to receive that anointed word because of doubt, fear, worry and distractions. I'm not sure this man even heard the prayer I spoke over him. **Has prayer become something people do with no real expected outcome?**

To be carnally minded is death but to be
spiritually minded is life and peace. Romans 8:6

A roman centurion said to Jesus:
Just say the word and my servant will be healed. Luke 7:7

We have to do our part, which is to receive the word from God, that's our responsibility. Remember when Jesus asked the man at the pool, *"Do you want to be healed?" (John 5:6)* That seems like an odd question to ask a person who's sick. Wouldn't anybody want to be healed? **Our part of receiving a healing is to DELIBERATELY CHOOSE TO BE HEALED and to not doubt that Christ has already accomplished the healing work for us! God's answer to every one of our healing prayers is YES! If you don't believe this, then you're mixing your prayer with doubt and unbelief. When it** comes to healing we need to BELIEVE it, COMMAND it, RECEIVE it, WALK in it, ACCEPT it, and be CONFIDENT and SECURE in it. We need to choose to be healed and accept nothing less than a complete miracle every time.

I've heard many people say, "We just can't understand God's ways. We can't always see the big picture in life. God's will is hard to figure out. We just have to accept the fact that we don't know why God heals some people and others he doesn't." There's a huge portion of the Christian community that is misinformed and confused when it comes to the atonement of Christ. They're confused about their salvation, healing, their born-again spirit, their anointing and God's love for them.

Don't be ignorant about what God's will is for your life. Ephesians 5:17

It's never God's will for us to be sick. He wants every person healed every time. If the Lord did not require our cooperation, then everyone would be healed. John 14:12, Acts 10:38

The Greek word *sozo* is used over a hundred times in the New Testament. It usually refers to salvation, specifically "to be saved". *Sozo* was used as the word "save" thirty-eight times in reference to the forgiveness of sins. Sozo was used fifty times as the word "saved" (pass tense). Many people aren't aware that sozo was also used in the scriptures as the word "healed." Finally, *sozo* was used as "made whole" or "wholeness" in many other scriptures. The same powerful word *sozo* with an identical message, SAVED, HEALED and MADE WHOLE.

My children, I wish above all things that you would prosper and BE IN HEALTH, even as your soul prospers. III John 1:2

Christians have *already been healed* of every disease, sickness and infirmity that tries to latch on to them. It's similar to how sin tries to come upon us. Sin cannot have me because I have died to sin. It cannot latch onto my spirit anymore. The price has already been paid in full, through Christ's saving work on the cross. I am free from; sin, sickness, cancer, tumors, headaches, depression and anything else that tries to attach itself to me. In Matthew 13:22 it says that the cares of this world CHOKED OUT THE WORD OF GOD. Find out what's choking the life out of your prayer. It could be any number of things, such as;

DOUBT	UNBELIEF	WORRY
A HAUGHTY SPIRIT	JEALOUSY	LUST
THE LOVE OF MONEY	COVETING THINGS	BITTERNESS
BUSYNESS	UNFORGIVENESS	CONFUSION
EMBARRASSMENT	IGNORANCE	THE FLESH
CARNAL THINKING	YOUR EMOTIONS	
WORLDLY DISTRACTIONS		

(and the list goes on and on.)

Is God amazed at your faith...or is he amazed at your lack of faith?

Believe God's word and that he will perform it, so God can glorify himself IN YOU, THROUGH YOU and ALL AROUND YOU.

PRAYER POWER
God wants to confirm his word IN US...so he can perform it THROUGH US.

The disciples went out and preached everywhere and the Lord worked in them and confirmed his word by wondrous signs and miracles that accompanied their faith. Mark 16:20

Christians have much more power and authority than they realize. We are just scratching the surface when it comes to using the spiritual gifts God has placed in us. Have you ever wondered, "Where's all my prayer power at?"

- Your prayer power is in your ability to forgive.
- Your prayer power is in your willingness to love others unconditionally.
- Your prayer power is directly proportional to your humility.
- When Christians remain teachable they have prayer power.
- You maintain your prayer power when you are not easily angered and offended.
- You erupt with prayer power when you love your neighbor.
- You have prayer power when you pray for those who despitefully use you.

This is all part of God confirming his word in us. **Your entire life needs to come in alignment with God's word, not so you can get the things you ask for, but so you can become the person God wants you to be. Your Christian life is more about being than doing.** You're already IN CHRIST in your spirit, but in your mind, you may not have a complete revelation of what exactly that means. Everyday crucial information is being revealed to us by the Holy Spirit. **When you're a Christian you are always in the learning stage because God is always trying to teach you something about you and him being united together in one spirit (I Corinthians 6:16).** When Christians remain teachable they have prayer power. If you let the truth of God's word change you, then it will change HOW, WHY, WHEN and WHERE you pray. That's how he confirms his word in us. If we allow the truth of his word to come in and change our attitude, words and thoughts, then there is no reason why when we pray for something, that his word will cease to confirm itself in us. **Does your pray life basically consist of you trying to get things from God or is it about enjoying God's love, presence and companionship throughout the day?**

If you remain in me and my words remain in you, then you
can ask for whatever you wish and it will be given to you.
This is to my Father's glory, that you bear much fruit and
show yourselves to be my disciples. John 15:7 & 8

Allowing God's word to *remain in us* means we allow it to; teach us, change us, transform our mind (Romans 12:2), our mouth, our motives and our methods (James 4:3). Then you can ask for whatever you wish and it will be given to you. Does that mean I can have a million dollars, a sports car and a house on the ocean in the Caribbean Islands? No…it means you can have everything that was secured for you through the atonement of Christ. If you think that doesn't sound as good as the car, house and money, then you haven't renewed your mind enough in God's word. As we read God's word his desires will become something we treasure.

The disciples spent considerable time there speaking boldly
for the Lord, who confirmed the message of his grace by
enabling them to do miraculous signs and wonders. Acts 14:3

The power comes from God, but he chooses to work through us (his creation) because it pleases him to do so. You see the world gauges power in measurements of volts, amps, watts, horsepower, joules, calories and British Thermal Units (BTU's). God's power is not gauged by a physical measuring device because it would blow away any chart a scientist could create. We can hardly comprehend God's supernatural, out of this world, life transforming power. Here are some things that are accomplished through prayer. In Ephesians 3:14-21 it says that:

- Prayer strengths us with power through God's Spirit. (verse16)
- God's Spirit planted in us gives us greater revelation of how much he loves us. (verse 17)
- God fills us with a greater measure of himself every time we pray. (verse 19)

Ephesians 3:14-21 uses the word power three times. God wants you to have a fresh revelation of the power you have in you. **I want my prayer and God's power to connect in such an incredible way, that the world will know beyond any doubt that God is Lord of my life.**

According to God's eternal purpose and mission for us (which was fulfilled by Jesus Christ) we have boldness, access and confidence by faith in him. Ephesians 3:11-12

My interpretation of this scripture is this:

Through the Lord Jesus Christ we have BOLDNESS before the world, ACCESS to God and CONFIDENCE in what our new born-again spirit is capable of releasing.

THE FOUNDATION OF PRAYER

If God has so many wonderful things for us to enjoy, then how come they're not being released when we pray? Could it be your prayers are starting from a position of unbelief? Is your prayer life mainly about you and what you want or need? Is it all about what God needs to do for you? Let's examine some biblical truths under a brighter light through the Holy Spirit's influence.

God has already responded to every person through the new covenant he made with mankind. Jesus secured everything for us through this new covenant. God's answer is YES to us through the work of the Lord Jesus Christ (II Corinthians 1:20). Through Jesus there is now peace between God and you and unconditional acceptance into his family. The healing power of God is in our fingertips and all his blessings have been deposited in our spirit. We already have all the anointing we need to do the things he's commanded us to do. We have the exact same faith as Jesus Christ. God wants us to understand that there's fruit that's been deposited in our spirit and it can only be released into this world through our positive faith-filled words. If we would just understand these concepts, then we would stop praying for all the many things that God has already deposited in us. For example:

- Don't pray for God to <u>send revival</u>, it's already in you. God sent the power of his spirit into you (Galatians 4:6). If you're not revived after that encounter with God, then nothing on this earth will ever be able to revive you. **We need to get excited about what God has already deposited in us.** When we stir our spirit with this knowledge, then it will bring life changing revival into our lives. Acts 1:8

- Don't pray for God to <u>bless you</u>, you're already blessed with all spiritual blessings. God has already commanded his blessing to come upon his children. Once our mind figures out they're already in our spirit, then we can release them through our positive faith-filled words. Ephesians 1:3

- Don't pray for God to give you <u>more anointing</u> or a double potion of his anointing. The anointing you have in you right now would bankrupt Heaven if you released it all at once. Your anointing would make Elisha and Elijah jealous (Matthew 11:11-14). We need to release the anointing that's already in us as we go and do the things God wants us to do. I John 2:27, II Corinth.1:21, Luke 4:18

- Don't pray to God to make <u>the devil leave you alone</u>, resist him yourself and he will flee from you. James 4:7

- Don't pray for <u>souls to be saved</u>. God already wants them saved more than you do. Asking God to save someone is going to accomplish nothing. Speak the real truth of the gospel message to them that's not performance-based, but instead is Christ based, sealed by the new covenant of his blood. Unbelievers can only believe when they hear the truth (Ephesians 1:13, I Peter 1:23, I Timothy 2:3 & 4). The thing we can do is bind the spirits that have blinded the hearts of unbelievers. II Corinthians 4:4

- Don't pray for <u>money</u>. *God has given you power to acquire wealth (Deut. 8:18).* God has placed his power in you to prosper you. Psalm 35:27 says that, *"God delights in the prosperity of his people."* God is not going to print money in Heaven and have it fall from the sky. He uses people to supply your needs (Luke 6:38). *God already knows what your needs are (Matt. 6:8). Seek first the kingdom of God and all these things (food, clothing and shelter) will be added to you. Matthew 6:33*

- Don't pray for <u>God's presence</u> or for God to come and be with you today. God literally lives in you and he said he would never leave you or forsake you. Corinthians 3:16, 6:17, Hebrews 13:5

- Don't pray for <u>more faith</u>. You already have the same faith as Jesus Christ (II Peter 1:1). *God has dealt to every born-again Christian the full measure of faith (Romans 12:3).* You may not be releasing the power of that faith the way Jesus did, but it's still there in you. You just need to learn how to release what you've already got.

- Don't pray for a <u>clean heart</u> like David did in Psalm 51. Your spirit has been cleansed, anointed, purified, purchased, redeemed, saved and then it was sealed after all that! David lived under an Old Covenant; you live under a New Covenant. You're filled with God's Holy Spirit. God responds to us radically different than he did towards the Old Testament saints under the law. *Moses administered an Old Covenant under the Law, but the Lord Jesus Christ sealed a New Covenant of grace, mercy and love between God and mankind. John 1:17*

- Don't pray for God to <u>heal someone</u>, come into complete agreement with Christ's atonement and command them to be healed (Acts 3:6, Matthew 10:8). God wants that person healed more than you do. God loves that person infinitely more than you do. God sent his Son to die for us, so there's nothing he would ever withhold from us (III John 1:2, James 5:15 & 16, I Peter 2:24). Stop releasing what's in your flesh and in your emotional realm and start releasing what's in your spirit.

- Don't pray to God for <u>more power and victory</u>. You have the exact same power in you that raised Christ from the dead. You just need to learn how to release it out of your spirit. Eph.1:19, I John 5:4, Acts 1:8
- Don't pray for God to <u>love you more</u>. Come into agreement with what the scriptures tell you about God's love (I Corinthians 13:3-8). God has completely filled your heart with his love through the Holy Spirit (Romans 5:5). Christians don't have a God not loving them problem...they have a knowledge problem.

We have received the Spirit of God in such a way, that we might know all the things he has freely given us. I Corinthians 2:12

God must really be confused sometimes when he hears our prayers. Christians spend a lot of time asking God for things that he's already given them. He's already commanded his blessing upon us. All these truths are in God's word, but they need to be properly taught, interpreted and understood before they can set us free in our spirit. All these blessings are already in you. Knowing this and operating in these truths is how we release them out of our spirit. Philemon 1:6

Thanksgiving is a powerful attribute to mix with prayer. Not just thanking God for the things we're blessed with. But thank him for all the spiritual blessings (listed previously) that he has deposited in us. **Thanksgiving is an awesome way to release something out of your spirit, because it's a positive response to what God has already done by grace.**

We should always abound in faith with thanksgiving. Colossians 2:7

For example: Instead of praying for souls to be saved, start thanking God for the blood of Jesus. We don't need to ask God to do something so people will be saved. He's already done something miraculous so they can receive his salvation. Start thanking the Lord that all mankind has been reconciled to him through Christ. Praise God that the war is over between God and mankind.

A Prayer of Salvation

God I know you no longer hate people because of their sin. You want them saved more than I want them saved. You love them infinitely more than I could ever love them. They're actually already saved, they just don't know it. A decision is the only thing standing in the way between them and you. Lord I'm going to go and do what you commanded me to do. I'm going to go and tell people about the good news of the gospel message. I'm going to extend to them mercy and grace until they see you in me. I'm going to show them your love and speak the truth of your word to them. Your word is like a seed planted in their heart that can produce salvation for anyone who will receive it (Ephesians 1:13, I Peter 1:23). Your word reveals the truth about your nature and salvation. Thank you for filling me with your Holy Spirit. Thank you for giving me the boldness, confidence and the compassion I need so I can be a minister of reconciliation for others.

This prayer does not ask God to do something. It boldly proclaims what he's already done. That's an incredible foundation to build your prayer life on. We need to thank God for Christ's atonement. We need to come into agreement with what he's already accomplished for the lost. This prayer will release love and power out of your spirit to go and do the things he's already anointed you to do.

THE POWER OF THE HOLY SPIRIT

The word of God is living and active, it's sharper than any double-edged sword. It penetrates and divides our soul and spirit. God's truth judges the thoughts and attitudes of our heart. Nothing in creation is hidden from God's sight. Everything is uncovered and lay bare before the eyes of God. Hebrews 4:12 &13

I know this scripture is speaking of God's word but it is also true in our prayer time with God. The word of God was inspired by the Spirit of God. The Holy Spirit is like a double edge sword. The Holy Spirit penetrates our heart when we humble ourselves before God. He spends a lot of time, encouraging, repairing, counseling, teaching and healing us, when we allow him the opportunity to do so. **God created you because he desires to have intimate communion with you. If you will desire the same from him, then you'll have it. Hebrews 11:6**

The Holy Spirit wants to filter your thoughts, help you process information and then teach you how to react to life, other people and God. The Holy Spirit would like to be involved in everything you do throughout your day. Even the small things like going for a walk or having a conversation with a friend. I've even invited the Holy Spirit into my dreams and I've had some of the best sleep in my life after praying that. The Holy Spirit changes every area of your life that you invite him into. I dare you to invite him into your worship time. He'll turn that soft spoken song into a WAR CRY! So who's stopping him? We already know the answer to that...IT'S US! **Do you allow the Holy Spirit to be an active participant in your thought life, attitude, emotions and words?** When we don't allow him to do what he was sent to do then he is very sad.

Did you know that you can greave the Holy Spirit? Ephesians 4:30
You can put out the Spirit's fire. I Thessalonians 5:19
You can quench the Holy Spirit. I Thessalonians 5:19
You can resist the Holy Spirit. Acts 7:51
You can lie to the Holy Spirit. Acts 5:3

God is trying to influence us all the time. He wants to speak to you and through you. He wants to use your mouth to speak out his wonders. The Holy Spirit wants to pray God's perfect will through you. He is a phenomenal helper that we have constantly with us. ISN'T THAT FANTASTIC! God knew we needed his Holy Spirit to walk with us throughout our day. He guides us, helps us, directs us, teaches us, encourages us, ministers to us and counsels us. All of those job titles require a second person (us) to have influence over before he can be effective. The Holy Spirit is entirely about you being intimate with God. That's why God didn't wait for us to get to Heaven to fill us with his Spirit. He knew we needed him immediately. Jesus told the people to wait for the Holy Spirit and you will be endued with power from on high. Luke 1:35

Have you ever experienced the power of sitting on a motorcycle and throttling it out all the way? Or the power of speaking into a live microphone and your voice is amplified through the speakers so loud that you can feel the sound waves bouncing off your chest? Have you ever felt the power of a jet engine as you're taking off at the airport? Most of us have experienced some type of physical manifestation of power in our lives, but have you ever felt God's supernatural power literally flow through you? Has God's power ever knocked you off your feet and you spoke wonders out of your mouth that you didn't understand? Have you ever experienced the presence of God so strong that you couldn't even stand up and walk? Have you ever felt the power of God when you were praying and you knew without any doubt that the Holy Spirit was praying God's perfect will through you?

The Holy Spirit wants to be an active participant in your life. He will humble you when you worship God. He will do spiritual surgery on you when you read the word of God. We need to be sensitive to him and his mission. **He knows who you are and he knows who you are becoming and he's come to lead you there. We are a temple for him to reside in (I Corinthians 6:19). He's trying to break you out of that religious mold you've been stuck in. He's trying to teach you the mysteries and wonders of God's true nature. There's a lot on his agenda that he's trying to accomplish in your life, but he's waiting for your cooperation.**

HOW MUCH SURRENDER ARE YOU SURRENDERING?

How much of yourself will you give to the Lord? That's a huge question for you to consider. It's a question that can take a lifetime to answer. How long will it take you to understand that the fullness of God lives in you? His nature is in your new nature. How long will it take you to comprehend everything that you possess by being IN CHRIST? Hopefully, since you've almost completed this book, you have a new revelation of the these truths.

Your faith will begin to work when you understand and declare to the world every good thing God has deposited in your spirit. Philemon. 1:6

When you accepted Christ into your HEART, God completely transformed your spirit. Your mind, thoughts, words, mouth and actions are continually learning about your *new nature*. Your old nature doesn't please you any more, you hate it. Infact, it no longer exists. You do still have lingering old thoughts and habits that were influenced by that *old nature*. But the good news is your *new nature* will guide you in new thoughts, words and actions, as you allow the Holy Spirit to lead you.

Wouldn't you love to sit down and talk to some of the smartest people in the world, pick their brains and listen to them? Millions of high school students flood into colleges and universities all over the world to gain knowledge...but the God of the bible is forsaken. Only a few are doing any research to find out more about him. People seek after man's knowledge and worldly wisdom while God's truth is forsaken. The Apostle Paul said:

The world's wisdom is foolishness to God. I Corinthians 3:19

Take a close look at the absolute perfect design of all the systems of the human body. Consider how complex and intricate the human eye is. A person studying to be an optometrist will spend most of their life studying the eye, but they may know nothing about the God who created and designed it. Going to school and learning is an excellent choice. But a college degree will not draw you closer to God or get you into Heaven. **You could possess all the knowledge that the best universities have to offer. But if you don't do any research regarding your creator then you're a fool. Your eternal security with God is the most important topic you could ever research. It would be of no benefit to you to gain all the wisdom and treasure of this world and in the end...lose your own soul? Mark 8:36**

I want to spend time with the one who has all this creative power.
I want to know what God knows.
I want to know everything he knows about me.
I want wisdom beyond my years.
I want to understand everything about God's nature.

*Those who seek me will find me when they
seek me with all their heart. Jeremiah 29:13*

Sometimes seeking God is scary. It's kind of like when you were little and first started to ride and balance your bike with no training wheels. You had to really trust the person that was teaching you because you didn't want to get hurt. It's also kind of like when you first learned to swim. You may have been afraid of the water but you trusted the person that was with you coaxing you along. God is with us when we take those crucial steps of discovery about him. He's not going to force us, but he will encourage us as we take those steps of trust.

---

*Our small efforts are what God uses to demonstrate
his mighty wonders. All God expects us to do is the little
things we know how to do, then he can do his part...
the miraculous, wonderful, magnificent and amazing part.*

God has done many miraculous things in my life and he's always required me to take that first step of faith. Look at all the mighty things God has done throughout the bible through simple ordinary people. Those people were very similar to you and I. They had the same fears, worries and doubts. They didn't want to be laughed at by others. But they reached a point in their lives where they decided that what God thinks is more important than what people think. So they trusted God with that first crucial step of faith. All of God's biblical principles and promises require that we believe and trust God with our lives and our circumstances. Steps of faith involve; praying, believing, obeying, loving others, standing firm, trusting, praising God, shouting, dancing or any number of things the Holy Spirit prompts us to do. When we do these little things unto the Lord, they become big things in the supernatural arena. It's like lighting a fuse in this physical world that leads to an explosive charge in the supernatural world.

When we step out in faith, then God can step in with power.
When we praise God for his grace, mercy and love, then he fills
us with the peace that surpasses all understanding. Philippians 4:7
When we charge after our spiritual giants,
then God will slay them before us. I Samuel 17
When we give our tithes and offerings based on the love we have
for God, then he will open up the windows of Heaven. Malachi 3:10

God's always looking for our steps of faith so he can glorify himself through us. God is mighty, powerful and sovereign. God has given us all the faith that we need for this journey through life. Now give that faith back to him so he can reveal his glory through you.

The Holy Spirit longs to complete the connection in YOUR MIND regarding what God has already accomplished in YOUR SPIRIT.

When we make the connection and understand, then rapid transformation begins in our actions.

- The Holy Spirit comes out of our voice with a song, a word of truth or a shout from our spirit.
- He makes himself known to the people around us with our loving actions.
- The Holy Spirit is evident in our attitude with our mysterious and confident smile.
- He speaks his wonders out of our mouth and guides our hands to serve. The Holy Spirit wants to lead you into a faith-filled, mountain-moving prayer.
- He causes us to see and hear things beyond our physical world and wants us to command these things to come forth from our spirit.

Just give him an opportunity and be ready to be amazed. The Apostle Paul wanted us to know that: *Faith without any actions prompted by the Holy Spirit is dead (James 2:26).* So trust God and take those initial, crucial and powerful steps of faith.

A GUILTLESS PRAYER LIFE

With all the millions of prayers that go up to Heaven everyday, why
don't we see millions of examples of God's miraculous power everyday?

Can you count on your fingers how many minutes you spend in prayer a day? The average Christian only prays about three to eight minutes a day. Maybe the sad thing isn't so much the lack of *time* in prayer; maybe it's the lack of *passion* for prayer that is so disappointing. Or maybe it's a lack of *thanksgiving* in prayer that confuses God. Your prayers could have a little too much doubt and unbelief mixed in with them. Don't pollute your prayer life with pride, selfishness, bitterness or unforgiveness. The answer to your prayer could be, "Soon, just be patient." Confused and disappointed you think God didn't hear your prayer. No matter what the combinations of reasons are, the problem is always us. It's never God who is slow or indifferent towards us. He is passionate and attentive towards our situation. His answer is always YES to us.

What's your motive during prayer…is it selfish?
Are you praying for the will of God in your situation?
Is prayer to you a way to motivate God to respond to you?
Do you begin your prayer with thanksgiving?
Does your prayer life consist of mainly updating God about your
situation, as if he didn't already know what your needs are?
Is you're prayer life mainly about begging God for something?
Do you allow the Holy Spirit to search your heart and pray through you?

When you ask, you do not receive because you ask with wrong motives.
James 4:3

I keep coming back to *us* when it comes to hindered prayers. That's because the problem is always *us!* The solution to answered prayer is about Christ. Don't ever ask God for anything based on what *you've done.* Everything we will ever receive from God is based on what was accomplished for us at the cross, at the curtain and finally at the tomb. The power comes from God through us. It's our responsibility to make sure we are not hindering the flow of God's power. Many times we tie the hands of God before we even kneel down to pray to him.

Jesus could not do many miracles in his own hometown
because their faith was hindered by their flesh. Mark 6:6

- We take away his life transforming power through unforgiveness and bitterness.
- We close off the peace that surpasses all understanding through our negative thought life.
- We kill the miraculous healing power of God through doubt and unbelief.
- We stifle the Holy Spirit through fear and embarrassment of what people will think.

If you're praying to God and you're just not feeling an exchange between you and him, then stop right there and ask God to reveal to you what's blocking your prayer. The Holy Spirit wants to lead you in prayer, so be sensitive to him. You may have a long list of things to bring to God in prayer, but God may have one thing he wants to speak into your soul that could change all your priorities.

Story - A Prayer Life Saturated With The Love Of God

God showed me this one day when I was praying to him. I remember being frustrated when I was praying. I felt in my spirit like nothing was being accomplished. I thought, "What's going on Lord?" I felt like I couldn't go any further in my faith. I felt empty and dry. Then the Lord began to reveal his love to me in a greater way. He touched my heart and I began to understand his love at an incredible new level. I began to know with certainty how great his love is for me. I got so busy with my life (and ministry) that I forgot to enjoy the journey. I forgot to enjoy God. I forgot to soak in his love on a daily basis. God had been trying to communicate this to me for some time. **I read about God's love in the bible on a daily basis so I had the knowledge. But I needed a fresh revelation in my mind of the fullness of God's love in my heart. I needed that information to become a reality in my life.** I don't remember asking God for anything after that phenomenal moment with him. My long list of questions, concerns and problems just fell to the floor. I had everything I needed from God the moment I was saturated with his love.

Faith works by love. Galatians 5:6
Without God's love working in me…I am nothing. I Corinthians 13:2

When it comes to our faith, everything rises and falls on the knowledge, understanding and complete revelation of God's love. Knowing God's complete nature is a mind blowing experience. Knowing his love intimately is what releases every good thing that

he has deposited in our spirit. Knowledge is power and knowledge about God's true nature towards us, releases supernatural power and revelation from our spirit. Understanding God's complete and unconditional forgiveness towards us also helps us to approach him with confidence, security and boldness.

When you kneel down before God in prayer ask him this question, "Lord what is the most important thing right now between you and me?" If you feel condemnation from sin that you seem to be struggling with then release them to God. Lay them at the cross where they belong and where they are covered in the blood of Christ.

<u>The enemy brings up the past and tells people:</u>

You failed God because you did that!
Look at how filthy your language is
and you're supposed to be a Christian!
You have too many bad habits for God to accept you, fellowship with
you and truly love you. You'll never be able to break those habits!
You won't ever be free from sin because it's apart of who you are.
It's engrained into your character.
You're still a sinner, you always will be
and you know that's never going to change.

None of these statements that the enemy whispers in your mind are true. Don't ever let the enemy attack your identity. **Your *new birth* in Christ determines how God responds to you.** Here is a short description of the supernatural attributes of every born-again Christian.

<u>IN CHRIST YOU ARE (In your spirit):</u>
You are a new creation, born of an imperishable seed from God.
I Peter 1:23
You are the righteousness of Christ. We are 100% righteous in God's sight (Romans 5:19). This righteousness is not based on any of our virtues or actions. It's based on our position and inheritance transferred to us through Christ.
You have been freed from sin (Romans 6:6). Your spirit can no longer sin. I John 3:9
Your old nature no longer lives in you, but CHRIST lives in you. Romans 8:10
You have been born-again, you are now a completely new person. II Corinthians 5:17
You have the spirit of God living inside of you and God certainly cannot sin. Only your mind and body can sin, but that will change as you renew your mind. Romans 6:11, 8:9
You have been brought from death to life. Romans 6:13

Sin is no longer your master. Romans 6:14
Condemnation has been erased from your heart. Romans 8:1
Nothing will ever separate you from the love of Christ. Rom. 8:35 & 39

There are many bookmarkers in the collection I've written that will remind you of your new identity. IDENTITY IS EVERYTHING! **God responds to our born-again spirit based on what Christ has accomplished for us in the atonement.** God responds to you the same as he did with Jesus, because Christ earned the adoption papers for us and sealed them with his blood. **You are a part of God's family now and you have all the benefits, rights and blessings that come with your family position.** As far as God is concerned, you are his child not his step-child. You were literally born from his supernatural seed. I Peter 1:23

Don't let the enemy quench your prayer life through condemnation.
We have been forgiven and therefore we live
in a forgiven state. The devil likes to bring up our past
but the Holy Spirit is preparing us for our future.

Sin is the only leverage Satan ever had on mankind. Christ destroyed that holding power at the cross. Accept the blood covering of Jesus Christ as the full payment of sin. Now walk away in freedom and confidence in the completed work of Christ. Do what Jesus said to do in John 5:14 and John 8:11; *"Go and sin no more."* Because you no longer have to serve sin like a slave serves a master. Romans 6:16

Christians confront the POWER OF SIN everyday.
It shows up in people through:

JEALOUSY	UNFORGIVENESS	DECEIT
RAGE	BITTERNESS	SELFISHNESS
ANGER	SELFISHNESS	PRIDE
ARROGANCE	SEXUAL IMPURITY	BOASTFULNESS
GREED	HAUGHTINESS	GOSSIP
ENVY	HATRED (MURDER)	ADULTERY

Christians may involve themselves in any of these sins. But remember, that's not your identity anymore. These are extremely bad choices people make that don't align with their new born-again spirit.

...sin is crouching at your door, it desires to have you,
but <u>YOU MUST MASTER IT.</u> Genesis 4:7

If you're free from sin, then why does it have so much power over you? The simple truth is, because you allow it to have power over you. You think about things for an extended period of time that you should have ejected from your brain long ago. You used to be a slave to sin before the cross of Christ. NOW YOU HAVE THE ABILITY TO MASTER OVER IT! Did you know you have that power inside of you? You didn't have that ability before. Your identity used to be sinful so you sinned without any reservations. You thought about whatever you wanted to think about. Now your identity is completely different. You're IN CHRIST. That new spirit living in you will produce love, joy, peace, patience, kindness, goodness and self-control. Will you sin some days? I don't know, that will be your choice to make. It depends on what you've been filling your mind with. It also depends on which direction you allow your thoughts to take you. Christians meditate on some awful things that they should have ejected from their mind the moment that thought formulated. If you do sin it won't be because you are a dirty rotten sinful Christian. It will happen because you gave in to the external power of temptation when you mixed it with some of your old desires and old habits (which you still may have) that were driven by your old nature (which you don't have anymore).

If you're a born-again Christian you are no longer evil, sinful or dirty. **God doesn't call us righteous and then hope we will get there one day. WE ARE THE RIGHTEOUSNESS OF CHRIST! It was supernaturally imparted into your spirit.** You can't earn it through behavior modifications. Christ earned it for you. You're covered in his righteousness and his blood. Don't let the enemy fool you into thinking you're a dirty, sinful, evil, failure and why did God even take the time to save you. You're a saint of God. You're a temple that the Holy Spirit lives in. Your God's child now and Satan is mad that you're no longer his.

Christians feel horrible when they sin, but don't base your identity on that fall that happened. You are not sinful because you sinned. **That's what the blood of Christ was for, to not only cover your sins but to destroy, completely obliterate and pulverize your *sin nature*.** Release that guilt, frustration and pain to God. **God's love for us is not based on our perfect performance or our failures. God loves us because of who he is.** So walk in your new identity that Christ established for you. Then go and sin no more like is says to do in John 5:14

PRAYER AND RELATIONSHIPS
Extending forgiveness to others validates the
richness of God's grace and mercy in your heart.

Knowing that God has completely taken care of your sin, by way of the Cross of Christ, makes it easier to forgive others and mend relationships with them. **Having the complete confidence that the relationship between me and God has been reconciled, is my foundation for doing everything within my power to reconcile with others.** I believe we need to take care of any fractured relationship issues because we love God and his people.

If you are offering your gift at the altar and you remember that
someone has something against you, leave your gift there at the altar
and first go and make every effort to be reconciled to them,
then come and offer yourselves to the Lord. Matthew 5:23 & 24

It's important to God that we do everything in our power to resolve any issues between each other. If you're a born-again, blood-bought, child of God, then you are an ambassador for him. You are a minister of reconciliation. You are his representative to other people.

If you want God to show himself strong in YOUR LIFE,
then you need to show yourself strong in HIS WILL.

Do everything without complaining or arguing, because you are
a child of God. You stand blameless and pure before him. We live
in a dark, crooked and depraved generation and God wants us
to shine like stars in the night sky. Philippians 2:14 & 15

I want you to reread the scripture above. Now I want you to read it again. Read it until it begins to sink into your mind, heart and mouth. For some of us, if we obeyed this scripture alone, it would eliminate more than half the conversations we have with people. It's through our loving actions and words that we stand out from the rest of the world and shine like stars in the night sky. Go make amends with the people around you. Also go to anyone who has sinned against you or offended you and amend that relationship as well. Don't be against other people because God's not against them. **God is entirely about mending broken relationships, first vertically through you and him (which has already been settled through Christ's blood) and then horizontal through you and others.**

Confronting people and doing this is going to be a hard thing to do depending on how willing you are to humble yourself. We know God wants us to do it; therefore he will give us the ability and strength to do it. Many of you may have not talked to some of your family members for years. Maybe you had a horrible divorce and said some things you shouldn't have. We've all said stupid things to people that we didn't mean. Could it be those little offenses that are weighing down your prayer life? Think of how proud God is going to be when you humble yourself and do what you can do to make amends with others. That's going to show God how much you love and trust him. It shows God how much you value the forgiveness he has extended to you.

PRAYER AND THANKFULNESS
With thanksgiving present your request to God. Philippians 4:6

If you want to take someone's spiritual pulse just listen to how thankful they are. Never underestimate the supernatural power inside of you called thanksgiving. Being thankful is a powerful attribute to mix with your faith. Being truly thankful shows God the condition of your heart. We need to show genuine and passionate appreciation for the goodness of God. It's an attribute he loves for us to enjoy.

When you begin to pray to God, start thanking him for your salvation, a home in Heaven, Jesus, the Holy Spirit, for the cross, redemption and forgiveness. Thank him for the people he has put in your life; your pastor, your church, your spouse, your children, friends, family and co-workers. Thank him for your health and for the beauty of the earth for us to enjoy. The truth is we can never stop thanking God enough for his favor, blessings, mercy and grace. Is God going to advance you to more when you haven't thanked him for what he's already done? **Thankfulness is our positive response to what God has already done by grace. Being thankful is an incredible way to release God's power and blessings from your spirit.**

A heart full of thanksgiving is the perfect way to begin a conversation with God. So give thanks in all circumstances. I Thessalonians 5:18

A lot of us start out our day with very busy schedules. Then a negative thought may come into your mind. That negative thought could lead to another negative thought and so on. It might even develop into a whole avalanche of dark thinking and frustration. STOP RIGHT THERE! Start running in the other direction in your thought realm. Start thanking God for anything and everything that comes to your mind.

Thank him for that grouchy boss. Having a grouchy boss means you have a job you should be thankful for. Instead of being frustrated because you have a messy house, start thanking God that you have a home to clean and enjoy. Maybe you're getting older and you have a few aches and pains that you like to complain about to everyone. You may need to take a field trip to the hospital, there are plenty of patients there who can't walk, can't see and can't breathe. Seeing those people will remind you of what to be thankful for. Someone always has it worst then you do.

My wife took care of a lady who had stomach and intestinal cancer. She was a diabetic and she had an open wound on her leg that hadn't healed in years. She also had a colostomy bag. Unfortunately she was so obese she could hardly move. Even though she had all this pain and anguish in her life, she still praised God and thanked him daily. She was always a grateful and thankful woman of God. My wife said after visiting her you always walked away renewed, energized and blessed. It was part of her countenance. God gave her this peace, contentment and joy that the world could not steal from her thankful heart.

As I said before, someone always has it worse than you, but that's not even the right premise for being thankful. A thankful spirit is grateful all the time, regardless of the circumstances or events of the day. A spirit of thankfulness is something you determine your going to walk in at the beginning of the day. Make a decision that you're going to be thankful today, and the world is not going to steal that from you.

STORY - The Lost Oven Rack

One time my wife took our oven rack to Home Depot to see if she could buy another one just like it. Unfortunately she accidentally left it there in the bottom of a shopping cart, so we went back to the store that night before it closed to look for it. My wife went into the store to talk to the employees and I started checking the hundreds of carts at the front of the store. Do you know how many shopping carts Home Depot has? I would guess about five hundred. It would have taken both of us hours to look through them all. Since the situation was hopeless and it would take a miracle to find it, I decided to call on someone I know who's in the miracle business. God has deposited in me his phenomenal Holy Spirit and nothing is hidden from his eyes. I said to the Holy Spirit,

"You know exactly where that oven rack is. You have all wisdom, knowledge and understanding and I need some of it right now. Please help me."

The Holy Spirit is our helper, teacher and counselor for any situation we ask him to be involved in. Was it a life threatening need or an absolute emergency where we needed to see God's miracle working power? NO! I just needed to find our lost oven rack. So I invited God into my situation. Before I even started looking through the carts at the front of the store, I was led by the Holy Spirit outside where another few hundred carts were lined up next to the building. I really didn't want to look through all of them either. I turned to my left and there was my oven rack leaning against the building. PRAISE THE LORD!

Being negative and complaining would have killed any hope for a move of God in my situation. I could have gotten mad and yelled at my wife. I could have thought, "WE WILL NEVER FIND THAT THING!" I could have excluded God from the situation but I choose to live my life as a child of God. When I cried out to him with joy and thanksgiving he helped me. The Holy Spirit gave me the knowledge and direction I needed.

Nothing is too big or too small to involve God in. If your little toe is hurting, then God is just as concerned about it as you are. **Dear saints of God, we need to invite the Holy Spirit into our situation, life, dreams, conversations and song. Create an atmosphere around yourself where God can move and operate freely.**

Be careful what you let come out of your mouth, evil words are not appropriate for a child of God. Let your words be sweet like honey, full of thankfulness and glorify God all day long. Ephesians 5:4

You might be thinking, "I don't speak evil, satanic, demonic words I'm a Christian." Well, that's who this scripture is talking to. An evil word could come out of a Christian's mouth in the form of being argumentative, opinionated, controlling or negative. I want God's presence in me, around me, above me and below me. The spirit of God literally lives in me. That means I'm completely full of love, joy, patience, kindness, goodness, faithfulness and self-control. I am not about to let a lost oven rack change that atmosphere around me. God is too precious to me to allow that to happen. I need the peace that surpasses all understanding in this dark world. I need him close to me. I need God to be just a whisper away. Don't give the presence of God away for anything. **Does this carnal world we live in dominate you or**

does your spirit bring life and peace into this world? Be determined in your mind that your attitude and emotions are going to glorify God and please him in everything you do.

I will praise the Lord with a song from my mouth
and glorify him with thanksgiving from my lips. Psalm 69:39

DON'T GIVE AWAY YOUR PRAYER POWER

Have you ever been angry at some other driver for doing something stupid on the road or in a parking lot? You may have called them a name or even cursed at them. Maybe this subtle rage began to build up inside of you because that driver caused you to have to stop at a traffic light or be late for a meeting. Maybe you just really wanted the closest parking spot to the door. What happened to the peace that surpasses all understanding that Philippians 4:7 speaks of?

One time my wife and I lived in an apartment complex and we had a car load of groceries. I really wanted a close parking space so we didn't have to carry our groceries so far. My wife said, "I hope we can get a close space." I responded, "We'll never get a close spot!" WOW! Why did I say that? Since I'm a child of God, shouldn't I expect God's best? Shouldn't I expect God's blessings to flow out from me? **My positive words should be intertwined with expectation so God's power can be released from within me. Negativity will never release faith from your spirit; it's one of the laws of faith that God has established. In fact, negativity pulls against your faith. Folks, we have enough of the world pulling against us. Don't let this world give you a rotten attitude; we need to change this world's attitude. The church needs to saturate this world with positive faith-filled words. You are a supernatural channel for God's goodness to be released through and the world desperately needs us to release the power of God on them.**

Christ literally lives in you...no matter what.
Whether or not he lives through you at any given moment...
is a choice that Christians make everyday.

We make right choices when our actions align with our new identity. We make wrong choices when our actions don't align with our new identity. The fruit of the spirit is not; anger, rage, bitterness, selfishness and arrogance. Those were some of the attributes your old nature participated in. The fruit of having God's spirit in you is LOVE, JOY, PEACE, PATIENCE, GOODNESS, KINDNESS and SELF CONTROL. These are the attributes of your *new nature* and you are not lacking in any of these qualities. **You have a whole orchard full of *The Fruit of the Spirit* in you. Now that you understand this, let it come out of you. Let Christ come to the surface and allow him to reveal himself in your thoughts, words, attitude, emotions, facial expressions, actions and laughter.**

We need to operate in what God has already given us. The very first thing God has given us is salvation through the Lord Jesus Christ. **If we choose not to forgive others, even though we were completely forgiven of our sins, then that shows very little appreciation for the sacrifice that was made for you by the Lord Jesus Christ.** We can't move forward IN CHRIST until we understand and leap over that trap of being offended and unforgiving. This is what I mean by operating in what God has already given us. Our minds need to fully understand that God wants us to walk in his power, blessings, favor, forgiveness, provision and anointing. We can lose our prayer power through lack of self-control. That's a trap to keep us ineffective for the kingdom of God. The enemy loves when we lack self-control. He knows there is plenty of frustration in this world to keep you anxious, up-tight, worried, angry and bitter. This guilt and frustration will hinder your faith and prayer life.

Let the peace of Christ rule in your heart. Colossians 3:15

WOW! Are you receiving this word into you spirit?
Here is my interpretation of that scripture.

Let the peace of Christ rule, reign, over power, minister, evaluate, possess, control, influence and dictate to you how you will respond to every person, situation and emotion that comes into your life.

I want this kind of peace! We need this kind of peace! Don't give it away over some bad driver, a lost oven rack, a grouchy boss, an irritated spouse or a parking space.

One time my wife and I where going through some spiritual battles for her soul. The enemy always fights the hardest when a spiritual break through is about to happen. He knows every sold-out, born-again, fire-baptized Christian has phenomenal potential to damage his kingdom of darkness. He's not going to just stand by and lose a worker of iniquity and watch them become a saint of righteousness.

I was praying over my wife as she laid there asleep in bed. Then I saw in the spirit realm that we were both in a heavenly place. We were at an altar on our faces before God. Then a river of gold colored liquid came down from the top of the altar and flowed over us. It was strange, but I knew something was happening to us in the supernatural realm.

Then I noticed all these warring angels in two lines on either side of us. They were holding these large intimidating spears. Then, I saw a dark evil spirit there with us. This demon was terrified and kept trying to flee but he couldn't. The angels leaned their staffs forward and opened their mouths with a loud, long, steady shout. They sounded like they were all in perfect key and pitch with each other.

Then the demon went berserk. He was holding his head and screaming. He was trying to get away but something held him there. I noticed he was getting smaller and smaller. I knew he was dying. The angels kept that same loud tone with that same steady pitch singing out of their mouths. The demon continued to get smaller and smaller. I held out my hand and the demon landed in my palm. He was almost lifeless now. I closed my hand on him and squeezed. Then I opened my hand and he was gone. REMOVED FROM EXISTENCE FOREVER!

I opened my eyes and thought, what just happened here? Did this really happen in the supernatural realm, or was I just going crazy? I believe I was so weighed down and burdened in prayer for my wife; I so desperately wanted to see her be victorious through Christ; that God opened up a supernatural window for me to see what my prayers were accomplishing. Five months after that event my wife got saved, filled with the Holy Spirit, born-again, baptized and completely turned her life over to the Lord. I realized then that I had engaged the enemy in spiritual warfare AND THE ENEMY LOST! I seen the enemy die in the palm of my hand. God has reminded me many times what he accomplished that day in the palm of my hand. When I look at my hands it's a reminder in the physical realm, of what God can accomplish through faith in the spiritual realm.

Our struggle is not against flesh and blood, but against rulers, authorities and the dark powers of this world. The war against these evil forces will be fought in the spirit realm using our minds. Ephesians 6:12

We demolish arguments and every evil force that aligns itself against the truth of God's word when we take captive every thought and make it submit to the truth of the Lord Jesus Christ. II Corinthians 12:5

If we really understood what was being accomplished through our prayers, we would be interceding for everyone and for every need all the time.

STORY - Go And Possess The Land

One time I was outside at night finishing up some yard work and I began thinking about the older couple who lived next to us. As I walked along the edge of our property, the Holy Spirit led me to begin praying for them. It wasn't an ordinary prayer; it was a fervent passionate prayer from my spirit. It wasn't the time for a general prayer that you lightly sprinkle on the top of people. It was time to GO TO WAR! As I began to pray for them the Holy Spirit spoke to me and said,

"You're on the wrong ground.
I want you to pray on their property.
I WANT YOU TO POSSESS THE LAND!"

WOW! That was different! The Holy Spirit never spoke to me that way before. So I went over to their property and began praying for my neighbors. As soon as I stepped on to their land I felt something leap in my spirit. I began to pray differently. God was moving, directing and orchestrating every word that came out of my mouth. The words that I spoke were filled with life and power. I knew God was there and he was working things out. Awesome things were being accomplished in the supernatural realm.

A few days later I saw my neighbor outside and I stopped to talk to her. She told me how her husband had been sick and was actually in the hospital these past few days. She told me everything that had happened to him. Just before I left I said, "Can I pray for you and your husband." That was the first time I ever had the opportunity to pray with my neighbor. I reached out my hands to her and she reluctantly took hold of them. I made sure I prayed about everything God wanted her to hear. After I finished praying we talked about God for a while, then I said, "Good evening" and walked away. As I was walking to my front door the Holy Spirit spoke to me and said,

"Turn around…do you see where you where just standing?"

My neighbor and I had just prayed on her property
at the exact same place I had prayed a few nights ago!

Christian soldiers, we need to go and possess the land. Our feet need to walk on it. Our prayers need to cover the earth. **The Christian community has an untapped resource of power locked up inside them, waiting to be released through their positive faith-filled words and actions. Will you be a channel for God to flow through is a question we answer everyday by what we believe, say and do.**

Don't worry about anything but instead pray about everything.
Tell God what you need and thank him for all he's done. If you do this
you will experience God's peace, which is far more wonderful than the
human mind can comprehend. His peace will guard your heart
and mind as you enjoy complete rest in him. Philippians 4:6-7

The Apostle Paul tells us to pray about everything. Those are very clear directions. Don't just pray for the sake of praying to pass the time or to fill a required time slot that you feel will please God. Don't fall into a rut of praying those GIVE ME THIS, GIVE ME THAT, and GIVE ME MORE type of prayers. God has a solution to everything that we come in contact with, so we should be praying about everything we encounter.

God wants us to be changeable and teachable. Kneel before him with thanksgiving. Be quiet before the Lord, he may have something important to say. Read I Peter 3:8-12 regarding what happens when we align our mind, attitude and mouth with God's agenda.

All of you should be of one mind, full of compassion toward each other, loving one another with a tender heart and humility. Don't repay evil for evil. Don't retaliate when people say unkind things about you. Instead, pay them back with a blessing. This is what God wants you to do and he will bless you for it. Turn away from evil and do good. Work hard at living in peace with others. The eyes of the Lord watch over those who do right and his ears are open to their prayers. I Peter 3:8-12

There are eleven things listed in this scripture that God asks us to do. If we will put forth the effort and show God we are serious about changing; then he will do two things according to this scripture; he will *hear our prayers and bless us.* I not only want my prayers heard but I want the blessings of God chasing after my prayers. I want the blessing of his presence, power, healing, favor, provision and anointing in my life. Does God require absolute perfection from us, of course not, that's not even within our reach. He wants us to remain teachable and willing to be molded into the image of his Son.

When our will aligns with God's will, he will perform his word. Once you've experienced it, you'll never want to be without it. If you really want God's will in your life, then his will is for you to change, grow and mature IN CHRIST.

CHAPTER 10

IN THE HANDS OF THE MASTER

People spend a lot of time, energy and money *getting* married, but they don't spend a lot of time and energy *staying* married. People usually look at the divorce rate as an indicator to how marriages are doing in society. The fact remains that there are plenty of couples who have physically and emotionally divorced their spouses, yet they remain legally married for different reasons.

The adversary has injected unforgiveness, lust, selfishness, envy and greed into the hearts of many married couples, non-Christian and Christian alike. Satan has successfully destroyed countless marriages. Remember when Jesus addressed divorce to the Pharisees. He said, *"This is not how it was in the beginning, it was because of the hardening of your heart" (Matthew 19:8).* So divorce became a condition of humanity by the hardening of people's hearts. This happens when we reject God's word and ignore the Holy Spirit's promptings on how to *be* and *stay* happily married. If your marriage was like a small sailboat, then God is like the force of the wind that pushes it along. The wind takes the sailboat different places and God will take your marriage from where it began to where it needs to go. Without wind the sail boat would have no direction, purpose or destiny.

Don't sever your marriage from your creator.
Your marriage is like a rope braided with three cords.
This includes YOU, your SPOUSE and the LORD.
(A cord of three strands is not easily broken. Ecclesiastes 4:12)

Many couples try to fulfill their marriage dreams through their own strength, power and love. God is not at the center of their marriage. He seemed to be at the beginning; after all, most people get married in a church, by a priest or pastor, they made a commitment or vows before God and other witnesses. But God wants to be involved in your marriage everyday, not just on the day of your wedding.

Take healthy, spirit-filled marriages out of the foundation of the home and our churches and communities will soon crumble. The home will no longer be a refuge from the world, but a place of strife and unrest. This occurs when the husband and wife are divided in their spirit and in their purpose. With broken, disillusioned church members, the church will not be able to function the way God wants it to. The gifts of the Spirit will not be poured out and active in the church and its members will soon surrender to mediocrity. Can God's church be rendered useless with no power? No, it cannot! Remember the gates of Hell shall not prevail against the church of God (Matthew 16:18). The church is not a building structure; the church is a body of believers. Believers are Christians who:

- Stand on the promises of God's word. They read, believe, memorize and speak God's word. They are not deterred by their circumstances. They are not doubters and are not discouraged by negativity. They are hopeful and persistent in their faith and in what God wants to accomplish in their lives.
- They're prayer warriors. They know the voice of God when he speaks to them. They spend time in their prayer closet with God and they are completely confident that God hears them and he knows what's best for them.
- The praises of God are continually on their lips. They know praise is a spiritual weapon and a supernatural shield. Through praise they overcome and sickness and depression (Proverbs 17:22). They know they were created to praise the Lord.

This is the kind of believers and the kind of church that the gates of Hell will not prevail against. These types of believers have THE POWER OF GOD working on the inside of them. They have spiritual authority over the enemy and they're not afraid to use it. In fact, they're ready, willing and excited to release it. They have wisdom and revelation from God regarding his nature, plan and provision. The Holy Spirit has completely engaged their soul to accomplish God's supernatural objectives. These are the people who call down the power of Heaven into their lives and into their marriages.

Jesus is in the soul repairing business and a marriage consists of two souls that need restoring. Jesus Christ wants to pick up all the shattered pieces of your marriage and create something whole out of it. If you will cry out to him together as husband and wife, he will not only put it back together, but he'll make it stronger than it ever was before. The bible says, *"That the two will become one flesh (Ephesians 5:31)."* He will give two individual people one united spirit with common desires.

The Holy Spirit filled family unit is a stronghold against the devil.

IN THE MASTER'S HANDS
by Eric Johnson

There was a table in the center of the dark cold room.
My spouse and I walked up to the table and saw a
tall glass vase with a candle at the bottom of it.
We both reached down into the opening of the vase
and as we touched the candle, a flame jumped to life.
The entire room was filled with a brilliant light.

After a while a dark shadowy figure came into the room.
He walked around us and then over to the table.
He came very close to the glass vase almost knocking it over.
We cringed as he nearly brushed up against it a second time.
I wanted to run over to the vase and grab it
and protect it from this sinister being.
He started to walk away from the table.
Then he swung his arm back and knocked the vase into the wall.
It shattered into hundreds of pieces.
He left us there in the dark cold room.

This symbol of our marriage had been shattered.
With down cast faces we separately left the room.
Why did this have to happen?
I could feel a cold chill flow into my heart.
My love and joy were leaving my spirit.
I wandered around in a dark fog for a long time.
I cried out to God, "I want to love again with passion!
I want a heart that cares, forgives and loves!"

I went back to the room and looked through the door.
A light was coming from the center of the room. IT WAS JESUS!
He picked up all the pieces the enemy had shattered.
As he placed each piece back together,
it seemed to glue itself in place.
Jesus looked at me, smiled and said,
"I HEARD YOUR PRAYER AND
I AM THE RESTORER OF YOUR SOUL."

I came back the next day and peeked into the room.
Jesus' hands flowed over the vase and a brilliant
fire made the vase glow red hot. Jesus
had not only repaired the glass, but he was
tempering it to make it stronger than it was before.
Jesus looked at me and said,

"SEE, I MAKE ALL THINGS NEW.
YOUR MARRIAGE IS IN MY HANDS NOW!"
At that moment, I felt something leap within my soul.
I left the room thanking and praising God.
The next day I could hardly wait to get there.
I peeked through the door and saw a beautiful sight.
Half of the vase was now tinted with an array of colors.
As Jesus touched the small pieces of
newly repaired glass they changed to a unique color.
Jesus said, "I'm almost done, GO GET THE ONE YOU LOVE."

I found MY LOVE slumped down in the shadows of life.
I extended my hand out and said,
"Let's see what can become of our marriage
IN THE MASTER'S HANDS."

We went back to the room and it was very dark again.
I could see an outline of the table and there was the vase.
We walked up to it and then we reached down into the vase together.
When we touched the candle the flame came to life again!
The light got brighter than ever.
The vase was stunning and the colored glass was incredible!
It was even more beautiful than before.
We looked around the room
and the colored lights danced everywhere.

Jesus made something whole out of our broken mess.
In the HANDS of the MASTER our marriage
was a brilliant shimmering rainbow of light,
FOR ALL THE WORLD TO SEE.

God's perfect design of marriage is a man and a woman coming together as one flesh. They share their thoughts, ideas, dreams and love. Two separate individuals coming together and uniting with one purpose and mission. That's why marriages don't work when people are selfish and self-centered. In a spouse-centered marriage, your thoughts are on your spouse and their needs. If you married someone for what they can do for you, then you got married for the wrong reason. It's easy to GET married, but most people don't have the commitment to BE married and to STAY married. **Most people don't understand the amount of love, attention and sacrifice a marriage requires to thrive.**

Jesus came to be a sacrifice. He said, *"I did not come to be served, but to serve and to give my life as a ransom for many" (Matthew 20:28).* Love is demonstrated by sacrificing something. If you're not giving up something, then you're not sacrificing anything and you're not loving the way God wants you to. You may have to sacrifice some of your time, energy or money to express love to your spouse. You may have to sacrifice your Saturday afternoon college football time to go on a walk with your spouse. Is your spouse a distraction for you or an attraction to you? Most of the time, expressing love to your spouse will not be so much about what you're willing to DO, but it will be more about what you're willing to GIVE UP. You're going to have to sacrifice something from yourself, something that's valuable to you to really show that you love them.

Divorce isn't killing marriages, its lack of forgiveness that's killing marriages. Selfishness is squeezing the life out of marriages. Spouses are hateful, angry and frustrated because they can't control the other spouse. The "I LOVE CHOCOLATE CAKE" kind of love, will not sustain your marriage. It takes something much deeper than that. It takes a love that looks out for the welfare of others rather than yourself. Most marriages today have reached a point where they simply tolerate each other. Worldly love does not produce thriving marriages. Most couples don't have a clue as to the type of love it's going to take for their marriage to heal, grow, thrive and prosper. Many couples have settled for a sub-standard, loveless, conditional, performance based life with their spouse.

Marriages in today's society are considered lucky just to be able to exist together. Many married couples live in the same house together, but that's it. They don't share anything else, they live completely separate lives. Living happily ever-after is just a story book fantasy that dissolved after their first few years together. **Many spouses don't possess the love that's necessary to serve the other spouse unconditionally.** The bible says that a man and his wife need to become *one flesh.* That means two individual people had to die so they could now live for each other. This is accomplished by serving each other, nurturing each other, loving each other and being patient with each other. Couples need to be SPOUSE-centered rather than SELF-centered. They need to be OTHERS-centered rather than ME-centered. This is the kind of love the Apostle Paul talks about in I Corinthians 13.

When you love your spouse, you'll enjoy learning about them and responding to their needs. Spouses need to develop the commitment and patience necessary to learn about and love the intricate details of each other.

I framed a picture of a rose for my wife with these words written down the edge of the flower.

THE ROSE
by Eric Johnson

*Here is a rose for you dear. It's drawn with a crayon.
It may not look like much. But follow me into my heart and
hold my hand as we walk through a bright forest.*

*At the end of the forest is a valley filled with millions of roses
rolling through the countryside as far as you can see.*

*This describes my love for you and what's in my heart.
I wish I could fill our home with all of them.*

*But here is a picture of one of the roses
picked from the millions in the valley of my heart.*

I asked my wife for permission to make THE ROSE into a bookmarker so other spouses could convey to their loved ones how much they admire them.

With all the busyness and distractions of this life, we all fall short of the mark when it comes to conveying to our spouses how much we truly love them. **Folks we need to shower our spouses with the love that God has placed in our heart.** Do things specifically for them simply because they're special to you. Let them know you're thinking about them and they are continually on your mind. Tell them and show them you love them everyday. You don't have to spend a lot of money to let them know they're loved and special to you, but you do need to be passionate about what you're doing. A simple love note for your spouse, purposely placed so they will find it later, is a fantastic reminder of how much they mean to you. The more creative you are the more they'll know you really mean it.

---

*Husbands: If you'll treat your wife like a queen in your thoughts
and actions...then you'll be a king in her heart.
Wives: If you'll treat your husband like a king in your words
and deeds...then you'll be his queen forever.*

STORY – Loving Your Spouse...God's Way

One time I used a lawn mower to tell my wife I loved her. In the back yard I mowed all the grass except for a strip shaped like the letter "I" and then I left some tall grass next to the "I" in the shape of a heart and then I made the letter "U" at the end of that. I told my wife to come and see what a great job I did mowing the lawn. When she saw the tall grass she was confused. She said, "This looks awful!" I told her to READ WHAT IT SAYS. Then she got the message. She was so excited that I wrote a love letter to her at such a grand scale. It's been over twenty years since that day and she still tells people that her husband mowed a big I LOVE YOU in the lawn for her. It only took about ten minutes to do that for her and that message is still radiating from her heart today. **The love of God flowing out of your spirit will show you how to be creative when loving your spouse.**

Husbands continually give special honor to your wives. Treasure her, study her and understand her as you live together. She may be weaker than you are physically, but a woman is just as strong as a man in her spirit and in the spiritual realm. She is your equal partner and companion for experiencing God's gift of new life together. If you don't treat her as you should, your prayers will be hindered. I Peter 3:7

God designed the marriage between a man and his wife to replicate the reflection of love between Christ and his bride (the church). One time in the bible, when Jesus was talking to a crowd of people he said, *"You adulteress generation!"* Why did he say that? Had everyone under the sound of his voice committed adultery? No, but they didn't truly love God anymore, they gave their heart to another. Their heart chased after the world and not the face of God and his true nature. They seemed to honor God with their lips (in their words) but their hearts (their passion) were far from him. Matthew 15:8

Whatever you treasure in this life...
is what your heart will focus on. Matthew 6:21

God wants to make something whole out of your broken mess. If you'll just agree together and give God a chance, he'll transform your marriage into something it could have never been under your own power and will.

Just as God has a purpose and destiny for his church,
he also has a purpose and destiny for your marriage.

That purpose will fuse two separate individuals together to become one in spirit. You can either hinder or help the flow of God, it's that simple. The choice is yours. Let Jesus transform your marriage into a brilliant shimmering rainbow of light for everyone to see.

THE SNOWFLAKE
by Eric Johnson

One snowy afternoon, my daughter
and I were doing a craft together that
involved cutting, gluing and drawing.
My daughter looked out the window and
said, "Daddy the snow is so beautiful."
I said to her, "Let me tell you a story
about one of those beautiful snowflakes."
I took a clean white piece of paper and said,
"Let's pretend this piece of paper is your dad's life."
I folded the paper in half, three times.
Then taking the scissors I said,
"Sometimes bad things happen to us in life,
kind of like these cuts I'm making in the paper."
I began cutting pieces out of the folded
paper and she watched them fall to the floor.
I told her, "When something awful happens in your life,
you feel like someone cut a big piece out of you."
She watched another piece drop to the floor.
"Other days life just seems to make
even more cuts into you.
Bad news seems to come from every direction
and my life certainly looked like a mess
with all those pieces missing.
But when you have faith in the Lord Jesus Christ,
you are a part of God's family,
and when you believe the truth of
God's word and do what it says,
then God always protects his children.
As you see when I unfold the paper,
what the world used to harm me,
God used to refine me and turn
my life into a beautiful snowflake.
You see dear, each snowflake that falls from
Heaven is a reminder to everyone, that God
can make something beautiful out of your life."

This was the very first message the Holy Spirit ever inspired me to write. After I told my daughter Erika about it, I began teaching other children and adults the lesson the Holy Spirit gave me. It's a rather simple object lesson with a clever and memorable message. I hope the next time you see it snowing you're reminded of this story.

No matter how the enemy uses the world or other people
to attack you, stand firm on God's promises.

God will turn your PAIN…into POWER.
God will turn your MESS…into a MIRACLE.
God will turn your TEST…into a TESTIMONY.
God will turn your PROBLEM…into a PRAISE SONG.

Don't fear people or the world system, for I am with you. Do not be down cast and depressed, for I will strengthen you with my power and uphold you with my strong hand because I am your God. Isaiah 41:10

The Lord says, "Because you love me, I will rescue you. I will make you great because you trust in me. When you call to me, I will answer you. I will be with you in times of trouble and rescue you. You will enjoy a long and happy life full of the salvation of the Lord. Psalm 91:14-16

Count it all joy when you face trials in life. Because the testing of your faith develops patience and patience must finish its work in you so you may become mature and complete, not lacking anything. James 1:2-4

My wife and I recently planted a wild flower garden. We put some commercial quality weed guard down to keep the weeds out and to keep it nice looking. I was glad that we took the extra time to do it right and cover everything thoroughly with two layers of weed guard. After a few months, I noticed a weed had sprouted up right through all that weed guard. I moved the wood chips to see what happened. A weed had pierced the weed guard like it wasn't even there. I also noticed a similar incident one summer when my daughter and I went bike riding. In this one section of new bike path there were weeds that had actually grown STRAIGHT UP THROUGH THE PAVEMENT! I had never seen anything like that before. How did those plants grow through three inches of new solid pavement? WOW! I thought that was amazing! If only our faith was as determined as those little plants to reach for the sky. The enemy, the world and your flesh will come in and try to keep your faith down.

They will try to convince you that you can't grow.
Why bother putting roots down…look what's over you.
Look at the challenges ahead…you can't make it.
You're going to drive yourself crazy
trying to follow and understand God.
You've disappointed God too much to be able to please and serve him.

But God has given each of us a measure of faith (Romans 12:2). It's like a seed that he plants in each of us (I Peter 1:23). Many people think, "What could God ever do with my little seed of faith?" Just prepare yourself Christian soldier, read God's word, pray, seek his face and give God the praise he's due. That's how we send down our roots. The enemy tries to extinguish your faith before it even has a chance to sprout. But God has planted in you a faith that reaches for the sky. Pavement is very hard and thick and a plant is soft and fragile. Yet those plants managed to grow right up through that thick, hard, black, hot pavement. Never stop reading, praying, changing and growing. Grow in the knowledge and grace of the Lord Jesus Christ. He will cause your faith to blast through any obstacles in life.

God specializes in surprise endings. That way everyone will know it was him that did the work and he will get the glory for it. God doesn't want the glory given to someone or something else. That's why we have to wait on God. **Waiting builds up our faith. The more desperate we get, the more faith it takes to believe for the impossible. It's not that God gives us more faith, it's that we rely more heavily on the faith that he has already given us.** God has already given every Christian the full measure of faith that they need to live an abundant, victorious, joyful life that glorifies him.

Just like _THE SNOWFLAKE_ story says:

God is patiently waiting to make something beautiful out of your life.

CHAPTER 11

READING GOD'S WORD

I will never forsake your commandments Lord. I treasure the words from your mouth, they're more important to me than my daily bread.
Job 23:12.

Satan doesn't mind when we carry our unread bibles to church every week. Satan doesn't mind that you have a big family bible sitting on the end table at home. He loves the fact that you haven't opened it in decades. He doesn't mind when we have bible studies. He doesn't even mind that you vaguely know of two or three bible verses. What he doesn't like is when you *believe* what you read in the bible and allow it to influence the way you live. There is a tremendous difference in knowing what the bible says (biblical knowledge) and believing, meditating on and speaking the word of life from your heart (biblical wisdom and supernatural application).

If Jesus is your savior and the Lord of your life, if he has redeemed you from your life of sin and placed you in his kingdom of light, then guess what? Reading about his life, his character, the things he did while he was here on earth and the things he proclaimed about himself, will be a pleasure. It won't be boring, IT WILL BE EXCITING! **Reading your bible is going to be one of the most life changing events in your time with God.** You see the bible was written by the Spirit of the living God and you are filled with that same spirit. When those two spirits connect something leaps inside of us. It's God in the supernatural realm connecting with us in the natural realm.

STORY – God Still Speaks To Us

My wife was going down the wrong road in sin and heavily addicted to prescription drugs. My prayers began to surround her and cover her with protection. She actually had to leave the house and go live with her aunt and uncle so they could keep an eye on her. When I packed some clothes for her I also put her bible in her suit case. Yes, she was a bible owner, but the bible didn't own her. She looked good carrying it into the church on Sunday, but it never carried her. She wasn't a bible believer, at least not yet. You see my prayers had brought her to her knees. My prayers chased my wife towards God. Now she needed to feed from the word of God and allow it to save her, change her and transform her.

While she was staying at her uncle and aunt's house, God brought a scripture to her mind in the middle of the night. It was Deuteronomy 1:6. My wife had barely ever read the bible, but she was aware there was a book in the bible called Deuteronomy. The next morning, she still remembered the scripture reference God had given her. When she went into the kitchen her aunt said, "Your husband brought a suit case full of clothes for you last night." So she went into the bedroom and prayed to God.

> "Lord I feel your presence and if this is really you and it's not just something I'm making up in my head, then my bible will be in this suit case when I open it."

She unzipped her suitcase, flipped open the lid and there was her bible right on top of her clothes where I placed it. The first scripture she looked up was Deuteronomy 1:6 and it says:

> *You have been on this mountain long enough.*

Folks, we've been away from the heart of God for far too long. Many times we choose a path and a direction for our lives, but it's not necessarily the way God wants us to go. We're so busy with everything this life has to offer. We need to turn back to God and surrender to him. You've been wandering around the same mountain long enough. Going around a mountain in circles means no growth and no maturity. **We grow when we change, we change when we learn and we learn when we read.** We mature in our faith when we read God's word. Reading God's word is not a waste of time. It's not a boring mundane ritual. **When we read God's word we begin to discover the truth about God and the depth of his nature towards us.**

When we read the bible, the Holy Spirit begins to perform spiritual surgery on us. The bible says the Holy Spirit will reveal the deep things in God's heart to us (I Corinthians 2:10). The Spirit of God teaches, counsels, encourages and renews us when we give him our heart and our mind.

Give him your mind and he will give you WISDOM.
Give him your pain and he will give you HEALING.
Give him your weakness and he will give you his STRENGTH.
Give him your humanity and he will give you his DIVINITY.
Give him your body and he will make you his TEMPLE.
Give him your heart and he will give you his LOVE.
Give him yourself and he will give you a RELATIONSHIP
with him that you'll never forget.

In just one moment of time God can give you a revelation about his nature that will change the way you think for the rest of your life. A life spent chasing after God and learning about him is a fulfilled, satisfied, complete and abundantly overflowing life.

Husbands love your wives just as Christ loved the church and gave himself up for her to make her holy. Cleansing her by washing her with water through the word, and to present her to himself as a radiant church, holy and blameless without stain or wrinkle. Ephesians 5:25-27

Reading the Holy Bible (the truth) creates right thinking in our minds about who God is and his *new spirit* that lives in us. If we will submit ourselves to the Holy Spirit, who wrote the bible, then he will come in and do a supernatural cleansing in our minds. You see our mind didn't get saved. Our minds are still filled with a lot of junk from the past. We still remember our old nature, habits and sins. After our salvation experience (the born-again experience that Jesus told Nicodemus about in John 3:3) we became a different person in our nature. The Holy Spirit came to live in us so he could minister to us constantly. His job is to teach us about our *new nature* and how to use that *new spirit* in us to respond to life, God, redemption, other people, sin, righteousness and healing.

The Spirit of God (in us) is continuously trying to teach us. The rate at which we mature in our Christian life, is directly proportional to how much we surrender to the Holy Spirit's promptings. Unlimited humility and surrender on our part, equals unlimited understanding, growth and wisdom from God.

It is so important to get your mind right. When you're about to swim in a certain direction, the first thing you point in that direction is your head. You don't point your head one way and swim another way. Whichever way your head is pointed, that's the direction your body follows. I can't express enough how important your thought life is. **Your mind will choose every path that you take in life.** You are a child of God, holy and dearly loved and we need to get our minds going in that direction by saturating ourselves with the truth of God's word.

Meditating on God's word and surrendering to the authority of that truth, allows God the opportunity to manifest himself in that promise.

I've wasted enough of the time God has given me on wrong thinking, self-centeredness, self-righteousness, rotten attitudes, regretful actions and negative words. I want a free flowing river of God's gifts in my life which include his; power, anointing, favor, blessings, provision, protection, peace, presence, direction, healing and love. The mouth of this supernatural river begins to flow by surrendering to the truth of God's word.

LET THE HOLY SPIRIT READ GOD'S WORD WITH YOU

When you read a verse in the bible ask yourself the following questions:

Do I really believe what that scripture says about me to be true?
Do I really believe that message and believe
what it means for me today in my life?
Do I really believe what God promised me in that verse?

Don't move on to the next verse until you believe what that verse says about you is true. Otherwise the bible has just become recreational reading. God's word is like living water, it's food from Heaven. It's like a double edged sword that reveals to us who we are deep within our core. It's more than just a nice peace of historical record. **When we read the word of God, we need to allow the Holy Spirit to cut deep into our hearts and do the work he was sent to do. The word of God**

is a powerful seed. It will produce something spectacular in you if you allow it to. It will produce life and peace in every area of your life (Romans 8:6). When we read God's word the Holy Spirit is constantly whispering in our ear:

> This is what that scripture means specifically for you.
> Here is where you need to apply it in your life.
> This is what I want you to speak boldly.
> Here is an area that you haven't surrendered to me.
> You might not be doing these things right now,
> but you're in the process and that's good.
> These truths are your destiny.

When we read God's word we need to listen to the Holy Spirit's voice that's whispering in our ear and receive that supernatural revelation. **Without application the bible is just words without power, but with the right application you can release an avalanche of universe creating power that's locked up within you.**

God's word comes alive in us and it radically changes our character. It's sharp like a sword and cuts deep into our soul and spirit. It transforms the thoughts and attitudes of our heart. Nothing in all creation can be hidden from God's truth. All of the many secrets in our heart are completely exposed before him. Hebrews 4:12 & 13

The Spirit of the living God wrote the bible as he moved upon people. We are also filled with the Holy Spirit. When the Holy Spirit that's in us, collides with the Spirit of God that wrote the bible, then that moment becomes a phenomenal manifestation of truth in our hearts and minds. The words from the bible seem to leap off the pages and into our spirit. **We begin to realize that we're reading about who we are (right now in our spirit) and who we are becoming (our destiny).**

God will captivate and amaze you when you read his word. When you read your bible God surrounds you with his nature and presence. God is a supernatural being, so you can't use the world's perspective or your flesh to seek after him. You'll never understand him that way. You have to perceive God by your spirit.

Proper interpretation of the TRUTH will set you free in your mind.
Proper application of the TRUTH allows you to take advantage of
that freedom and run towards your divine destiny. John 8:32

God wants you to experience your new identity IN CHRIST. **Knowing we have God's unconditional presence and love on the inside of us brings us security and confidence to trust him completely.**

Everyday God whispers in our ear:

- Learn about who you are IN CHRIST and the fullness of my presence in you.
- Now that Christ is living in you, you just need to be yourself and I will be in every action and word that comes out of your new spirit.
- Allow me to influence your thoughts, words, emotions, attitude and actions.
- It pleases me to see Christ coming out of you.

When you read your bible listen to that whisper next to your ear. This new information about you will bring about changes in how you think about yourself, thereby changing your actions. The Holy Spirit speaks specifically to us individually as we read our bibles. Everything the Holy Spirit says to you will be an encouraging word about your new identity. Look at what happens to people who closed their heart to the voice of God.

You hear but never understand, you see but never perceive.
Your hearts have become calloused, so you can no longer hear with
your ears. Your eyes are wide open but you can't see anything.
If you would turn from your carnal thoughts, then I would give
you spiritual vision so that you could see clearly and I would open
your ears so you could listen and understand. Matthew 13:14

*If you really desire to know God better...THEN YOU WILL...
because he rewards those who diligently seek him. Hebrews 11:6*

<u>When we first accepted God into our heart:</u>

His spirit made a home in us. Galatians 4:6
His light removed the scales from our eyes. Acts 9:18
God whispered into our ears and we clearly heard his voice. Jn. 10:27
He opened up our mind so we could understand the truth. Philip. 2:5
His glory was deposited in us. Ephesians 1:18

*When we read God's word we begin to understand his character,
thoughts, desires and the truth regarding his love, grace and
forgiveness towards us. When his desires become our desires then he
will give us the desires of our heart. Which were his desires first for us.*

*Jesus said, "Whatever you desire when you pray, believe
that you have received it and you shall have it. Mark 11:24*

A roman guard had strict orders to go and arrest Jesus. He went determined to carry out the orders his commander gave him. Weapons were in hand and his troops were behind him. But when he came to the crowd were Jesus was, he stood there and listened to him talking to the people. Jesus' words were loving, gentle and true. His words cut into the Roman guard's spirit and enlightened him. How do we know this? Because the soldier went back to his commander and said:

I've never heard anyone speak the way this man does. John 7:46

What! You're going to go back to your commander and tell him that! He disobeyed a direct order and risked his position, reputation, imprisonment and possibly death! His comrades were probably very confused. The truth and love from Jesus' words changed this Roman guard's hard calloused heart and he was willing to accept any consequences for his actions. Those must have been some convincing and convicting words Jesus spoke that day. Jesus' words were sharper than their swords and his truth penetrated their armor. We need to read the words that Jesus spoke. They had power in them two thousands years ago and they have just as much power in them today as well. Jesus said,

The words that I speak to you are full of life and power. John 6:63

<u>People who don't read the bible use excuses like this:</u>

There just isn't enough time in my day (week, month, life).
I hate history. It's boring. I'm too busy. I can't find my bible.
I don't have the time or patience.
The language is so old, I don't understand it.
I don't believe it's going to make any substantial changes in my life.
How could a bunch of old philosophies from
an old book affect my modern day life?

*They will call to me, but I will not answer, they will look for me,
but will not find me, because they despised my words
and did not accept my truth. Proverbs 1:28-30*

WOW! Those people are on dangerous ground! Look at what the first and second chapters in the book of Romans tell us about rejecting the truth of God's word.

*The wrath of God is being revealed from Heaven against all the ungodly
people who suppress the truth by their wickedness. Romans 1:18*

They exchanged the truth of God for a lie. Romans 1:25

*Because of your stubbornness and your unrepentant heart, you are
storing up wrath against yourself for the day of God's wrath,
when his righteous judgment will be revealed. Romans 2:5*

*For those who are self-seeking and who reject the truth and follow evil,
there will be wrath and anger. There will be trouble and distress
for every person who does evil. Romans 2:8*

<u>THE POWER OF GOD'S WORD IN US</u>

STORY – Royal Ranger's Rainbow

One time my church was going on a Royal Rangers (the Christian version of The Boy Scouts of America) weekend camping trip. The boys were ages eight to twelve years old. There were about twenty-five boys and seven adult commanders going on the trip. As we began to drive to the campsite, the weather began to get lousy, dark and rainy. I knew this was going to be a disaster when we reached our campsite if this weather persisted. I quieted the boys down in the van and we all prayed over our trip, the weather and God's favor. When we reached our campsite the rain had completely stopped, PRAISE THE LORD!

We began unloading our supplies, tents, food and tables. Then I stopped dead in my tracks and saw the hand of God all over our campsite. The entire camp was filled with brilliant sunlight. The dark clouds were literally being pushed away from us and a bright blue sky was all that was left behind. I looked straight up above me and there spanning the entire sky was the prettiest rainbow I had ever seen. It spanned the entire sky and it was directly over us. We had to look straight up above us to see it. WOW! THE LORD IS GOOD! I had never seen weather change so drastically. God did a miracle at our campsite that day. We went there to shine the light of his glory to those boys and God shined the light of his glory on us.

Skeptics may say, "You simply drove out of the storm and rainbows do many times accompany thunderstorms." They have a good point. It could have been a coincidence that we prayed thirty minutes before we got to our camp site and the rain completely stopped when we pulled into the park. It could have been a coincidence that the storm seemed to be pushed away from us as we were unpacking. Maybe it was a coincidence that we had a completely blue sky after the storm and for the rest of the weekend. It could have been a coincidence that we had a big beautiful rainbow directly over our campsite.

But it also could have been the mighty hand of God!

You see a supernatural element was introduced into our situation. It's called THE PRAYER OF FAITH. Now that a Christian person's faith has been introduced into the situation, even the skeptic has to admit there is a possibility that God intervened. You see even a skeptical person doesn't have all knowledge. They don't know everything about everything. A skeptic might say, "Well neither do you!" But we do have the Holy Spirit living inside of us and GOD HAS ALL KNOWLEDGE ABOUT EVERYTHING. When we compare our knowledge with God's wisdom: It would be like us taking one small baby step to cross a universe that's a billion light years wide. That's how little we know in comparison to God. I don't think any comparison is justifiable. God knows everything there is to know about everything and he also knew how to create everything from nothing. We have God's Holy Spirit inside of us, giving us the knowledge we need for any situation. The Holy Spirit will reveal to us the depth of God's nature. WOW! THAT'S AWESOME!

The secrets of the kingdom of Heaven have been given to you.
Matthew 13:11

God will destroy the wisdom of the wise, the intelligence of the proud will bow down to God. Where is the wise man? Where is the philosopher? Where is the scholar who will exchange words with God? The knowledge of this world is foolishness when compared to God's wisdom. I Corinthians 1:19, 20 & 25

If any of you lacks wisdom simply ask God for it and you shall have it. James 1:5

You may be smart based on the world's standards, but if you know nothing about God's love, forgiveness, salvation and grace, then you missed the most important information about the most important relationship you'll ever encounter.

God can make you wise faster than anyone on the planet. Having the Holy Spirit inside of us is a tremendous resource of knowledge, wisdom, security and comfort. He will divinely influence you when you invite him in to your situation.

God's Holy Spirit gives us supernatural wisdom and profound understanding in our heart. I Corinthians 12:8

Since the day we heard about you, we have not stopped praying for you and asking God to fill you with the knowledge of his will through all spiritual wisdom and understanding. Colossians 1:9

Be encouraged in your heart and united in love, because you have the full riches of complete understanding and know the mystery of God and his son Jesus Christ. In him you'll discover a wealth of valuable information. I tell you this so no one may deceive you with their persuasive arguments. Colossians 2:2-4

These scriptures all confirm that God can give us divine knowledge about any specific situation through his Holy Spirit. The Holy Spirit is always ready to let you know how you're supposed to think, act and what to say in any situation. The bible says:

Jesus got up and rebuked the wind and the raging waters, and the storm subsided and all was calm. "Where is your faith?" he asked his disciples. In fear and amazement they asked one another, "What kind of man can command the wind and the water to obey him?"
Luke 8:24 & 25

Whatever you ask in prayer, believe that you've received it and you shall have it. Mark 11:24

So that's what I did. I rebuked the storm that was threatening our camping trip for the weekend. I didn't rebuke the storm so we could have a nice camping trip. There were boys there that needed God in their lives. There were boys there that didn't have a father to love and encourage them. God wanted to glorify himself that weekend through men that wanted to shine the light of Christ to these boys. As our hearts touched God's heart, his glory came down around us. God can move in that environment and he literally did move on the environment.

STORY - Walk For Jesus

Years later there was another weather miracle that happened to a large group of us. It was at a world wide event called *Walk For Jesus*. Basically it was a one day, world wide, coordinated event to go out into the city streets and glorify God and honor Jesus Christ.

There was an extremely heavy down pour the morning of the event. It was raining so hard that I had to stop and purchase a rain coat and pants or else I was going to get drenched. There was absolutely no way this event could happen that day during this torrential down pour. I thought maybe they would just cancel the event. As I was sitting in my car watching it rain, something rose up in my spirit and I began to speak to God,

"Your not going to let it rain on us today are you Lord? This WALK FOR JESUS event is to honor and glorify you and your son. I just can't believe that you're going to let it rain on us as we set out to do this. I feel you speaking something into me right now and I'm going to have faith in you for what seems to be impossible."

I went to church full of peace and assurance that God was in control of the situation. We met at the church before we went down to the city wide event. I asked them if they brought any suntan lotion because we were going to need it. They laughed as if I was joking, but I wasn't. Something was nudging me in my spirit saying God is in control. As we looked out the window into the rain, the phone rang and we were informed that the event was not going to be canceled because of the weather. When I said, "It's going to clear up anytime now," I got some strange looks...but I knew what God had spoken to me earlier.

When we got to the downtown area, people were getting out of vans and busses with their umbrellas up and their raincoats on. We all waited under a parking structure watching the rain begin to slow down. At 10:00 AM we all stepped out to WALK FOR JESUS. We all had our raincoats and umbrellas, but we didn't need them. It stopped raining right at ten o'clock!

We walked the route they had planned for us and it was still very dark and cloudy. It looked like it could begin raining again at any time, but it never rained one drop. At the end of our walk the entire group of about two hundred people met on the top of the parking structure. There was a large stage and seating for the city wide event. A pastor came out and began to pray. THEN IT HAPPENED! With my eyes still shut I felt the warmth of the sun hit my face. It was like the hand of God had brushed up against me. I didn't open my eyes; I just stood there in his presence. Tears began to roll down my face as I began to remember what God had spoken to me early that morning. God heard the cries of his faithful ones that day and he revealed himself to us at that precious moment. What he confirmed in my spirit early that day had come to pass. It wasn't really the sunshine we needed, it was him that we needed. God wanted to see who would cry out to him and who really trusted him with steps of faith as they walked for Jesus. As I opened my eyes I could see the entire city around us. There was a circle of clear blue sky about a quarter mile wide directly over us. God loves to see the kind of faith that steps out into the middle of a storm and says,

"MY HEART IS AT PEACE...BECAUSE GOD IS IN CONTROL. "

Wow! What a day to remember. God can certainly alter the creation he has made. So get yourself an experience with the word of God. I'm just simple enough to believe God with all my heart.

God wants us to be saved, healthy, prosperous, joyful, blessed and healed. That doesn't mean we're not going to have trials, difficulties or low points. But those are the times when we prepare ourselves and mature for even greater opportunities in the future. You're just going to have to step out and get an experience with the word of God for yourself. **I've come too far and you've come too late to tell me God doesn't perform miracles or still speak to us today.**

You won't ever succeed at anything if you don't take a chance on failing. Take a chance on God's promises. Some people don't step out in faith because they're afraid God will not be in it and then what will they look like. They won't look like people of faith or they will look like their faith is weak. Do you see the problem with this type of thinking?

You're worried about what you will look like,
rather than what God wants to do through you.

Being extremely self-conscious (carnal) has stifled a lot of people's faith. One of the scriptures to counter this problem is found in Colossians 3:2, "*Set your mind on things above, not on earth below.*" Your earthly mind thinks about your needs, wants, desires, goals and plans, but God has a plan for you that completes you and fulfills your destiny. You won't be happy doing anything else in life until God is at the center of your life. A heavenly minded person thinks about God's will, his plan and his desires. When you listen to the Holy Spirit, supernatural doors will open, divine opportunities begin to unfold and God will pour out his spiritual gifts on you in a new and marvelous way.

The bible is filled with promises which are for us to
STAND ON, BELIEVE IN, SPEAK OUT and RECEIVE.

The world is not going to stand on the promises of God. So don't look to them as your example on how to trust, love, give and hope. It's the Christian community that needs to speak out the wonders of God. On the day of the *Walk For Jesus Event* it was raining very hard. The weather was awful, but I believed for something awesome to happen that day. Yes, this was kind of a crazy thing to do. My physical senses were telling me this rain is never going to stop. But my spirit was telling me something different. I chose to perceive life through my spirit that morning. People could have said that I was a Jesus freak. You could end up looking ridiculous, but remember; it's not your name that's on the line. It's God's name that's on the line and he will fulfill his promises every single time to his children. People are going to look at you funny or maybe even think you're strange. But God is looking for faithful people who will look directly into the storm and say, "PEACE BE STILL." God loves when we mix our faith with hope, trust, confidence and thanksgiving. Those are miraculous laws of faith to live by. The Apostle Paul said it so simple:

Faith without actions is dead. James 2:17

(My interpretation of this scripture is this)

Every Christian person's actions should be propelled by what's true about them in their new born-again spirit.

You have all the faith that Jesus Christ has; it's in your spirit. Whether or not that faith rises up out of your spirit and into your mind, mouth and actions is a decision you make everyday. Will God be glorified today by your thoughts, attitude, thankfulness, personality and emotions? Your faith mixed with these attributes: expectation, boldness, confidence, encouragement, hope, love and trust, will turn this world upside-down. When the Holy Spirit tells you to step out of your comfort zone and do something for God, then allow what's in your spirit to overcome your fear and insecurities. Faith will put your mind, body and mouth into motion in an extraordinary, life altering way. James 2:17

We have complete confidence in this...when we ask God for anything that glorifies him...he will grant our request. I John 5:14-15

You see when your desires become his desires, then God can operate in that type of humility and submissiveness. When God's word abides in you, then God's power can be released through you.

That's one of the keys to answered prayers...
your desires becoming his desires.

God wants to be glorified on the earth by his creation through our attitude, mouth and actions, as we listen to and follow the leading of his Holy Spirit.

God desires to hear his name lifted up by his people. He wants to see your faith moving throughout the earth and establishing his kingdom. God wants you to walk over to your neighbor's house and let them know that you found God (not religion) through the Lord Jesus Christ. While you're at it, hand them a bucket of fried chicken or a plate of warm cookies. They'll remember that blessing and what you said. People are not as likely to refuse the Lord Jesus Christ when you present them with the physical evidence that God loves them and that you love and care about them also.

> *God's will is that Christ lives in us in such a radical way, that he expresses himself through us in amazing and miraculous ways.*

Jesus said, "Speak to the mountain that's in front of you and it will collapse into the sea. Do not doubt in your heart, but believe that what you say will happen and you shall have whatever you say." Mark 11:23

Never underestimate the power of GOD'S WORD IN YOUR MOUTH! Jesus wants us to have awesome confidence in *our words* as we speak *God's word*. This is the confidence that I John 5:14-15 is talking about.

When my truth becomes alive in your spirit, then you can ask for whatever you want and you will have it. John 15:7

Do these scriptures mean I can have whatever I want? NO! You can have whatever God wants you to have. Specifically, you can have everything that Christ secured for you through the atonement of his sacrifice. When you align your life with the word of God, his desires will become your desires. Jesus said to his father, *"Not my will but yours be done" (Luke 22:42).* You'll be able to look at a situation and know what God's will is...and you'll want that...and then he'll give you the spiritual desires of your heart.

Jesus said, "The farmer sows the word. People are like seed along the path where the word is sown. As soon as they hear it, Satan comes and twist the word that was sown in them. Others are like the seed sown on rocky soil; they hear the word and at once receive it with joy. But since they have no root, they last only a short time. When trouble or persecution comes they quickly fall away. Still others are like seed sown among thorns, they hear the word; but the worries of this life and the desire for worldly things comes in and chokes out the word making it unfruitful. Others are like seed sown on good soil, they hear the word, accept it and produce a healthy crop of thirty, sixty or even a hundred times more than what was sown." Mark 4:14-20

God wants us to act on our beliefs and put some motion behind our faith. A daily intake of the word of God will completely change you in every way a person can be changed. Allow God's word to cut into your spirit and new revelation will flow out of your soul, mind, body and mouth.

HEARING AND DOING
Don't just be hearers of the word...but be doers of the word. James 1:22

Many modern day Christians have lost their sensitivity to God's word and his spirit that lives in them. People have rejected God's promptings so many times that their ears have become deaf and their hearts have become calloused. Have you ever left some clay out accidentally with the lid off the can? After a day or two it gets hard and crumbly. After a week you might as well forget it, it's as hard as a rock. This is what happens to a person who has desensitized themselves to the Holy Spirit. They're no longer pliable and they will not allow themselves to be shaped and formed by the hands of their creator. God says a person like this has a cold hard heart. **A Christian person can reject the promptings of the Holy Spirit just as much as an unsaved person. They shouldn't, but it happens. Christian's get busy, distracted, offended and can miss years of growth that God is trying to lead them into. Christians have become so comfortable operating in a world that easily meets the needs of their five senses. But it's going to take faith to operate in the supernatural realm.**

You are not controlled by the sinful nature but by the Spirit, because the Spirit of God literally lives in you. The Holy Spirit will help you when you are tired, weak and burdened. Romans 8:9 & 26
The Spirit intercedes for us in direct alignment with God's will. Rom. 8:27
Because the Holy Spirit lives in us, we have access to his miracle working power. The Holy Spirit will reveal to you all the many layers of God's love. Romans 15:19 & 30
The Holy Spirit searches, heals and renews our heart. I Corinth. 2:10
The Holy Spirit was sent to give you wisdom from God. The Holy Spirit gives us the very thoughts of God. I Corinthians 2:6 & 11
The Holy Spirit gives you faith-filled words to speak. I Corinthians 2:13
The Holy Spirit empowers you with the gift of healing. I Corinthians 12:9

The Holy Spirit has a lot of work to do IN US, WITH US, FOR US and THROUGH US. Christians must be sensitive to what the Holy Spirit is saying. Jesus said he was going to send the Holy Spirit for us and to wait on him (John 16:7). Don't do anything without the Holy Spirit. He's our direct connection with God's love, thoughts, plan, nature and power.

I Thessalonians 5:19 warns us, *"Do not put out the Spirit's fire."* Which is the same as having a hard heart or deaf ears? When you allow God's Spirit to speak to you, then God can work through you and it will be the most remarkable thing you've ever experienced. Jesus always said to the crowds of people:

Those who have ears...let him hear. Mark 4:23

What an unusual statement he made to the people. You have ears, now you need to use them to hear with your heart and understand in your mind. There is a big difference between hearing and listening. Jesus said it like this:

The people's hearts have become calloused, they hardly hear with their ears and they have closed their eyes. Otherwise they might see with their eyes, hear with their ears, understand with their hearts and turn and I would heal them. Matthew 13:15

Be Open:

First, we need to open our BIBLES and read God's word.
Then we need to open our EARS and hear what God is saying.
We need to open our HEARTS and understand God's nature.
We need to open our MINDS and meditate on God's wisdom.
Then we need to open our MOUTHS and speak out God's promises.
We need to open our EYES and supernaturally see what God is doing.
Finally, we need to open our SPIRIT and unleash God's love,
power and truth on this world.

God is light and in him there is no darkness. If we claim to have fellowship with him but walk in darkness, then we are confused about who we are in our spirit. But if we walk in the light of God's presence, then we'll have fellowship with one another and the blood of Jesus purifies us from ALL SIN in our spirit. I John 1:5-7
Since some did not think it was worthwhile to retain the knowledge of God, he gave them over to a depraved mind, to do what ought not to be done. They have become filled with every kind of wickedness, evil, greed and depravity. They are full of envy, murder, strife, deceit and malice. They are gossips, slanderers, God-haters, insolent, arrogant and boastful. They disobey all authority. They are senseless, faithless, heartless and ruthless. Romans 1:28-31

This is what happens when people suppress the truth of God's word instead of responding *to it*. Their thinking becomes futile and their hearts become darkened. When people reject the truth of God's word and believe the lies the enemy tells them, they become double-minded, foolish and perverse in their thinking. A downward spiral begins to take place in society when people reject the word of God. They have no benchmark for truth to determine right thinking from wrong behavior. They just exist. They're dead in their spirit. Like a cow grazing in the pasture waiting to be devoured by the world (I Peter 5:8). They have no life, no passion, no purpose and no hope. That's not the life God has planned for his creation.

Go to a nearby lake and jump in the water. Then live the rest of your life under the water like a fish. Well, after about a minute or less you would come bursting to the surface for a huge breath of air. God designed us to be air breathing people. In the book of Genesis 2:7 God breathed into Adam *the breath of life*. God gives our spirit life when he breathes into us. It's time for the world to come to the surface and breathe in that fresh breath of air full of life, forgiveness, reconciliation and hope.

When God's spirit is intertwined with our spirit, then we will enjoy the abundant life he has planned for us. It's at that born-again moment that God fills us with himself; his love, joy and peace beyond measure. John 6:63, Romans 8:2, 6 & 11

This is what happens when people get saved. They are literally born-again in their spirit. Not in a natural way by a woman or from the seed of a man. It's a supernatural birth by our heavenly Father. People weren't designed to live underwater like a fish. God wants them to come to the surface where he can breathe the breath of life into them. **God created you to be his; full of life, love, passion, wholeness, greatness, authority, enthusiasm, joy and power. God designed you to overflow with these divine character attributes (John 7:38). People need a serious revelation of God's nature so a revolution can begin within them.**

God wants us to read, hear, understand, believe, apply, meditate on, speak and pray his word. You can plant the word of God into your life and reap a harvest of supernatural blessings, or you can choose to not listen with your ears and not understand with your heart and reap from that. It's your choice. You can choose to humble yourself before the mighty hand of God like the bible says, or you can choose not to humble yourself before God. I believe it really is just that simple. **The choices we make will determine the changes we experience in life. Galatians 6:7 & 8**

Even though this universe is a billion light years wide, God's ear is just inches from our lips, waiting to hear from us.

CHAPTER 12

A CLOSE EXAMINATION OF ISAIAH 55:6-12

Seek the Lord while he may be found, call on him while he is near. Let the wicked forsake their ways. Turn to the Lord and he will have mercy on you and he will freely pardon. My thoughts are not like your thoughts, neither are your ways like my ways, declares the Lord. As high as the Heavens are above the earth, so are my ways greater than your ways and my thoughts higher than your thoughts. As the rain and the snow come down from Heaven and do not return without watering the earth and making it bud and flourish. In the same way my word will not return to me empty, it will accomplish what I desire and achieve the purpose for which I sent it. You will go out in joy and be led forth in peace, the mountains and hills will burst into song and all the trees of the field will clap their hands. Isaiah 55:6-12

What an awesome word from God. There is so much knowledge and wisdom we can glean from this. Let's examine Isaiah 55:6-12

1. Seek the LORD while he may be found. Isaiah 55:6

Folks, we've wasted enough time haven't we? We wasted enough of the time God has given us in rebellion, fighting with each other, angry, not loving each other, not extending the forgiveness that was freely given to us. Wouldn't you agree with me that it's time to change, grow and mature? This is our season to submit ourselves before the mighty hand of God. **Let's surrender ourselves to God totally and see his wonderful and miraculous power unleashed from within us. We are here to promote the greatest kingdom that has ever been established in the history of the world.**

2. Call on him while he is near. Isaiah 55:6

God wants to hear from you. He created you. You're his child. So go and spend some time with your heavenly Father. One of the most powerful bookmarkers I've compiled is the I AM / HE SHALL BE

CALLED bookmarker. I've definitely read this one the most because it reminds me of everything that I am IN CHRIST. It gives me complete assurance that the fullness of God lives in me. I Corinthians 6:17

My wife came up with an idea to print out and laminate signs with the individual words on different sheets from the I Am/He Shall Be Called bookmarker. Then she hung them in our Sunday school room at church. All four walls are completely filled with the words that are on the I Am/He Shall Be Called bookmarker. It is an awesome room to see. You just stand there reading about who you are in Christ and how much you're loved by God. Everywhere you look in the room you can read scriptures about the deeper relationship God is seeking between you and him. **You see if God can convince you of how much he truly loves you, then you'll begin to act differently based on that new belief about yourself.** Because of what we put on the walls, our Sunday school classroom has become the most exciting room in the church to be in.

You might not feel worthy of being loved by God, but that's because people simply don't understand the complete nature of his love towards them. **God's love is unconditional in its application and unlimited in its supply.** That's why I like to spend time in my Sunday school room. I can't tell you how many times I've just walked around the room reading the walls. When I do this, God always gives me a greater understanding of how passionately he's pursuing after me. Knowing that kind of love and receiving it into your heart is going to change how you love God back, and loving God is going to disassemble you and then rebuild your passion and your entire foundation for life.

Many times people build invisible walls around themselves and they won't let others get to close to them. This is usually because they have been hurt in the past. Many times if you build enough walls around yourself, you'll discover you're living in a box. The world is moving around you and you're safe inside your shelter. The world can no longer hurt you, but you can't love people from within a box. **You can't have a deep relationship with God or people when you put an impenetrable force field around yourself. Living this life with just a few superficial relationships is not a life that glorifies God. That box you're in is built out of pain, suffering, offense, unforgiveness, abandonment and rejection. God doesn't want you to live like that. God is a master counselor when it comes to your emotions. It's time to come out of the box and allow yourself to experience the complete, unconditional, pure and perfect love of the Lord.** Repeat this in the mirror to yourself on a daily basis:

God you love me unconditionally because I'm your child. I am the apple of your eye. I am cherished by you and I have been adopted into your family. You are my heavenly Father and your favor surrounds me like the air I breathe. You love me and accept me because of who you are, not because of my perfect performance. You will never leave me or forsake me. I am inseparable from your love and attention.

The reason you need to look in the mirror and say these words is so you will start believing those words are true about you. **God wants his opinion of you to be far more valuable to you than anyone else's opinion on the face of the earth.** When we go before God in prayer, he will listen to every problem, situation and care you have. He will not only hear you, but he will speak words of life and power into your heart. Every word he speaks to you will be a positive, encouraging, uplifting word.

Before you call to me, I will answer you, before you even speak a word, I have heard the desires of your heart. Isaiah 65:24

When God whispers in your ear, you'll never forget his voice. The moment he places his fingerprints on you, you'll never forget that touch. Imagine this, someone placing a dictionary on the top of your head and saying, "Receive this now into your thoughts." Then all those pages of information begin to flow into your mind. That's how it is when God gives you greater knowledge and understanding about his love, his forgiveness, his peace and his inner nature. It's going to blow you away! You'll walk away from that experience transformed in your mind, renewed in your soul and awakened in your spirit.

3. Let the wicked forsake their ways and evil thoughts. Let them turn to the LORD and he will have mercy on them and God shall freely pardon them. Isaiah 55:7

There are three golden rules of writing:
The first is to tell your readers what you're about to say to them.
The second rule is to say what you want to say to them.
The third rule is to tell them what you just said to them.

A good writer uses repetition to teach their readers. God repeats himself over an over in the bible on the subjects of repentance, forgiveness and love. Repentance must be genuine and heart felt when people come before God. Repentance bridges the gap between what God wants and what you need. When people repent of their sins, then this supernatural God makes a direct connection with his creation. Supernatural life begins to flow because your spirit has been touched by God. Your life will begin to flourish like a garden with new God glorifying fruit.

God is the one who came up with the plan of salvation. People shouldn't be embarrassed or ashamed to come to God. Know this...GOD LOVES REPENTANCE! Repentance is like a gate at the front of the salvation bridge leading to God. Opening that gate (your heart) will lead you into God's presence and salvation. God has made a way for people to cross over to him and it all begins with repentance. That's the most important message you could ever share with the lost.

When Jesus died on the cross his last words were, "IT IS FINISHED!" He paid your fine. He canceled the debt of sin against mankind for every sin that was ever committed (former sins) and for every sin that will ever be committed (future sins). People who admit, accept, and confess the truth about what Jesus accomplished for them become BORN-AGAIN in their spirit.

Jesus is the propitiation for the sins of the entire world. I John 2:2

In the temple there was a large curtain separating the altar area from the holy presence of God. The curtain was made of multiple layers of thick fabric stitched together. It was very strong and it was made to last for centuries. This seventy foot high curtain separated the people from the presence of God. Only the priest could go behind the curtain and ask God for the forgiveness of everyone's sins. The priest had to do this continually because people sinned continually. Let's read what the bible says happened at the exact moment Jesus died.

Jesus cried out in a loud voice and gave up his spirit and died. At that moment the curtain in the holy temple was torn in two from top to bottom. The earth shook and split open. Many tombs broke open and the bodies of many holy people, who had died, were raised from the dead. When the centurion and others who were guarding Jesus saw the earthquake and all that had happened, they were terrified and exclaimed, "Surely he was the Son of God!" Matthew 27:50-54

Notice the curtain that had separated the people from God was torn from the *top* to the bottom. Only God could have grabbed hold of the fabric from the *top* and ripped it with his mighty hands. **He did this as a sign to ensure to us that we have complete access to him. No priest is ever going to have to go into the temple ever again and shed** any more blood for the sins of the people. **Under the Old Covenant the blood of animals covered sin temporarily, under the New Covenant, Christ's blood actually took away sin (Romans 11:27, Hebrews 10). God did this to announce to all people to come to him directly, sin is not going to separate you from him any longer (Hebrews 4:16, Romans 6:14).** Don't be embarrassed or ashamed because of your sin. God has already completely and thoroughly dealt with it (II Corinthians 5:19). God is not dealing with sin anymore; he is completely pleased with the payment for sin through the atonement of the Lord Jesus Christ (Isaiah 53:10). Jesus Christ took care of your sin at the cross and God took care of your sins at the curtain so that people could draw close to him. That's God deepest desire.

4. My thoughts are not like your thoughts, neither are your ways like my ways declares the Lord. As high as the Heavens are above the earth, so are my ways greater than your ways and my thoughts higher than your thoughts. Isaiah 55:8 & 9

Saints of glory, we're never going to understand everything there is to know about God. Don't wait to come to him until you analyze and understand everything about him. It works just the opposite way. When we come humbly before God, then he will reveal himself to us in a way we can understand.

Without faith it is impossible to please God, because anyone who comes before God must surrender their whole heart to him. When you finally discover that it is the Lord who is God, then he will reward those who have been desperately seeking after the truth about him. Hebrews 11:6

How do we capture God's thoughts and understand his ways? By reading what he wrote, The Holy Bible. Supernatural understanding will begin to blossom in our mind when we water it with the truth of God's word.

The truth of my word is so powerful, that when it touches your spirit, it will accomplish miraculous things. So glorify me by speaking it out of your mouth. Isaiah 55:11

WOW! What a phenomenal word from God! The reading of God's word will always produce something in us. Something in our soul begins to bud and flourishes when we read it. God's word really is like nourishment for our spirit. Reading God's word divinely positions us to accomplish what we could have never accomplished on our own. Blood bought saints of God, everyday God's agenda should be on our minds. Here are some examples of what God's agenda is for you:

...to be thankful always. I Thessalonians 5:18
...to love one another deeply. Romans 12:10
...to forgive as Christ forgave you. Mark 11:25
...to cast all your cares upon him for he cares for you. I Peter 5:7
...to let the peace of God rule in your hearts as you trust in him. Col. 3:15
...to assemble together with other born-again believers. Heb.10:25

God's will is found in his word.
God's will is found in his nature.
God's will is found in Christ's actions.
God's will is literally in YOU!

Here is just a small list of God's daily agenda for you, found in
I Thessalonians 5:6-23

Be alert and self-controlled. (verse 6)
Put on faith, hope and love. These three will surround you like an
impenetrable suit of armor. (verse 8)
Encourage one another and build each other up with positive faith-filled
words. (verse11) Live in peace with each other. (verse 13)
Encourage the timid, help the weak and be patient with everyone. (v14)
Be kind to each other. (verse 15) Pray continually. (verse 17)
Give thanks in all circumstances. (verse 18)

Staying focused on God's agenda EVERYDAY...
will produce fresh supernatural results EVERYDAY.

5. *You will go out in joy and be led forth in peace, the mountains and*
hills will burst into song before you and all the trees of the field will
clap their hands giving praise to God. Isaiah 55:12

How can we not also burst forth in song? God saved us, he listens
to us and he's prepared a home in Heaven for us. He's given us an
abundant life here on earth to experience. A life filled with supernatural
peace and joy that the dictionary can't even begin to define. If the trees,
rocks, flowers, mountains and all God's creation are going to praise
him, then we certainly need to praise him as well. We have so much to
praise God for. All of us are behind in our praise and thanksgiving. **If
you don't have anything to praise God for, then you don't
understand what he's done for you. You don't understand how
much he loves you. A greater understanding of why God does the
things he does, will change why you do the things you do.** I hope
these words challenge you to hunger and thirst for God in a way that
you never have before, because anyone who thirsts after righteousness
will be filled. Matthew 5:6

<u>Here is a list of things that we need to "BE":</u>

Be filled with the Spirit. Ephesians 5:18

Be lead by the Holy Spirit. Acts 13:4

Be sensitive to God's voice. Acts 9:31

Be transformed by the word of God. Romans 12:2

Be loved. John 3:16

Be thankful. Colossians 3:15

Be forgiving. Ephesians 4:32

Be free from sin. Romans 6:19

Be in prayer continually. I Thessalonians 5:16

Be a praise warrior. (The book of Psalms)

Be joyful always. Psalm 68:3

Be in close fellowship with God. Ephesians 2:13

Be victorious in Christ Jesus. I Corinthians 15:57

Be united together in God's love. Colossians 2:2

A FOURTH DIMENSIONAL RELATIONSHIP

God has reconciled us to himself through the Lord Jesus Christ. Don't be embarrassed or ashamed to come before God. Just come to him as humbly as you know how, repent and he will receive you. **God is the one who designed, built and paid for the *salvation bridge* that spans the gap between you and him. All God requires us to do is walk across it.**

Jesus Christ came into the world to save sinners. I Timothy 1:5

God wants everyone to be saved and understand the truth about his nature. I Timothy 2:4

God doesn't want anyone to perish, he wants everyone to experience eternal life with Christ. II Peter 3:9

God did not send his Son into the world to condemn the world, but that the world through him, might be saved. John 3:17

You used to be far from God but now you have been brought close to him through the blood of his son. Jesus made peace between God and us by tearing down the wall of separation between God and us. Ephesians 2:13 & 14

He himself bore our sins in his body on the cross, so that we might die to sin and live for righteousness. By his wounds you have been healed. I Peter 2:20

You were like sheep that had lost their way, but now you have been found by your shepherd. Isaiah 53:4-6

MY SHEPHERD
by Eric Johnson

As I rose from my bed on the ground, I could smell the fresh mountain air. I could hear my shepherd calling because it was time to move on. I often wondered what life would be like outside the flock. I could run free and do whatever I wanted to do. As my shepherd and the flock disappeared over the hill, I galloped out of sight. Being free to wander wherever I wanted was new and exciting to me. I was now the master of my destiny. It quickly got dark so I found a place to bed down for the night. I could hear wolves howling in the distance and it made for a restless night of sleep. For the first time that day, I wished I had never left my shepherd.

I suddenly woke up startled. I heard the sound of wolves close by. I bolted out of the woods back to the open field. When I reached the top of the hill I was completely out of breath. I turned, and to my horror, saw a pack of wolves bounding out of the woods toward me!

I ran for my life down the other side of the hill. I dove into some tall grass and didn't move an inch. I could hear them zigzagging through the grass. One came sniffing very close to me. Then he lunged at me and bit me, but I kicked him off! I ran as fast as I could through the tall grass, but the wolf was close behind me. Then I came to an open area, I knew the end of my life was only moments away. The large black wolf burst out of the grass at full speed, only to receive a fierce hit to his head from the staff of my shepherd! MY SHEPHERD HAD FOUND ME!

He knelt beside me and put his arms around me. He said, "Didn't you know that I would leave the entire flock and come look for you?" I buried my head in his arms. The wolf he had hit lay motionless beside us. The other wolves began to surround us. My shepherd raised me up on his shoulders. I knew he was going to do whatever it took to save me. He yelled and swung his staff close to the other wolves' heads. They seemed like they were ready to attack, but when they saw the dead wolf at my shepherd's feet, it was enough to deter them and one by one they left. He carried me back to the safety of the flock.

My shepherd was willing to lay down his life for me. I never really knew how much he loved me until that day. That night I slept next to MY PROTECTOR, MY DELIVERER, MY SHEPHERD.

Jesus is like a shepherd to us; he loves us, cares for us, provides for us, directs us and protects us. Jesus is the good shepherd who chose to lay his life down for us. John 10:11

If a shepherd owns a hundred sheep and one of them wanders off,
he will leave the others and go look for the one that wandered away?
When he finds the sheep that wandered off,
he picks them up and rejoices all the way home. In the same way
your heavenly Father does not want any of his children to
wander off, be lost and perish. Matthew 18:12-14

The Son of Man came to seek and save the lost. Luke 19:10

Out of you Bethlehem will come a shepherd...
who will lead God's people. Matthew 2:6

People spend a lot of time and money to go and talk to psychiatrist or therapist about their problems and how to fix them. Usually the psychiatrist spends a lot of time in the first few sessions getting to know the person so they can have a complete picture of their specific challenges. HELLO! GOD CREATED YOU! He understands everything about you in advance. He understands the complex areas of your mind and character that even you don't understand. **He knows how to fix the things in you that you don't even know need fixing.** That's the Holy Spirit's job to help you and counsel you. He's really good at it if you'll just spend time listening to him.

God knows you better than your family and friends could ever know you. Some things you can hide from people, but you can't hide anything from God. He can give you spiritual insights, visions and supernatural life transforming power. We live under the umbrella of his unconditional love and grace. **When you became a child of God you became a joint-heir with Christ (Romans 8:17). Everything God's son has, you have right now here on earth. It's in your spirit; the saved, sanctified, righteous, anointed, blessed, perfect, pure, sealed, and redeemed part of you.** Doesn't that close bond with God sound better than any other relationship you've ever had in your life?

God is an expert at communication and relationships.
He's ready to listen to you.
He created you and already knows everything about you.
He knows what's bothering you and who hurt you.
He knows why you've hardened your heart towards him.
He knows clearly the condition of your heart and soul.
He knows how to heal your brokenness.

Do you see the words *he knows* repeated over and over? Since God knows how many hairs are on the top of your head (Matthew 10:33) I would say he knows you pretty thoroughly. Isn't that what close relationships are all about? Close relationships happen when people exchange deep intimate information about each other. We want that person to know our likes and dislikes. We want them to be a good listener. Since God created you, I would say he knows you better than anyone. Here is a phenomenal collection of scriptures that God has directed me to compile so you can understand how much God knows you and loves you.

GOD KNOWS MY NAME

Lord you know my heart and you know everything about me.
You know when I sit down and when I stand up.
You know all my thoughts throughout the day.
You know the path ahead of me and show me
where to kneel and rest in your presence.
You watch over me wherever I go.
You know every word that comes out of my mouth.
You go ahead of me to guide the way
and chase after me when I wonder off.
Your hand of blessing is always on my head.
Your knowledge is too wonderful for me to understand.

I never want to escape from your presence.
If I go up to Heaven, you are there.
If I go down to the depths of the sea, you are there.
In the morning you're there to greet me.
If I go to a far away country your strong hand guides me.
If I find myself in darkness, you are a light to my path.

In my mother's womb you formed all my inner most parts.
I will praise you because I am fearfully and wonderfully made.
Your workmanship is marvelous, how well I know it.
You knew me before I was born,
every moment of my life was laid out before you.
How precious are your thoughts about me,
I can't even count them, they out number
the grains of sand on the seashore.
You are my God and you're always near.
Search me Lord, know my heart and reveal
to me your new spirit that lives within me.

(Adapted from Psalm 139:1-23 and complied by Eric Johnson)

That's a creator that knows his creation! God doesn't want us to have any doubts that he knows us completely, he loves us unconditionally and wants to care for us forever. God is right there next to you, close to you and whispering to you. He knows you and he wants you to know him. He wants us to chase after him and pursue him relentlessly everyday just as passionately as he does us.

A RELATIONSHIP SATURATED WITH INTIMACY

Christians and non Christian alike have a difficult time understanding how you can have a relationship with God. He is an invisible supernatural being. You can talk to him but you don't know if he really hears you. Sometimes people wonder if he really exists at all. Have you ever seen those people who go out and hug and kiss trees? They put their arms around them and hug the trees for hours. They want to have a relationship with a tree or Mother Nature or something. But the tree never responds to all the love that they're giving to it. It takes two people willing to communicate and respond to each other to have a thriving relationship.

God desires to have a close, intimate connection with you. He pursues after that relationship with us because he loves us. Do you desire to know God intimately? A relationship consists of two people willing to communicate, learn about each other and love each other. God is already doing his part. The statement I made earlier is worth repeating.

You're as close to God as you want to be.

Have you ever been in a relationship where it seems like one person is putting forth all the effort and the other person is doing as little as possible? We need to pursue after God just as passionately as he pursues after us. **I wish for one moment you could feel all the love God has towards you.** God loves you and admires you...because you're his.

I challenge you and propose this to you today, you can have
a more fervent, intimate, life changing relationship with God
than you can with anyone else in this physical world.

Have you ever been talking to someone and you discovered that they're really not listening to you at all. You wanted them to pay close attention to you and understand you. You wanted them to care about you and your situation, but it just wasn't happening. They may have allowed their minds to wonder off during the conversation. Many times you think people are listening to you, but actually they're thinking about what they're going to say next and sometimes they interrupt you to say what their thinking. One time I was talking to someone and then all of a sudden they abruptly interrupted me to give some input in the conversation that was happening next to us. Their eyes were looking right at me but their ears were pointed in a different direction. Your undivided attention, time and interest are key elements for a thriving relationship.

Take a close look at your own relationships. How many really close relationships do you have? We all have people around us that we love and communicate with everyday. But many of those relationships are to a certain degree, quite shallow. Have you ever had someone want to spend the entire day with you, just so they could be around you, because they loved you and were interested in knowing more about you? They wanted to do whatever it was that you were doing. As long as it involved being with you, they were happy. That's how it is with God. That's how much he adores us. The communication and intimacy between you and God can be like no other relationship you've ever had.

THE POWER OF THE MOST HIGH
Luke 24:49

I love the story of *The Woman With The Issue Of Blood* in Mark 5:25. Here are some key points in that story:

- She spoke her miracle out of her mouth before she received it.
- She exhausted the world's remedies and knew she needed a supernatural solution.
- She mixed confidence and hope with her faith.
- She had to push her way through the crowd.
- She stopped worrying about what people thought of her.
- When she touched Jesus she felt power leave him and enter her.

Jesus said to her, *"Your faith has healed you."* Ask yourself these questions:

- When was the last time power left Heaven because of your faith?
- When was the last time power burst out of your spirit because of what you believed?
- When the last time God's power was interwoven with your positive faith-filled words?

- When was the last time the power of the Holy Spirit was manifested in your song?
- When was the last time the anointing came flooding out of your prayer like a raging river?
- When was the last time you reached out to God in a way that it commanded the attention of Heaven?
- When was the last time the power of God flowed through you in such a way that every word, thought and action was completely directed by God's Holy Spirit?

Jesus said, "I tell you the truth, anyone who has faith in me, will do the same things I've been doing, and they will do even greater things than what I've done, because I'm going to my Father and I am sending his power back to flow through you." John 14:12

I have given you authority to overcome all the power of the enemy so that nothing will ever be able to harm you. Luke 10:19

God has unlimited power, but unfortunately we are the ones who limit his power. God has already transformed you into a Holy Ghost filled, fire-baptized, demon crushing, doubt killing, praise warrior; with angels waiting for your call, that will charge towards the enemy with you. NOW THAT'S A TRUE REVELATION OF THE POWER THAT'S IN EVERY BORN-AGAIN CHRISTIAN! Unfortunately most Christians have never released this power from within them. They feel that it's out there in the heavenly realm behind the sun, or it's in God's hands waiting to be dispensed to us. We have access to the most incredible power source in the entire universe and it was deposited right here inside of us, in our spirit. Jesus said:

I will clothe you with power from the Most High. Luke 24:49

This miracle working power will manifest itself when our beliefs come into agreement with the truth of God's word. When we align ourselves with God's will, that's when all Heaven breaks loose with a shout for us and angels are sent out on our behalf. It's our responsibility as born-again bible believing Christians, to be a channel for God's power to flow through. We need to lift our hands to Heaven, surrender to God and say:

Here I am Lord, your servant. Channel your love and power through me in such a life altering way that your glory surrounds me everywhere that I go. I am yours and you are

mine and I want to see your wondrous works abound in my
life.

You will receive power when the Holy Spirit is deposited in you. Acts 1:8

*I continually ask God to give you the Spirit of WISDOM AND
REVELATION, so you may know him intimately. I pray that your heart
will be enlightened so you will know the HOPE you have in him, the
RICHES of his glorious inheritance IN US who believe, and his
incomparably GREAT POWER FOR US. That power is like the working
of his mighty strength, which he exerted in Christ Jesus when he raised
him from the dead and seated him at the right hand of God.*
Ephesians 1:17-20

WOW! The apostle Paul wants us to know God intimately through
WISDOM AND REVELATION. That's so we will fully understand the
HOPE we have in Jesus Christ. Only then will we fully comprehend the
magnitude of the POWER that is available in us. **This scripture
promises us wisdom, hope, power, spiritual vision and a glorious
inheritance right now here on earth for us to enjoy. WOW! Praise
the Lord! Are you receiving this truth into your spirit? Your spirit
should be jumping up and down, running, leaping and doing
cartwheels right now!**

*The weapons that Christians fight with are not mechanical in nature.
They're similar to the weapons in this physical world because they have
great power to destroy the enemy. Our weapons are mighty and
powerful in the supernatural realm that God controls.
They are designed to completely obliterate the enemy's kingdom.*
II Corinthians 10:4

**Are you getting the impression that God doesn't want his
children just sitting around doing nothing with their inheritance?
Don't let yourself be deceived, we have a wealth of supernatural
power and God has given us authority to rise up, be bold and speak
out the wonders of God into this physical world.**

STORY – The Little Frog

One day I was pulling up vegetable plants in our garden in
my back yard at the end of the growing season. I saw a slim fast
frog jump out of the garden. It wasn't a toad; he was a beautiful
frog with lots of vibrant green colors. I tried to catch him, but he
was just too fast. When I did manage to grab him he just slipped
out of my hands. He was full of energy and determined not to be

caught. When he was about to jump out of my yard through the chain-link fence, I lowered my hands around him. Then I began to pray to God,

> "Lord this frog is one of your creatures. You know every detail about this frog and why he does what he does. I just want to look at him Lord, up close so I can see the beauty of your marvelous creation. I can't stop him from jumping away, but I'm asking you right now to cover him with your peace and let him not fear me."

I slowly brought my hands up under the frog and to my surprise; he didn't jump away this time. I put both my hands under him and lifted him up off the ground. I just looked at how perfectly designed he was. I got to closely examine his little feet, his eyes and the beautiful colors on his skin. Do you know what happened next? He just sat there in the palm of my hands! He didn't jump away! He just sat there! My face was so close to him I could see him breathing. I was amazed that this little frog sat in my hands for such a long time. He could have jumped away at anytime. Nothing was keeping him there.

EXCEPT FOR THE SUPERNATURAL HAND OF GOD!

God created that frog. He knows all the inner workings of a frog and why they jump when they sense danger. Who told that frog he was not in any danger? I know it was the PEACE OF GOD that I prayed for, that came over him and kept him there in my hands.

Peace I leave with you, my peace I give to you. The Lord your God will give you a supernatural peace that cannot be explained. Do not let your hearts be troubled, do not be afraid. John 14:27

Since God can calm the fear and anxiety of a little backyard garden frog, then how much more will he do for me and you? **God's peace is phenomenal; it's inside of every Christian's spirit (Galatians 5:22).** Let it come out of you in such a profound way that it can literally be felt when people walk up to you. It's the kind of peace that even a little backyard frog can sense from you. Allow it to surround you and flow out of you and into others.

One time I was looking for something in my 3,600 square foot, two story barn. I looked and looked to no avail. After about thirty minutes of searching I finally prayed:

Lord you know all things. You have put your Holy Spirit inside me. The Holy Spirit knows all things. I need some information that you have to come out of me so I can find this thing I've lost. Please Lord, glorify yourself through me in every way. In Jesus name…Amen.

This may sound silly, but I don't care. I held out my hands and I began moving them all around. I allowed the Holy Spirit to take control of my hands. My hands mysteriously went over my head up high and there between my hands I saw the object I was looking for on a shelf near the ceiling. There where literally a thousand different places it could have been. But I found it the moment I invited God into my situation. PRAISE THE LORD!

The Holy Spirit wants to reveal to you how to glorify God in everything you do. We need to start leaning on the Holy Spirit heavily. He wants to be involved in every area of our life, even if it's just looking at a frog or trying to find something you've lost.

The Holy Spirit was sent into you, to fill your spirit will all God's divine uniqueness. The fullness of God's nature literally lives in every born-again Christian. We are never alone…ever…for the rest of our lives. The core of our being has been indwelt with the universe creator. All the power of Heaven is in us. As we begin to understand these truths in our mind, believe it in our heart and release it out of our spirit by faith, then the earth will experience Heaven and all its glory. Mankind will be able to touch the face of God. Sickness will bow to the healer and death will meet the author of life.

One time I prayed for my wife's severe neck pain. I prayed:

Lord we want you involved in every area of our lives. What we think about, what comes out of our mouths, our attitude and everything else we've committed to you. We want you so involved in every area of our lives that this pain cannot attach itself to my wife in any way. We are people of *the word*, people who are connected to the *Cross of Calvary* for life. We are people of *the way*. We are your children. Christ has already accomplished all that was required for our healing and we thank you for that right now. Lord your grace towards us is overwhelming. Your answer to our prayers is not based of what we've done for you, but because of what Christ has done for us. So we release positive, thankful, faith-filled words out of our mouth and we refuse to let any doubt, unbelief or fear oppose this manifestation. In Jesus name…Amen!

A few minutes later my wife said, "WOW! PRAISE THE LORD! My neck is completely better!"

Do you see why I had to write this book? God just amazes me everyday with himself. God has healed me, saved me, blessed me, anointed me and he loves me more completely than anyone has before. It's no wonder I praise him all day long for his goodness. He just blows my mind away with his awesome glory, power and nature.

I have probably written a hundred times in this book:

God loves you.
God loves us.
God loves his creation.

His love is amazing. God's love is indescribable, but if you'll ask him, he'll describe it to you with extreme detail. Jesus said,

"Whoever drinks the water from the earth, will eventually get thirsty again, but whoever drinks the supernatural water that I give, will never be thirsty again." John 4:13 & 14

God's divine character and power has given us everything we need to live this life and glorify him. II Peter 1:3

God has given us many blessings in life to enjoy. Life is full of opportunities to release those blessings and glorify him. Don't let those opportunities slip through your busy fingers. Don't miss out on them by being overwhelmed and distracted. Later in life it will be those God glorifying opportunities that you reflect back on the most. Time is an extremely valuable gift God has given us. We only have a certain amount of it here on earth. God wants to fill those precious moments of time with his life quickening spirit and then you'll be empowered to unleash grace, love and forgiveness on others.

I know I am writing this book for you to read and encourage you in your journey of faith. But the truth is, writing this book has done more for me than anything else. While writing this book, I have scanned the entire bible multiple times over and over. I have read and re-read thousands of scriptures. This has caused me to be bold in my faith which releases God's power. Also, recalling what God has done for me in the past has brought all those supernatural stories back to my mind. Saturating my mind with those miracles, God's word, his love and his grace has stirred my spirit to love God even more. Reading God's word and spending time in his presence is the most fulfilling thing you will ever do in life. Understanding God's nature towards me has radically changed my life. I now have hope, confidence and security to my relationship with God.

I hope this book has stirred your spirit and quickened your perception of God. I hope the Holy Spirit is speaking to your heart right now and prompting you to go further, higher and be bolder in your faith. Now is the time born-again believer, to join together like a mighty army does. It's time to give the world a radiant revelation of the new nature God has placed in you.

I hope this book has encouraged you to pursue God relentlessly. God will satisfy your hunger and thirst for him, when you hunger and thirst for more of him (John 6:35). I've drawn closer to God over these past ten years than I ever have in my whole life. God has given me spiritual visions and supernatural dreams that have blown me away. He wrote a personal message to me, with his own hand, right when I needed it. He's given me wisdom beyond my years and peace beyond my tears. **God has manifested his divine nature in my life so many times, that my main focus everyday is to live a GOD GLORIFYING LIFE.** I'm not starting my day without him! He has saved me in every way a person can be saved. He has given me a purpose and he's given me positive faith-filled words to speak over my life and other people's lives. The great news is, every bit of what God has given me, is available for everyone!

God has never stopped operating in my life
since the moment I said, "I WANT MORE".

I hope this is not simply the end of another Christian book for you. I hope it's the beginning of a new spirit-filled journey IN CHRIST. I hope, one day, you'll also write a book about God's indescribable, unconditional, never ending love and you'll fill the pages with testimonies, miracles and the wonders of God. LET CHRIST...THAT IS IN YOU...COME OUT OF YOU! Engage your faith with a new found boldness and God will take you places you thought were never possible.

May the word of the Lord prosper in our hands together.
May his face radiate in your countenance.
May the Lord cradle you in his loving arms all the days of your life.

Writings from the GOD STILL SPEAKS TO US series:

All of these ministry resources are a part of the
GOD STILL SPEAKS TO US COLLECTION
Published by New Vision Ministries.

Made in the USA
San Bernardino, CA
23 February 2015